D1246630

The Burned-over District

The Burned-over District

THE SOCIAL AND INTELLECTUAL HISTORY

OF ENTHUSIASTIC RELIGION IN

WESTERN NEW YORK, 1800-1850

WHITNEY R. CROSS

Cornell University Press

ITHACA AND LONDON

Copyright 1950 by Cornell University

All rights reserved. Except for brief quotations in a review, this book,
or parts thereof, must not be reproduced in any form without
permission in writing from the publisher. For information address
Cornell University Press, 124 Roberts Place, Ithaca, New York 14850.

First published 1950 by Cornell University Press.
Published in the United Kingdom by Cornell University Press Ltd.,
Ely House, 37 Dover Street, London W1X 4HQ.

First printing, Cornell Paperbacks, 1982.

International Standard Book Number 0-8014-9232-7
Library of Congress Catalog Card Number 50-12161
Printed in the United States of America

MILSTEIN
BR
555
, N7
C7
1982

This book is a print-on-demand volume.
It is manufactured using toner in place of ink.
Type and images may be less sharp than the same
material seen in traditionally printed
Cornell University Press editions.

For Ruth

For precious, immortal soul, I pray thee consider: thou art but a man, a worm of dust as well as I and the list of thy fellow mortals tabernacling here in clay. Thy breath is in thy nostrils. Remember thou art still in the body, liable to temptations as others are, and therefore not sufficient in and of thyself to determine what shall be done with offenders. For if thou canst determine [sentence?] upon one, thou may as well upon all thou imaginest to be guilty, whether they be so or not. . . . —MEHITABLE SMITH TO ABNER BROWNELL, AUGUST 30, 1782.

PREFACE

BURNED-OVER DISTRICT was a name applied to a small region, during a limited period of history, to indicate a particular phase of development. It described the religious character of western New York during the first half of the nineteenth century. Time, subject, and area have thus all combined to confine the scope of this book. The study has nevertheless seemed rewarding, mainly because its implications transcend all three limitations.

The meaning expands in a geographical sense because this one area provides a case history in the westward transit of New England culture. Likewise, it is representative as a sample of the change from youth to maturity in a single section affected by continuing westward movement. The subject of religion has broader significance in this period and locality than might at first appear. This section was the storm center, and religious forces were the driving propellants of social movements important for the whole country in that generation. As far as time goes, this book is an illustration of the way in which the minds of one era help to form the destinies of succeeding generations. Neither the causes of the Civil War nor the origins of national prohibition, to cite only two prominent examples, can be thoroughly understood without reference to the Burned-over District.

Microcosmic study has definite advantages. This limited territory I have come to know intimately, perhaps thus achieving more careful analysis than I could have hoped for with a larger expanse. In the small theater of investigation, integrated treatment of cultural, social, economic, political, and ideological causations may be more satisfactory than in larger ones. My motivation, in any case, has been no glorification of the locality, no devotion to regional patriotics, and, most emphatically, no yen for antiquarian lore. Rather, I have tried by the microcosmic approach to produce a reliable and broadly meaningful bit of general American history.

My obligations in developing the volume are multitudinous. Professor Arthur J. May directed my attention to local history in my first excursion into the past of Rochester, New York. Dr. Blake McKelvey has more recently aided me in interpreting not only that city, on which he has written some of the ablest volumes of urban history, but also the whole of western New York. He has read and criticized the manuscript, entire. So also has Professor Louis Filler. Professors Arthur M. Schlesinger, Perry Miller, and Frederick Merk in courses at Harvard University greatly stimulated me to broaden my background for this work. Professor George H. Sabine and other officials at Cornell University were notably generous about time for research during my employment there, which was in a capacity that incidentally enabled me to travel extensively in, and greatly enrich my understanding of, western New York. Travels farther afield searching out sources brought rich acquaintanceships and fertile suggestions from a number of experienced historian-collector-librarians. I am especially indebted to Dr. Lester J. Cappon, Dr. Randolph G. Adams, Dr. Thomas P. Martin, Dr. Clifford Shipton, Dr. Clarence S. Brigham, Dr. R. W. G. Vail, Mr. Edward C. Starr, and Mr. E. R. B. Willis.

Studies without which this one could not have been undertaken have been published by the late Dixon Ryan Fox, Robert S. Fletcher, the late Gilbert H. Barnes, Everett Dick, Dwight L. Dumond, John A. Krout, Charles Keller, David M. Ludlum, Paul D. Evans, Ralph V. Harlow, Lewis D. Stilwell, Fawn M. Brodie, and Robert F. Nichol. Their work merits recognition of my heavy obligation, beyond routine references to their books. Like all scholars in the period, I am basically indebted to Frederick Jackson Turner. In addition, I have profited from various suggestions made by President-Emeritus O. R. Jenks, Professor Glyndon Van Deusen, Dean Carl Wittke, Professors Richard Power, David Ellis,

and Neil McNall, the Rev. Frederick Kuhns, and Mrs. Edith Fox.
I wish also to acknowledge generous permission to use studies still in manuscript form by Professors Howard F. Bennett, Arthur E. Bestor, Jr., F. L. Bonner, Merrill E. Gaddis, Reuben E. E. Harkness, and Miss Christine Zeh. Miss Louise J. Hitchcock, Mr. Charles D. Osborne, and Mr. James A. Jackson have made accessible original manuscripts in their possession, and Miss Anna Hulett accorded me permission to use the Lewis Tappan manuscripts at the Library of Congress. The New York State Historical Association has allowed me to use material under its copyright that I originally contributed to *New York History*, and permission to quote from George W. Noyes, ed., *John Humphrey Noyes: Putney Community* (Oneida, N.Y., 1931), has been granted by the copyright owner.

Library and manuscript depository staffs have been universally courteous, patient, and helpful. The number forbids personal mention of my many benefactors at the following libraries:

Colleges and universities:—Aurora, Chicago, Colgate, Connecticut, Cornell, Dartmouth, Hamilton, Harvard, Michigan, Oberlin, Princeton, Rochester, St. Lawrence, Smith, Syracuse, Tufts, and Yale.

Public libraries and historical associations:—The New York, Boston, Rochester, Auburn, and Penn Yan Public Libraries; Grosvenor Library, New York State Library, and Library of Congress; American Antiquarian Society, New York State Historical Association, New-York Historical Society, Buffalo Historical Society, Tompkins, Cortland, Onondaga, and Ontario County Historical Societies.

Theological school and denomination depositories:—Andover, Chicago, Colgate-Rochester, Crozier, and Newton Theological Seminaries; Congregational House, American Sunday School Union, Presbyterian Historical Society, American Baptist Historical Society, Universalist Historical Society, New England Methodist Historical Society.

To three unfailing critics and advisers throughout a prolonged period, I owe my greatest debt. My mother, Helen Rogers Cross, and my mentor, Professor Arthur M. Schlesinger, have struggled to increase my literary skill, while inspiring my thinking constantly. My wife, Ruth Whipple Cross, has typed, criticized, and borne more than a half share of all the burdens, direct and indirect, which the work imposed. These advisers merit the greater credit for whatever value the book possesses. Its shortcomings rise from limitations of mine which their efforts could not overcome.

WHITNEY R. CROSS

West Virginia University, 1950

CONTENTS

List of Maps   xiii

BOOK I.   ORIGINS: 1800–1825

Chapter *1*.   The Great Revival   3
Chapter *2*.   Yankee Benevolence   14
Chapter *3*.   Premonitions   30

BOOK II.   ENVIRONMENT: 1825–1850

Chapter *4*.   Canal Days   55
Chapter *5*.   Social Patterns   78

BOOK III.   PORTENTS: 1825–1831

Chapter *6*.   The Martyr   113
Chapter *7*.   Yorker Benevolence   126
Chapter *8*.   The Prophet   138
Chapter *9*.   The Evangelist   151

BOOK IV.   GENESIS OF ULTRAISM: 1826–1837

Chapter *10*.   New Measures   173
Chapter *11*.   New Men   185
Chapter *12*.   New Ideas   198

BOOK V.   HARVEST: 1830–1845

Chapter *13*.   A Moral Reformation   211
Chapter *14*.   Perfect Sanctification   238
Chapter *15*.   Schism   252
Chapter *16*.   The Pattern of Dispersing Ultraism   268

CONTENTS

BOOK VI.   AFTERMATH: 1840–1850
Chapter 17.   The End of the World
322
Chapter 18.   Utopia Now   287
Chapter 19.   World without End   322
Chapter 20.   The Passing Era   341
                                                     353
Appendix.   Notes on Maps
                                                     358
Index
                                                     363

LIST OF MAPS

I.	Population Density in 1820	57
II.	Population Growth between 1820 and 1835	58
III.	Dollar Value of Manufactures, 1835	60
IV.	Farm Area Served by Chief Canal Cities	61
V.	Yankee Nativity	68
VI.	Isms and Economic Maturity	77
VII.	Home Manufactures, 1825	85
VIII.	Home Manufactures, 1825–1845	86
IX.	Common Schools, 1829	90
X.	Common Schools, 1839	91
XI.	Common Schools, 1829	94
XII.	Common Schools, 1839	95
XIII.	Private Education, 1845	96
XIV.	Libraries	97
XV.	Illiteracy, 1850	99
XVI.	Illiteracy, 1840	100
XVII.	Antimasonry, 1828	118
XVIII.	Antimasonry, 1829	119
XIX.	Early Branches of the Mormon Church	147
XX.	The Finney Revivals, 1831	157
XXI.	Liberty Party Poll, 1842	227
XXII.	Antislavery in the Churches	228
XXIII.	Adventism	289
XXIV.	Fourierism	330
XXV.	Spiritualism	350

The Burned-over District

BOOK I

Origins: 1800-1825

The Baptists generally in this Western Country . . . are of the opinion, that Ministers should take no thought how, or what they should speak . . . for it is not they that speak, but the Spirit which speaketh in them. And one of the Ministers told me that "I must let the Holy Ghost study my sermons for me."

—DAVID RATHBONE, SCIPIO, MAY, 1812, TO JOHN WILLIAMS

Chapter 1. THE GREAT REVIVAL

ACROSS the rolling hills of western New York and along the line of DeWitt Clinton's famed canal, there stretched in the second quarter of the nineteenth century a "psychic highway." [1] Upon this broad belt of land congregated a people extraordinarily given to unusual religious beliefs, peculiarly devoted to crusades aimed at the perfection of mankind and the attainment of millennial happiness. Few of the enthusiasms or eccentricities of this generation of Americans failed to find exponents here. Most of them gained rather greater support here than elsewhere. Several originated in the region.

Some folk called it the "infected district," thinking mainly of the Antimasonic agitation which centered west of Cayuga Lake. Critics chiefly concerned with the habitual revivalism occurring in a much wider area came to call it the "Burnt" or "Burned-over District," adopting the prevailing western analogy between the fires of the forest and those of the spirit. Charles Grandison Finney, the greatest evangelist of the day, helped give the term its customary usage when he applied it to localities between Lake Ontario and the Adirondacks where early Methodist circuit riders had, he thought, left souls hardened against proper religious tutelage.[2] Yet these very people proved in fact thoroughly adaptable to his own exhortations, as did others farther afield.

---

[1] Carl Carmer, *Listen for a Lonesome Drum: A York State Chronicle* (New York, 1936), 115.

[2] Charles G. Finney, *Autobiography of Charles G. Finney* (New York, 1876), 78.

3

The history of the twenty-five years following Finney's early campaigns suggests that the burning-over process fertilized luxuriant new growths rather than merely destroying old ones. The epithet, in any case, like so many others originally intended to condemn, was in time adopted by those against whose practices it had been directed. It became a hallmark of upstate New York. No exact geographical sense can be assigned to the phrase. It simply meant the place where enthusiasts flourished. But convenience dictates an arbitrary boundary located to include the major expressions of the spirit identified by the term. For my purposes I have defined the Burned-over District as that portion of New York State lying west of the Catskill and Adirondack Mountains.

A solid Yankee inheritance endowed the people of this area with the moral intensity which was their most striking attribute. It was only to be expected that emigration would carry the old traditions westward, most abundantly in the region wherein the migrants settled most thickly. But this natural legacy was reinforced by the purposeful activity of those who remained in the land of steady habits; and a swelling resurgence of evangelistic religion coincided with the period of migration. Consequently, fervent revivalism concentrated in western New York as in no other portion of the country during its pioneering era. Emotional religion was thus a congenital characteristic, present at birth and developed throughout the youth of the section.

Settlement beyond the Appalachian Mountains began about 1790 in this latitude. Although New Englanders were destined to dominate immigration for nearly a half-century, others also were attracted to the fertile new land. Especially before adequate roads stimulated wholesale infiltration by way of the Mohawk Valley, a reasonably large proportion of folk came up the Susquehanna from Pennsylvania. The numerous branches of that river provided natural highways eastward and westward over the southern tier of New York State. Many persons crossed the gentle hills from which those tributaries flow, to descend into the middle Finger Lakes country. This migration was sizable for several decades, though it dwindled gradually before the growing Yankee tide. Its effects can be discerned as late as 1845. Ten counties, forming a triangle in the middle of western New York, with its apex on Lake Ontario and its base on the Pennsylvania border, show in that year a notably lower percentage of New England nativity than do the neighboring counties on either side.[3] Eastern New Yorkers also moved across the mountains and joined the Yankees and Pennsylvanians in the western part of the state. Many of them were twice instead of once removed from ancestral New England soil. Finally came some foreigners, but only in small numbers before 1825.

The predominant Yankees swarmed from Connecticut and Massachusetts into the upper reaches of the Mohawk Valley and over the western slopes of the Catskills. Farther north, Vermonters simultaneously moved around the Adirondacks, populating stretches of the flat St. Lawrence Valley on their way to the Black River and the eastern shores of Lake Ontario. By 1800, the two streams had come together in central New York and flooded westward to the Genesee country. Here, among the knolls and hollows at the bases of the western Finger Lakes and across to the Genesee River Valley, lay the richest soils of the state. Settlement advanced more rapidly here than upon the Military Tract just to the east, where folk from south of the border were mingling with New Englanders. When the Peace of Ghent removed threats of border warfare, when better roads and the projected canal promised both transportation to market and a less rugged initial journey, the pace of the Yankee advance redoubled. The Ontario plain north of the Finger Lakes country filled rapidly, as did the Holland Company acres west of the Genesee River, as soon as land values rose substantially in the first-occupied neighborhoods.

Some few New England villages moved as units, but large family groups comprised the bulk of the westering horde, and many a man followed his own personal initiative. Yet it would not be a distortion to consider the movement one of communities more than of individuals. "Genesee Fever" struck entire neighborhoods. No matter how he might travel, the pioneer preferred to buy land of someone he had known at home, to settle near acquaintances already established at the destination. Land company agents generally maintained New England contacts; several of the speculators

---

[3] See map V. A slightly different analysis appears in Frederick Jackson Turner, *The United States, 1830–1850: The Nation and Its Sections* (Avery Craven, ed., New York, 1935), 97.

themselves were old neighbors. The voyager could always locate former friends, since the many men who went west for the summer land-clearing and back east for the winter several times before their final trip constantly carried letters and messages between the new and the old New England. Thus, within a large region whose entire population was Yankee in the majority, notably homogeneous districts and towns developed. Jefferson and St. Lawrence counties were the new Vermont. Oneida was the new Connecticut. Farther west, Genesee, Wyoming, and Chautauqua contained people of considerably mixed local New England derivation, scarcely tinged by other strains. In areas less dominantly Yankee, certain communities like Rochester, Auburn, Manlius, Homer, Ithaca, and Prattsburg had similar unilateral origins.

This wholesale emigration served to select a group of transplanted Yankees who would be on the whole more sensitive to religious influences than their kinfolk in the homeland. Those who went west were, first of all, younger sons for whom the scrubby farms held little opportunity. The youths, too, had greater ambition and lust for adventure than their elders, who either had substantial stakes and compelling social ties in the old land or had already compromised upon mere existence in the hard struggle for a competence. Although two-thirds of all Vermonters were twenty-five or under in 1800, the emigrants were, on the average, still younger.[4]

A geographical selection accompanied the age differential. Western New York drew its population chiefly from hill-country New England. Bostonians, even at this early date, seldom budged without serious provocation. The number interested in leaving the prosperous lower Connecticut Valley was likewise negligible. A reasonable proportion of Rhode Islanders and New Hampshire folk chose to move, but an overwhelming majority hailed from the western hills and valleys. Litchfield County in Connecticut, Berkshire in Massachusetts, and the western tier of Vermont counties led all Yankeedom in "go-outers."[5]

Since these were the very regions inhabited by "come-outers," a

[4] Lewis D. Stilwell, "Migration from Vermont (1776–1860)," *Proceedings of the Vermont Historical Society*, n.s., V, no. 12 (June, 1937), 66.

[5] Dixon R. Fox, *Yankees and Yorkers* (New York, 1940), 211.

third sifting principle came into operation, one involving the criterion of a religious tradition.[6] The emotionalism of the Great Awakening in the 1740's had permanently split the historic Congregational Church. One branch, emphasizing the intellectual qualities held in balance with spiritual zeal by the original Puritans, had early adopted the Half-way Covenant, which permitted children of church members to become full-fledged members themselves without a demonstrable experience of conversion. This branch, centering about Boston, drifted in time toward Unitarianism. The "New Light" school, on the contrary, resented the declining zeal marked by the Half-way Covenant. Their leader, Jonathan Edwards, supported the enthusiasm of the old faith upon new foundations constructed from eighteenth-century psychology and philosophy, paradoxically using the greatest intellect of colonial America to reinforce that religious doctrine which would in practice stress emotionalism at the expense of reason. Edwards and the New Lights made conversion the exclusive test of church membership.

These enthusiasts of the Great Awakening had, for religious or economic reasons or both, moved westward, and northward into Vermont. The Congregationalists and the Separatists alike residing in the western hills remained in the Edwardean tradition, denying the Half-way Covenant and resisting deism and irreligion during the era of the American Revolution. In these younger, poorer, more isolated sections revivals had continued from time to time, bridging the gap between the religious fervor of the 1740's and that following 1790. Here it was, chiefly, that the "Second Awakening" made thorough and permanent conquests, far beyond its effect on the rest of New England. Indeed, this was far more significant, albeit less sensational, than the contemporary Kentucky revival of much greater renown. Wave upon wave of seasonal enthusiasm swept the Yankee hill country until long after 1825.[7]

The lad who emigrated from these neighborhoods could hardly

6 The coincidence is particularly noted by Turner, *Nation and Sections*, 41–43; David M. Ludlum, *Social Ferment in Vermont, 1791–1850* (New York, 1939), 12–15.

7 Ludlum, *Social Ferment*, 12–15, 42; Charles R. Keller, *The Second Great Awakening in Connecticut* (New Haven, Conn., 1942), 37, 193–194; Vernon Stauffer, *New England and the Bavarian Illuminati* (New York, 1918), 74 ff.

have escaped at least one such revival, whether he left his hillside home or valley hamlet as early as 1795 or as late as 1824. He was perhaps not himself a convert, though he had always gone to church and had scarcely considered doing otherwise. He awaited the day when the Holy Spirit would marvelously elect him to church membership. In the new country he might temporarily violate the Sabbath, swear, or drink too heartily, but he always expected another revival to change his ways. His adolescent mind readily lent itself to religious excitement. He probably married a "professing" Christian, who constantly warned him of his dangerous position, and he certainly intended to rear a family of respectable, churchgoing children.[8]

It mattered little whether he was nominally Congregational, Baptist, or Methodist. He might in the young country change affiliation several times as one sect or another held services nearby, or seemed to enjoy particular manifestations of heaven-born agitation.[9] Had he perchance left the old home before the revivals of the nineties reached that vicinity (or if he were one of the rare "village atheists" who aped Ethan Allen and attracted notice out of singularity rather than influence), still he could scarcely evade a religious experience in New York. For ten years at most he might dwell in some isolated spot, but settlers inevitably arrived, churches formed, and revivals occurred. These occasions provided the same theology, the same techniques, the same habits and mannerisms as did the simultaneous episodes in the parent section.

Here, of course, as at home, practices differed somewhat among the denominations. Methodists held camp meetings and permitted physical exercises upon which Congregationalists frowned. Freewill Baptists inclined to tolerate such activities, while Calvinist Baptists were more strict. Methodist and Baptist preachers enjoyed rather less of education than Presbyterians and Congregationalists. The last-mentioned church may have maintained more effective control of a member's behavior, but such a distinction can easily

---

[8] Much of the supposed irreligion of the New York frontier originates in the prejudices of missionaries, taken without the necessary grain of salt by later historians. Comments of the same kind were similarly made upon New England in the period of the American Revolution. See Stauffer, *Bavarian Illuminati*, 26–33.

[9] George Peck, *Early Methodism within the Bounds of the Old Genesee Conference*, etc. (New York, 1860), 126, 226–229, 280–281, 345.

be overemphasized. All sects tried as they did in New England to exercise discipline; if temporarily exercised with less success in the youthful region, it increased with years, population, and the growth of evangelistic fervor. A person could change his affiliation more conveniently than under the rigid New England establishments, but he probably gained little leeway thereby for heretical or immoral practices.

Theological differences also existed, but apparently not in such a way as to affect religious emotionalism. All the major denominations (the Episcopal Church was relatively weak in this area) and most of the smaller ones were strongly revivalistic. Congregationalists, soon Presbyterian under the Plan of Union,[10] were accustomed to social dominance just as they had been in New England. They consequently initiated revival campaigns in which other sects followed, as they had in the home region. Methodists and Baptists, more literal, more emotional, and better understood by common folk, increasingly "strung Presbyterian fish" and gained adherents more rapidly, just as they had at the expense of the established New England church.

Evidence concerning the development of the Burned-over District churches before 1825 is unreliable, but it suffices to indicate similar patterns of growth among the several denominations. In periods of awakening all increased rapidly; in times of quiet all grew slowly. Prior foundation in particular vicinities gave one or another sect special local strength, but in the region as a whole they appear to have maintained uniform patterns of expansion. Their history can be told as one tale.

The winter of 1799–1800 was in western New York long called the time of the Great Revival, just as it was in Kentucky. But the violent sensationalism of the southern frontiersmen repulsed the relatively staid Yankees, whose experiences, because more calm, have been the more easily forgotten by historians. Additional factors conspired to diminish the fame of the northern awakenings which occurred throughout western New England and New York in scattered places, in various seasons. The one winter represented a culmination and peak of a period of several years, rather

---

10 See below, pp. 18–19.

than a single, climactic outburst. The preaching techniques and excitement-breeding expectation, which long use would eventually make habitual, had been more completely out of style in New England than in Kentucky. The Great Awakening of the colonial period had come later to the South than to New England and memories were the fresher there on that account. Slow travel and imperfect communications prevented the immediate infection of large areas which would later become customary. Indeed, appearances could easily justify the feeling of conservative clergymen that the spasmodic nature of this Great Revival showed that it came unsought from Heaven, while later ones seemed more directly the work of human agents.

Yet, in proportion to the slight population of upstate New York, the Great Revival must have justified its name. Most of the settled neighborhoods participated. The more homogeneous Yankee centers provided leadership, and strongholds of Congregationalism developed in the towns of the Genesee country. Oneida and Otsego counties farther east shared equally, along with other communities sprinkled between these two population centers.[11] The Methodists seem to have gained over 1,500 members in the one year. Two years later, Lorenzo Dow first visited the village of Western, where Charles Finney would commence his triumphs in 1825. Dow converted a hundred sinners in a single three-hour meeting at nearby Paris Hill. Western itself, after a three-day camp meeting involving over twenty preachers of various sects, became the base of the key Methodist circuit for central New York. Here also "Crazy" Dow met and married his "rib," Peggy, and here he returned four times before 1817 to reinvigorate the locality.[12]

After 1800 excitement diminished, rose again to a lesser peak in 1807–1808, and slumped once more during the war years. But even the least promising seasons saw awakenings in a few localities.

---

[11] Rev. James H. Hotchkin, *A History of the Purchase and Settlement of Western New York and . . . of the Presbyterian Church in That Section* (New York, 1848), 36, 37, 122; P[hilemon H.] Fowler, *History of Presbyterianism . . . of Central New York* (Utica, 1877), 168–172; George Punchard, *History of Congregationalism*, etc. (5 vols.; Boston, 1881), V, 36, 37.

[12] Peck, *Early Methodism*, 179, 195–203; Lorenzo Dow, *The Dealings of God, Man, and the Devil, as Exemplified in the Life, Experience, and Travels of Lorenzo Dow*, etc. (New York, 1849), I, 95, 106, 109, 253.

Meanwhile, fresh migration from New England constantly added to church membership and to the general desire for spiritual satisfaction. The Great Revival, operating in New York upon early arrivals and in New England on those to follow, provided continued religious sensitivity during the formative years of the Burned-over District.

The religious upheavals following the War of 1812 surpassed all previous experiences. Although the proportion of converts in the entire population may have been smaller than in 1800, settlement had increased enough to give an impression of greater magnitude. Those accustomed to such events may have seemed less impressed than upon the earlier occasion, but this revival did spread more widely and abundantly than had the one at the turn of the century. Yankee towns which featured in the earlier awakening again stimulated similar communities more recently founded. The Presbyterians of Utica made nearly as many converts in 1815 as in the Finney revival a decade later, and added large numbers again in 1819 and 1821. Many of the places which would later contribute to Finney's renown, scattered from the Catskill foothills to the St. Lawrence River, were similarly affected during these years. Again the excitement ran through the Finger Lakes and Genesee countries, but now it extended through younger settlements westward to Lake Erie. Baptists followed the Presbyterian example. Particularly intense campaigns centered in Ontario and Monroe counties. For the first time extensive Freewill Baptist revivals appeared in southern Erie County, along the shore of Lake Ontario, and in the Susquehanna Valley. The Methodists gained 16 per cent in the single year of 1818.[13]

These postwar waves of enthusiasm demonstrate clearly for the first time what may have been true as well in 1800, that western New York was more intensively engaged in revivalism than were other portions of the Northeast. One listing of local episodes in the three years following 1815 includes 6 Rhode Island towns; 15

---

13 Fowler, *Presbyterianism*, 180–188, 222–223; *Evangelical Recorder* (Auburn), II (Feb., Nov., 1820), 104, 150 ff.; *Western New York Baptist Missionary Magazine* (Norwich, Morrisville), I, II (1818, 1819); I. D. Stewart, *The History of the Freewill Baptists for Half a Century* (2 vols.; Dover, N.H., 1862), I, 322–324; *Minutes of the Annual Conferences of the Methodist Episcopal Church* (New York, 1840), I, 312 ff.

in Connecticut; in eastern New York, Pennsylvania and New Jersey, 21 each; in Vermont, 45; in Massachusetts, 64; and in the Burned-over District, 80.[14] Population in several of the compared regions exceeded that of this area at the time, so the case cannot be dismissed as a matter of numerical ratio. No noticeable theological novelty arose to confuse the question. Nor does explanation lie in the frontier element, for neither within nor beyond this particular locality did excitement prevail more generally in the younger communities; in fact the reverse seems probable. Even at this date, then, western New York exhibited an unusual degree of religious fervor.

The crest of postwar revivalism highlights another developing characteristic of equal importance. At first, little uniformity in timing had been apparent, but with each succeeding wave, the tendency grew toward simultaneous operation over an extensive area. Contagion became the more significant as improved communications made each vicinity more conscious of the moral and religious state of its neighbors. Most of western New York during these years experienced revivals at the same times.

Since the first climax of 1800, distinct peaks of fervor had now occurred twice with intervals of quiet interspersed. Another low point in the cycle was destined to follow 1820. The automatic tendency for enthusiasm to wax and wane found reinforcement in the parallel variations of economic trends. Then, as now, many people sought God more earnestly in adversity than in prosperity. The postwar years had been a time of depression, but buoyant expectations of the building Erie Canal now strengthened the rising curve of business activity. Excitements of other types were always potential competitors for religious fervor. But the standardization of the revival cycle was not yet complete. Isolated neighborhoods which lacked the stimulus of the canal often continued ablaze in the five years following 1820, when much of the region remained uninspired.

Most Methodist circuits showed declining membership in two of these five years and only slight growth in a third. But substantial gains came in 1821, and in 1824 rapid development began once

---

[14] Joshua Bradley, *Accounts of Religious Revivals in Many Parts of the United States from 1815 to 1818* (Albany, 1819), vi–x.

more, led by the district about Western, in Oneida County. Regular and Freewill Baptists both enjoyed noticeable, if isolated, awakenings centering about Cortland and southern Erie counties. Since the peak of fervor reached in 1826 is often attributed to Charles Finney's single-handed influence, Presbyterian revivals in the immediately preceding years are particularly significant. James H. Hotchkin, a close and accurate observer, reported on a region entirely west of Oneida County. While he considered it a time of indifference, he listed fifty-two towns which had healthy revivals. A missionary from New England who traveled over the neighborhood east of Lake Ontario two years before Finney's campaigns there observed extensive awakenings throughout the territory. In early 1825, just before Finney's revival at Western began, a flurry of excitement passed through the churches along the south shore of Lake Ontario.[15]

The series of crests in religious zeal begun by the Great Revival formed the crescendo phase of a greater cycle. Strenuous evangelism mounted irregularly from the 1790's to reach a grand climax between 1825 and 1837. The Burned-over District experienced in these years a gradual transfer westward from New England of the center of gravity for spiritual stimuli. Accompanying the migration as it did, the transfer seems upon first sight to have been a fortuitous process without purpose or encouragement, which centered upon this one area because population flow did likewise. So it was in fact to a substantial degree. But the automatic, natural development of religious sensitivity in western New York was reinforced by a more conscious and deliberate system of indoctrination from the Yankee homeland.

---

15 *Methodist Conference Minutes,* I, 345, 346, 366, 384, 408, 409, 446; *Baptist Missionary Magazine,* III (May, 1820), 60; Stewart, *Freewill Baptists,* I, 399-412; Marilla Marks, ed., *Memoirs of the Life of David Marks,* etc. (Dover, N.H., 1847), 27-32; Hotchkin, *Western New York,* 135, 136; Fowler, *Presbyterianism,* 189-192, 194-196; *New York Observer,* III (March 5 and April 30, 1825), 31, 69.

Chapter 2. YANKEE BENEVOLENCE

THE New England conscience was ever an idiosyncrasy of ample proportions; when migrant sons, relatives, and neighbors wandered westward all the purposefulness of Yankeedom exerted itself to see that these departing loved ones should continue to walk straightly in the accustomed faiths.[1] No deliberate plot aimed at making New Yorkers more pious than others who went farther afield. Probably contemporaries could not realize the extent to which missionary enterprises tended to concentrate in this single region. Certainly the homelanders failed to anticipate the brood of isms which would result from the overconcentration. Nevertheless, as the several denominations extended themselves into this new New England, they did succeed in focusing their proselytizing activities upon this one section in thoroughly remarkable fashion.

One major evangelical denomination in the Burned-over District, and that one alone, failed to share equally in the New England heritage. The early Methodist circuit riders came from the south by way of the Susquehanna, Delaware, and Hudson valleys. Methodism had come to New England too recently to have developed a surplus of native leaders. Later on, recruits to the clergy came from every circuit, and a fair proportion must have sprung from Yankee stock. But even the earliest preachers noted the superior interest in religion of the New England pioneers, compared with

---

[1] Committee of the General Association of Connecticut, *An Address to the Inhabitants of the New Settlements*, etc. (New Haven, Conn., [1793]), 6.

others of their flocks.[2] Before long most Methodist ministers were bound to be serving a clientele with a Yankee majority.

Nevertheless, the Methodists had a less homogeneous membership than other sects. They also had an episcopal organization and adhered to a doctrine which permitted easier release of emotional stresses. Others accused these Arminians of noise, wildness, and extravagance. In the early days they probably were more given to muscular practices than the more dignified sects with larger strains from Calvinism in their theology. But Methodism rapidly became respectable, while other denominations learned gradually to cater to popular tastes and came to exceed those they had accused in enthusiastic methods.[3]

Muscular enthusiasm and heterodox doctrine are quite different phenomena; moreover, they are not always found in combination. Methodism, whatever its practices, produced little discoverable leadership toward heresy in this period and region. Individuals left this church to join every eccentricity, and each popular crusade created internal pressure which threatened clerical authority. But these occurrences came after the fervent movements had gathered momentum and aroused the basic susceptibility of the Yankee-bred members of the church. It is not primarily among the Methodists that the sources of Burned-over District peculiarities are to be found.

A number of smaller sectarian groups which came here from New England played a somewhat larger role in the development of the distinctive mentality of the region. The Freewill Baptists and the Christians were sectarians descended from the Separatists of the Great Awakening and developed in the late eighteenth century on the northern frontiers of New England. The former retained Baptist usages but maintained an open communion and an Arminian doctrine of salvation. The latter (not to be confused with the Campbellites or Disciples of Christ, also often called Christians) might properly be called Unitarian Baptists. They disclaimed creeds and believed in the unity of God, but emphasized regen-

---

2 George Peck, *Early Methodism within the Bounds of the Old Genesee Conference*, etc. (New York, 1860), 53, 125, 134; Rev. F. W. Conable, *History of the Genesee Annual Conference of the Methodist Church*, etc. (New York, 1876), 331.

3 [Calvin Colton], *A Voice from America to England*, etc. (London, 1839), 64, 67.

eration by conversion, immersion, and a literal reading of the Bible. These groups, always in close sympathy with each other, provided a large proportion of emigrants to western New York, where they flourished chiefly in isolated rural areas and probably retained the relatively low cultural and economic stations in society which they had occupied in the homeland. Their clergymen had little schooling and often followed a trade for support. Moving westward like other craftsmen and farmers, these preachers pursued their clerical duties as an avocation, picked up whatever followers they chanced upon, and eventually founded churches. Possibly occasional fellowships moved en masse to the younger land.[4]

An abundance of personnel existed within these sects, ready to respond to any spiritual stimulus but lacking the initiative to originate or direct novelties. Here were to be found recruits for Mormonism, Millerism, spiritualism, and various social experiments. If these folk provided leadership in unorthodoxy, reliable data fail to substantiate the fact. Their discoverable behavior suggests the contrary belief. They held revivals upon the heels of other denominations, borrowed the camp meeting from the Methodists, and supported Antimasonry, temperance, and abolition without noticeable participation in their origins. They were of course free of hierarchical control, and probably quicker to respond to any leadership or pressure toward heresy than were the members of the Methodist Church.

The New England branches of these sects presumably did what they could to send ministers to the emigrants. The process seems to have been a casual one, lacking the planning and organization which the larger churches utilized. But even if the missionary work was not systematic or adequately financed, it was remarkably effective. By 1827 the Freewill Baptists apparently had nearly as many churches and probably over half as many preachers here as in New England, where the sect had flourished some time before settlement in New York began. Of 143 Christian elders in the country in 1823,

---

4 Marilla Marks, ed., *Memoirs of the Life of David Marks,* etc. (Dover, N.H., 1847), 27–45; I. D. Stewart, *The History of the Freewill Baptists for Half a Century* (2 vols.; Dover, N.H., 1862), I, 319–409, *passim; Minutes of the General Conference of the Freewill Baptist Connection,* etc. (Dover, N.H., 1859), vii; *Gospel Luminary* (West Bloomfield), II (Aug., 1826), 177.

7 served in New Jersey, Pennsylvania, and Ohio; 9 in Virginia and Kentucky; 47 in New York; and 80 in New England, where the northern branch of the church had begun about 1780.[5]

The Friends in western New York likewise came chiefly from hill-country New England. Strong communities developed rapidly in the Finger Lakes country and in more scattered fashion elsewhere. Seven quarterly meetings organized before 1825, and two of these in the Genesee country only two years later had gathered over four thousand members.[6] Quakers came to be represented in many experiments of Burned-over District history, but they did not share the state of mind engendered by the revivalism of the other religious groups. Since they had no professional clergy and lacked a degree of organization permitting policies which can accurately be called denominational, they defy authoritative placement among the sects of the region. They did, however, share in the Yankee inheritance, as they probably did in the New England-motivated campaigns to develop religion in western New York. In the Hicksite controversy of 1828, they anticipated the schismatic tendencies which would characterize this area. They contributed strongly to the social enthusiasms of the day, as well as to the religious experiments which rose from the minority antirevivalist tradition of the area.[7]

The Universalists, too, shared abundantly in the Yankee heritage and exhibited enthusiastic response to those movements whose rationale was sympathetic with liberal theology. But most of the majority manifestations of the common mind, growing out of revivalistic beliefs, drove them into violent opposition. A healthy minority opinion, propagated with forthright zeal, often serves to develop strength in the majority group by furnishing a definite antithesis to be controverted. More than the Catholics in western New York did the Universalists serve as this kind of foil for the evangelists, stimulating them to ever-more-heroic efforts. Thus a thriving Universalist Church served a dual function, irritating the

---

[5] *Quarterly Register and Journal of the American Educational Society* (Andover, Mass.), I (Oct., 1827), 26; Stewart, *Freewill Baptists*, I, 414–415; *New York Observer*, I (Dec. 27, 1823), 127.

[6] Elbert Russell, *The History of Quakerism* (New York, 1942), 269, 270.

[7] See below, chapters 13 and 19.

revivalists to action while providing a stimulus for alternate types of enthusiasm.

This Yankee church, the rural equivalent of urban Unitarianism, entered the Burned-over District several years after the Great Revival and developed rapidly only with the increased tide of hill-country New Englanders who migrated in the years following 1815. Its emissaries were rugged itinerants, who roamed isolated country regions trading blows in kind with their evangelistic opponents. Although churches rose slowly in urban centers, about village and farm success was remarkable. By 1823 nearly ninety congregations had taken root in western New York, with strength centered in the lower Black River Valley and in the Finger Lakes and Genesee countries. In the following year, the sect was supporting periodicals at Watertown, Buffalo, Rochester, and Little Falls. Two of these, removed to Auburn and Utica, claimed circulation totaling nearly eight thousand copies by the end of the decade. A theological school had by this time appeared at Clinton, which would later remove to Canton and become St. Lawrence University. By 1845 this church had nearly as many congregations as had the Episcopalians, and twice as many as had the Catholics in the Burned-over District.[8]

If the smaller sects flourished in the new territory without much conscious direction, the larger ones enjoyed a thoroughly systematized evangelism. The Methodists, here as elsewhere, employed their circuit plan most effectively. Baptists and Congregationalists, lacking such machinery, substituted a confederation of missionary societies. This development, originated by the Connecticut Congregational Association and eventually copied by the Baptists, derived its major energies and its predominant aims from a remarkable nation-wide co-operative agreement between the Presbyterian Church of the Middle States and the Congregationalists of New England.

This Plan of Union of 1801 grew from the similarity of doctrine between the predominantly Scotch-Irish Presbyterians and the Edwardean branch of New England Congregationalism. The two churches faced together their two great problems: the threat of deism and Unitarianism, and the difficulty of supplying ade-

---

[8] *Census of the State of New York, for 1845* (Albany, 1846), *passim.*

quately trained clergymen to maintain doctrinal standards and yet achieve expansion in the growing frontier areas of the country. The agreement divided missionary enterprises at the New York–New England line. New churches to the east would join Congregational Associations. All to the west were expected to become Presbyterian under the "accommodation plan" which allowed Congregational bodies some latitude of internal structure, while bringing them under presbytery control. The two denominations would contribute jointly and individually to missionary enterprise as circumstances dictated, but the pastors would exchange affiliations as they crossed the geographical demarcation line.

The Plan of Union provided only a loose working agreement without consolidated management. The churches of New York and regions to the west usually joined the General Assembly at Philadelphia, but the energy and money which created them came primarily from New England. Organized societies, synonomous with, but independent of, the various Congregational Associations of New England, took the place of direct interdenominational controls for missionary undertakings. These societies, which rose out of the Great Revival, paved the way for the Plan of Union itself. They assumed a nonsectarian form and made general appeals for funds. In time they federated to achieve national scope and came to derive support more from the "New School" Presbyterians of New York and the West than from New England.

Connecticut churches began sending missionaries to the western emigrants as early as 1784. Ten years later the practice had become state-wide, had received the endorsement of the legislature, and had come to support at least eight "ministers of reputation" in the west.[9] Four years later the organization had developed which was soon to become standard for all benevolent societies. The General Association (the Connecticut Congregational Church) authorized formation of the independent Connecticut Missionary Society, with a board of directors composed of six laymen and six clergymen. The membership (open to all who paid a modest fee) included the entire clerical profession and most of the prominent laymen of the state. In time, honorary and life memberships at higher

---

9 Committee, General Association, *Address*, 4 and *passim*.

figures provided added revenues. The efficient enterprise thus established lent prestige to and gained support from talented businessmen, while it capitalized upon the fervor, ability, and direction to be gained from the clergy. The Connecticut Society so flourished under this design that by 1814 its revenues approximated four thousand dollars a year.[10]

Although the society's funds went into three fields of service—Vermont, western New York, and the Western Reserve of Ohio—in proportions which shifted more heavily westward with the passing years, a full half of the total for the first sixteen years poured into the Burned-over District. And even as late as 1823, long after most parts of New York equally merited support on grounds of recent settlement, a good 15 per cent still came in this direction. Such undue concentration of financial aid seems to trace to the fact that the western New Yorkers themselves contributed to the Connecticut itinerants more generously than did either Vermonters or Ohioans, and far more consistently. When the funds had to be stretched broadly and thinly among many missionaries, a reasonable amount of local support constituted a real attraction. So it happened that to those who had less need more was given.[11]

The first Connecticut evangelists had taken short leaves from home churches to tour in the west, but after the society was established it hired full-time itinerants. Soon after the turn of the century, most preachers found a station to provide local support and continued their itineracy from such a focal point. After 1829 they usually worked in a single community, with a portion of their salary underwritten by the home society. These early Connecticut clergymen exerted a profound influence on western New York. They settled as soon as local conditions permitted and cast their fortunes with the younger section. They led their colleagues in the ministry and guided the affairs of their communities. They introduced the Great Revival in the region and founded under

---

[10] Charles R. Keller, *The Second Great Awakening in Connecticut* (New Haven, Conn., 1942), 74–86.

[11] *A Narrative on the Subject of Missions: And a Statement of the Funds of the Missionary Society of Connecticut for the Year 1804* (Hartford, Conn., 1805); *Ibid.*, 1805–1808, 1810–1819 (title varies slightly); Rev. James H. Hotchkin, *A History of the Purchase and Settlement of Western New York and . . . of the Presbyterian Church in That Section* (New York, 1848), 178; *New York Observer*, II (March 27, 1824), 49.

its stimulus strong and growing Congregational churches which even after thirty years could be distinguished from others in size, vitality, support of benevolent enterprises, and aptitude for evangelistic enthusiasm.

The Connecticut Society was probably the most important single religious influence in the early days of the Burned-over District. It was also the first organization of its type, a model for the other groups which came to share the evangelizing campaigns in the region, and in every respect except the larger scale of its operations it may be considered typical. Three other New England Congregational societies, working on a smaller scale, poured their total effort into this one area for more than twenty years. The Massachusetts Missionary Society provided support for thirty preachers in 1814, four fewer than the Connecticut body; the Hampshire Society, of the Connecticut Valley neighborhood of Massachusetts, sustained at least fourteen men here the same year; while the Berkshire and Columbia Society (named for counties straddling the New York–Massachusetts line) had sent at least sixteen in all by that date. Other groups of the same nature, such as the New Hampshire Society and the Westchester and Morris Counties Associated Presbyteries (Congregational schismatics in southern New York and New Jersey), contributed similarly in smaller amounts.[12]

Despite these Yankee-driven missions, the Presbyterian General Assembly at Philadelphia soon began to operate in the field. The funds for this activity came primarily from the orthodox, Scotch-Irish branch of the church in the middle and southern states, but most of the missionaries proved to be New Englanders. This conservative wing was much less vigorous on all frontiers, but it sent the same undue proportion of its men into the western New York area as did the Yankees. In 1817 eight of a total of forty-four, and the next year nine out of thirty-six, worked in this single region,[13] and the same degree of support continued long after subsidiaries

---

12 Rev. James H. Dill, "Congregationalism in Western New York," *The Congregational Quarterly* (Boston, April, 1859); *Annual Report of the Trustees of the Hampshire Missionary Society,* etc. (Northampton, Mass., 1809); Hotchkin, *Western New York,* 32–88, *passim.*

13 *The First Report of the Board of Missions to the General Assembly of the Presbyterian Church in the United States of America for 1817* (Philadelphia, 1817); *Second Report, 1818.*

of the American Home Missionary Society had come to dominate the area.

Along with the organizations from the east and south, local bodies, patterned on the Connecticut model, grew up in New York to underwrite missions in their own vicinities. By the twenties these native groups dwarfed those of external origin and exceeded any corresponding activity in other parts of the Yankee mission field. The local movement developed gradually after 1810, nourished by the contemporaneous revivals and feeding them in return. The great number of separate societies in the Burned-over District gradually federated, until they joined in creating the American Home Missionary Society in 1826.[14] Since an article in the constitution of the national body allowed auxiliaries to designate where their funds should be spent, approximately the same distribution of activity continued under the new arrangement as had prevailed before the federation.[15] The first A.H.M.S. report showed 169 missionaries in the whole country. Of these, 120 were in New York State, 101 of whom had previously enjoyed the support of local societies. While these proportions continued practically unchanged for the next five years, the donations to the national society from this state still customarily exceeded expenditures here by about eight thousand dollars. By 1835 emphasis on western New York had declined substantially, yet 134 preachers still received aid in the western half of the state, and 45 in the eastern, of a total of 719 in the country.[16] The Western Agency reported without exaggeration upon the effect of the Missionary Society on western New York:

Its importance, practicability, and usefulness, have been fully established. Within nine years it has nurtured and strengthened more than two hundred different Presbyterian and Congregational Churches in the seventeen western counties of the state. It has bestowed upon these churches four hundred years of missionary labor, at an expense of $40,000. Many of these churches are now sustaining the Gospel without missionary help. . . . It has rendered essential aid in laying deep and broad foundations for a religious community; has done much to pro-

---

[14] Hotchkin, *Western New York, passim.*

[15] *First Report of the American Home Missionary Society* (New York, 1827), 69.

[16] *A.H.M.S. Report* (1827), 42–43; (1828), 48–50; (1835), 11–54.

mote the virtue, intelligence, and consequent prosperity of this part of the state, and to make it a delightful residence for the Christian, and for the lover of order.[17]

The report omitted the fact that the A.H.M.S. was a Plan of Union enterprise whose predominant backing came from New York State. It had, indeed, sprung full grown from local organizations whose development had been constant for fifteen years. The report did not note, as it might have, that the boasted prowess was really a tribute to the overwhelming extent of spiritual interests among New Yorkers themselves. Within the state, much of the revenue came from the wealthier eastern half, but the greater proportionate income, considering its youth, originated in the section west of the Catskills. Here the Yorker Yankees, under the stimulus of the Great Revival and succeeding awakenings, had long outrun the eastern area, as well as other states, in demand for religious satisfaction and in efforts to convert their neighbors and the world. Even in 1824, before the Finney revivals enhanced the tendency to concentrate energies here, and before the A.H.M.S. became the keystone of full organization, nearly half the Presbyterian clergymen in the country labored in this one state, while over a fourth of the national total served in the Burned-over District.[18]

The proportionate number of Baptists in the state was equally remarkable, and the missionary campaigns of this church before 1825 were exceeded only by the Presbyterian efforts. In both New York and New England, the Baptists lagged behind Congregationalists and Presbyterians in joining the interdenominational benevolent groups. In home missions, as well as in ministerial education, they preferred for the most part to play a lone hand. If their missionary work was less substantial because of slighter denominational cohesion and slimmer budgets, their opportunity in the Burned-over District was greater in another respect. The Separatists and Baptists of New England had been particularly strong in the very neighborhoods from which emigration to western New York was heaviest. Perhaps they also had greater initial

[17] *A.H.M.S. Report* (1835), 77.
[18] *New York Observer*, II (June 12, 1824), 96.

success in the early revival waves of this region. Whatever the reason, they gained at a faster rate than the Presbyterians and by 1825 had 40,000 professing members. No adjacent state had over 12,000 Baptists, and only Virginia and Kentucky had over half as many as New York.[19]

The first New England Baptist itinerants left for New York in 1792. Organization of the work began ten years later with the formation of the Massachusetts Baptist Missionary Society, and was reinforced by the addition of a Connecticut society in 1811. The New York Baptists, like the Presbyterians, soon undertook this work themselves in similar groups and rapidly outdid the parent section. The Baptists shifted center to the west even more prominently. Soon a far larger segment of the church existed here than remained in New England itself. The Hamilton Society, established in 1807, came within twelve years to support 21 itinerants for a total of 134 weeks in the area about Oneida and Madison counties. This group developed subsidiaries, evolved into the New York State Baptist Missionary Convention, and finally sponsored a national organization. In 1838, auxiliaries of the American Baptist Home Missionary Society helped support 48 churches in the Burned-over District, and maintained 18 missionaries in addition. As late as 1844, the national body and its subsidiaries still aided 110 men in the state, 62 of whom functioned in the western half. This compared with sponsorship of 38 men each in Pennsylvania and Ohio, and smaller numbers sprinkled over the other states of the Union.[20] Thus the Baptists, like the Presbyterians, through their organized missionary work succeeded in creating a disproportionately strong religious interest in western New York.

The home missionary societies worked at supplying clergymen, but other benevolent organizations performed functions of nearly equal importance. Just as the A.H.M.S. was predominantly a Plan of Union order with mere appendages beyond New York State, so was the whole associated train of would-be national benevolent

---

[19] *New York Observer*, III (June 18, 1825), 97.

[20] *Western New York Baptist Missionary Magazine* (Norwich, Morrisville), III (May, 1822), 289–292; *Baptist Register* (Utica), II (June 10, 1825), 59; *Annual Report of the American Baptist Home Missionary Society* (New York), no. 6 (1838), 21 ff.; no. 12 (1844), 24–36.

organizations conceived on one side of New York's eastern border and reared on the other. Like the mission enterprises, these sister activities also had grown extraordinarily in western New York and were fully organized locally before they achieved national federation.

Largest of these groups, and oldest of the domestic ones, was the American Bible Society. At least seven auxiliaries within the Burned-over District had preceded the formation of the national society. By 1829 a sixth of the subsidiaries in the United States, about a hundred, operated in this state. New York in twenty years bought over twice as many Bibles from the parent body as did New England and donated more cash for its support than came from Massachusetts and Connecticut combined.[21] The two regions together accounted for a preponderant majority of the total business.

The two American Tract Societies in Boston and New York grew likewise out of earlier local groups. The New York City body was far the larger, encompassing all activity beyond New England. Since circulation corresponded roughly to the strength of the various auxiliaries, the position of the New York State unit is indicated by the fact that in 1822 it had published three-fourths of all tracts issued in the country. During the two years following its foundation in 1825, the American Tract Society (New York) printed forty-four million pages, of which only a million crossed the Allegheny Mountains. In ten years it published thirty million tracts, nearly a million *Christian Almanacs,* and over two million miscellaneous magazines, books, and pamphlets. Probably not more than a quarter of this output left the confines of the state. The Baptist General Tract Society, formed in 1824, had one semi-independent branch in Rochester with half as many auxiliaries as belonged from the whole country to the parent body (136), and another in Utica, second only to the Rochester unit.[22]

Besides these bodies mainly concerned with publishing, other

---

21 *Journal, American Education Society,* II (Aug., 1829), 31, 51; *Western Recorder* (Utica), II (Jan. 25, 1825), 14; *Twenty-first Annual Report of the American Bible Society* (New York, 1837), *passim.*

22 *First Annual Report of the American Tract Society* (New York, 1826), 15; *Journal, American Education Society,* I (July, 1827), 13; *Tenth Report, American Tract Society,* 1835, 24; *Journal, American Education Society,* II (Aug., 1829), 40; *Baptist Register,* IV (April 18, 1828), 31.

benevolent societies engaged in printing incidentally. All the home mission groups contributed to religious literature. The Methodist book concerns and periodical presses sent their products out in the saddlebags of the circuit riders. The colonizationists, seaman's friends, and later the Sunday school, temperance, female reform, antislavery, and other organizations helped to build up a huge total of religious propaganda whose circulation in all likelihood followed the same distribution lines as those of the major publishing groups, farther developing the concentration of religious influences in western New York.

A different enterprise developed to maintain a supply of men upon which the A.H.M.S. might draw. The American Education Society, like its fellows, superimposed federal unity upon previously operating concerns. Its largest auxiliary, the Western Education Society of New York, had collected locally nearly thirty thousand dollars during 1819 to aid indigent college and seminary students. After its juncture with the national body in 1827, this unit remained independently active, supporting up to a hundred ministerial candidates besides its contributions to and proportional withdrawals from the parent society. The Baptists, unwilling to trust the advertised nonsectarianism of this group, maintained a separate education society in the state.[23]

These various benevolent orders had no official interrelationship, but their directorates often interlocked, their memberships were substantially identical, they flourished in the same areas, and they contributed strength to each other while deriving support from and lending encouragement to the contemporaneous revival campaigns. The Baptists and Methodists maintained forthright denominational connections, perhaps limiting their appeal by so doing. The Plan of Union groups, in part perhaps because of their nonsectarian make up but probably more largely because of the wealth and prestige of their Congregational and Presbyterian members, had far greater influence in western New York. These societies appear to deserve primary responsibility for the phenomenal

---

[23] *Evangelical Recorder* (Auburn), II (June 19, 1819), 44–45; Hotchkin, *Western New York*, 261; Charles W. Brooks, *A Century of Missions in the Empire State*, etc., (sec. ed., Philadelphia, 1909), 75; *Twenty-second Annual Meeting of the Baptist Education Society of the State of New York* (Utica, 1839), 20.

growth of New School Presbyterian churches, for the successful operation of the Plan of Union itself, and for the unique concentration of religious zeal in the Burned-over District.[24]

The forthcoming expressions of this concentrated energy would doubtless have been far different, had the doctrinal similarity upon which the Plan of Union was founded remained constant as the benevolent movements expanded. In fact, the movements themselves assisted the evolution of a new theology, quite different from either the Presbyterian or the Congregational at the turn of the century. The New School beliefs penetrated completely the Plan of Union churches of the westering Yankees, but they affected New England Congregationalism much less and Scotch-Irish Presbyterianism scarcely at all. By the 1830's controversies raged between the New England conservatives and the westerners, while the Presbyterian denomination suffered complete schism in 1837.

The Edwardean traditions of New England Congregationalism were even in 1800 more liberal and flexible than those of the Princetonian Presbyterians of Scotch antecedents. Edwards' successors had developed distinctive aspects of his thought in two opposite directions. Timothy Dwight and, later, Nathaniel Taylor of the New Haven theological seminary gradually warped the New England theology in the Arminian direction, away from the notion of predestination and toward free will. This tendency, continued by Lyman Beecher and Charles Finney, approached the Methodist position that anyone who willed to do so could choose to be holy rather than sinful, while it minimized the Puritan emphasis upon the independent workings of the Holy Ghost in the process of conversion. The other school, typified by Samuel Hopkins and Joseph Bellamy, placed increasing emphasis upon the total sovereignty of God and the absolute powerlessness of the individual being before Him. Because man must love God totally in all His grandeur, do His will whatever it might be—even to glory in damnation, if that be one's lot, in order to demonstrate His power—this tradition came to foster the "disinterested benevolence" which would grow

---

[24] Oliver W. Elsbree, *The Rise of the Missionary Spirit in America, 1790–1815* (Williamsport, Penna., 1928), and J. Orin Oliphant, "The American Missionary Spirit, 1828–1835," *Church History*, VIII (June, 1938), 125–137, best summarize the benevolent movements.

into movements for moral reform. Revivalists caught up a part of this emphasis along with the other and bred of the two an illogical, but effective, doctrine.

Man's ability to be saved was a matter of his own will, yet actual conversion was supposed to be exclusively the work of the Holy Spirit. Complete submission to the will of God would somehow put one in the way to be saved. Righteous behavior was both a token of the person's correct state of mind and a symbol of Heavenly favor. This doctrine justified a revivalism of increasing strenuousness and sensationalism and placed the evangelist in a continually more responsible position. It made him God's agent and interpreter, who could tell one how to be saved, yet torment one with threats of damnation. Once the individual was converted, the evangelist indicated what kind of behavior was the will of God. At this last stage, the New School theology expanded religious energies into a host of crusades, aimed at the redemption of sinners but in the process invading fields of social reform.[25]

Whether a certain brand of theology was instrumental in creating evangelistic excitement and benevolent activity, or whether the emotion and social emphasis generated the theology in justification, is ultimately to be decided only by a subjective judgment. Many church historians answer the question one way, and most secular scholars, the other, each according to preconceived notions. In actual occurrence, both processes may have gone on together, reinforcing each other. The benevolent societies, however, did begin as natural extensions of the home missionary movement. This in turn developed out of the Great Revival, before the greater changes in the New England theology had occurred. Westward migration, neighborly concern for the welfare of emigrants, the concurrent development of economic maturity and of political democracy, and the tendencies to humanitarianism those two growths fostered—all these circumstances seem nearly sufficient to explain the nature of the benevolent movement, even if its theology

---

[25] See Keller, *Second Great Awakening;* Elsbree, *Missionary Spirit;* the various works of Charles Finney; Charles Beecher, ed., *Autobiography, Correspondence, etc., of Lyman Beecher, D.D.* (2 vols.; New York, 1863), especially a letter to the Rev. A. Hooker, March 13, 1825, II, 25; and Sidney E. Mead, *Nathaniel William Taylor, 1786–1858: A Connecticut Liberal* (Chicago, 1942).

may have been designed as much by after- as by forethought. In any case, the benevolent groups had succeeded by the mid-twenties in creating a phenomenally intensive religious and moral awareness in the Burned-over District.

Chapter 3. PREMONITIONS

INCREASING revivalism and growing benevolent operations demonstrate that the evangelical movement begun in the Great Revival was surging toward a crest throughout the first quarter of the nineteenth century. The full tide of religious agitation would not affect the Burned-over District until after 1825. But minor swirlings and bubblings, slight tokens of greater experiments and excitements to come, can be discerned among the first generation of western New Yorkers. Such early manifestations of enthusiasm may in some cases have been direct inspirations for ensuing developments. More certainly they provide a gauge to measure the early steps of a more general phenomenon: the growing appetite of the region for exhibitions of zeal.

Several types of these manifestations appeared. The Shaker communities at New Lebanon and Sodus Bay and the colony of the Universal Friend on Keuka Lake were importations, already established faiths when they entered the area in its earliest days. Less distinctive but perhaps more significant, since they illustrate more broadspread native impulses, were a number of scattered eccentricities whose histories were as transitory as they were local. Still more indicative of the future character of the section were innumerable episodes, presumably typical, which illustrate the competition between the various denominations struggling for mastery over western New York. The bitterness engendered and the complexity of doctrine produced by an unremitting warfare of theologies would have much to do with the greater spiritual upheavals of the future.

Mother Ann Lee, prophet and founder of Shakerism, crossed the Atlantic from England with a small group of followers in 1774. Her adherents, first assembled at Watervliet two years later, soon moved to New Lebanon, where they established a communal enterprise in 1787. Although greater growth occurred in the communities found in New England during the nineties, and in the Ohio Valley after the turn of the century, the first-built colony near the eastern boundary line of New York remained the largest single society and the first family of the church. While the essential doctrines of the church had been fixed by Ann Lee and her few English disciples, she and her original followers had died before the growth which came with the Great Revival guaranteed that her innovations would survive. Some modification of belief and practice undoubtedly accompanied the period of expansion under American leaders, so Shakerism may be considered a partially native religion, as well in ideas as in membership.

Like a number of novel beliefs yet to arise, Shakerism was established upon a theory of the Second Coming and the millennium. Ann Lee represented the second embodiment in human flesh, this time of the feminine spirit of a bisexual God. Her followers lived in a new dispensation. Community of interest, celibacy, nonresistance, full equality of woman in both physical and spiritual life, the direct guidance of the Holy Ghost in personal and community worship, an extremely perfectionist code for individual behavior, mystic powers of healing—these and other Shaker doctrines impossible of execution by unregenerate man could be carried out in the life of this millennial society.

Despite, or perhaps because of, the Pentecostal orientation of Shaker beliefs, they included elements which tended to make for greater liberality than did the orthodox theologies. Punishment of the wicked was not to be everlasting. Predestination and original sin were abandoned. Baptism, the Communion, and concepts of the Trinity and the atonement, alike were discarded. Literal adherence to the Bible was supplanted by direct revelation. The chaste, honest, industrious, and saintly life a person led, rather than any sacrament or creed, was his chief claim to sanctification.

It involved among other things eschewing tobacco, alcoholic beverages, war, politics, and corporal punishment, while it demanded the discharge of all debts and the labor of one for all.[1]

The absence of orthodox dogmatism and the presence of a communist system may well explain why some fifty members of a failing Owenite colony [2] and a man of agnostic bearings like Frederick W. Evans should be attracted to New Lebanon. The great majority of converts, however, apparently throughout Shaker history as well as during the inaugural years, came from the major Protestant denominations. They joined after times of general revival, when emotions had been excited, convictions of latter-day immanence roused, and hopes and expectations of personal holiness kindled. The most earnest seekers after a more intense spirituality, disappointed by declining zeal, regularly found final refuge in the various Shaker communities sprinkled from Maine to Kentucky.[3]

Shakerism thus remained throughout the first half of the nineteenth century a kind of ultimate among enthusiastic movements. It likewise incorporated several ideas which were to become characteristic of various future enthusiasms. In one sense, then, it may be considered a model for the more eccentric developments of Burned-over District history after 1825. Germs of communism, premillennialism, spiritualism, and perfectionism could from existing Shaker communities infect larger movements.

Inhabitants of central and western New York knew something of this people. How much and how accurately they knew seems impossible to determine, for Shakers lived much unto themselves. One community did grow up and remain through the period in the western part of the state, but it was one apparently smaller than most of the other units and little noted in Shaker annals. The people involved in a revival at Sodus Bay in 1826 sent to New Lebanon for assistance. A group from the mother colony responded, and at least six remained to guide the new venture. Ten years later,

---

[1] *Autobiography of Mary Antoinette Doolittle*, etc. (Mt. Lebanon, N.Y., 1880), 35 ff.; [Benjamin S. Youngs, *et al.*], *Testimony of Christ's Second Appearing*, etc. (4th ed.; Albany, 1856), *passim*.

[2] Anna White and Leila S. Taylor, *Shakerism: Its Meaning and Message*, etc. (Columbus, O., 1904), 159.

[3] Doolittle, *Autobiography*, 9–30; White and Taylor, *Shakerism*, 35–37; Marguerite F. Melcher, *The Shaker Adventure* (Princeton, 1941), 20, 35, 59.

when a Sodus Canal was being agitated, the group removed to a site near Groveland in the Genesee Valley to remain at least until after 1850.[4] The first location later fell into possession of the Sodus Fourierist Phalanx. Mops, seeds, and presumably other Shaker products found a market in western New York towns,[5] but cultural exports are more difficult to trace. Any direct influence from Shakerism upon later religions in the region must apparently be assumed rather than proved.

The Community of the Publick Universal Friend, planted first on Seneca Lake in the present town of Dresden in 1787, and soon after removed to Jerusalem, Yates County, had much in common with Shaker colonies, though it was quite certainly an entirely independent development. The founder was a woman, known before her religious experience as Jemima Wilkinson or Wilkerson.[6] Her early life, like Ann Lee's, was spent in the Friends' meeting. Her converts were at first chiefly Quakers, but like those of the Shakers included persons both within and beyond that church, reared in the Separatist traditions of the Great Awakening in New England. She, also, emphasized celibacy, equality of the sexes, and a modified communism. The same millennial note was present, though not stressed, but The Friend never laid claim to divinity or even to prophethood. She did believe that after her conversion in 1777 a new spirit inherited the body of Jemima Wilkinson, a messenger from Christ, destined to proclaim "News of Salvation to all that would Repent and believe the Gospel." She preached, apparently with great effect, from Bible texts, and had won a numerous and influential following in Rhode Island, Connecticut, and Pennsylvania during the first ten years of her ministry.[7] Unlike the Shakers,

---

[4] Doolittle, *Autobiography*, 32; White and Taylor, *Shakerism*, 154–157; Arthur E. Bestor, Jr., "American Phalanxes: A Study of Fourierist Socialism in the United States (with Special Reference to the Movement in Western New York)" (2 vols.; MS at Yale University, 1938), I, 20, 21, 115 ff.

[5] *Rochester Daily Advertiser and Telegraph*, March 27, 1830; *Daily Advertiser*, Oct. 4, 1830.

[6] Her will is signed by mark, but must have been written by an intimate companion. Here the name is clearly spelled Wilkerson. "Will of the Universal Friend, 25, 2nd month, 1818," Jemima Wilkinson Papers, Cornell Collection of Regional History.

[7] Stafford C. Cleveland, *History and Directory of Yates County, Containing a Sketch of Its Original Settlement by the Public Universal Friends*, etc. (Penn Yan, 1873), I, 19–50; "Journal of Ruth Spencer, 1792–1817," Wilkinson MSS.

the followers of The Friend exerted a demonstrable influence upon the Burned-over District.

Her advance guard was the first group of settlers known to have wintered west of Cayuga Lake. The prosperous Yankee Quakers among her disciples bought extensive tracts of land in the Genesee country, in addition to that purchased for the community and partially divided among the contributors.[8] Her people were the first whites to raise crops in the area, probably built the first mill, and helped to feed the early settlers brought by Charles Williamson to the lands of the Pulteney Estate just west of them. The Friend herself joined the colony in 1789 and lived there until she "left time" in 1819. Lawsuits between her heirs and several opposers and apostates dragged in the courts until 1828. Her appointed successor, Rachel Malin, apparently held at least a core of the society together until her death in 1843. A number of families in and about Penn Yan today trace their descent from persons originally members of the community.

The entire venture has suffered in reputation from malicious gossip, probably devised originally to prejudice the courts handling the protracted suits which were the colony's nemesis. Most commentaries which have been perpetuated find their origin in a single scurrilous attack published in 1821.[9] Credible contemporary witnesses, with one exception, support the dignity of The Friend's character, note her personal beauty, charm, and effective leadership, and explicitly or implicitly deny the monstrous fabrications of modern folklore.[10] Apparently her preaching emphasized the

---

[8] James Parker, Jerusalem, 17, 9th month, 1788, to the Publick Universal Friend, Wilkinson MSS.

[9] David Hudson, *History of Jemima Wilkinson: A Preacheress of the Eighteenth Century*, etc. (Geneva, 1821); and another edition, published as *Memoir of Jemima Wilkinson*, etc. (Bath, 1844).

[10] Carl Carmer, in *Listen for a Lonesome Drum: A York State Chronicle* (New York, 1936), acknowledged use of the Potter family Wilkinson manuscripts, but his story bears no relationship beyond personal names to the information he claims to have utilized. The exception among contemporaries who met her is Duke de La Rochefoucauld-Liancourt [François Alexandre Frédéric], *Travels through the United States of North America . . . in the Years 1795, 1796, and 1797*, etc. (2 vols.; London, 1799), I, 110–124. Compare George Peck, *Early Methodism within the Bounds of the Old Genesee Conference*, etc. (New York, 1860), 125–127, 250, which has the original impressions of two circuit riders in 1797 and 1805; Marilla Marks, Oberlin, Dec. 5, 1843, to Margaret Millen, Wilkinson MSS; and Robert P. St. John, "Jemima Wilkinson,"

gentler and more liberal doctrines to be built from the Scriptures rather than the more harsh and limiting ones then in style. She probably preached love, charity, resignation, unlimited salvation, and good works. In any case, persons once in her society proved singularly resistant to the less gentle persuasions of Calvinist ministers.[11] Rachel Malin herself befriended David Marks, a pioneer Freewill Baptist itinerant in western New York, and his wife. James Parker, one of the wealthiest, most accomplished, and most staunch supporters in the early days, quarreled with Jemima in 1800. He became an ordained Freewill Baptist minister of some prominence, but in 1811 he joined the Universalists and assisted materially in establishing that church in the Genesee country. He entertained a Methodist preacher cordially even in 1797 and was at that time interested in Swedenborg. He may at one time later in life have made a Swedenborgian affiliation, but he died a Methodist.[12] At least some of the society became interested in Antimasonry and later in abolition.[13]

It seems fair to conclude that if later prophets or eccentrics learned anything from Jemima's example, it was from their false conception of her nature rather than from the actuality. On the other hand, the gradual dispersion of her followers into the more liberal churches may have greatly strengthened opposition to revivalistic excitement in their vicinity, while reinforcing reform movements aimed at more definitely social or political objectives. The communist impulse to be derived from this example was certainly very slight, if it existed at all. The Friend's system allowed private property complete freedom; she merely herself maintained

New York State Historical Association Quarterly Journal, XI (April, 1930), 158–175, who reviews other evidence to the same effect.

11 James Rowlett, Jerusalem, March, 1832, to Miles P. Squier, Corresponding Secretary, Western Agency, American Home Missionary Society, American Home Missionary Society Papers, Chicago Theological Seminary.

12 Parker had been a magistrate for twenty years and state treasurer of Rhode Island. He negotiated the purchase of the colony lands and directed settlement until Jemima arrived. References to him in Cleveland, *Yates County*, I, 6, 7, 26, 65, 67, 69; Peck, *Early Methodism*, 125–127; *Memoirs of the Life of Nathaniel Stacy*, etc. (Columbus, Penna., 1850), 238–245, and his letters to The Friend establish his complete integrity.

13 Richard Mosely, Thompson [Conn.?], April 2, 1829, to James Brown, and Marilla Marks, Oberlin, Dec. 5, 1843, to Margaret Millen, Wilkinson MSS.

a "family" which presumably depended for support on some voluntary labor by others upon the land placed in her name. Her will only commanded Rachel and Margaret Malin to see to the employment and support of her "family" and to provide "assistance, comfort & support during natural life" for "all poor persons belonging to the society of the Universal Friend." [14] Her mixed system of community and private enterprise failed completely, in a tangle of bitter litigation.

The colonies of the Shakers and The Friend contributed character to the Burned-over District. They were not, however, bred in the region. Nor can they be deemed typical of frontier society generally, regardless of their specific location. But the first generation of western New Yorkers included its share of individual eccentrics: the sort which appeared spasmodically on every frontier, gathered sometimes a small following, and usually soon lost identity with the advance of more mature civilization. Only presumably representative samples can at this late date be discovered; yet, whatever their number, such peculiarities doubtless had some part in forming the traits of the rising generation.

Undoubtedly many individuals or families buffeted by an adverse fate in the unkind environment of the frontier were driven to novel expedients which affected their religious beliefs. Most cases passed into oblivion with the persons who experienced them, or with their children. One family tragedy, perhaps unique in its exact nature, will nevertheless serve to show how rugged, sane, God-fearing pioneers could under duress wrench their thoughts into unaccustomed paths.

Benajah McCall was a Yankee of Scotch-Irish antecedents, a soldier in the Revolutionary army, and progenitor of a family later to achieve some local distinction in western New York. His second wife, with a family of stepchildren to rear, soon after the war "by an unskillful physician and the use of calomel lost her sight and the use of her limbs. The cords of her limbs were drawn up in a sitting posture." Retaining her other senses, she lived thus for eleven years, while the family took up its military land in the wilds of the upper Delaware Valley. Under these circumstances, Benajah

---

[14] "Will of the Universal Friend," Wilkinson MSS.

began to imbibe sentiments + sometimes to argue that polliggamy was right that it was not prohibited in the Old Testament nor interdicted in the new. his friends laboured with him, and his Brethren of the congregational church but to no effect, he Brought into the house a widdow whose character was bad . . . to the great grief + mortification of his family. . . .[15]

Unrecorded individual cases bred of conditions on this order may explain, as much as does the existence of more organized heresy, an apparently large proportion of excommunications in the early churches of western New York.[16]

Clergymen as well as parishioners braved the perils of the wilderness and met their share of adversity. Personal situations may have compelled doctrinal innovations, or relative freedom from a community of clerical minds may have released inborn tendencies to visionary speculations. Whatever the reason, an apparently plentiful sprinkling of preachers inaugurated unusual beliefs in the early history of the Burned-over District. Shifts from one sect to another were frequent. Exclusions, suspensions, or excommunications from the ministry, seemingly quite numerous, undoubtedly reflect these changes of affiliation as well as transgressions from the very narrow path necessarily trod by clergymen of that day, and outright religious novelties in addition. At least two Methodists on the Holland Purchase were frankly called eccentric.[17] Possible traces of other unusual personal clerical histories, otherwise buried, are indicated in the plentiful reports from several neighborhoods of abundant errors, heresies, or irreligion; but one who reads enough of contemporary sources to learn the attitude of the various sects toward each other cannot take such reports too seriously.

One practice which probably was a recent innovation, whether or not it particularly prevailed on this frontier, should however receive emphatic notice. At least two women preached regularly

---

[15] James McCall, Rushford, N.Y., to Ansel J. McCall, copy of first letter in a series, dated 1843, in copybook no. 1 of Ansel McCall, James McCall to Ansel [second letter, Jan., 1843], undated, Ansel J. McCall Papers, Cornell Collection of Regional History.

[16] Rev. James H. Hotchkin, *A History of the Purchase and Settlement of Western New York and of the . . . Presbyterian Church in That Section* (New York, 1848), 129; A. Russell Belden, *History of the Cayuga Baptist Association,* etc. (Auburn, 1851), 40–41.

[17] Peck, *Early Methodism,* 239.

in western New York before 1825, one in the Methodist and one in the Freewill Baptist Church. Women certainly constituted a majority of the memberships of most early churches. They began early in the benevolent movement, here as in New England, to form female societies which often proved the main support of the various local chapters.[18] Churches accustomed to women's preaching could scarcely deny their feminine members full participation in the meeting, and those which sponsored women's charity organizations were well on their way to the same position at a very early date in western New York history.

Nor did the ministry of the Burned-over District completely escape early manifestations of mass tendencies to change the religious status quo. A group of sixty New York preachers met, probably during the year 1825, to protest the evils of the Methodist episcopacy and make friendly gestures toward the Christian Connection.[19]

Whatever the significance of such hints of strange religious leadership, a few more distinct tokens of nonconformity have survived to suggest the nature of others only vaguely ascertainable. Just as the mass of people came from east of the Hudson River, so also did their early eccentricities, stemming from a continuous Yankee tradition of irregularity which stretched back to Anne Hutchinson in the early seventeenth century. Thus, some of the illustrative cases which have most nearly approached the light of historical investigation happen to find their chief locale farther east than the Burned-over District proper. About Guilford, Vermont and Leyden, Massachusetts, during the 1790's, an ex-officer of the British army assumed prophetic gifts and established some type of politico-religious movement. This experiment apparently soon foundered and its members dispersed, presumably westward.

Near Middletown, Vermont, during the Great Revival, there bloomed another sect with extraordinary doctrines, apparently involving millennial expectations and direct revelation as well as some mysterious treasure hunting. One of the two leaders, named

18 *Ibid.*, 239; I. D. Stewart, *The History of the Freewill Baptists for Half a Century* (2 vols.; Dover, N.H., 1862), I, 408; Charles R. Keller, *The Second Great Awakening in Connecticut* (New Haven, Conn., 1942), 234.

19 *Gospel Luminary* (West Bloomfield), II (Aug., 1826), 190.

Winchell, and a follower, named Oliver Cowdery, moved to Palmyra, New York, where the latter in time became Joseph Smith's clerical assistant. During the next significant time of revival following the War of 1812, a group calling themselves Pilgrims migrated from north of the Vermont line in Canada, through Woodstock, where at least a hundred converts were gathered, to the vicinity of Troy, New York. Later they moved by gradual stages to Missouri.[20]

About the same time Talcott Patching, a war veteran originally from Saratoga Springs, moved to Boston, Erie County, and experienced conversion in the Baptist Church. He advocated receiving into membership the sprinkled as well as the baptized, disapproved of the Bible and church government, and relied for guidance upon the infallible inner light. It may be significant that Boston was from the beginning predominantly a Quaker settlement. Patching gathered adherents from most of the Baptist churches in the Erie Association, influenced a number of preachers, and kept that denomination in the area somewhat upset until he migrated to Texas in 1834. Perhaps similar, or even connected, was a movement in the Ontario Freewill Baptist Quarterly Meeting which came to a climax about 1825, when at least two churches, in Lyons and Williamson, suffered disfellowship. A more infamous, or perhaps merely more investigated, prophet, named Matthias, was about the same time disturbing churchly peace in Albany and New York City.[21]

Further investigation might bring a larger number of the heretical movements of western New York's first generation into an area of knowledge from the present one of supposition. But the unreliable data to be discovered would at best leave their details still in question and their significance in doubt. Whether any greater number of such events occurred here than elsewhere could in all probability never be satisfactorily determined. To guess with admittedly slight evidence, it seems likely that these aberrations of individual church members, parsons, or prophets should be con-

---

20 David M. Ludlum, *Social Ferment in Vermont, 1791–1850* (New York, 1939), 239–243.

21 Stewart, *Freewill Baptists*, I, 405–412; Hiram Smith, Collins, N.Y., to Miles P. Squier, Sept. 21, 1831, A.H.M.S. MSS; Theodore Schroeder, "Matthias the Prophet (1788–1837)," *Journal of Religious Psychology*, VI (Jan., 1913), 59–65.

sidered typical at least of the New England-settled frontiers generally throughout American history. Perhaps such minor eccentricities, seldom widely adopted or long preserved, though they may be encouraged by a frontier society, happen in all times and places for reasons beyond the possible scope of historical analysis.

These normal agitations of the frontier era, and the colonies of the Shakers and the Universal Friend as well, help to explain the growth of a distinctive quality in the Burned-over District. The more significant fact is that none became large-scale movements before 1825. After that date, when the frontier days were fairly closed, the region earned its reputation for peculiar innovations. The distinction must be clearly made between the occasional unexplainable eccentricity of a single or a few minds, happening at any time or place without integral connection to a particular society, and the kind of general upheaval which could take place when one of these isolated phenomena coincided with a cultural situation which made it catch on, gain wide support, and flourish for a respectable length of time. The latter type of movement grew out of western New York only when its civilization had passed early youth. It was sired much less by the kind of events just reviewed than by another enthusiastic element in the character of the early Burned-over District: one nearly universal in the area, bred into its life from the first settlements, and apparently quite distinctive.

The conditions of frontier life probably worked toward cordial interdenominational relations. The entire evangelical movement of the first quarter of the century seemed in many respects to stress piety rather than sectarian peculiarities. The Plan of Union itself evinced an early desire to redeem sinners without undue creedal emphasis. The whole string of benevolent societies was nondenominational in form, nondoctrinal in bearing, and at least officially directed toward common Christian goals. Yet warfare between sects, perhaps common in type, but definitely uncommon in intensity, raged increasingly in western New York, long before the excitements which followed after 1825. It is paradoxical that purportedly nonsectarian revivalism and benevolence should encompass much of the spirit they professed and yet engender interdenominational strife of a bitterness scarcely to be paralleled. Resolution of the paradox requires a rather close examination of the process by which Burned-over District churches developed.

The test of conversion for church membership, common to all the evangelistic denominations in the region, created a condition little known in recent times. An overwhelming majority of western New Yorkers sympathized with the churches and attended meeting regularly. Relatively few, however, "professed" religion, attended Communion, or belonged in a legal or religious sense to the church proper. This situation was indicated by the phrase "the church and society" regularly used in ministerial correspondence. A reliable witness once estimated the normal proportions of the two groups in the Presbyterian Church (nationally) at 250,000 members to 2,000,000 "allied population." A Baptist, writing in 1817 from an Ontario County town, probably described a not uncommon congregation:

I do not administer to a church in this Neighborhood where I live, for there is none—my congregation has . . . some nominal Baptists, presbyterians, congregationalists; and some of them have been . . . deeply tinctured with Arminianism; several Universalists; and there are a number of nothingarians, and profane vulgarists . . . that sometimes attends my preaching. . . .[22]

Revivals did not customarily bring outsiders into the church so much as they promoted the hopeful onlookers to the sanctity of church membership. Most of the persons usually described by Baptist and Presbyterian clergymen as irreligious, immoral, or profane went to church regularly and expected at some future time to experience conversion during a revival. This allied population also contributed regularly to the budgets, through pew rents, collections, and pledges for buildings and salaries.

In pioneering days, while ministers and church members remained thinly scattered and local transportation was difficult, professors and sympathizers of all denominations perforce attended the nearest church. Most Baptist and Presbyterian pastors addressed at least two congregations, on alternate Sundays. The Methodist circuit riders held meeting whenever they arrived at a

---

22 Calvin Colton, *Thoughts on the Religious State of the Country; with Reasons for Preferring Episcopacy* (New York, 1836), 63; Elkanah Watson, Phelps, April 23, 1817, to John Williams, John Williams Papers, American Baptist Historical Society, Crozier Theological Seminary.

given spot on their rounds, leaving class leaders to conduct Sunday sessions when no other service was held in the neighborhood. School houses in completely rural vicinities often harbored Methodist service on one Sunday, Baptist, the next, and perhaps Presbyterian, the third. As often as not, the first church building in a town was erected by general subscription and shared on alternate Sundays by at least two sects.

Under these circumstances, when a revival commenced it automatically became interdenominational. If one minister presided at the beginning, the others participated during the following weeks. The meeting which exhibited the first token of awakening usually included at least the most active members of the church which would conduct service the next week. Once the revival gained momentum, all the preachers in the vicinity would drop other business to attend the one agitated neighborhood, for the constant hope of each church was to increase sufficiently to build its own meetinghouse and support its own pastor. The struggle for converts followed; but during the active season itself, co-operation could be complete, for the interests of all were served in the proportion that enthusiasm flourished.[23]

A wise, cautious, tactful clergyman could rapidly build a vigorous "church and society," minister to the spiritual needs of his community, keep the sectarians in his own congregation on friendly terms, and preserve cordiality among his rival colleagues. In certain areas within the Burned-over District this type of development occurred and continued. In Norwich, for instance, as late as 1826, the Baptist church entertained the village at a series of plays given by the youths of the locality, while the Presbyterians gladly lent their building for a Methodist Quarterly Meeting. Luther Lee, beginning his ministry on the Malone circuit in the mid-twenties, found his injured horse providentially replaced through the charity of a prominent Presbyterian. At Avon, in 1828, the minister announced, "This is a free church," and invited Christians of all denominations to attend Communion.[24]

---

[23] Peck, *Early Methodism*, 356, 367–368; *The Life and Times of Rev. George Peck, D.D., Written by Himself* (New York, 1874), 22 ff.; William Reed, *Life on the Border, Sixty Years Ago* (Fall River, Mass., 1882), 42–43.

[24] *People's Advocate* (Norwich), May 21, Oct. 7, 1826; Luther Lee, *Autobiography*,

Although these are not isolated cases, they unfortunately represent the minority practice. Luther Lee regarded Malone circuit as a very poor one, and both Avon and Norwich were among the river towns of which Presbyterians complained because of their heterogeneous populations, moral laxity, and spiritual deadness.

Probably in other regions where revival fervor was less intense and benevolent societies less developed church practices proved more consistent with their professions. Here they nurtured a zeal which, interdenominational and noncreedal as it might be at the height of a revival, often relentlessly and increasingly sharpened sectarian antagonisms. The consequent warfare was not a free-for-all among numerous independent, equal interests; rather it comprised a complicated array of distinct campaigns, each with a different combination ranged against the enemy.

The different campaigns made up a sectarian hierarchy. All Protestant churches united in condemning Catholics. All evangelical sects united, too, against Universalists and Unitarians. Methodists, Baptists, and Presbyterians could share their hatred of Christians. Baptists and Presbyterians co-operated in damning Methodists and Freewill Baptists. Presbyterians all too often proved disagreeably intolerant of Baptists. To cap the climax, both Baptists and Presbyterians, particularly the latter, maintained a constant and bitter strife between the enthusiasts and the conservatives in their own ranks.

It is not to be supposed that these hostilities were unique in kind within western New York. They were unique in intensity, in the same proportion that revivalism and the benevolent operations concentrated in this region. Presbyterians might on occasion accuse their fellow churchmen or Calvinist Baptists more gently than they did Universalists or Catholics, but none of their epithets were carefully weighed in any circumstance. Their very scruples shock the modern observer—whom they would have called an immoral infidel. A few cross sections of these antagonisms will adequately represent the temper of all.

The Universalists came late to the scene and had to battle an already popular revivalism. Upon first reaching a place the itiner-

---

etc. (New York, 1882), 40; James Stuart, *Three Years in North America* (3 vols.; Edinburgh, 1833), I, 129.

ant usually gained a fair reception. Then, "fears would begin to be excited . . . the alarm would be sounded by the clergy, and the congregation would suddenly drop down . . . and sometimes entirely dwindle out." In the country some recovery gradually took place, as a few bold farmers slipped away from watchful wives to satisfy their curiosity.[25] But in most towns opposition was especially strong. Ellicottville was "as very a sink-hole of bigotry and intolerance as a narrow and priestly rule could make it." Utica was "one of the most perfect hot-beds of Calvinist superstition and Orthodox dogmatism that could be found on the continent of America."[26] New converts in revivals regularly found themselves advertised as former Universalists, made wicked by that evil doctrine, and now regretting their former wallowing in sin. Universalism was practically made to appear "the *original sin* with which infants came into the world, and possibly which the devil committed in Paradise . . . although everybody knew these professions to be false, yet everybody affected to credit them!"[27] Debates held between Universalist and orthodox preachers were of course boasted as orthodox triumphs. Methodists, Baptists, and Presbyterians alike won their spurs in the ministry by their lectures and publications to disprove this supposed libertarian heresy. The religious press constantly labeled criminals prominent in the news as Universalists, suggesting that without the fear of eternal punishment one could not remain moral. School houses, court houses, and other public places were usually closed to Universalist and Unitarian meetings alike, and in some places the appropriateness of allowing Universalist testimony in court was debated.[28]

Despite such obstacles, Universalists gained strongly in due time. If the testimony of orthodox preachers is credible on the subject, they controlled the wealth of many vicinities. It may at least be true that substantial farmers joined them, leaving their wives to attend orthodox meetings without the means of making equal con-

---

[25] Stacy, *Memoirs*, 116–117.

[26] [George Rogers], *Memoranda of the Experience, Labors, and Travels of a Universalist Preacher, Written by Himself* (n.p., 1846), 340, 343.

[27] *Ibid.*, 132–140.

[28] *Herald of Salvation*, etc. (Watertown), II (July 3, 1824), 69; *Rochester Observer*, Jan. 16, March 13, April 24, 1829; Stacy, *Memoirs*, 167; Peck, *Early Methodism*, 229–230; Peck, *Life*, 77; and Joel Parker, *Lectures on Universalism* (Rochester, 1830).

tributions. Some of the spirit of lay revolt against clerical control in the evangelistic sects, soon to be strongly exhibited, may have risen from experience with the questions raised at Universalist meetings or debates. The editor of the *Gospel Advocate* probably came near the truth when he reported in 1825:

Many places west of Cayuga Lake have often been represented as being destitute of a preached word. . . . The picture . . . has often been exhibited to those living at a distance from us, until tears, groans, cloth, mittens, shirts, and even *rags* have been extorted from the dupes of a cold-blooded priestcraft. . . . It is not for want of information that the people here reject the wicked dogmas of Calvin . . . but the *reverse:*— they are generally too well informed . . . to swallow down the disgraceful absurdities of Andover Seminary. . . . The moral condition of this section . . . is not a whit behind that of other places where much is said and done to stigmatize the inhabitants of the West with heathenish epithets and clerical slanders.[29]

Methodist doctrines approached far closer to those of Baptists and Presbyterians than did Universalist, but treatment of the two denominations can often scarcely be differentiated. In Buffalo during 1818, Presbyterians monopolized the court house and Episcopalians, the school house. Methodists could meet only in the latter place at sunrise or sunset. After a successful revival this sect was forced to build its own church. In Ithaca, no Methodist preached until 1817, when "every family of influence and means was fast in the Presbyterian Church." In few districts in Madison County, where the school teachers were usually Presbyterian or Baptist, could Methodists use a school house. At Cazenovia, the Baptists appropriated a vacated court house, mainly to exclude a Methodist church; but with the aid of a prosperous miller the poorer Arminians outbid them at a public auction. When Luther Lee first visited Adams, Jefferson County, he looked so young that the local Methodist church, struggling "under the very shadow of a large Presbyterian Church," dared not chance ridicule by allowing him to preach. Examples could be multiplied indefinitely. The prevailing attitude of the Calvinist clergymen was probably accurately reported by Horace Galpin from Lakeville: "one great difficulty

---

29 *Gospel Advocate* (Buffalo), III (Dec. 9, 1825), 379–380.

is that they can have the preaching of the Christ-ians + the Methodists for nothing, to the subversion of the regular ministry + consequently the promotion of the blessed Gospel of our Savior." [30]

At the fountainhead of all the streams of intolerance, flowing at different levels, stood the Presbyterians and Congregationalists. They boasted the nondenominational character of the Plan of Union and the benevolent societies which they controlled. They decried the bigoted sectarianism of those other denominations which failed to co-operate in home missions, education, Bible, tract, and Sunday-school organizations. This self-vaunted broadmindedness could easily be made to appear as deliberately hypocritical as their contemporary rivals thought it to be. But the contradiction between profession and practice indicated no lack of sincerity. The Presbyterians of western New York had as good intentions as did other sectarians, and pursued them with rather more energy than did most others. Their membership and allied population having comprised from the start the best educated, most prosperous, and socially most established class of Yankee migrants, their assumption of superiority was strongly inbred. It was reinforced by their position in the young communities of the new section. Their pastors were educated and on the whole distinguished beyond even the ambitions of any other sect but the Baptists. In most sizable villages and towns they had founded the first church. Members and ministers alike had been reared in the special privileges of New England establishments. Their doctrine was the one historically orthodox in the parent section. It was habit and circumstance rather than malice which made the competition of any other denomination seem to be either heretical, wild and extravagant, or at the least, unethical.

Fixed in dominant position in the large older settlements, the Presbyterians found themselves losing ground to others in the countryside and the younger towns.[31] This loss may be ascribed to their insistence upon an educated ministry, their emphasis upon

[30] Peck, *Early Methodism*, 350–352, 400–404; Lee, *Autobiography*, 32; Horace Galpin, Lakeville, Nov. 1, 1828, to Miles P. Squier, A.H.M.S. MSS.

[31] By 1825, Baptists and Methodists, approximately equal in number, each exceeded the combined memberships of Congregational and Presbyterian churches. *New York Observer*, II (June 12, 1824), 93; III (June 18, 1825), 97; *Minutes of the Annual Conference of the Methodist Episcopal Church* (New York, 1840), I, 446.

settled pastors rather than itinerants, and their conservative, limiting theology. In part consciously, but more largely unconsciously, they set out to overcome these handicaps by zealous effort and by compromise. In rural and youthful areas they had before 1825 gone from the defensive to the offensive in sectarian competition.[32]

The predecessors of the A.H.M.S., later to become auxiliaries, were the heavy artillery of this offensive, and the Bible, tract, and education societies were the accompanying lighter weapons. Apparently it simply did not occur to the rulers of these benevolent groups that the process of collecting funds under nonsectarian auspices to spend upon the advancement of a single denomination involved hypocrisy. They were striving for the redemption of sinners, aiming at the conversion of the world. All should cordially contribute to such a noble end. Of course, if Baptist or Methodist doctrine was questionable, the money should be spent on the approved church. Who could educate clergymen adequately but Presbyterians or Congregationalists? Youths of all persuasions were freely admitted, nay, even urged to Auburn Seminary, as children of all churches were welcomed to Sunday schools operated by Presbyterians. Bibles and tracts contained no churchly creed; what harm if Presbyterians pressed the true religion with their literary donations? Who could possibly be more liberal and nonsectarian?

The American Home Missionary movement in western New York was the primary source of bitter sectarian warfare. It encouraged the multiplication of churches, and consequently the rivalry of opposed faiths, in neighborhoods which would never adequately support more than one or two and where the financial burdens would never have been assumed without external aid. It maintained full-time pastors in places which could not support one and forced rival sects to add to their commitments in self-defense. These circumstances created lay pressure upon ministers of all denominations to induce revivals, to make converts, and to get them away from other churches.[33]

Since the church and pastor must demonstrate need to the na-

---

[32] George Still, Mendon, Feb. 8, 1825, to Matthew Bruen, M. L. Farnsworth, Mayville, Jan. 19, 1829, to Miles P. Squier, John W. Adams, Syracuse, Feb. 14, 1828, to Absolom Peters, B. C. Creasy, Auburn Theological Seminary, Dec. 25, 1828, to Squier, and A.H.M.S. MSS, 1816–1835, passim.

[33] Baptist Register (Utica), II (April 1, 1825), 18, XI (Aug. 15, 1834), 70.

tional society in order to get aid and prove substantial results in order that it be continued, the missionary automatically emphasized the situation of "moral waste" before his arrival, the obstructions thrown about him by his opponents, the erroneous and ineffective work of other churches, and his own successful revivals. Edited to eliminate positive libel and to demonstrate the good works accomplished by the benevolent contributors, his reports were printed in the society's journal. They circulated in the religious press generally, roused the bitterness of those he unfairly accused, and made a reputation for perpetual revivalism which his fellow missionaries and his competitors must strive to surpass.

Two magnified illustrations of this regular phenomenon may demonstrate in caricature how the system operated. A Niagara County report, printed in Boston in 1827, said that five towns were "destitute of the stated ministry of the gospel, of every denomination. . . ." It developed upon further discussion, however, that two Baptists had full-time pastorates there, while Methodists held thirty-nine services a month in the neighborhood. This supposedly depraved society was nevertheless "enlisted in the cause of Jesus Christ" by a Presbyterian revival in 1830.[34] In 1825 a Monroe County town, reported in the *Western Recorder* of Utica to be a moral waste, proved to have a population of over sixty per square mile, with four active churches and numerous Methodist class meetings, all of which had been functioning for years. Even though A.H.M.S. pastors worked here in the interval, it was still being reported three years later as "destitute of both religious, and moral principles," in order to justify external financial aid.[35] This mechanism for compounding religious excitement functioned more smoothly under the American Home Missionary Society than it did before the federation of 1825, but operated with considerable efficiency from 1815 on.

---

[34] Rev. F. W. Conable, *History of the Genesee Annual Conference of the Methodist Episcopal Church*, etc. (New York, 1876), 261–263; *Priestcraft Exposed and Primitive Christianity Defended*, etc. (Lockport), I (Aug., 1828), 61; George Colton, Royalton, Jan. 11, 1828, to J. F. Schermerhorn, R. G. Murray, Niagara Falls, Nov. 1, 1831, to Miles P. Squier, A.H.M.S. MSS.

[35] *Gospel Luminary*, II (March 26, 1826), 72; John C. Morgan, Perrinton, Oct. 26, 1825, to Matthew Bruen, John Taylor, Mendon, Aug. 5, 1828, to Miles P. Squier, and P. S. by Squier to Absolom Peters, A.H.M.S. MSS.

One attempted transaction of the organization, typical in spirit though not in result, must suffice to demonstrate its temper, though further illustrations abound in the New York State papers of the A.H.M.S. Silas Hubbard, missionary at Centreville, Allegany County, in 1825 called the attention of the secretary in New York to the hundred-acre donation the Holland Company would give for new churches. The matter must be handled delicately, for "If it is held up publicly . . . it will excite jealousy in the minds of other denominations, cause them to rival us in this business, and perhaps defeat the object." Samuel Mills of Moscow, Livingston County, interviewed the agent, Jacob Otto, and reported back: "The greatest number of grants, have been made to *presbyterian* societies. . . . [Otto] signified that he took a deep interest in the establishment of religious societies . . . + that he should be very glad to have communication with you on the subject." But Mills misjudged his man. The next month came a letter from Otto himself, whose wording reveals the kind of letter he must have received from New York City:

We have uniformly left the people to organize their own religious institutions, and in order to extend our aid . . . we occasionally, grant them small donations in land; the extent of which is altogether discretionary in us. . . . Much to our regret we find these liberal donations . . . perverted and misapplied. Our settlements, notwithstanding are by no means destitute of religious instruction; our people are as moral and industrious as any in the United States. . . .[36]

Even within the denominations involved in the Plan of Union or intimately connected with the A.H.M.S., the allotment of funds provided a heavy pressure in one direction and a source of bitterness and controversy between and within the sects. Small portions of aid went regularly to a few Dutch Reformed churches in the Mohawk Valley, but very little to the numerous Congregational churches which preferred not to join the presbyteries in western New York. The excuse that they were too feeble to justify expenditures does not bear comparison with action toward Presbyterian churches. Even meetings retaining Congregational form under the

---

[36] Hubbard, May 20, Mills, July 20, Otto, Batavia, Aug. 25, 1825, to Matthew Bruen, A.H.M.S. MSS.

accommodation plan were forced at times into full Presbyterian organization by the missionaries.[37]

Within the single denomination, the upstate agencies trod a difficult path between enthusiastic and conservative extremes. Up to the early thirties, when extravagant emotionalism began to prevail, revival men who tended to liberalize on the question of the individual's power to put himself in a way to be converted were systematically favored over conservatives. They had to be favored if growth was to occur. But after the Finney revivals A.H.M.S. policy tried to put the brakes on excitement. Even on occasion during the twenties appear hints for a need of caution against excessively liberal theology and itinerancy.[38]

Thus it was that the tendency toward liberal nonsectarianism, implicit in the normal religious arrangements of a frontier society and equally imbedded in the revivalism and benevolence of the evangelical awakening, became distorted in this particular region, until results became exactly the opposite of those expected. The Baptists contributed to this situation, as did the Presbyterians, but in smaller measure and partly in response to the competition of the A.H.M.S.

The nature of this development is quite clear. But whether it was the exclusive, final cause of unusual excitability in the area after 1825 may fairly be doubted. Perhaps the very fact that this excessive proselytism followed upon a pioneer era when all church members experienced some preaching of other sects may be significant, as Luther Lee suggested. While all were attending the alternating school house meetings, "the members . . . would report to their preacher what had been said against their doctrine, and a reply would be hurled back, and a constant religious warfare was maintained." [39]

---

[37] Benjamin B. Smith, South Bristol, Dec. 10, 1829, no addressee, Richard Dunning, Buffalo, Oct. 15, 1835, to John Murray, D. T. Wood, South Middletown, Dec. 2, 1835, to Absolom Peters, A.H.M.S. MSS. The Congregational form left the minister less power. Before 1830, the proscription probably recommended itself to the A.H.M.S. because of the relative conservatism of the old Congregational churches. Afterwards, the Congregational form permitted too free play for radicalism.

[38] Absolom Peters, Buffalo, Sept. 8, 1829, to Charles Hall, A.H.M.S. MSS; William Wisner, Ithaca, Sept. 9, 1824, to Samuel Miller, Samuel Miller Papers, Princeton University Library.

[39] Lee, *Autobiography*, 50.

Probably also, an unusual religious sensitivity existed from the earliest settlements and helped to create the peculiarly intensive development of missionary societies in the first place. Direct and indirect testimony from all denominations suggests such a special spirit in the region early as well as late in the pre-Civil War period. The presiding elder of the Genesee country in 1797 was a calm, modest man. Upon his first appearance a subordinate prayed: "O Lord, bless our new elder and give him more religion. . . ." to which a multitude of the audience responded: "Amen!" William Shaw, minister at Fall Creek, Tompkins County, protested in 1823 that William Burchard was unfit for his home missionary agency, for he failed to make "such an appeal to the heart as would have brought the people to take hold of the missionary cause. . . ." Baptists in the region expected that ministers would "let the Holy Ghost" prepare their sermons. David Millard, a Christian itinerant and editor, discovered when touring Pennsylvania in 1833 that: "In proportion to population, fewer persons profess experimental religion here, than in New York. Professors are more formal, less zealous, and revivals less frequent and extensive, than in New York, or New England." Charles Finney found in Boston that he "could not learn that there was among them anything like the spirit of prayer that had prevailed in the revivals at the West and in New York city." Religion there did not exhibit "that freedom and strength of faith which I had been in the habit of seeing in New York." [40]

This peculiar growth of the Burned-over District was destined to bear abundant fruit in the second quarter of the century.

---

[40] Peck, *Early Methodism*, 119–120; Joshua Deane, with P.S. by William T. Shaw, Fall Creek, Nov. 21, 1823, to the United Domestic Missionary Society, New York, A.H.M.S. MSS; *Gospel Luminary*, n.s., VI (April, 1833), 241; Charles G. Finney, *Autobiography of Charles Grandison Finney* (New York, 1876), 314.

BOOK II

Environment: 1825-1850

What New England was fifty years ago, the western section of New York . . . has in many respects already become. Her population . . . are now the most enterprising[;] all that is requisite to make them "the happiest loveliest land of all," are the good old New-England habits, and New England society. But . . . emigration is yearly, yes . . . almost daily, rolling on to the new west.

—Orleans Advocate (ALBION), AUG. 29, 1827

Chapter 4. CANAL DAYS

THE wave of evangelistic fervor surging toward a peak in the mid-twenties probably constitutes the major explanation of the religious peculiarities which followed. But why should such phenomena have been markedly stronger and more numerous in western New York than in other sections which in considerable degree shared the same religious experience? Information on this question must be sought in the structure of society here during the climactic years of spiritual change. That social conditions played some causal role may be assumed. Just what that role was, just how far religious events can be explained by sociological determinants, is a problem to be solved finally only by individual opinion. Yet suggestions pointing toward a more generally valid conclusion may fairly be attempted.

The year 1825 marks a distinct turning point in the history of upstate New York. It serves in most of the region to set off the pioneering first generation from the second. It dates completion of the Erie Canal, which speeded the economic maturity of the entire state. In matters religious and moral, it separates the period of scattered, episodic eccentricities from the era of major, significant enthusiasms. Between this date and the panic of 1837 came twelve crowded years: years in which a series of startling events revolutionized life in the western half of the state. It was the mentality then fixed upon the adult and the rising generations which determined the unusual character suggested by the phrase "Burned-over District." New crusades developed after the ensuing depression, to be sure, but their existence depended upon preceding movements and upon a state of mind continuing from the thirties. Not only did these twelve years establish a culture which would lag behind some of the circumstances of its creation; their basic economic condition also tended in many respects to persevere, despite constant, slow change, until after 1850, when the regional peculiarities may properly be considered to have run their course. The dominantly rural, water-power manufacturing economy which achieved maturity by 1837 was not before the Civil War seriously encroached upon by the advance agents of an urban, industrial age.

The Erie Canal quickly introduced western New York into a period of relatively stable agrarian maturity. During the twenties population grew more rapidly here than in any other part of the country. Albany gained 96 per cent, Utica 183, Syracuse 282, Buffalo 314, and Rochester 512. The entire five counties surrounding the western half of the canal increased 135 per cent in the decade.[1] The canal's value as a route between the seacoast and the Great Lakes often obscures its continuing commercial significance within the state itself. Through trade grew constantly both absolutely and proportionally; but only once during the first quarter-century of complete operation, in 1847, did tolls on shipments from the West exceed collections along the canal line.[2] Within New York the great ditch provided the principal transportation for several reasonably distinct circles of economic activity. Rochester, specializing in flour, Syracuse in salt, and Utica in cloth, all exported their products eastward to the seaboard and brought westward in return commodities from beyond the region.

A substantial volume of business also moved on a scale even more local. The several urban centers collected and processed farm harvests for distribution beyond their immediate area. It turn they sold farmers manufactured goods, partly imported but increasingly made in the city itself, and at the same time furnished pro-

---

[1] Caroline E. MacGill et al., History of Transportation in the United States before 1860 (B. H. Meyer, ed., Washington, 1917), 85–86; Thomas F. Gordon, Gazetteer of the State of New York, etc. (Philadelphia, 1836), 350, 446, 531, 563, 576, 586, 612, 763.

[2] Report of the Auditor of the Canal Department of the Tolls, Trade and Tonnage of the New York Canals (Albany, 1854), 10.

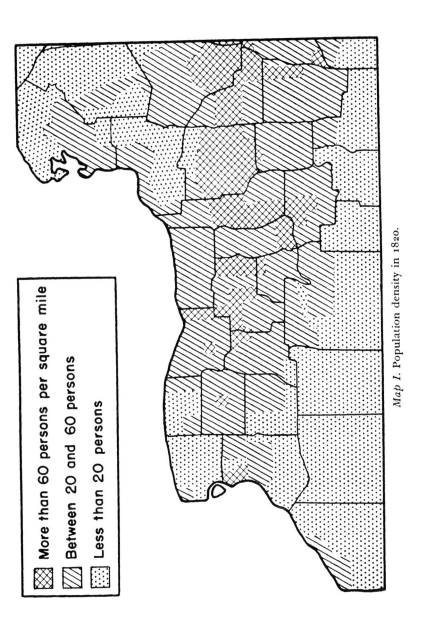

Map I. Population density in 1820.

More than 60 persons per square mile

Between 20 and 60 persons

Less than 20 persons

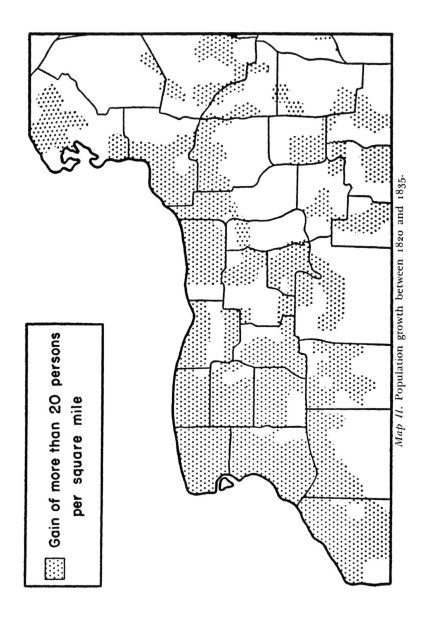

Map II. Population growth between 1820 and 1835.

Gain of more than 20 persons per square mile

fessional services to their hinterland. The canal was not only the importing and exporting facility which enabled the city to serve its market area; it acted besides as a short-haul line between city and hamlet or farm, and between adjacent economic territories within the upstate region.[3] The Burned-over District may thus be thought of as a series of trading spheres, each subsidiary to one or several local towns destined for urban development.

The effect of the canal on these several spheres was not concentrated in one sudden burst in 1825; instead it came to each one separately in a series of impacts striking successively across the state over a period of fifteen years. Thus Utica's boom was over before Buffalo's began. Even before construction began in 1817, improvements along the Seneca, Oswego, and Mohawk rivers contributed to upper Mohawk Valley prosperity. Thereafter, portions of the Erie were pressed into use as soon as they could be navigated. Tolls on the Erie and the earlier Mohawk canals together came to $28,000 by 1820. Three years later construction crossed the Genesee, and in the next season 10,000 boatloads paid $300,000 in tolls.[4] People streamed into each area as transportation reached it—indeed, even before. Many a canny Yankee scented approaching opportunity and preceded it to a good location. Thus was the canal boom anticipated, prolonged, and made progressive from east to west.

Utica and Rome, twin centers of the easternmost trading sphere, commanded an area immediately tributary consisting of Oneida and Madison counties, and less immediately a larger sector stretching southward down the Chenango Valley to Pennsylvania and northward through the Black River Valley to the eastern end of Lake Ontario. Excellent bottom lands, punctuated with gentle, rather fertile hills, lay along and south of the Erie route. Today both truck and dairy farms flourish in this central portion of the Utica territory. The northern half of Oneida County was and is far less richly endowed, but with the extra stimulus of forest enterprises it could maintain a good number of small farmers, at least

---

[3] Detailed relationships between city and farm for one economic sphere appear in Whitney R. Cross, "Creating a City: Rochester, 1824–1834," (MS at University of Rochester, 1936), 31–102.

[4] MacGill, *Transportation*, 178–192.

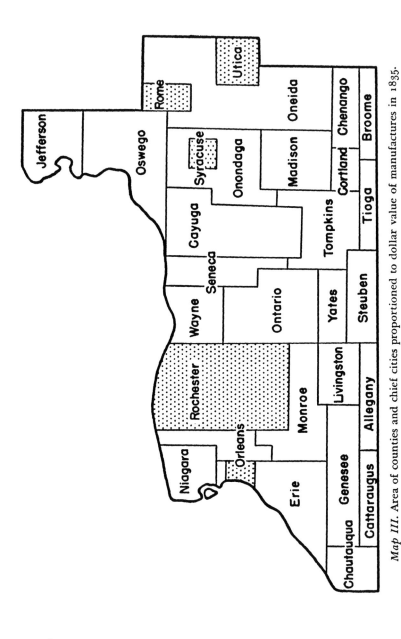

Map III. Area of counties and chief cities proportioned to dollar value of manufactures in 1835.

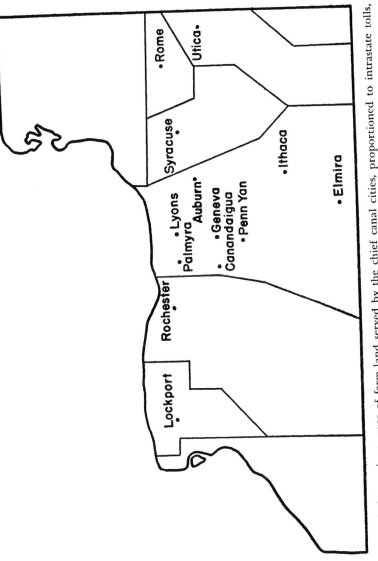

Map IV. Approximate area of farm land served by the chief canal cities, proportioned to intrastate tolls, averaged for 1837, 1845, and 1850.

in the pioneer generation while virgin trees and original leaf mold survived. Proximity to transportation made neighborhoods near the canal temporarily more inviting, so that they tended upon the waterway's arrival to catch up with the portion just to the south which had been earlier settled.

Growth of the canal towns and a short-lived expansion of tillage to the north account for most of the population increase in Oneida and Madison counties after 1820. Their better lands had long since been occupied. Their farmers had profited from early river improvements and from the nearly completed Erie Canal eastward, as early as 1820. Even at that date, the agricultural county of Madison supported a population larger than that of 1940, and Oneida, a population over 75 per cent as great. Twenty years later the latter county also exceeded its corresponding 1940 figure.[5] The saturation point for a rural economy had thus early been reached. Further growth would depend on industrial cities with enlarged markets.

Beyond the immediate vicinity lay the broader hinterland, dependent upon lateral canals or railroads to bring it into the same trading area. By 1836 the Chenango Canal had been completed to Binghamton. Its traffic was never heavy (tolls were not 25 per cent of Utica collections on the main canal) but it provided an outlet for farm produce from a rather extensive if not extraordinarily fertile stretch of land. In this southern sector, the excellent valleys grew progressively deeper and narrower and the hillsides more steep and rockbound as they approached the Pennsylvania mountain ranges. Here, too, settlement had been early and, in proportion to the fewer arable acres, as complete before 1820 as in the upper Mohawk Valley. What growth the branch canal did bring largely preceded its completion. Chenango County increased only slightly before 1835 and gradually declined during the next twenty years.[6]

The Black River country to the north had previously been less developed than the rest of the Utica sector. Whatever degree of early prosperity it promised to pioneers accustomed to scrubby

---

[5] Gordon, *Gazetteer*, 523, 576; E. Eastman Irvine, ed., *The World Almanac and Book of Facts for 1942* (New York, 1942), 619.

[6] *Report of Canal Tolls* (1854), *passim*; Gordon, *Gazetteer*, 393; J. H. French, *Gazetteer of the State of New York*, etc. (Syracuse, 1860), 231.

Vermont was probably illusory, but the routing of the Erie far from its limits reinforced a natural tendency to stagnation and it was left isolated from the chief streams of settlers and commerce until 1850. The Black River Canal, projected over virtually impossible terrain in 1838, had just been finished after twelve years, when a railroad arrived to render it obsolete. During the interval before the mid-century most of this territory had to ship by road to Rome, while the lower valley became tributary to Oswego and Rochester by lake transport. Jefferson and Lewis counties, presumably compensating for previous under-settlement, gained rapidly until 1830, after which their rate of increase was slight and concentrated mainly within easy reach of Lake Ontario.[7]

New York's early railroads suffered from canal competition, except where they could profit as feeders for existing waterways. Utica and other towns, however, optimistically plotted radiating lines to increase their market areas, while equally sanguine farmers took up land on the proposed routes. Five such lines had been chartered about Utica by 1834, but none did business before 1850. The one successful road of the period, the Utica and Schenectady, reached Utica in 1836 and Syracuse three years later. Even this was only a passenger line, since state law at first prohibited rail shipments and later required payment of canal tolls in addition to the rail freight tariff. Free competition came only in 1851.

The Utica agricultural province was a mediocre source of produce and markets. Its average prosperity was probably below that of any section to the west except the southern tier.[8] Its lateral transportation lines failed. Toll collections at Utica and Rome, and on the Chenango Canal in addition, ordinarily amounted to much less than those of either Buffalo or Rochester, and were even somewhat smaller than those of Syracuse, and of Oswego after 1840.[9]

---

[7] Dorothy K. Cleaveland, "The Trade and Trade Routes of Northern New York from the Beginning of Settlement to the Coming of the Railroad," *New York State Historical Association Quarterly Journal*, IV (Oct., 1923), 223 ff.; MacGill, *Transportation*, 200; Gordon, *Gazetteer*, 492, 504; French, *Gazetteer*, 364, 380.

[8] Based upon an index of per capita personal and real property, from financial figures for 1842 and population figures for 1840. O. L. Holley, ed., *The New York State Register*, etc. (New York, 1843), 67; Joel T. Headley, ed., Franklin B. Hough, Superintendent, *Census of the State of New York, for 1855*, etc. (Albany, 1857), xxxiii.

[9] *Report of Canal Tolls* (1851), *passim*.

Their central, inland position denied the Oneida County towns opportunity to become great commercial marts. Early settlement and gradual stimulus from the canal guarded them from the extreme booms and the ensuing reactions of their more westerly competitors. Growth was relatively steady, solid, and unspectacular. The cities, like much of their countryside, reached an early stability.

Because it gained urban proportions before the western canal towns, Utica had certain advantages over them. Manufacturing started early enough to establish leadership. Madison and Chenango counties led the Burned-over District in sheep raising. Consequently Utica and its suburbs began a flourishing woolen industry, besides developing the greatest upstate cotton mills. The flour mills of Oneida and Madison ground the local grain. Oneida contained also the largest foundry business west of the Hudson. Likewise, utilizing the resources of the forest and of more nearly subsistence-type farms to the north, the county led western New York in dollar value of output from saw mills, tanneries, distilleries, and breweries. Thus, Utica, Rome, and several smaller towns could offer finished products to their own region and more distant ones in sufficient quantity to maintain an increasing prosperity, while the countryside stood still.[10]

In the same fashion, Utica established cultural enterprises before other towns could do so and tended to retain leadership once it was established. In recent years Syracuse has become the customary meeting place for state-wide groups, but in the 1820's population was distributed more heavily to the east, while Syracuse itself was barely emerging from a neglected swamp. Political and religious convocations naturally therefore gathered in Utica. Here also they printed their journals, pamphlets, and handbills. Thus developed a publishing and book trade which would lead upstate New York for a decade or more. When the first partial comparison becomes possible in 1855, the Oneida County press (chiefly in Utica) circulated nearly 6,000 copies of four daily papers. This more than doubled the Onondaga circulation centered in Syracuse, but failed to approach that of Monroe (Rochester) and Erie (Buf-

---

10 See map III.

falo) counties. More significant is the semiweekly and weekly circulation which reached the rural folk. In this category Oneida County ranked next to Monroe, with thirteen papers going to 56,000 people. Onondaga's nine totaled 29,000 and Erie's fifteen, only 34,000.[11]

The extent of a city's cultural ties with its hinterland is an important index for measuring its own susceptibility to emotional movements which were primarily rural. On the other hand, a dominating city might help materially to determine the character of rural society in its own province. Within the western half of New York State, the two localities surrounding Utica and Rochester reflected isms more consistently than did others. Between the two lay a variegated territory in which enthusiasm had a less universal appeal.

To the north in this middle sector lay the rich lowlands of the Ontario plain. Fever-breeding swamps, however, had discouraged early settlement, as had remoteness from trade routes and fear of British excursions on the lake shore. To this region the canal proved extremely beneficial, for between 1820 and 1835 most townships jumped from around twenty to about sixty inhabitants per square mile.[12] The great artery ran horizontally through the middle of the area, leaving few portions inconveniently remote. Palmyra, Lyons, and the Montezuma Swamp ports became reasonably important outlets for local produce. The main-line towns built flour mills, but other crops and presumably even much of the grain went by canal to Rochester or Syracuse. Little other manufacturing developed and goods for the farmers came from the two cities.

The boom here for fifteen years was so pronounced that by 1835 the rural saturation point had been reached. The villages often continued to grow, but with larger nodes conveniently on their right and left less than fifty miles away, they were not destined for urban proportions. The delayed completion of its branch canal postponed a few years the entire cycle of growth, but eventually made of Oswego a commercial center almost equal to Syracuse. Yet by 1840 even this hinterland had developed to the capacity of its agrarian resources.

---

11 *Census, 1855*, 496–497.
12 See maps I and II.

The mucks, glacial sands, and moderating lake breezes which have combined to make the Ontario plain an abundant fruit and vegetable producer in recent times did not so well suit the agricultural styles of the early nineteenth century. This region failed to produce wealth comparable to that of the more rolling country adjacent to the south. Wayne and Oswego counties barely reached over half the prosperity of their southern neighbors, as measured in value of dwellings, real property, and personal estates. Yet, given a reasonably stabilized rural society, isms could flourish regardless of wealth—in fact, they often shied away from it. The canal and lake-shore sector of midwestern New York had little part in the enthusiasms of the twenties and early thirties, but made up for lost time in the forties.

Before the canal came, the main east-west route had crossed just north of the Finger Lakes, while the southerly routes, which perhaps handled more freight, ran through the larger lakes, over portages to branches of the Susquehanna River, and on to Baltimore and Philadelphia. The gentle hill country between Auburn, Geneva, and Canandaigua on the north, and Ithaca, Watkins Glen, and Bath on the south, had from the date of first settlement been the focus of activity for all western New York. Most of this region and its eastward extension through Onondaga and Cortland counties into the Utica area harbored about sixty persons per square mile as early as 1820. With the main-line canal passing it by, this belt of land still retained and increased its prosperity. But it could not compete in commerce or industry with the towns on the Erie nor experience any sudden expansion. Its farms, fully occupied, in semi-isolated agrarian wealth watched the world go by farther north.

This was nearly as fine farming country as the famed lower Genesee Valley, and far more extensive. The western half of it was in fact usually indicated rather than the Genesee Valley itself, when the early New England emigrants headed for what they called the Genesee country. Even hilltop acres long since covered with briars and second-growth timber seem to have flourished, probably at the expense of their present condition. Canalized Finger Lakes oulets afforded good transportation, available to so many localities that no one village could become an economic capital. The several inlet, lake, and outlet communities all did some manufacturing and forwarding, but could become at best smaller nodes, themselves dependent upon the main canal-line cities. By water their produce flowed toward Syracuse, but the flour city on the Genesee probably drew more of the wheat for which the countryside gained such renown. Rochester capitalists early planned the Auburn Railroad, finished in 1841, possibly in part for this very purpose, though attraction would be exercised rather by passenger than by freight service for several years.[13]

According to the economic symptoms which apply elsewhere, this sector should have been fascinated with the enthusiasms of the period. Parts of it were. Three factors help to explain the fact that the appeal was not universal. The triangle of Pennsylvania migration extended into the heart of the region. Seneca County, for example, had the lowest percentage of Yankee nativity in western New York and also registered resistance to most religious and reform movements of the evangelistic type. Again, the lake villages were the country seats of gentleman landlords, descended from the eighteenth-century aristocracy of New York, Pennsylvania, and Virginia, who generally attended the Episcopalian Church, which maintained a cool dignity amidst the fiercest storms of fervent revivalism. Finally, a sufficient number of the more substantial Yankee farmers espoused Universalism to make this the center of strength for that liberal denomination in the Burned-over District. The balance of the New England-born farmers, however, and many of their village kin, were excellent subjects for the excitements.

At the northeastern edge of this rich section, bordering on the Ontario lowlands, the Seneca and Oswego rivers converge and turn north to the lake. From the earliest days the salt works here at Salina had prospered, but Manlius, Pompey, and Skaneateles, south in the hills on the stage route, had attracted greater populations. The present city of Syracuse did not exist until the advent of the canal. Starting as it did from nothing, the boom of the twenties left Syracuse still behind Utica and Rochester. The town was only gradually able to assume the urban responsibilities which the other

13 MacGill, *Transportation*, 376; Blake McKelvey, *Rochester: The Water-Power City* (Cambridge, Mass., 1945), 224, 225.

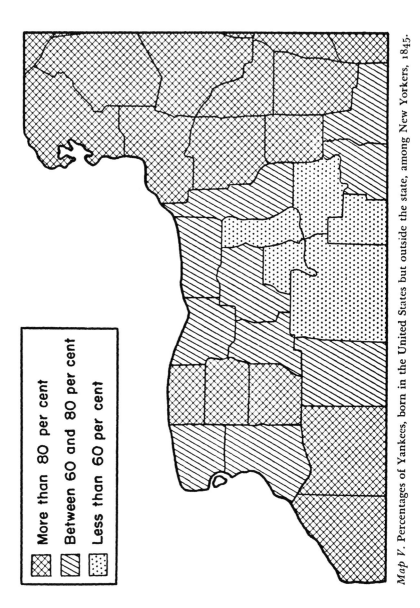

Map V. Percentages of Yankees, born in the United States but outside the state, among New Yorkers, 1845.

More than 80 per cent

Between 60 and 80 per cent

Less than 60 per cent

two undertook earlier. It became a secondary market for Finger Lakes produce, a trans-shipment point for Oswego and Canada, and a nationally known salt producer. Its destiny lay, consequently, in commerce rather than in industry. Aside from the salt business, one relatively independent of the countryside, its manufactures never before 1850 approached those of the other canal towns.[14] Its rate of growth was often higher, but considerably less regular, than that of Rochester and Utica. It achieved stability more slowly, and not until its preoccupation with physical growth diminished would it have much to do with revivals or reform movements. Toward the end of the period it grew more like its neighbors and shared more largely in nonmaterial excitements. Oswego repeated practically the same evolution, retarded a few years.

The limits of the Susquehanna watershed closely skirt the upper ends of the Finger Lakes and protrude northwards between them in marked salients. From this divide southward the terrain changes character, as plateau-like hilltops rise toward the Appalachian highlands. Glaciated soils quickly give place to bedrock only thinly surfaced with eroded shales, clay, and humus. As elevation increases, the Susquehanna tributaries continue downward, confined in ever-narrower valleys with steepening walls. In the broad upper reaches of these southward-facing valleys and about the glacial moraines which often form the divides above them, keeping their waters from draining toward the St. Lawrence, there are still, and presumably have always been, numerous acres of prime fertility. Nearer the Pennsylvania line, also, there frequently occur plains which present or prehistoric river junctions dug from the hills, superb stretches of alluvial richness. But on the whole, opportunity for agricultural prosperity in the southern tier was limited.

Here then was a region far less peopled in 1820 than those to the north, except along the arteries which had crossed it to reach the Susquehanna and the seaboard. Vacant lands abounded, especially in the west. The twenties and thirties brought men to occupy and clear them in the full confidence that branch canals or the Erie Railroad would soon connect to, or supersede, the northern route of trade. But their hopes were long forlorn. Before 1850

14 See map III.

much of the area remained submarginal, in terms of availability to market as well as because of poor natural endowment. The Chemung Canal and the Ithaca and Owego Railroad further developed vicinities which had grown from the beginning, but neither was ever an overwhelming success.[15]

A trans-Appalachian railroad would release the entire southern tier from its vassalage to the northern cities by providing a direct outlet to New York. But although agitation for such a project began in 1826 and a charter was granted only four years later, so unfortunate was the financial history of the Erie Railroad that a complete line from the Hudson to Dunkirk came only in 1851.[16] The Susquehanna-drained sector of western New York thus failed to achieve economic maturity before the mid-century mark. Its people were less predominantly Yankee than were those elsewhere in the Burned-over District. Only in the homogeneous New England townships along the divides grading off toward the Finger Lakes did the inhabitants exhibit a strong susceptibility to isms.

The western half of the Finger Lakes section was throughout the second quarter of the century tributary mainly to Rochester. The Genesee Valley itself, and most of the land to the west up to a vague line just east of Buffalo, rounded out the flour city's sphere of influence. The lower valley, with salients stretching east to Canandaigua and Palmyra and west to Batavia, contained exceedingly rich land which had been very early occupied. Its population failed to grow substantially when the canal came, but as in the companion hill country just to the east its wheat crops gained fame and wealth.

At the opposite end of the prosperity scale was the part of the southern tier between the Canisteo Valley and the Lake Erie watershed. This sector had been pioneered as lately as 1825 and advanced only slightly in the quarter century. Except for the relatively narrow upper Genesee and Allegheny valleys it contained the poorest land in western New York, and was in addition virtually isolated. It was the only part of the Burned-over District which can fairly be called frontier after 1825. It likewise exhibited the most complete indifference to the religious and social excitements of the time.

---

[15] *Report of Canal Tolls* (1854), *passim;* MacGill, *Transportation*, 372.
[16] *Ibid.*, 336-371.

A succession of hills and valleys run in north-south parallels between the Genesee River and the Lake Erie plain, descending gradually in elevation from central Allegany and Cattaraugus counties to the Ontario lowlands. Less thoroughly glaciated and less amply watered, this terrain afforded somewhat less fertile land than did the corresponding section east of the Genesee. Its small streams provided no comparison with the freight-bearing Finger Lakes. Settlement before the advent of the canal had been relatively slow; in consequence, opportunity for rapid development came after 1825. Buffalo did little to reach this countryside, but Rochester led the western part of the state in rail-laying calculated to enlarge its granary and its market.[17] Among other projects was the Tonawanda road, which reached Batavia in 1837 and soon continued to Attica. This came rapidly to command Genesee County and the valleys descending to it from the south.

During the decade after 1825 the hill country southwest of Rochester filled speedily. Rural growth thereafter was negligible; since many of the farms proved disappointing and tenure was often uncertain, the section became almost immediately a leading reservoir for migration farther west. The antirent squabbles of the thirties betokened much turbulence and change, in part the harvest of earlier latitudinarian leasing policies which had drawn a more restless, less stable brood of Yankees than had the lands to the east.[18] Antimasonry here raised agitation which lasted longer than in neighboring areas. Replete with excitements bearing on more material concerns, the territory had little appetite for intensive religion and reform until the forties. Unlike the companion country across the Genesee, however, these lands drew even their earliest settlers during the period of dominantly New England migration. This population was consequently more purely and more freshly Yankee. Once the folk could settle down to normal living they would become as fertile with isms as any people in the Burned-over District.

Through the Ontario lowlands the canal wended its way from Rochester toward the Niagara Frontier, where it mounted to the Erie level and turned southwest to the Buffalo harbor. Lockport was built on the escarpment. On the business it garnered as a mill-

---

17 *Ibid.*, 374–378; McKelvey, *Rochester*, 224.
18 Paul D. Evans, *The Holland Land Company* (Buffalo, 1924), 324–418, *passim*.

ing and shipping point for neighborhood produce, this new community rapidly became the major town between Rochester and Buffalo. In time it came to serve in a smaller way the same kind of urban purpose as did Rochester, Utica, and Oswego, in contrast to the more purely commercial nature of Buffalo and Syracuse. As this sector was even more sparsely settled when the canal came than the corresponding region east of the Genesee, so its growth was proportionally more startling up to 1840. Like that section, too, its wealth continued to be slighter than that of the higher lands to the south. It compared, however, with Wyoming County rather than with Wayne, in its large proportion of Yankees as well as in its share of the rent troubles of the Holland Company and successors.

Rochester commanded an immediate agricultural area larger and wealthier than did any other canal town. Less directly, its market spread from Lake Ontario to Pennsylvania and from the middle Finger Lakes to the edges of Chautauqua County. Its lake port gave entrance to Canada besides, while its railroads successfully tapped neighborhoods not accessible by water. The Genesee Valley Canal, virtually a failure as an outlet for the Allegheny Valley and the West, nevertheless improved upon the earlier trade routes along the lower Genesee. Much of this hinterland was superb wheat country. The river at Rochester lent ample water supplies, more manageable than a torrent like Niagara in that day of simple engineering techniques. These circumstances combined with canal transportation to make the city the primary milling center of the country for many years.

More significant to the social historian is the extent to which Rochester emulated Utica, manufacturing for its nearby farm areas and exchanging ideas along with products throughout the countryside. By 1835 the mill city produced goods worth more than two and a half times those made in Utica and more than eleven times those of Buffalo or Syracuse. The total, indeed, nearly reached that of Buffalo, Syracuse, Utica, Albany, and Troy combined. Flour, of course, accounted for this overwhelming superiority, but other businesses were by no means negligible. In the same year, Monroe County ranked second in the Burned-over District in foundry products, third in asheries, fourth in woolens and breweries, seventh in distilleries, tenth in tanning, and eleventh in saw milling. Even omitting flour, Rochester yielded place only to Utica as an all-around manufacturing town.[19]

Though its first settlers had arrived in 1812, the village remained insignificant for five years. The decision locating the canal-river junction there, however, started off a boom whose climax came with, not after, completion of the new waterway. By 1828 the phenomenal growth with which the town led the United States for the decade had run its course. Careful reading of contemporary papers shows not only a slackening to a more stable rate of growth, slight depressions in 1830 and 1834, and retarding effects from two cholera epidemics, but also an increase of service occupations, educational facilities, aspirations for cultural improvement, and the preoccupation with religion and reform which normally came to Yankee communities when they relaxed to customary modes of life.[20]

Rochester's bonanza period preceded that of Syracuse and Buffalo. Thus it was able, like Utica, to take priority in establishing habits of cultural leadership. Persons west of the Finger Lakes who had special interests to discuss found it natural to travel in the channels of trade and to convene at the junction of the canal and the river. Such groups tended in due course to let printing contracts at the seat of their conferences. Pure coincidence made this the principal center of Antimasonic journalism at just the right moment to elevate a possibly temporary tendency to the position of a fixed habit. In addition, the milling center logically became the fount of agricultural advice. The *Genesee Farmer* and the *Anti-Masonic Inquirer* alike were early and pre-eminent in their respective fields. They probably circulated more thoroughly among the rural folk of western New York than any other two papers. By 1855 the seven nondaily journals published in the town reached more than 65,000 copies per issue. This approximated the nondaily circulation of Buffalo and Syracuse combined and exceeded by 9,000 that of Utica.[21]

The territory remaining to accept Buffalo's leadership was slight.

---

19 See map III.
20 Cross, "Rochester," *passim;* McKelvey, *Rochester,* 163 ff.
21 *Census, 1855,* 496–497.

Stretching southward along Lake Erie, however, there is a gradually widening plain which includes the fertile lands of Chautauqua County. Dunkirk and the lesser lake ports served much of this province as local depots, sending their exports to be transferred to the canal at Buffalo. The canal terminus consequently had little contact with the original agricultural producers. Buffalo was the gateway to the West, the trans-shipment point for through canal traffic. Its destiny for the time lay far more in commerce than in industry. Starting later, it grew only less than Rochester during the twenties and continued its extravagant expansion longer. Its dependence on western trade brought the panic of 1837 down upon it in fuller force than upon any other canal town. Thereafter an even greater boom set in,[22] so that few of its people inclined to spend much thought on nonmaterial concerns before 1850.

Chautauqua and southern Erie counties, however, shared the characteristics of the neighboring hill country on the east. Their population spurted until about 1835 and then stood virtually constant in rural areas. They contained a folk as exclusively Yankee as did Wyoming County. They shared in Antimasonry and in the agrarian unrest of the thirties, but the forties found them ripe for a harvest of religious excitements.

The relationship of Burned-over District enthusiasms to specific sociological conditions could easily be overdrawn. Religious zealots were in no conscious fashion motivated by calculations of their economic or social interests. They found direct inspiration in the Bible and aimed at some kind of millennium within their own time. They may well have been as little driven by outward circumstance as any group of persons in history. No rigid determinism can be applied to men who sought always the right and never the expedient, according to insights which were invariably individualistic. Still, they lived in an environment whose influence they could scarcely escape, however much they might disregard it. No direct cause of an economic or social nature can be therefore ascribed to the whole mass of movements, or to any one of them; but the culture which produced them did create fairly definite limitations within which they operated.

---

[22] Gordon, *Gazetteer,* 446; French, *Gazetteer,* 294.

Charles Grandison Finney, for instance, shook the very foundations of Rochester society with a renowned revival in 1831, as he had done in Utica five years earlier. Josiah Bissell, Jr., pillar both of the Presbyterian Church and of the Genesee Valley entrepreneurial community, had brought the evangelist there with an eloquent plea recounting the evils of life on the canal. No economic factor had much directly to do with the revival, but if Finney had happened upon Utica in 1822, perhaps, or upon Rochester about 1825, neither town would have been so well prepared to listen. He struck postfever states in both places, when economic booms had declined and stability had arrived.[23] Even such a righteous reformer as Bissell may very well, like his fellow citizens, have been far too busy in 1825 to worry about the sins of the "canawlers." About thus far, and little farther, may economics interpret religious forces.

Mapping the concentration points of all the enthusiasms within the Burned-over District demonstrates that such excitements were chiefly rural.[24] Utica and Rochester reflected the rural mind, but Buffalo did not and Syracuse did so in limited degree. Farther east, the industrial town of Troy was warm and the commercial town of Albany, cold. Lockport, Oswego, and Rome, among smaller places, fall in the first category, Elmira and Binghamton in the second. Thus it seems reasonable to conclude that two types of urbanism existed: the manufacturing town served a farming area while the commercial town handled commodities headed farther afield. Furthermore, the new, rapidly expanding town was too active to be concerned with spiritual motives, while the more stable community took thought for its moral and religious welfare.

The excitements of the twenties, excepting Antimasonry which had a political angle, focused in the regions settled before 1800. Places more recently occupied, like the south Ontario shore and Wyoming and Chautauqua counties, became enthusiastic over religion only when they had reached a corresponding age and development. Thus the phenomena of Burned-over District history

---

[23] Josiah Bissell, Jr., Rochester, Sept. 15, 1829, to Charles G. Finney, Charles Grandison Finney Papers, Oberlin College Library. Finney's visit to Buffalo in 1831, there a boom year, achieved no especial renown.

[24] See maps XVII–XXV.

belong to a stage of economy either of full or of closely approaching agrarian maturity. The portions of the southern tier which retained genuine frontier conditions had therefore little part in this history. Areas whose prosperity failed to approximate advance expectations, like the triangle between Lake Ontario, the Black River, and Oneida Lake, and to some extent many of the Holland Company lands, provided a fertile soil for isms. On the other hand, the landed aristocracy of inherited wealth, Yankee or not, controlling such vicinities as lower Livingston County and the environs of Canandaigua, Geneva, and Bath, resisted such movements heartily. Gerrit Smith was the rule-proving exception.

A view of the other sections of the country to which these movements spread confirms the propriety of designating them as concomitants of a fully developed agrarian society. Antimasonry, antislavery, and temperance; revivalism, perfectionism, Millerism, and spiritualism—all of these flourished in the Yankee belt extending from New England into the Middle West. Their strength in most cases was greatest, after New York, in New England, next being northern Ohio and eastern Michigan. Farther west all dwindled gradually to insignificance. The Mormons on first sight seem to be an exception, for they increased as they moved west. But they were eastern people in the first place, while eastward-wending missionaries long continued to convert more new adherents in New York and New England than in the Middle West.[25] Measured in terms of its appeal to new recruits, the Church of the Latter-day Saints conforms to the pattern of its companion Burned-over District novelties.

---

[25] See below, pp. 148–149.

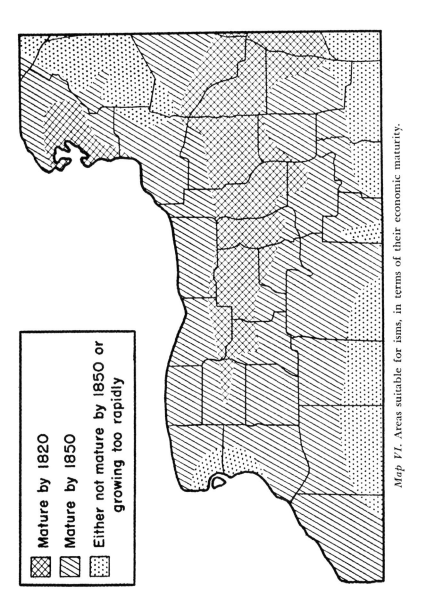

Legend:
- Mature by 1820
- Mature by 1850
- Either not mature by 1850 or growing too rapidly

Map VI. Areas suitable for isms, in terms of their economic maturity.

Chapter 5. SOCIAL PATTERNS

SINCE western New York achieved a substantial degree of economic maturity within ten or twelve years of the Erie Canal's
completion, the transformation from pioneering days had been
accomplished very rapidly. Such speedy change could hardly be
comprehensive, affecting equally every social habit and condition.
Definite vestiges of youthful character therefore remained evident
in 1835.

The main and branch waterways, their railroad connections,
and the older turnpikes provided a transportation network which
must have been extraordinarily complete for that period. Still,
good local roads permitting easy and frequent trips to a neighboring village at all seasons of the year had as yet scarcely been imagined. Although even the cultivators of new clearings could get
produce to market and lay in necessary staples on occasional jour-
neys, few men living any distance from town are likely to have
made such excursions very often. Their wives, if they went at all,
undoubtedly did so at even greater intervals. The kind of loneli-
ness suffered when the family next door dwelt several miles away
had certainly forever departed, but the type of isolation would
long remain which threw a few men and women from a limited
farming area almost exclusively upon each other's society. The
church at a central trail or road crossing was the focus for neighborhood sociability throughout much of the nineteenth century.
Its ruins, yet witnessing former needs, now crumble on remote by-
ways in nearly deserted valleys.

Ideas and tastes changed slowly, just as did the unit of rural friendliness. A naive optimism characterized Americans generally in Jacksonian days. The rapid growth and enhanced wealth introduced by the canal could only strengthen this buoyantly youthful mode of thought. Although the majority of Burned-over District folk customarily voted for what turned out to be the conservative political party, opposing the more hopefully egalitarian Jacksonians, their poll was determined rather by accident than by principle. The emigrants from the minority sects and the rugged hills of western New England had been bred in the Jeffersonian opposition to Yankee Federalism, but upon reaching New York they found many of the landlords' agents and other scions of aristocracy associated with the Democratic Republicans. Many also proved to be Masons. Antimasonry seemed a more genuine vehicle of optimistic democracy than the Democratic Party itself.[1] Many upstaters failed to perceive the gradual drift of their ebullient movement toward Whiggism.

In religion, optimism took the form of belief in an early millennium. Just as the American political system would lead the world to equality and justice, so would American revivals inaugurate the thousand years' reign of Christ on earth before the Second Coming and the end of the world.[2] Millennial revivalism flourished more strongly here than in any other part of the country, bespeaking a correspondingly sanguine disposition. Though not a frontier region at this time, the Burned-over District certainly exhibited a disproportionate amount of optimism, at least as compared with New England.

The elements of gracefulness which grew with eastern urbanism evidently filtered only gradually into the developing upstate cities, and even more slowly into their hinterlands. Folkways which grew in prevalence toward the West—tobacco-spitting, heavy drinking, freedom of the streets for livestock, the bolting of meals without accompanying conversation, lack of regard for the privacy of trav-

---

[1] Paul D. Evans, *The Holland Land Company* (Buffalo, 1924), 334 ff., 369; Dixon R. Fox, *The Decline of Aristocracy in the Politics of New York* (New York, 1919), 53, 288, 307; and "New York Becomes a Democracy," *The Age of Reform* (Alexander C. Flick, ed., *History of the State of New York*, VI, New York, 1934), 12.

[2] Calvin Colton, *History and Character of American Revivals of Religion* (London, 1832).

elers—the survival of such traits indicated the continuation of youthful awkwardness in western New York.[3]

Again, the folk of this region identified themselves with West more than East in their persistent superstition and credulity. Cosmopolitan influences spreading along commercial routes would gradually undermine the more extreme gullibility of the countryside, but even the sophisticated among the area's citizens remained amazingly uncritical. President Eliphalet Nott of Union College voiced the classic statement of a prominent temperance doctrine, that alcohol in the stomach might be ignited by spontaneous combustion and blow up the inebriate. One of Theodore Weld's colleagues described an experiment, supposedly most scientifically conducted, which proved that hairs in water "first change their color from black to a kind of brown or drab, then begin to move, squirm, crawl, etc." Gerrit Smith, upon Angelina Grimké's advice, carried a horse chestnut to cure his piles; and L. D. Fleming recommended for William Miller's boils, *"one pound of shot . . .* [boiled] in a quart of sweet milk down to one *pint,"* taken in small quantities several times daily. Thurlow Weed recorded a boyhood excursion to dig gold in the moonlight, when "the throat of a black cat was cut, and the precise spot was indicated by the direction the blood spurted." Even a Universalist preacher had "engaged the services of one of those imposters who, by looking into a mysterious glass, or rather stone, pretended to be able to discover hidden treasures." [4]

Legends of buried treasure were indeed widespread, dignified by a lineage rejuvenated by the fame of Captain Kidd, but reach-

---

[3] Captain Basil Hall, *Travels in North America,* etc. (2 vols.; Edinburgh, 1839), I, 138; [Isaac Candler], *A Summary View of America,* etc. (London, 1824), 59; and Harriet Martineau, *Society in America* (3 vols.; London, 1837), III, 260–262.

[4] John A. Krout, "The Genesis and Development of the Early Temperance Movement in New York State," *New York State Historical Association Quarterly Journal,* IV (April, 1923), 90; G. H. Barnes and D. L. Dumond, eds., *Letters of Theodore Dwight Weld, Angelina Grimké Weld, and Sarah Grimké* (2 vols.; New York, 1939), I, 53; Ralph V. Harlow, *Gerrit Smith, Philanthropist and Reformer* (New York, 1939), 36; L. D. Fleming, Newark, May 21, 1843, to William S. Miller, William Miller Papers, Aurora College Library; Thurlow Weed, *Autobiography of Thurlow Weed* (Harriet A. Weed, ed., Boston, 1884), 7; Christian Schulz, *Travels in an Inland Voyage through the State of New York,* etc. (2 vols.; New York, 1810), I, 16; *Memoirs of the Life of Nathaniel Stacy,* etc. (Columbus, Penna., 1850), 172.

ing back to the first explorers of the American continents. Joseph Smith's method of establishing his prophethood was by no means peculiar and quite naturally seemed authentic to ordinary folk among a generation whose sages would soon experiment with table tipping. Even more common, if less sensational, was a belief, respectable at least as early as William Penn's day, that the Indians or a previous race now extinct developed from the lost tribes of Israel. Educated European travelers and authorities in American anthropology alike called attention to pre-Indian remains in New York and Ohio.[5] Neither Solomon Spaulding, for whom some have claimed authorship of a manuscript which became the basis of the *Book of Mormon*, nor Joseph Smith required any originality to speculate in this direction. Their writings would scarcely seem fanciful, possibly not even novel, to their contemporaries. Neither in any case need have borrowed from the other.

The whole tribe of Yorkers exhibited a trait which bears on the nature of Burned-over District credulity. It ranks in importance with the canniness and moral intensity customarily attributed to Yankees and relates to both, but has been less noticed because it is difficult to define and isolate. Against the "holy enterprise of minding other people's business," [6] which produced a marked community-mindedness, these folk balanced a stubborn introspection in the fashioning of personal beliefs, which recognized no authority this side of Heaven. Frank curiosity, pride in independent thinking, a feeling that action should be motivated by sound logic and never by whimsy, a profound skepticism of any rationalization looking to less than the supposed ultimate good of society, and, once arrived at, an overweening confidence in one's own judgment —all these attitudes differently demonstrate the same trait. The mores of the community must definitely be observed when established and agreed upon, but in practice they remained forever open to challenge and subject to revision. No apology was required for

---

5 E[manual] Howitt, *Selections from Letters Written during a Tour through the United States*, etc. (Nottingham, England, 1820), 161–165; John M. Duncan, *Travels through . . . the United States and Canada in 1818 and 1819* (2 vols.; Glasgow, 1823), II, 91–112; Timothy Dwight, *Travels in New England and New York* (4 vols.; New Haven, Conn., 1822), IV, 188–189; Josiah Priest, *American Antiquities and Discoveries in the West*, etc. (Albany, 1833).

6 Dixon R. Fox, *Yankees and Yorkers* (New York, 1940), 3.

unorthodoxy dictated by conscience in conference with Scripture;
rather, any difference from custom created a compelling obligation
for the individual to press toward conformity with his own new
light.[7]

In New England this trait had always mitigated the repression
so often made to seem the dominant folkway of the Yankees, though
much of the time and in many localities the combined pressure of
church and state had sufficed to suppress irregularities. Possibly the
lack of a church establishment in New York helped weight this
side of the balance against conventionalism. More probably, the
freer reign of optimism in the younger section provided release
needed for the tendency to grow. For whatever reason, the New
York descendants of the Puritans were a more quarrelsome, argumentative, experimenting brood than their parents and stay-at-
home cousins. As compared with non-Yankees they were credulous
in a particular way: they believed only upon evidence. Their
observation, to be sure, was often inaccurate and usually incomplete, but when they had arrived at a conclusion by presumably foolproof processes their adherence to it was positively
fanatic.

Much of the isolation, optimism, crudity, superstition, and
credulity characteristic of a young section thus remained during
the second quarter of the century. If these were the primary causes
of isms, however, western New York should have been much less
"burned" than other territories farther west, instead of itself
earning the designation, "Burned-over District." In fact, this region
during the era of its renowned enthusiasms progressed rapidly from
its pioneering characteristics toward new ones of an eastern stamp.
The survivals of earlier manners have some part in explaining its
habits of mind, but the newer traits seem more important.

---

[7] Approaches to this trait are made by Frederick Jackson Turner, *The United States,
1830–1850: The Nation and Its Sections* (Avery Craven, ed., New York, 1935), 72, 98–
99, 114; John A. Krout, *The Origins of Prohibition* (New York, 1925), 227; George
Combe, *Notes on the United States . . . during a Phrenological Visit,* etc. (2 vols.;
Philadelphia, 1841), I, 146, 164; *Autobiography of William H. Seward from 1801 to
1834, with a Memoir of His Life and Selections from His Letters,* etc. (New York,
1877), 312; and William H. Dixon, *New America* (Philadelphia, 1867), 414. Certain
angles of it survive the generations of Yankee descendants, and my discussion of it is
based in part upon observation of acquaintances, my family, and myself.

Westward migration continued through this area for many years. Some Yankees during the thirties went directly to Michigan or Illinois, but others stopped here to buy out earlier settlers who moved on in turn. Still others had stopped earlier in eastern New York and now moved on within the state. The transients headed for more distant parts were ordinarily the restless, the less educated and propertied, the more optimistic folk, who preferred a rough frontier to the adjustments which civilization required. Ambition for material success when inadequately satisfied in New York drove them on; so they probably had less religious inclination than did the persons they left behind, who had achieved a degree of worldly position and could well look to their eternal welfare. The second wave of Yankee migrants had been not so quickly persuaded to leave reasonably satisfactory stations in New England as were the first wandering sons and customarily had become more accomplished and substantial farmers in their new locations than their predecessors. Thus the continuing flux of migration left western New York more sensitive to religious influences than it had been before.[8]

Another immigration, beginning to swell as the canal approached completion and continuing to grow throughout this period, soon outnumbered the incoming Yankees: the foreign-born workers, who preferred cities to farms and stuck close to the main commercial artery. Their heritages denied them any potential interest in the isms of New England derivation, so their relationship to radical religion is a negative one. Many were Catholics; some, free thinkers; practically all resisted the temperance movement, the Puritan Sabbath, and other shibboleths of the Yorkers. Antipathy between the two groups was nearly inevitable and would find expression in various forms. Nativism in the strict sense, however, dependent upon the concentrated settlement of significant numbers of recent arrivals, never gained the general appeal it had on the seaboard but limited its appearance to the canal-line towns. At its height in the fifties, when it became a political alternative for abolition agitation, it held little appeal for the zealously antislavery Burned-over District; but during the earlier, more purely

---

[8] Turner, *Nation and Sections*, 98, differentiates between the types who migrated farther and those who remained.

anti-Catholic stage of the thirties it became one of the minor religion-dominated isms of the region.[9]

The presence of European-Americans in its cities identified this section with the coastal region and with the developing industrialism whose opportunities the immigrants were best prepared to grasp. The same growth of manufactures had an even more significant consequence for western New York's religious history. Canal transportation facilitated a reciprocal trade between city and country. When the farmer could sell rather than eat his crops, his wife could buy textiles instead of spinning and weaving. Home crafts passed in the same evolution which ended subsistence farming. This evolution, of course, proceeded more rapidly near the larger towns and in the most-matured rural neighborhoods than in more remote provinces. The counties exhibiting the steepest decline in household production of yard goods prove to have been also the very ones most susceptible to isms.[10]

It would be absurd to deduce from this change a vastly augmented leisure for farm women. They continued to raise, feed, and clothe large families with few mechanical aids and probably helped with chores and cultivated the vegetable garden besides. Still, they had won an advance from the age of homespun. The ladies of the country villages more certainly gained time for church socials and the other busynesses of a feminine leisure class. And in the textile cities, chiefly Utica and Rochester, an alternative to marriage, albeit a poor one, had been created.

Although women had reached the threshold of their modern freedom, they were still so much the forgotten members of society that little satisfactory direct evidence about them has survived. Properly, they should dominate a history of enthusiastic movements, for their influence was paramount. One early investigator who approached the subject with an unusual degree of detachment believed that "Spiritual Wifery," as variously seen in perfectionism, Mormonism, and spiritualism, should be ascribed to the scarcity of women in the American population.[11]

---

[9] Ray A. Billington, *The Protestant Crusade, 1800–1860: A Study of the Origins of American Nativism* (New York, 1938), 40 ff., 380, 390–399.

[10] See maps VII and VIII.

[11] Dixon, *New America*, 268.

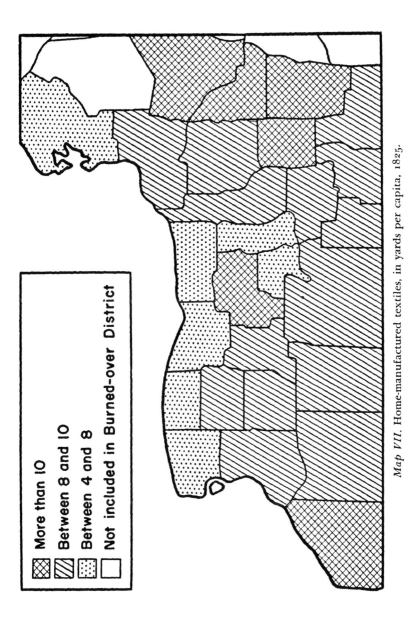

Map VII. Home-manufactured textiles, in yards per capita, 1825.

More than 10

Between 8 and 10

Between 4 and 8

Not included in Burned-over District

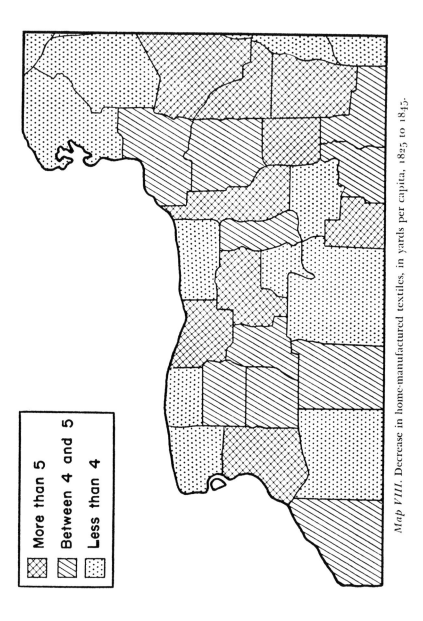

Map VIII. Decrease in home-manufactured textiles, in yards per capita, 1825 to 1845.

More than 5

Between 4 and 5

Less than 4

A national disproportion between the sexes may have contributed to the temper of the times, providing leverage for the growth of feminine prestige, but local conditions fail to support this thesis. In fact, spiritual wifery and religious eccentricity generally prevailed rather as women became more plentiful. Younger counties and cities still in the bonanza stage had low feminine ratios, whereas mature farming neighborhoods and towns relaxed to normal speeds of growth had ratios approaching a balance, or even occasionally a surplus of women.[12] Perhaps more significantly, the proportion of married women to the total of females declined with the maturity of town and countryside alike. In the older localities marriage was longer postponed, educational facilities were more plentiful, alternative careers more possible, and the wherewithal to sustain leisure more generally available. Possibly neuroticism flourished as the number of young women with time to spare increased. More probably, these data are mere circumstances accompanying that stage of maturing society which could produce isms.

For at this period, in all parts of the United States, women led unexciting lives. In the East fashion dictated light exercise, stuffy rooms, tight stays and poor diet; the frontier demanded endless drudgery. Baths were none too frequent. Children came in all too rapid succession, often at considerable risk. Schoolteaching, the boarding house, or work at the mills might be substituted for marriage, but all three required hard labor for slight rewards. Indeed, wages in the mills often had to be supplemented by vicious avocations. Custom allowed girls more freedom than prevailed contemporarily in England or western Europe, but compensated by increased restraints upon married women. Many recreations existed for men only; others induced segregation of the sexes. Most people bred in the New England tradition still considered dancing, cards, and novels immoral, and outlawed similarly the stage, the circus, and most other public amusements, at least for females.[13]

Romantic sentimentality pervaded the entire subject of sex. Un-

---

12 *Census of the State of New York, for 1835*, etc. (Albany, 1836), *passim; Census of the State of New York, for 1845* (Albany, 1846), *passim.*

13 Frances A. Kemble [Butler], *Journal by Frances Anne Butler* (2 vols.; London, 1835), I, 165 note, 202, 256–259, 291–292; Martineau, *Society*, III, 128, 147, 151 ff.; Combe, *Notes*, I, 288 ff.

til they married, women must pose as protected, untouchable models of innocent virtue. Upon marriage they might suffer an even more serious application of double standards. The man had all the marital privileges, with little if any sense of sex requirements in the woman, who was supposed to be superior to base physical satisfactions. Unrequited desires of the male were considered detrimental to health, and wherever the local composition of society permitted it, custom was apt to sanction his resort to extramarital relief. But in the female anything like waywardness would be punished by the most severe ostracism.[14]

These circumstances pertained in no peculiar fashion to western New York. Most of them were, and had always been, universal. The Burned-over District could have been unique only in the manner in which it arrived at a point where women might reach toward freedom. Compared with the West, upstate New York in this period surely provided for greater leisure, more extensive educational opportunities, and a population unusually sensitized to social injustices. Compared with the East, there certainly remained more isolation and crudity, less opportunity for nonreligious pursuits, and slighter relaxation of the inhibitions surrounding feminine social life. Woman made a nearly exclusive avocation of religion throughout the country. On the frontier, however, she returned from camp meeting to thought-forbidding drudgery, while about Boston and New York she could indulge in innumerable secular activities. Perhaps only in the middle stretch of just-matured society, and within the belt of Yankee migration, could she attain the maximum concentration upon this one type of expression. Unconscious desires found outlet in revivals and in the busy campaigns of reforming crusades.[15]

In the still-mysterious inner sanctum of the human mind the psychological drives toward religion and sex are almost surely close affiliates. Consequently, the interpreters of religious heterodoxy have included a multitude of pseudo-Freudians who elaborate an amateurish, historical psychoanalysis pointing to the supposedly profound conclusion that sex caused it all.[16] If, however, we grant

---

[14] E. Douglas Branch, *The Sentimental Years, 1836–1860* (New York, 1934), 350.

[15] Comments abound in Martineau, *Society.* See III, 106, 109, 145, 265, 268.

[16] Robert A. Parker, *A Yankee Saint: John Humphrey Noyes,* etc. (New York, 1935);

that sex permeates large areas of behavior, and somewhat particularly the area of religious emotionalism, it still remains to analyze the other social factors upon which sex drives operated and to show how the interplaying influences brought forth their results.

Intellect must have been fully as important an influence in women as supressed desires. The state of mind would determine the kind of channel through which emotion could seek release and dictate the form of its final expression. Female seminaries, practically unknown in 1825, flourished in some number a quarter-century later, and a fair proportion of girls in this area attended them. Here was offered a training distinguishable from that of male academies chiefly in its emphasis on etiquette and housewifely graces at the expense of college preparatory curricula. Most schools, originating among religious groups, doubtless provided Bible reading, singing, and praying exercises. But theology, which observed Christianity as a system of thought and demanded some pretense to reasoning and analysis, gained no such attention as it held in the men's colleges and graduate seminaries.[17]

Few women in this generation, however, progressed beyond the elementary school. There girls enjoyed the same education as boys and probably attended more regularly since the boys dropped out for every important season of farm labor. The overwhelming majority of girls in western New York did go to school for some part of each year from their fifth to their sixteenth. Enrollment figures show that children of both sexes attended universally, except in industrial towns where immigrant groups suffered neglect.[18] The common schools taught the three R's, spelling, some geography, and occasionally history. The session was short, especially

---

Ernest S. Bates, *American Faith, Its Religious, Political and Economic Foundations* (New York, 1940); Branch, *Sentimental Years;* Gilbert Seldes, *The Stammering Century* (New York, 1928); William H. Dixon, *Spiritual Wives* (London, 1868); Theodore Schroeder, "Erotogenetic Interpretation of Religion," *Journal of Religious Psychology,* VII (Jan., 1914), 23-44.

17 Martha MacLear, *The History of the Education of Girls in New York and New England, 1800–1870* (Washington, 1926); Thomas Woody, *A History of Women's Education in the United States* (2 vols.; New York, 1929); Robert S. Fletcher, *A History of Oberlin College from its Foundation through the Civil War* (2 vols.; Oberlin, O., 1943), I, 290–316, and II, *passim;* and Whitney R. Cross, "Creating a City, The History of Rochester from 1824 to 1834," (MS at University of Rochester, 1936), 163–175.

18 See maps IX and X.

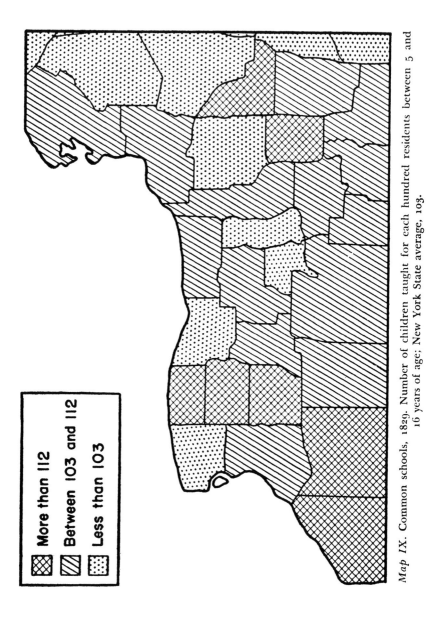

Map IX. Common schools, 1829. Number of children taught for each hundred residents between 5 and 16 years of age; New York State average, 103.

More than 112

Between 103 and 112

Less than 103

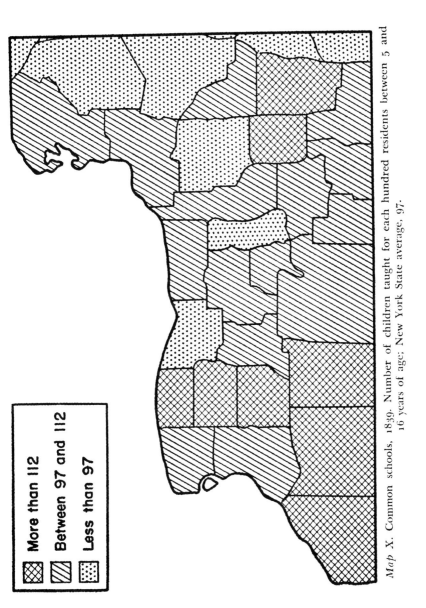

Map X. Common schools, 1839. Number of children taught for each hundred residents between 5 and 16 years of age; New York State average, 97.

More than 112

Between 97 and 112

Less than 97

in more newly settled areas, and attendance spasmodic, at least in farm districts, perhaps seldom exceeding 65 per cent. Teachers in all likelihood stimulated little zeal for learning, as their payment and training were alike poor. Yet very nearly the entire native born population had at least an opportunity to learn reading, writing, and simple figuring. It seems likely that the quality of this education exceeded that of any other available west of New England, while it probably at least equaled what the parent section had to offer.[19]

The curriculum contained no specific religious education, although the Bible often served as a reader, and teachers, judged by the local district's conception of character and morality, were apt in Yankee-settled vicinities to be evangelically minded church members. Presbyterian pastors, and perhaps others, assumed as much responsibility for the public school as community opinion would permit. Regular visits, sessions of prayer, distribution of tracts or magazines—these became points of duty whose exercise the A.H.M.S. ministers reported regularly to headquarters. That exertion of a more sectarian influence occurred at least occasionally is indicated by one report, unusually frank, but typical in tone:

Moral and religious instruction have . . . been imparted . . . with some degree of faithfulness. The difficulty in introducing catechetical instruction into our common schools is still greater than in establishing daily religious worship. This arises from the mixed character of the population, from the strong prejudices . . . against the Calvinistic and fundamental doctrines of the Gospel. . . .[20]

Thus the nonsectarian and secular principle of common school education often proved in practice to be nullified by disregard of the spirit if not the letter of the law.

New York's plan of state financial aid, posited upon the attainment of certain educational practices and the proportion of local

---

[19] [A. C. Flagg], "Annual Report of the Superintendent of Common Schools," *Documents of the Assembly of the State of New York*, 56th session, I, no. 17 (Jan., 1833), 68–70; A. D. Mayo, *Report of Commissioner of Education* (1897–1898), I, 437, quoted by Frank T. Carlton, *Economic Influences upon Educational Progress in the United States, 1820–1850* (Madison, Wis., 1908), 96; *Census, 1845, passim*. See maps XV and XVI.

[20] Phineas Smith, Portage, Nov. 4, 1829, to Corresponding Secretary, American Home Missionary Society Papers, Chicago Theological Seminary.

support in each district, was already warping the school system toward uniformity. Differences between various counties and sections in the state are naturally slight, but within such a standardized framework even small distinctions became the more indicative of fundamental dissimilarities of attitude. The Burned-over District consistently sent a larger proportion of its children to school than did the eastern half of the state. While the term was shorter in the younger, western counties, its length increased more rapidly than elsewhere. At least eleven western counties provided more local support than the median for the state, even as early as 1829, and ten years later only five of the twenty-eight counties in the western half fell below the state average. Private school attendance and library facilities in similar fashion indicate a superior educational opportunity in the very sections which also exhibited relative maturity, agricultural prosperity, Yankee predominance, and isms.[21]

Of course, many of the persons involved in enthusiasms had passed their school days by the 1820's and had enjoyed slighter privileges in youth than did their children. A minimum education, however, had long been a virtual birthright for New Englanders, and New York's common schools rose chiefly from the universal habit of those settlers to establish classes as soon as meeting had been organized. Men and women who were by no means learned, yet able to read their Bibles from childhood, definitely made the best subjects for religious excitement. At any given time or stage of the society's educational development they were apt to be a relatively educated class.

Although the case must be assumed rather than proved for the earlier years of the period, the New York common schools so broadened the bases of popular knowledge that by the time measurement can be taken very few native-born adults remained illiterate. In 1850, three western New York counties equaled or exceeded the Massachusetts literacy record for the native-born,

---

21 See maps XI and XII, XIII and XIV. [A. C. Flagg], "Annual Report of the Superintendent of Common Schools," *Legislative Documents of the Senate and Assembly of the State of New York*, 53d session, I, no. 31 (Jan., 1830), *passim.* [J. C. Spencer], "Annual Report of the Superintendent of Common Schools," *Documents of the Assembly of the State of New York*, 64th session, IV, no. 100 (1841), 22-24.

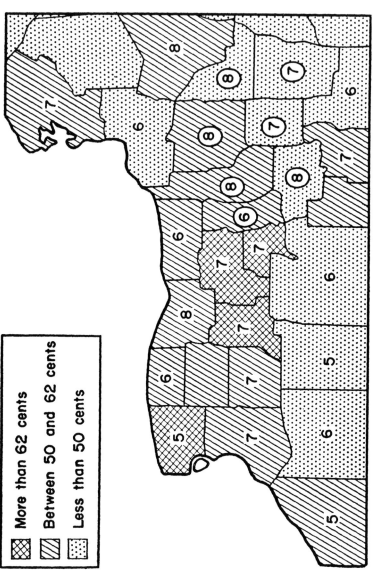

Map XI. Common schools, 1829. (1) Months of school session; state average, 8. (2) Amount paid per student beyond state and local public funds; state average, 62 cents. Counties in which the months of school session are circled had incomes from land sales

More than 62 cents

Between 50 and 62 cents

Less than 50 cents

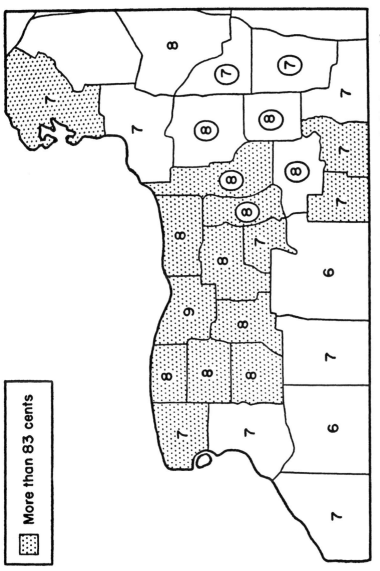

Map XII. Common schools, 1839. (1) Months of school session; state average, 8. (2) Amount paid per student beyond state and local public funds; state average, 83 cents. Counties in which the months of school session are circled had incomes from land sales.

More than 83 cents

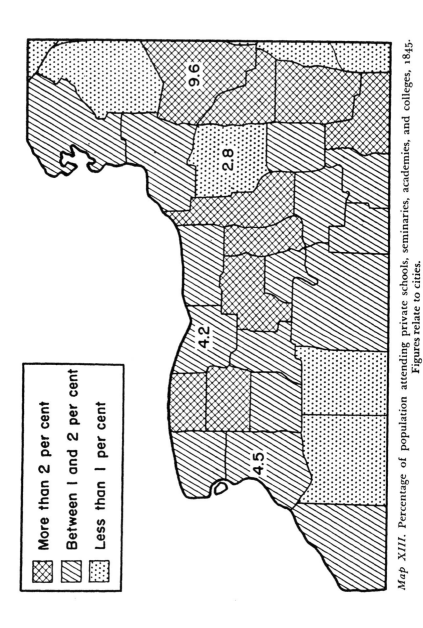

Map XIII. Percentage of population attending private schools, seminaries, academies, and colleges, 1845. Figures relate to cities.

More than 2 per cent

Between 1 and 2 per cent

Less than 1 per cent

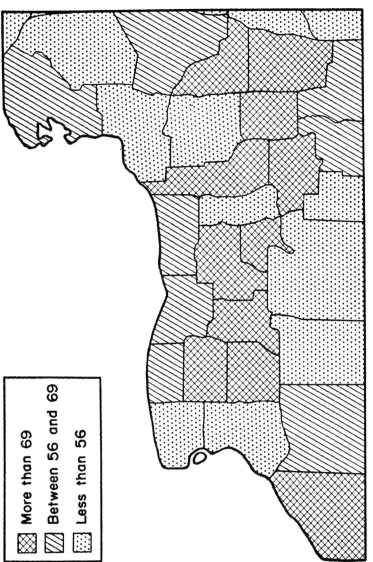

Map XIV. Books per capita in public, school, and Sunday school libraries, 1850. The Massachusetts average was 69 books per capita; New York, 56; Connecticut, 45; New Jersey, 17; Pennsylvania, 16; Ohio, 9.

More than 69

Between 56 and 69

Less than 56

highest of any state in the Union, while twenty of the twenty-eight counties west of the mountains surpassed the New York State average of 99 per cent. New Jersey, Pennsylvania and Ohio all had at least twice as many illiterate native-born citizens. Earlier census figures fail to isolate the foreign-born, who had little connection with religious enthusiasm, but an approximate estimate for 1840 suggests that the portions of western New York interested in isms even then contained fewer than 1 per cent of native illiterates.[22]

The aspirations of the rising folk demanded that every child should obtain the tools essential for making his own way in the world. These tools were simple ones, adequate only for a youthful society short of labor and overflowing with unexploited resources. Neither specialized vocational training nor even a facility for critical thinking could be considered vital for such an uncomplicated existence. Apprenticeship, not schools, led to trades and professional competence. A person's real education, once he could read and write, might satisfactorily be left—as indeed it still is in large measure—to his accumulating experience. The ideas and attitudes of that generation, probably even more than our own, took form not so much in the schools as in the various informal agencies of culture surrounding its members. Dominant among these agencies were newspapers, periodicals, groups and societies organized to influence opinion, the various learned professions, and especially the clergy, who by virtue of their highly esteemed public office had an unusual degree of influence upon those impressed more by the spoken than by the written word.

College attendance, also, indicates the nature of the Burned-over District's intellectual leadership, both clerical and secular. In the year 1829 more New Yorkers went to college than the number from Pennsylvania and New Jersey together. Except for New England, which exceeded the total from these three states, it is likely that no other part of the country could show comparable proportions. More than half the Yorkers remained in the institutions of their own state, while thirty-one went to Rutgers, Princeton, or other places to the south or west. Yale and the upland Yankee colleges of Williams, Amherst, Dartmouth, Vermont, and Middle-

---

[22] See maps XV and XVI.

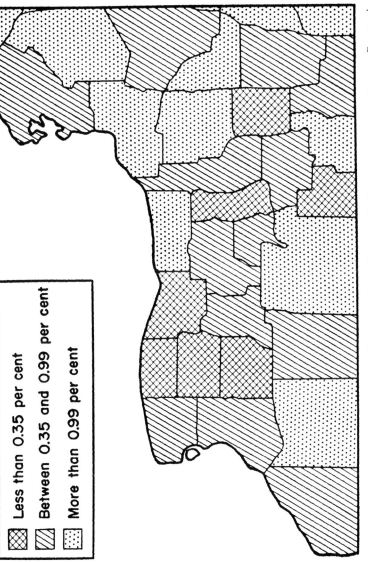

Less than 0.35 per cent

Between 0.35 and 0.99 per cent

More than 0.99 per cent

Map XV. Percentage of native-born illiterates, 1850. The New York average was .99 per cent; Connecticut, .35 per cent; Pennsylvania, 2.22 per cent. All counties are above the New Jersey and Ohio averages and all but one above Pennsylvania.

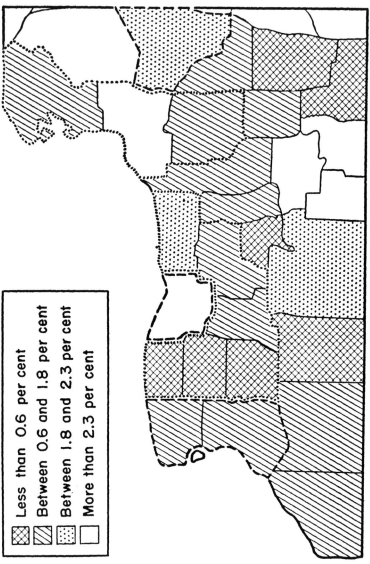

Less than 0.6 per cent

Between 0.6 and 1.8 per cent

Between 1.8 and 2.3 per cent

More than 2.3 per cent

Map XVI. Percentage of illiterates over 20 years of age, 1840. The New England average was .6 per cent; New York, 1.8 per cent; Ohio, 2.3 per cent. Line of dots encloses counties with over 5 per cent foreign-born; line of dashes, counties with from 5 to 10 per cent foreign-born.

bury, all strongly evangelical in tone, drew nearly a hundred, while Harvard footed the list with only four.[23] After Oberlin had been established under the aegis of Charles Finney and his New York City financiers, to bring eastern piety to the great "valley of dry bones," a substantial portion of men and a few women elected this more intensely religious education. More than two hundred students from western New York attended Oberlin College during the five years following 1835, about a third for college work and the others for preparatory or theological courses. This number approximated a fourth or more of the total college enrollment from the region, and may even have amounted to majority representation from several rural counties.[24]

Few professional men acquired institutional training beyond the college level, these few being for the most part ministers of two denominations, Presbyterian and Baptist. By virtue both of education and social position these were the very persons who provided effective leadership in creating an excitable state of the popular mind. Not only did they exercise a persuasive influence as preachers and pastors, as did other clergymen, but they also wrote the religious literature of the region. Many of these men were New England-born and most of the rest sprang from Yankee parentage.

The usual Presbyterian career may be indicated by a composite biographical analysis of thirty-six men, most of whom came early to the Burned-over District and enjoyed long activity there. Twenty-one hailed from Massachusetts or Connecticut; only four from Pennsylvania and New Jersey. Only two had not attended college; the majority had both undergraduate and postgraduate training, the former mainly in the western New England colleges, the latter mainly at Princeton, for some time after 1800 the only denominational theological school. Probably the personal eminence which helped these particular records to survive indicates greater education than average, but it is equally probable that the average rapidly approached this level during the second quarter of the century. Auburn Theological Seminary alone graduated 228

---

[23] *Quarterly Register and Journal of the American Education Society* (Andover, Mass.), I (April, 1829), 221–226.

[24] *Catalogue of the Trustees, Officers, and Students of the Oberlin Collegiate Institute* (Oberlin, O., 1835, 1836, 1838–1841); *Census, 1845, passim.*

candidates during the thirteen years following 1824, the great majority of them prepared at Hamilton and Union colleges. The shift from New England to New York institutions adequately suggests the growing cultural maturity of the younger area, but it probably meant little change in educational styles. The early upstate New York colleges and seminaries seem in most respects indistinguishable from the upland Yankee schools upon which they were modeled.[25]

Baptists had the same kind of origins and only less of the same type of training. Of thirty ministers prominent in the area, twenty failed to reach college but had gone to Yankee academies and experienced clerical apprenticeship at the feet of New England divines. Five of the ten college graduates were educated in the same section, four at Hamilton Seminary (now Colgate University) and one at Princeton. Only four were of other than Yankee derivation.[26] Baptists and Presbyterians thus maintained higher standards of preparation for the ministry than did other sects, and better standards in this region than they themselves did elsewhere, except in New England.

Higher education did not perhaps directly shape the popular mind, but it bred the small minority of cultured individuals who would by speech and writing create many of the thought patterns of the multitude. Newspapers and periodicals made a much more direct contact with the mass of literate folk than did colleges or theological seminaries.

Daily papers in cities and weeklies in the country undoubtedly provided the primary literary fare for the Burned-over District. During the second quarter of the century practically every village supported at least one news sheet. Publishing followed only after the meeting and the school in the order of Yankee cultural establishments. These people had an original predilection for justifying

---

25 William B. Sprague, *Annals of the American Pulpit*, etc. (II, *Trinitarian Congregational*, New York, 1857, and III, *Presbyterian*, New York, 1858); John Q. Adams, *A History of Auburn Theological Seminary, 1818–1918* (Auburn, 1918), 232; *Journal, American Education Society*, II (May, 1830), 248.

26 David Benedict, *A General History of the Baptist Denomination*, etc. (New York, 1848), 487; *Western New York Baptist Missionary Magazine* (Norwich, Morrisville), I (1814–1816), 332–334; II (1817–1819), 254; William B. Sprague, *Annals of the American Baptist Pulpit*, etc. (VI, New York, 1860), *passim*.

themselves in public, and New York State supplied an extraordinarily complex and turbulent political history to help fill the newspapers. It seems likely that the folk of this state had throughout the period a larger number and greater circulation of papers than did any other group of corresponding size and development in the country. Careful study of this proposition is possible only in 1850, at the end of a time of great journalistic growth, but the knowledge that the development was long and steady and the fact that at least 129 weeklies had commenced in the area before 1820 alike suggest that earlier years, could they be observed accurately, would exhibit the same proportional publishing eminence relative to other sections of the country. In the mid-century, this state published journals of all types in a larger number per capita than any other state except Massachusetts, which nearly doubled the New York figure of 37.2 a year. Pennsylvania was a close third and the only near rival.[27] It seems likely, moreover, that this pre-eminence rested more largely in the other two cases upon the printing business of their single metropolis, since the upstate New York cities had long grown more rapidly than secondary publishing centers in the other states.

Newspapers molded opinion on domestic and foreign politics and on many economic issues. Religious and social matters entered only when they assumed a political nature. Antislavery and temperance both took such a turn, but not until they had been substantially formed as emotional movements by other forces. In order to seek the sources of indoctrination for isms, therefore, one must look to the more specialized periodicals. Nevertheless, the great news circulation is highly significant, since it testifies more adequately than do figures on literacy and schooling to the fact that Yorker Yankees were extraordinarily wide-awake, well-informed, and ambitious for greater knowledge. Beyond the routine of formal education they were more alert than most other Americans.

---

27 The Antimasonic movement alone created fifty-two newspapers. Milton W. Hamilton, "Antimasonic Newspapers, 1826-1834," *The Papers of the Bibliographical Society of America* (XXXII, 1938), 74, note 10; Clarence S. Brigham, *History and Bibliography of American Newspapers, 1690-1820* (2 vols.; Worcester, Mass., 1947), I, 527-606, 707-757; J. D. B. DeBow, Superintendent, *The Seventh Census of the United States, 1850*, etc. (Washington, 1853), xxxiii, 60, 126, 199, and *passim*.

New York State probably exceeded even New England in its publication of other periodicals. Albany gave birth to the second agricultural journal in the country in 1819. Although this soon died, the Rochester *Genesee Farmer* and *Albany Cultivator* led their field nationally; upon their combination at Albany, a *New Genesee Farmer* rose on the banks of the river it celebrated to run a close second. The farm papers generally avoided controversial subjects, but did carry a quantity of reform literature of basically religious nature which doubtless gave their constituencies throughout the Northeast many of the germs of their social attitudes.[28]

A growing host of literary sheets permeated the upstate area from local as well as metropolitan sources. The local ventures seem to have been rather miserable specimens, for the section was not yet sufficiently mature to support a leisured class which might either patronize or create fine arts in adequate fashion. In addition, the idea that literary or artistic expression could be justified on aesthetic, rather than moral grounds met little approval in this society of Puritan derivation. So far as this kind of paper helped create Burned-over District thought-ways, it merely supported and reinforced the religious press.[29]

According to the census of 1850, religious periodicals in this state exceeded a fourth of the total newspaper circulation, providing 4.2 copies a person. Massachusetts still led New York, but by a far slighter margin than in the case of the total for all serial publications. Pennsylvania lagged considerably, and no other state remotely approached the three leaders. The census classification excludes many presumably semireligious journals by failing to separate the reform press from the "literary and miscellaneous" column. A more accurate grouping would doubtless make New York the more pre-eminent.[30] It is further likely, but beyond demonstration, that this state's proportionate superiority in clerical journalism was more marked during the twenties and thirties than in 1850,

---

[28] Albert L. Demaree, *The American Agricultural Press, 1819–1860* (New York, 1941), 13, 14, 53, 67, 77, 82, 94, 95, 336 ff.

[29] Bertha-Monica Stearns, "Reform Periodicals and Female Reformers, 1830–1860," *American Historical Review*, XXXVII (July, 1932), 678–699; *Rochester Gem*, etc., 1829–1831, 1830–1834.

[30] *Seventh Census*, xxxiii, 60, 126, 199, and passim.

for the literature of all the benevolent orders centralized heavily here in those decades, and several religious papers of obvious importance flourished during the period of revivals but declined or died before the middle of the century. It is a roundabout yet valid reasoning which credits the rise of religious journalism to enthusiastic religious movements, and yet claims for that journalism a dominant influence in forming the state.of mind from which enthusiasm grew. The written word reinforced the spoken and extended the audience for localized episodes and key thinkers.

A thorough analysis of Burned-over District religious literature would have to assess the effectiveness of tons of tracts, Bibles, pamphlet sermons, and periodicals. The *Home Missionary*, the Education Society's *Quarterly Register*, the *New York Observer*, and all their sister journals apparently circulated at least as widely here as elsewhere, as did also the national denominational papers from New York, Boston, and Cincinnati.[31] But this kind of organ had only a standardized influence, different quantitatively but not qualitatively from its impact on other parts of the country. A few local ventures occasionally attempted to serve the same general purpose, but most of them failed to compete with the metropolitan establishments. Conservatives or middle-of-the-roaders in religion could easily satisfy their tastes without organizing to publish in their own neighborhood. But the protestor, by virtue of his desire to alter the status quo, becomes invariably a more strenuous propagandist; so this region which bred unorthodoxies specialized in argumentative local journals, with radical purposes to champion or to defeat. Much of the controversy raged rather between conservatives and reformers than between denominations, focusing on such issues as strenuous evangelism, abolition, the alcoholic content of Communion wine, and denominational schisms.

The *Baptist Register* of Utica, the most influential local paper of the denomination, maintained considerable balance amidst the storms of the day but occasionally declared war on over-radical tendencies. Agitators in that church probably followed other leadership during most of the period. Excellent editorship, sane

---

[31] Six letters in one year, 1828, reporting from Elmira, Ithaca, Lockport, Ionia, Camillus, and Coventry indicate seventy-eight subscriptions to the *Home Missionary*, A.H.M.S. MSS.

conservatism, and connection with the Hamilton Seminary, virtual center of the church in this state, enabled the *Register* to achieve financial success. With over two hundred agents and a subscription list of five thousand by the early thirties, it paid about $500 annually into the coffers of the state convention to the end of its career in 1852. Only near the end did it receive a challenge, when the *Christian Contributor and Free Missionary* began publication as an advocate of radical positions.

A vigorous Universalist press also protested the excesses of enthusiasm in evangelical religion, in such combative fashion indeed as to come itself to the fore among controversialists. A number of early ventures gradually consolidated into two sizable organs in the late twenties: the *Gospel Advocate,* edited by Orestes A. Brownson at Auburn, and the *Utica Magazine,* which had the official sanction of the state convention. When Brownson flirted with Abner Kneeland's skeptical notions, and finally left both the church and the paper, the two publications united, to cover the state with a circulation of between four and five thousand copies.[32] Similarly, though with more orthodox theological accompaniment, the journal of the Christian Connection found itself ranged dogmatically against certain kinds of enthusiasm. First as the *Gospel Luminary* and later as the *Christian Palladium,* it served the denomination in central and western New York. Vigorously opposed to Presbyterian "priestcraft" and to much of the activity of several of the large benevolent societies, this journal was nevertheless warmly revivalistic in sympathy and took a radical position on reform movements, once they lost sectarian connotations. During the early forties, under Joseph Marsh's editorship, the *Palladium* became for a time virtually a Millerite sheet, until nonsympathizers removed him from his post.

Whereas other churches drifted toward the use of one paper, at least for one state or region, the Presbyterians developed an increasing diversity. Several dignified theological magazines struggled along even before 1825, but leadership soon fell to the more enthusiastic sponsors of the new revival spirit. The *Western Recorder* of Utica, begun "for the benefit of the Western Education

---

[32] *Utica [Evangelical] Magazine,* etc. (title varies), n.s., II (Jan. 9, 1830), 14.

Society and Auburn Theol. Seminary," soon became the great organ of the Finney evangelists in central New York and apparently flourished for six or seven years, though it ceased publication in 1834.[33] The *Rochester Observer*, started in 1827, came to parallel the *Recorder* in the western reaches of the state, attaining a circulation of nearly 3000 at its peak in 1832. Two years later it had reverted to earlier habits of fiscal loss and merged with the *New York Evangelist*.[34] Presbyterian schismatics, as they drifted in time into new interests, published zealously. Luther Myrick's *Union Herald* at Cazenovia circulated at least a thousand copies at its height, while John Humphrey Noyes's journal under its various titles may have come close to the same number in the mid-forties. William Goodell eked out an editorial salary of $52.00 from the *Christian Investigator*, printing 1500 copies, only a third of which represented paid subscriptions.

If Presbyterian heretics were on the whole more literary than others, each radical movement had at least one journal in the area. The *Friend of Man* (Utica), the *Cazenovia Abolitionist*, and the *American Citizen* (Warsaw, Perry, Rochester) stood for abolition; the *Voice of Truth* (Rochester), and the *Voice of the Shepherd* (Utica), for the Millerites; the *Spiritual Clarion* (Auburn), for spiritualism; and John Collins' *Communitist*, for the Skaneateles communist experiment. Many other papers of some slight temporary influence seem to have followed spasmodic careers all over the region, some leaving practically no trace of their brief existence.

Probably equal in influence with the local sheets was a series of radical publications originating elsewhere than in western New York. The upstate revivalists and reformers had connections throughout the Northeast and constantly strove for national status. For this reason and also because of the Tappan brothers' influence on a number of wealthy Gothamites, it often proved expedient to publish in the metropolis. *McDowall's Journal*, the *New York Evangelist*, and *Zion's Watchman* (antislavery Methodist) derived

---

[33] *Baptist Register* (Utica), XI (Dec. 26, 1834), 178; Fletcher, *Oberlin*, I, 13; *Western Recorder* (Utica), II (Dec. 20, 1825), 203, VI (Dec. 29, 1829), 207, VII (Jan. 5, 1830), 4; N. C. Saxton, So. Wilbraham, Mass., July 17, 1832, to Finney, Charles Grandison Finney Papers, Oberlin College Library.

[34] *New York Evangelist*, V (Jan. 4, 1834), 2.

substantial, and at times almost exclusive, support from their circulation in western New York. This was also true of the *Oberlin Evangelist* for many years, and of the Boston and New York Adventist and spiritualist journals in a slighter measure. The nativist papers of the metropolis, however, attained no more than a normal proportion of support in the Burned-over District.[35]

These magazines had a standardized composition, and all of similar interests copied extensively from one another. Their editorials, "arguing-down" opponents, occupied relatively little space, as most columns carried either articles by the editor's circle of clerical friends or personal accounts of religious experience.

Now that theology is a very nearly dead subject, one finds it extremely difficult to realize how such journals could have an extensive appeal. But appeal they did, in demonstrable fashion. The region's sanest religious editor believed in 1830 that "we need constant excitement. . . . And in what way can this be done so effectively, as by the circulation of a religious paper?" After ten years of bitter experience he regretted but reaffirmed the power of the press: "There is a prodigious deal of power . . . to sow dissention . . . and stir up desolating strife; . . . they may exert a discordant influence before they are aware, and raise a storm altogether beyond their power to control or calm." [36] Many of John Noyes's converts gained initial interest from perusal of a stray copy of his paper. Hundreds of western New Yorkers followed the *Oberlin Evangelist* with only the remotest interest in the institution. Many Methodist clergymen turned abolitionist as they read *Zion's Watchman*. Isolated bands of Millerites maintained their zeal by subscribing to the *Voice of Truth*.[37]

The puzzle of such an attraction solves itself in two ways. First,

---

[35] *New York Evangelist*, II (April 2, 1831), 1, V (April 26, 1834), 68; Thomas Kendall, New Lebanon, April 7, 1830, to Finney, N. C. Saxton, New York, Sept. 27, 1830, to Finney, Finney MSS; *Zion's Watchman* (New York), II (Dec. 30, 1837), 104; Fletcher, *Oberlin*, I, 419–420; Lewis Tappan, New York, Dec. 9, 1842, to Finney, Lewis Tappan Papers, Library of Congress; *Protestant* (New York), I (Jan. 16, 1830), 24, II (July 30, 1831), 241; *American Protestant Vindicator* (New York), II (April 6, 1838), 108.

[36] *Baptist Register*, VI (Feb. 19, 1830), 106; XVII (Feb. 28, 1840), 10, 11.

[37] *Spiritual Magazine* (Putney, Vt., Oneida Reserve), I (Oct. 7, Dec. 15, 1846), 121, 158, II (June 15, Aug. 15, 1848, Sept. 18, 1849), 63, 109, 255; *Zion's Watchman*, I (Jan. 22, March 16, April 20, Oct. 15, 26, 1836), 13, 41, 62, 158, 171, 177, II (March 4, 1837), 34; *Voice of Truth*, etc. (Rochester), VI (May 14, 1845), 52.

a continuing itineracy often accompanied the paper, making local friends who in turn urged its support. A train of camp meetings, revivals, conventions, and quarterly sessions also kept adherents in contact. To others beyond immediate reach, the magazine, even were its heavy doses of theology not read, could be a constant reminder of intellectual and spiritual ties, while some leisurely seepage of doctrine originally imbibed by ear might filter into the inner consciousness. But suggestion of such indirect influence begs the major question. It seems an inescapable conclusion that a considerable proportion even of laymen read and relished the theological treatises. Such folk formed a minority which thought seriously about religion and took pride in the ability to thresh things out for themselves. Readers of this sort must have tested each dissertation against their own knowledge of Scripture, although they may often have examined less critically than they supposed and in the process swallowed the editor's argument entire.

BOOK III

Portents: 1825-1831

The Lord rides upon the whirlwind and directs the storm . . . this excitement will yet in some way promote his glory.
—EBENEZER MEAD, ATTICA, OCT. 23, 1828, TO MILES P. SQUIER

Chapter 6. THE MARTYR

HISTORY seems often to glide in a smooth current for a time, until certain forces, gathering like a brewing storm, break forth to ruffle the surface and alter the direction of flow. Some dramatic event or masterful man, a product of the accumulating tokens of change, then sets off the reservoir of energy which whips the stream to turbulence till flooding waters dig new channels.

Such a quiescent period prevailed in the United States between the end of the War of 1812 and the appearance of Andrew Jackson in presidential politics. In the Burned-over District the same decade stored up the elemental forces which were to burst forth after 1825. Not one man or episode but five proved to be the portents of the coming quarter-century, the catalytic agents releasing these dynamic influences. Nor should these events be mistaken for the basic causes lying behind them, which naturally were deep-rooted and long-grown, and bound to set the broader tendencies of the future. Yet the more exact and intimate characteristics of life in the coming generation would in considerable measure be fixed by the nature of the introductory events and the way they reacted upon one another.

First of all, the Erie Canal arrived. It had been some time in partial use, and transportation of some variety would have developed in any case. But the fact of completion and the celebration of that event had galvanizing effects. Because it was a waterway and reached only certain places, avoiding others which might have profited more from roads or railways, it created a different detail in the region's economic pattern from that which might otherwise have been realized.

Similarly in noneconomic realms, climactic episodes picked out the smaller lines of a pattern of society whose bolder features had been predetermined by the Yankee traditions of religion and culture. Scarcely had furor over the canal subsided when William Morgan's disappearance aroused anew the western portion of the state. A hundred and fifty miles to the east Charles Grandison Finney was almost simultaneously inaugurating the revivals at Western which set churches ablaze over a wide area. In 1831 he lighted another greater conflagration at Rochester. While these excitements spread and grew, Joseph Smith founded the Mormon Church in the intervening territory. And amidst these occurrences came local expressions of the older benevolent movements, whose fervent crusading heightened to a furious pitch the rivalry between Presbyterians and those sects which feared a campaign to amalgamate church and state once more, as had been done in old New England. These were the major omens which foreshadowed the history of the Burned-over District.

William Morgan became a Mason in Rochester in 1823, but found himself excluded from the Batavia chapter when he moved to that community a short time later. Possibly for revenge, or perhaps in hope of securing a windfall, he wrote the *Illustrations of Masonry* and arranged for its publication by the *Batavia Advocate* press. The secret leaked out, however, whereupon the unfortunate author suffered a series of mysterious persecutions. First the authorities held him briefly on a debt claim, so that his lodgings could be searched for the manuscript. On September 8, 1826, parties of strangers, apparently from Buffalo, Lockport, and Canandaigua, began appearing in town. Their attempt at arson on the print shop failed. Then a trumped-up charge demanded Morgan's presence for trial in Canandaigua. While in jail there awaiting his hearing, he was kidnapped on the evening of September 12. His captors drove him in a curtained carriage through Rochester, by the Ridge Road to Lewiston, and thence to the Fort Niagara powder magazine. He may after a time have been released across the Canadian border. More probably he was tied in a weighted cable, rowed to the center of the Niagara River at its junction with Lake Ontario, and dropped overboard. In any case, it cannot be proved that he was ever seen again.[1]

The Morgan episode came at the peak of turbulent economic expansion in the area west of the Genesee River, and at a time when the common folk were rising to combat privilege of all types; they had already been keenly sensitized to rigid notions of justice and morality by their New England heritage. The event implicated Masons all the way from the Finger Lakes to the Niagara Frontier and gave many villages in that broad stretch a sense of intimate contact with the transactions leading to the crime. The mystery of Morgan's end, still and probably forever beyond solution, invested the consequent horror with enchantment.

The irresponsible action of the Masonic brethren demonstrated an excitability which would prove to be characteristic of the Burned-over District. Why, indeed, perform so hasty and dastardly an act, when revelations of Masonry had been published at intervals for centuries and might be obtained by anyone with a pressing curiosity? The same excitability induced non-Masons throughout the scene of the affair to add their private energies to those of a laggard law, in order that proper justice might be done. Increasingly it appeared that Masons held a monopoly of offices and juries, so that local trials had no chance of reaching suitable verdicts. When local citizens' committees induced the state legislature to consider a special investigation, their resolutions met such smacking defeats that a gigantic conspiracy seemed the only logical explanation. If corruption in high places extended over the whole state, surely the people must act. Thus by 1827 village committees from Rochester westward had begun to organize politically against the accused society. Within the year popular nominating conven-

---

[1] Charles McCarthy, "The Antimasonic Party: A Study of Political Antimasonry in the United States, 1827–1840," American Historical Association, *Annual Report for 1902*, I, 365–574, remains the standard monograph. Dixon R. Fox, *The Decline of Aristocracy in the Politics of New York* (New York, 1919), 339–371, and Glyndon Van Deusen, *Thurlow Weed: Wizard of the Lobby* (Boston, 1947), are able supplements.

tions had been used on a large scale for the first time in the United States, all over western New York, and fifteen Antimasons had been returned to the Assembly at Albany.

The history of Antimasonry in politics is a brief but interesting one, long adequately explored and familiar to historians. In part because Jackson was and John Quincy Adams was not a Mason (he volunteered to expose the secrets of the Phi Beta Kappa fraternity as his contribution to the movement); in part because the Albany Regency of Martin Van Buren had long been affiliated with landlord interests in the western section of New York State; and in part because of the astute management of such political leaders as Thurlow Weed and Francis Granger—for all these reasons and others the Antimasonic program gradually changed from a quest for equality into a businessmen's platform, disguising in more popular garb principles derived from bygone Federalism. In 1834 the party became the nucleus of the new Whig organization, made up of the various disparate oppositions of Jacksonian Democracy. The original emphasis of the western New Yorkers was thus eclipsed, though it never entirely disappeared. The Greeley-Weed-Seward (or old Antimasonic) wing of Whiggism remained the most progressive faction in this conservative party, contained the "conscience" Whigs during the days of political antislavery, and wound up as the radical core of the "Black" Republican Party in 1856.

New York's canal belt found the conservative emphasis of Antimasonic Whiggery perfectly suited to its growing prosperity and normally voted accordingly. Rochester, the center of Weed's organization, however, went Democratic in the 1830 election.[2] This exceptional event was induced partly by reaction from the excitement and demonstrates emphatically how rapidly the crusading fervor subsided in urban society.

But in the hill country farther south on both sides of the Genesee, the emotional spirit of the movement persisted. The rural folk were more sensitive to the appeal of an ism. Egalitarian democracy was either more strongly rooted or more easily nourished by clever propaganda there. The evangelistic churches, which took

---

[2] Whitney R. Cross, "Creating a City: The History of Rochester from 1824 to 1834" (MS at University of Rochester, 1936), 309 and ff.

up Antimasonry strongly, held more complete sway generally in country than in city. Probably lodges had prevailed only in the larger towns, and in so far as Masonry did represent a harbor of social or political privilege the farmer or resident of a smaller hamlet was the object of discrimination. Perhaps the movement may justly be described as an early evidence of rural jealousy toward urban superiority, or at least toward the controlling middle class of the larger villages and county towns. Clearly and strongly, it had an agrarian cast in that it aligned leaseholders and renters against the resident agents of absentee landlords. Thus a set of nonpolitical considerations served for many years to keep in the anti-Democratic column votes which on grounds of interest alone might well have joined the Jacksonians against the merchants and millers of the canal towns.[3]

In its original form, and persistently in rural areas, Antimasonry was a crusade, with marked affinity for most of the movements in religion and reform which would make western New York distinctive in coming years. The major issue seemed to be one of morality: Masonry was believed to have committed a crime. Its members had put their fraternal obligations ahead of their duty to state and society, sanctioning both a lawless violation of personal security and a corrupt plot to frustrate the normal constitutional guarantees of justice.

Once the institution was examined in this light, many other supposed immoralities appeared. Masonry had come to serve many persons in place of a church, to the exclusion of Christianity. Its oaths took the Lord's name in vain. At the very least, it interposed a prior association among certain church members, who were held to be bound equally with all regenerate humans in the exclusive fellowship of the Communion. The rumor that alcoholic beverages were used with abandon in its ceremonies irritated a growing sensitivity on the subject of temperance. Its titles and rituals smacked of monarchy as well as of infidelity. The very secrecy which required such reckless guarding suggested ignoble and dangerous designs. Whence, for instance, came the skulls, reputed to be used

---

[3] Frederick Jackson Turner, *The United States, 1830–1850: The Nation and Its Sections* (Avery Craven, ed., New York, 1935), 73; McCarthy, "Antimasonry," 546; *Orleans Telegraph* (Albion), Sept. 23, 1829.

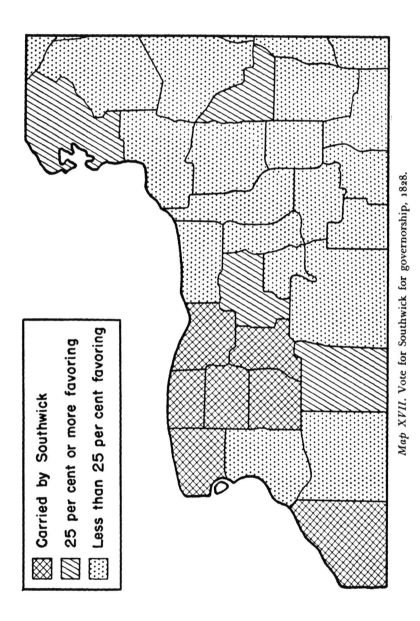

Map XVII. Vote for Southwick for governorship, 1828.

Carried by Southwick

25 per cent or more favoring

Less than 25 per cent favoring

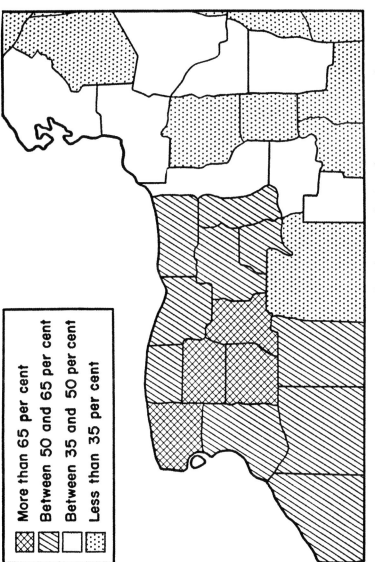

Map XVIII. Percentage of Antimasonic feeling shown in election of state Senators, 1829.

More than 65 per cent

Between 50 and 65 per cent

Between 35 and 50 per cent

Less than 35 per cent

for drinking vessels in the ceremony of the Royal Arch degree? Curiosity, fancy, and rumor thus multiplied the apparent threats of Masonry to the peace, order, and spirituality of society.[4]

Such reactions grew as expert propagandists played upon the fears and wonderment of the multitude. Since many existing newspapers had Masonic editors, a "free press" sprang up in every county west of Cayuga Lake, and less numerously farther afield. Morgan's widow needed the philanthropy of many collections. Pamphlets by seceded Masons and printed resolutions of the many popular conventions found a circulation patterned on the distribution of religious tracts. Ex-members opened and operated mock lodges in the public view. Lecturers roamed the countryside. Such publicity measures, already somewhat familiar in political and religious groups, experienced a decided development under the facile management of Thurlow Weed and his associates.

Although the Antimasonic excitement flourished because it combined many variant interests and soon disintegrated because of its centrifugal energies, its brief impact may well have been the most comprehensive single force to strike the "infected district" during an entire generation. Charles Finney later estimated that two thousand lodges and forty-five thousand members in the United States suspended fraternal activity. Most of the groups in western New York must have done so. Elizur Wright compared the affair's effect with the abolition controversy, but the editor of the *Baptist Register* pointed out that the later issue "never attained an equal unanimity with it in numbers." In fact, "had not the people discovered that designing ones were improving it for sinister purposes of personal elevation, the conflict would have been maintained to the present day [1840]." [5]

If, as may be, political expediency demanded that the issue be artificially enlarged and sustained, its growth and its somewhat persistent influence on the rural mind of western New York could

---

[4] McCarthy, "Antimasonry," 544 ff.; Elizur Wright, Jr., *Myron Holley: and What He Did for Liberty and True Religion* (Boston, 1882), 190; *Orleans Advocate* (Albion), Feb. 27, 1828; Fox, *Decline of Aristocracy*, 339; Joel Parker, *The Signs of the Times*, etc. (Rochester, 1828).

[5] Charles G. Finney, *The Character, Claims and Practical Workings of Freemasonry* (Chicago, 1887), 18; Wright, *Holley*, 155; *Baptist Register* (Utica), XVII (March 20, 1840), 22.

hardly have been accomplished by artifice alone. Fundamentally, the crusade depended upon its religious and moral energies, and these would seem to be the more permanently significant aspects of Antimasonry.

Previous students have discovered data, largely from other areas, to suggest a theological divergence between the adherents and the resisters of Antimasonic agitation, submitting that a larger number of prominent Calvinists protested, while Arminian or Arminian-tending sects promoted, the crusade.[6] This generalization proves very difficult to document in the Burned-over District itself. Myron Holley accused the liberal group of Presbyterian revivalists of staging religious awakenings to distract attention from their Masonic status. Among the A.H.M.S. pastors who commented on the controversy (persons with the same Arminian tendencies), about as many were Masons as were not. At the other theological extreme, Universalists seem to have been quite solidly ranged in the opposition, along with political Democrats and Masons, while the Methodists appear to have been the least-disturbed denomination throughout the episode. Petitions from local conferences for a church disciplinary rule on Masonic affiliation entertained no hope of passage, while in several localities individuals excluded from Presbyterian congregations on this count joined the Methodists with impunity. Christian assemblies probably on the whole failed to garner support for strong Antimasonic resolutions, but Freewill Baptists, not far separated in theology, generally did so. The regular Baptists probably responded most zealously and solidly to the issue, but they included at least as many fairly strict Calvinists as the Presbyterians.[7]

The denominational principle of analysis, as distinguished from

[6] Particularly, David M. Ludlum, *Social Ferment in Vermont, 1791–1850* (New York, 1939), 96, 104, 105; also McCarthy, "Antimasonry," 537.

[7] Wright, *Holley*, 181–184; Reports from Milton Huxley, Isaac Eddy, John Baldwin, Silas Hubbard in 1828, Sylvester Eaton, Lot Sullivan, Chauncey Cook in 1829, Daniel Washburn, 1830, Samuel White, 1831, and Coanrod Ten Eick, 1832, American Home Missionary Society Papers, Chicago Theological Seminary; *Gospel Advocate* (Auburn), V (Feb. 24, 1827), 63; Rev. F. W. Conable, *History of the Genesee Annual Conference of the Methodist Episcopal Church*, etc. (New York, 1876), 302–311; "Minutes, Naples Presbyterian Church," MS at Ontario County Historical Society; John C. Morgan, Naples, to Miles P. Squier, March 29, 31, Aug. 14, 1828, Squier to Absolom Peters, Aug. 18, 1828, A.H.M.S. MSS.

the theological, seems more rewarding in this particular region. Even more important is the distinction to be observed between certain classes. Antimasonic excitement brought a changed relationship between clergymen and laymen and tended to differentiate rural and lower-middle-class folk from their would-be social superiors. All of these discriminations bore on the history of revivalism in the Burned-over District.

Although Charles Finney and many other Presbyterians, conservative and liberal alike, had been Masons, it seems likely that this denomination had the smallest proportional clerical membership in the fraternity when Morgan was kidnapped, while Baptists more certainly had the largest representation. Back in New England in the years between the American Revolution and the War of 1812, Masonry had been associated by the fathers of Congregational orthodoxy and Federalism with the secret, infidel orders of Revolutionary France: with deism, radicalism, and terrorism. A miniature crusade against secret societies had in fact occupied considerable attention during the 1790's. At that time the Baptists, who suffered certain handicaps under the system of church establishment in the parent section, had generally been allied, as had Masonry, with Jeffersonian political groups, and early Methodists, Christians, and other dissenters were similarly inclined.[8] The New York descendants of Yankee Congregationalism thus inherited a bias against Freemasonry not shared by their companion evangelical sects. In so far as the clergy of the other churches continued their affiliations, they were quite apt to become Democratic in politics and Masonic in social orientation. It may be for this reason that a preponderance of Baptist ministers seem to have joined the order, while many fewer Presbyterians did so.

With different proportions of membership in the fraternity, reactions to the crusade against it were bound to differ also. Baptists, one of whose vaunted distinctions in church organization was the closed Communion, felt particularly oppressed by the interposition of Masonic ties among their clergymen and leading laymen. Apparently a great majority of the ministers, compensating for

---

[8] William A. Robinson, *Jeffersonian Democracy in New England* (New Haven, Conn., 1916), 86–135, *passim;* Vernon Stauffer, *New England and the Bavarian Illuminati* (New York, 1918).

past sins, renounced and denounced the fraternity. The two leading tracts by seceders in this region came from the pens of Baptist
pastors. The state denominational journal, somewhat distant from
the storm center, tried to moderate passions and prevent persecution of those who would cease Masonic activities without castigat-
ing the order, but it apparently had little success in the infected
region. William Miller, still farther east of the disturbance, rejoiced when Antimasonry died in his locality.[9] For the most part,
however, the Baptists near enough to be concerned at all seem to
have become for the time totally preoccupied with the movement,
almost to the exclusion of other interests.

Not so the Presbyterians. Their clerical members in the fraternity being relatively few, with many churches heavily indebted to
the Home Missionary Society in New York, their cue seemed almost without exception to be to quiet the controversy, oust Masons
without ado if necessary, and keep at the revivals and benevolences
which would increase the stability of their church.[10] Most of the
denomination in the locality sympathized heartily with the Antimasonic movement, but chose to make it rather a means to develop
universal revivalism and reform than an end in itself. Antimasonry
thus became another gun in the benevolent system's artillery to
convert the world and introduce the millennium.

Since about a fourth of all the Protestant ministers had probably
been Masons, whereas not more than a twentieth of church laymen
had been invited to join,[11] the vast majority of members in all denominations had Antimasonic leanings. Thus it seems more than
probable that lay pressure drove the entire movement, forcing
those clergymen who came to lead it into their prominent roles.
The democracy of the church meeting, no doubt in all sects alike,
was revolting against one form of professional privilege. With the
bit in their teeth, laymen would henceforth do a good deal of the

---

[9] *Baptist Register*, I (June 11, 1824), 184, IV (March 16, 1827), 10, V (Jan. 16, 1829),
186, VI (Oct. 9, 30, 1829), 130, 142, VIII (March 11, 1831), 9, and *passim;* Elder David
Bernard, *Light on Masonry*, etc. (Utica, 1829), v–x; John G. Stearns, *An Inquiry
into . . . Speculative Free Masonry*, etc. (5th ed.; Utica, 1829), vi; William Miller,
Hampton, Nov. 17, 1832, to Truman Hendryx, William Miller Papers, Aurora College
Library.
[10] A.H.M.S. MSS, 1828–1830, *passim.*
[11] Stearns, *Free Masonry*, 103, 104.

driving in matters of church policy, particularly in the way of encouraging the kind of revivalism which, for common folk, made religion live.

Whenever splits occurred in the various church meetings they probably emphasized divisions between different social classes within the congregations. Amos Brown of Moscow reported in 1828 to the A.H.M.S. that most of the land about his village was owned by wealthy, irreligious [Masonic?] men, and that "A strong prejudice against the village, prevails generally with the people of the town." In Clarkson, the new Antimasonic preacher reported the same year on the divisions surviving the departure of his Masonic predecessor: all men of Masonic leanings were now retaliating by withholding church support for three years. "As they are not religious men, they care not whether religious society is supported." In Attica, "Some of the principle [sic] subscribers to the support of the Gospel are Masons, and some of the leading members of the church are Anti Masons. . . ." At Stafford, a Masonic clergyman had the same classification in different terms. "Nearly, if not all of . . . the influential part of the community have subscribed more than usual for another year, yet . . . a multitude . . . under the influence of the late Morgan excitement . . . are glad of a pretense in order to oppose the preaching of the Gospel." [12] People of reasonably substantial property interests—and perhaps by the same token of reasonably good judgment—thus seem to have been driven from sympathy with churchly concerns by the fanaticism of Antimasonry. Their less prosperous fellows moved into command of the meeting and would henceforth freely underwrite religion pleasing to their own tastes and of a sort which might increase membership quickly, to relieve their own increased financial burdens, without the balancing influence of more conservative minds.

Such a more vigorous revivalism could scarcely coincide exactly with the height of Antimasonic furor. On the contrary, dissensions in all the churches meant that for the moment the "moral mercury . . . steadily ran down until it reached its zero. . . ." The

---

[12] Amos Brown, Moscow, Jan. 31, 1828, to Miles P. Squier, Benjamin Lane, Clarkson, Nov. 17, 1828, to Absolom Peters, Ebenezer Mead, Attica, Oct. 23, 1828, and Milton Huxley, Stafford, April 15, 1828, to Squier, A.H.M.S. MSS.

storm indeed poured its "maddening torrent into the very bosom of Christian Churches . . . [creating] laceration, distraction and desolation" among them.[13] But two years after the peak of the excitement the lines drawn between social groups during the controversy had become established divisions. Among the reformers could come a renewed dedication, heightened by guilt-consciousness and a reawakened aspiration for public rectitude. Some new diversion was in fact required by whetted appetites. The churchly pressure which helped to close the lodges had in the crusade grown powerful; now it was left dominant to consolidate its victory. But other events occurring during the excitement contributed much to the religious situation of 1831.

---

13 "History of the Baptist Church in West Middlebury," *Minutes of the Genesee Baptist Association, 1866* (Buffalo, 1866), 10; *Baptist Register,* IV (Sept. 14, 1827), 113.

Chapter 7. YORKER BENEVOLENCE

ANOTHER flurry of excitement simultaneously reinforced the consequences of the Antimasonic upheaval. Four benevolent movements experienced such sudden growth in western New York during the twenties and generated such controversies that they seem collectively to merit consideration as a major portent of the era to come. These were not complete innovations but had long roots in the past. They were not unique in this locality, for they claimed national scope. Yet the campaigns to circulate Bibles, to found Sunday schools, to encourage temperance, and to enforce Sabbath observance all spurted so suddenly here and so intensified and broadened their appeals in this region that they became in their proportions veritable peculiarities of this time and place in American history.

The first episode of the decade to concern the circulation of religious literature involved tracts instead of Bibles. When the state tract society organized in 1824, it prevailed upon J. V. N. Yates, then Secretary of State, to request systematic use of its publications in the common schools. Upon the petition of the inhabitants of Lebanon, Madison County, however, a legislative committee investigated the matter and early the next year announced that the Secretary-Superintendent had no authority to make such a pronouncement. While the original order stood, Presbyterians were charged with exerting local pressure for use of the tracts, and upon its cancellation they may have tried in some areas to prevent publication of the decision. Though this kind of issue failed to rise again and controversy soon centered rather about Bible distribution, the aggressive work of the Presbyterian-dominated tract society continued to antagonize some groups. By 1833 the Geneva agent managed to cover over two hundred towns monthly, reaching a half million people with four million pages in two years. Opponents taunted the Presbyterian churches for their Sabbath tract sales, charging that funds gathered at large were diverted to sectarian purposes. One A.H.M.S. pastor thought that "none of our benevolent operations have excited the rage of the wicked so much as this." Nevertheless, Baptists supported the enterprise, at least in its earlier years.[1]

So also did Baptists and other sects support the Bible societies. After all, the Bible contained material acceptable to all evangelical denominations. Monroe County, led by the Rochester churches, set off the intensive campaign in this direction. A census in 1824 having shown that twelve hundred families lacked copies of the Scriptures, during the next year the local group supplied that entire number. This episode seems to have received national publicity and to have been emulated far afield. At least, it was followed before 1830 by practically every county or town group in western New York.[2]

Despite the shock suffered by the religious-minded from the supposed large number of people without the Word, and all the excellent publicity brought to benevolent operations, more sober analysis suggests little basis either for the strenuous efforts or for the resulting great satisfaction of the campaign. The societies' own figures indicated that only a seventh to a tenth of all families lacked Bibles. Close checking in two spots further shows that the censuses were "pious frauds." One village with forty-three families in all, only six of them without Bibles, had been reported to need forty-

[1] *Gospel Advocate and Impartial Investigator* (Buffalo), II (Aug. 20, 1824), 253, III (March 18, June 3, July 1, 1825), 77, 168, 197; *Paul Pry* (Rochester), April 14, 1828; *American Revivalist and Rochester Observer*, III (Jan. 5, 1833), 1; Edwin Barnes, Boonville, Aug. 13, 1830, to Secretary Cushman, American Home Missionary Society Papers, Chicago Theological Seminary; *Baptist Register* (Utica), I (Aug. 20, 1824), 211.

[2] Blake McKelvey, *Rochester: The Water-Power City, 1812–1854* (Cambridge, Mass., 1945), 129; *Rochester Observer*, April 28, 1827; *Western Recorder* (Utica), X (July 2, 1833), 105; *Baptist Register*, I (Oct. 5, 1824), 275.

six. A county called on to furnish twelve hundred copies had no more than twenty-five literate families who needed them.[3] The sensational pleas for funds and the attention shed upon all the associated enterprises by such a campaign naturally antagonized skeptical-minded folk who could appreciate its distortions.

Sunday schools seemed at least on first sight as unexceptionable as Bible circulation, and Baptists as well as other church groups flocked to support the Presbyterian leadership which commenced to campaign for them about 1825. The Sunday school in the modern American style had its beginning in Connecticut around 1816, and a few specimens had appeared in western New York within two years. The early movement in Connecticut had been invoked in part to compensate for laws which secularized the common schools; and the more intensive drive of the mid-twenties in western New York seems not unrelated to the adverse decision on tract circulation for public education. The same years brought at least one protest against the use of state funds to aid denominational seminaries and colleges.[4]

By 1827 the Monroe Sunday School Union reported twelve units, all in Rochester: five of them Presbyterian with a thousand students, two Methodist with over a hundred, and five Baptist with just over five hundred. Nearly two thousand people attended the anniversary celebration two years later. In the state at large the campaign went almost equally well: by 1829 New York had twenty-five hundred schools and nearly seventy-six thousand pupils, more than all New England, and probably also more than the balance of the country to the west and south. By the same year the Sunday School Union had circulated over five million copies of various books through the medium of its member schools.[5]

It may well have been the defaulting of other sects rather than Presbyterian intention which made this an almost exclusively sectarian venture outside the larger towns. Between the efforts of Auburn Seminary, the Education Society, the Home Missionary

---

[3] *Gospel Advocate*, V (Sept. 8, 1827), 283 ff.; *Olive Branch and Christian Inquirer* (New York), I (June 7, 1828), 63.

[4] *Gospel Luminary* (West Bloomfield), II (Sept., 1826), 197 ff.

[5] *Rochester Observer*, Oct. 13, 1827, Oct. 9, 1829; *Quarterly Register and Journal of the American Educational Society* (Andover, Mass.), II (Aug., 1829), 34.

Society, and Oneida Institute, this one denomination had a greater supply of men in the area to become school agents and teachers, and its stationed clergy by virtue of superior education were the logical persons to run any such undertaking. Also, of course, the denomination held a dominant position in the Sunday School Union management. For all these reasons, the schools in rural sections invariably became Presbyterian, though they scrupulously received all comers. That the energy of the agents merited their high success is unquestionable. Gerrit Smith turned to a career of reform after his zealous year as president of the Western Sunday School Union. Ashbell Wells of Auburn Seminary founded fourteen new schools in six weeks in 1827. The next year, Auburn students helped the Genesee, Utica, Central, and Western Unions cover twenty-six counties, visiting every Presbyterian church and going from house to house to root out every available child in the parishes.[6]

That the agents preserved an appropriately nonsectarian attitude suited to the supposed purposes of the society is by no means so clear. Johnson Baldwin reported to the A.H.M.S. from York that he had a hundred and fifty in Sunday school, half from other churches, but he had just been forced to expel several adults in his congregation for attending Universalist meeting. Lyman Barrett wrote from Howard that "to these schools there has been a decided + persevering opposition from that class of people who say that this institution is founded exclusively on sectarian motives. . . ." Conversions from the schools to Presbyterian membership gave occasion for boastful remarks. A bitter opposition journal quoted the remark of a Methodist paper on the subject. "Whatever may be said . . . to relieve these *national institutions* from suspicion . . . they are *sectarian*. One denomination . . . has a preponderating influence . . . and just enough from other denominations are introduced . . . to save appearances . . . and to give a tone to the sound of catholicism."[7] In no matter how in-

---

[6] Ralph V. Harlow, *Gerrit Smith, Philanthropist and Reformer* (New York, 1929), 50–56; A. S. Wells, Auburn Theological Seminary, Oct. 17, 1827, to Smith, Gerrit Smith Papers, Syracuse University Library; Dexter Witler, April 9, 1828, and T. Stillman, April 1, 1829, Auburn, to Andover Society of Inquiry, Correspondence of Society of Inquiry at Andover, Newton Theological Seminary.

[7] Johnson Baldwin, York, July 22, 1828, and Lyman Barrett, Howard, Dec. 20,

nocent a fashion, the Sunday-school enterprise, like most of its fellows, served to antagonize many able and intelligent people.

In much the same manner as the Bible- and Sabbath-school operations, the early campaigns for temperance gained nearly universal support among church folk but fell under substantially sectarian management. The Baptists' journal in the state demanded a society exclusively for this purpose at a time when the Presbyterian sheet was still running liquor advertisements.[8] Several home missionaries testified to the co-operation of Methodists, Baptists, and others in the undertaking. Indeed, the temperance movement in the Burned-over District had a broader appeal than any of the other peculiar concerns of the religious minority.

Interest in the subject began here in emulation of the New England societies formed, largely upon Lyman Beecher's initiative, after the War of 1812. The movement gathered force gradually in the first half of the decade, developing organized form during the second half. A temperance lecturer reached Prattsburg in 1826. The next year saw societies formed at least in Warsaw, Perry, and Arcade. Meantime, the Ontario, Ogdensburg, Otsego, Watertown, and Cortland presbyteries adopted abstinence resolutions. At least seventy-eight groups in New York, probably the larger number in the Yankee-oriented western portion, preceded formation of the state society in 1830. Meetings, tracts, journals, and lecturers gradually increased, and in particularly favorable localities experiments took place with dry ordinances, restricted licensing, and temperance boats and hotels.[9] Although the pledges taken in this period received the appellation of "total abstinence," they usually meant the rejection merely of distilled liquors, except for medicinal purposes. Even hard cider was often excluded from the pledge. Aggressive the movement was from the start, but only occasional hints

---

1828, to Miles P. Squier, A.H.M.S. MSS; *Gospel Advocate,* VII (Oct. 3, 1829), 313; *Priestcraft Exposed and Primitive Christianity Defended* (Lockport), I (May, June, 1828), 10, 22.

[8] *Baptist Register,* I (June 11, 1824), 132; *Western Recorder,* II (March 22, 1825), 47.

[9] John A. Krout, *The Origins of Prohibition* (New York, 1925), 84–104, and "The Genesis and Development of the Early Temperance Movement in New York State," *New York State Historical Association Quarterly Journal,* IV (April, 1923), 87; Harlow, *Smith,* 74–80; McKelvey, *Rochester,* 133, 172, 179, 191, 192.

appear before 1831 to indicate the more radical kind of teetotalism which was to follow.

Had not the Presbyterian Church been simultaneously involved in Antimasonry, Bible and tract circulation, Sunday schools, and Sabbath-observance campaigns, it might have escaped criticism for its leading role in the early temperance movement, since its clergymen, however much they led the crusade, did not at this time carry it beyond moderate limits. But in the circumstances it was perhaps inevitable that opponents should react against a supposed oppression and intolerance from that denomination.

When in 1829, at the suggestion of several Presbyterian synods, the state legislature adjourned three days to honor a temperance fast, the Universalist *Gospel Advocate* seized upon the episode as a dangerous precedent, suggesting that such time might better be spent cultivating vineyards, so that "the plenty and cheapness of wine [might] force out of use all distilled spirits." [10] Home missionaries found their work impeded by resentment. One reported that "many who feel themselves secure in what they term a moderate or temperate use of the poisonous liquid, encourage . . . iniquity. . . ." More common was this complaint: "In short those who are not for us are against us. . . . And among us as in other places, we now hear the cry of Priestcraft! Church and State! + c." At Naples a crowd of prosperous nonprofessors "who would be thought temperate drinkers," moved to set up an Episcopal church. At a denominational temperance meeting in Orleans County "there came a sleigh load of men . . . [who] took a bottle from their pockits [*sic*] and went to drinking + c." Others tried "to force spirits down one of the members." The preacher at West Dresden made no "public effort in the cause of temperance, because . . . this cause is intimately connected with party politicks. One year ago, church and state resounded daily thro' our streets. But now . . . has nearly subsided. . . ." [11] Thus the temperance movement must take its place among the incitements to controversy.

Of all the benevolent movements, however, the crusade to en-

---

[10] *Gospel Advocate*, VII (Feb. 7, 1829), 42.

[11] Tenas Riggs, Danby, Aug. 11, 1828, Church Elders, Mendon, May 4, 1829, John C. Morgan, Naples, Sept. 14, 1830, Ebenezer Raymond, Murray, Jan. 27, 1831, and William Todd, West Dresden, March 1, 1831, to Miles P. Squier, A.H.M.S. MSS.

force Sabbath observance probably roused the greatest furor. Blue laws had of course been long established in New England, and petitions to the United States Congress to enforce similar regulations upon the nation had had spasmodic expression ever since Thomas Jefferson's election in 1800 frightened the religious community. But interest in the question had for the time subsided when completion of the Erie Canal thrust it anew upon western New York, which region attempted promptly and aggressively to thrust it once more upon the nation. Construction crews and boatmen followed different mores from those of the Yankee Yorkers, and as the waterway reached across the state place after place took alarm at miscellaneous immoralities in general, and at desecration of the Sabbath in particular. Palmyra, for instance, formed a society for the suppression of vice in 1823. Both the *Baptist Register* and the Presbyterian *Western Recorder* at Utica commented extensively on the problem at the time of the great canal celebration in 1825. The latter paper in the same year made what seem to be the initial suggestions both for a national order to promote sanctification of the Sabbath and for a concerted effort by all Christians to put only pious men in office, in order to reassert the clerical influence in politics which had declined since the French Revolution.[12] These two apparently separate propositions were to remain juxtaposed throughout the next five years, in the minds of advocates and opponents alike.

Little action developed for the moment, but two years later the Hudson and Erie six-day boat line began operating on the canal to interrupt the "constant stream of demoralization, which is perpetually deepening and widening its current."[13] Early in 1828, mass meetings in both Rochester and Utica organized movements to boycott boats and stages operated on Sunday. The opposition also rallied en masse, but the *Rochester Observer* only remarked calmly: "We have before mentioned that the ground which had been taken . . . would make the distinction more apparent between

---

[12] *Western Farmer* (Palmyra), Feb. 27, 1822; *Palmyra Herald*, Jan. 15, 1823; *Baptist Register*, II (Nov. 18, 1825), 150; *Western Recorder*, II (July 19, Nov. 29, 1825), 115, 192, III (Nov. 14, 1826), 182.

[13] *Western Recorder*, IV (Oct. 9, 1827), 162; *Rochester Observer*, I (March 17, 1827), 23.

those who serve God, and those who serve him not [;] . . . it will be seen that our prediction was correct." [14] Excitement grew when Utica and Rochester presbyter-capitalists started the Pioneer Line stages on the six-day principle during the summer. Immediately the Universalists laid down the gauge of battle with the Presbyterians:

There remains no doubt . . . that the "new line of stages" is *one* of the measures . . . designed as another step in the ladder of their preferment . . . a measure designed to limit our freedom and destroy the rights of the people.

Herman Norton wrote Finney: "From Albany to Buffalo the conversation of men, women and children is about the pioneer and the old line—opposition—tremendous and growing worse." [15]

Both enterprises grew in the main from the efforts of Josiah Bissell, Jr., of Rochester. Spark of the Monroe County Tract and Bible Societies and "chief pillar" of the Third Presbyterian Church, Bissell was also one of the wealthier real estate promoters of the Genesee town, the instigator of Finney's visit there in 1831, and a zealous Antimason. Opponents and even one Antimasonic colleague considered him a "make-or-break merchant, miller and land speculator" who "has not to this day been *accused* of engaging in *any cause* however specious, unless it had an intimate and close connection with his purse." Admirers thought "all western New York . . . indebted for an example of Christian zeal and energy" and that "society in Rochester would never outlive his influence." Speculator though he was, Bissell apparently invested according to religious rather than financial principles and relied on the Lord (in vain) to "sustain us in all these branches of His Cause . . . so mote it be." [16]

While direct action proceeded upstate, Bissell and his cohorts attended the May anniversaries of the benevolent societies in New

[14] *Rochester Observer,* II (Feb. 1, 8, 1828), 19, 22, 23; *Gospel Advocate,* VI (March 15, 1828), 95.

[15] *Gospel Advocate,* VI (July 5, 1828), 223; H. Norton, Utica, Sept. 3, 1828, to Finney, Charles Grandison Finney Papers, Oberlin College Library.

[16] McKelvey, *Rochester,* 188; Thurlow Weed, *Autobiography of Thurlow Weed* (Harriet A. Weed, ed., Boston, 1883), 99; *Priestcraft Exposed,* I (May, 1828), 3; Mary B. A. King, *Looking Backward* (New York, 1870), 117; Bissell to G. Smith, Oct., 1827, quoted by Harlow, *Smith,* 59.

York, and there led in the formation of the "General Union for promoting the observance of the Christian Sabbath in the United States." On an ostensibly national scale, church folk were henceforward to boycott Sunday conveyances. By sustaining "knowledge and virtue" and by the restraint of moral power, they should keep the United States from being "carried by the tide of a corrupting abundance to dissoluteness, effeminacy, and ruin." [17]

When the Pioneer Line failed to make profits, Bissell applied for the mail contract, and opponents warned him to "Remember the fate of that TRACT man, J. V. N. Yates." Early in 1829, with his bid refused and the Pioneer Line hotel in Buffalo up for sale, Bissell gave up economic coercion and entered the growing campaign to petition Congress for the closing of Sunday mails. Excitement rose through the early months of the year, until Col. Johnson's Senate report on the Sabbath mail petitions ended all hope of national action for the predictable future, and the flurry accordingly subsided. Nevertheless, the various Sabbatarian activities in the Burned-over District seem to have had considerable local effect. By 1831 Sunday observance had improved in marked fashion, and at least a substantial portion of church folk probably agreed as never before that "The Sabbath is the basis even of our *civil* privileges. Let it once be abolished from the land, and the nation is prostrated." [18]

The Sabbath mail argument above all others precipitated anxiety over the larger issue of sectarianism. As Orestes Brownson put it, stopping Sunday mails "is but a trifle. It is only designed by those who love our souls, but our *cash* more, to accustom our legislative councils to priestly influence and clerical dictation." [19] Ezra Stiles Ely, of Philadelphia, had turned the *Western Recorder's* suggestion into a national cause in a Fourth of July oration in 1827. Proposing "*A Christian party in politics*" which "all good men in our country should join," he declared, "The Presbyterians alone could bring *half a million of electors* into the field, in opposition to any

---

[17] *The Address of the General Union for . . . the Christian Sabbath*, etc. (New York, 1828), 9.

[18] *Priestcraft Exposed*, I (Dec., 1828, Feb., March, 1829), 121, 153, 169; *Rochester Observer*, June 19, 1829; *Western Recorder*, VII (Jan. 5, 1830), 3.

[19] *Gospel Advocate*, VII (Jan. 24, 1829), 31.

known advocate of Deism, Socinianism, or any species of avowed hostility to the truth of Christianity." Universalists pointed out that already "some of our courts have rejected important witnesses . . . because they either disbelieved the eternity of hell-torments, or the omnisciency of the Devil." [20]

Although Ely's proposals were promptly shouted down, certain moves seem to have been made in and about upstate New York toward the beginning of a consolidation of interests. He and Absolom Peters of the A.H.M.S. corresponded during 1829 in the hope of uniting the Presbyterian board of missions with the larger body. This move might well have succeeded had it not been for Presbyterian suspicion of the growing radicalism in upstate New York, and a desire to re-establish influence there, rather than to co-operate with the New York organization. Paradoxically, the local part of the conflict bore on the question of itineracy as a mission method, with the more conservative church body championing this device tending to radicalism, and the more progressive one holding to the fixed pastorate. With its hook baited with an itinerant system, the Presbyterian board won away several presbyteries north of Utica, and nothing further came of the proposals for unification.[21]

The agitations created by these various benevolent movements gained heat from their coincidence with the Antimasonic excitement. They also reinforced the same tendencies in religion which grew out of that greater controversy. Both denominational and interdenominational lines of conflict stiffened, perhaps even more in this case than in the other. The A.H.M.S. group of revivalist Presbyterians stood foremost in all the activist benevolences, and high in the lists of furious Antimasons. In equally consistent opposition stood Universalists, skeptics, Unitarians, Friends, Campbellites, many Christians, and most Episcopalians. Baptists, Freewill Baptists, and many Christians were violent Antimasons,

---

[20] Ezra S. Ely, *The Duty of Christian Freemen to Elect Christian Rulers*, etc. (Philadelphia, 1828), 8, 11, *passim;* see Arthur M. Schlesinger, Jr., *The Age of Jackson* (Boston, 1945), 137 ff.; *Gospel Advocate,* VII (June 27, 1829), 208.

[21] James Richards, Auburn, Aug. 9, 1826, John Frost, Utica, March 8, 1826, E. S. Ely, Philadelphia, Jan. 6, Feb. 12, 1829, Henry Dwight, Geneva, Feb. 24, 1829, Henry Davis, Hamilton College, March 2, 1829, S. C. Aikin, Utica, April 6, May 21, 1829, D. C. Lansing, Utica, Sept. 21, 1829, and J. R. Boyd, Sackets Harbor, Nov. 18, 1829, to Absolom Peters, A.H.M.S. MSS.

and at least on occasion aggressive reformers. Though they would resist obviously sectarian moves, their basic sympathies rested with the Presbyterian revivalists. Some minority of Baptists, however, and also of Presbyterians, drifted into the opposition as temperatures rose. Both sides recognized the increasing rigidity of their classifications. Both felt that anyone not fully with them must be against them, and indulged in persecution complexes. Methodists apparently avoided strict alignment by means of vigorous episcopal rule, but later schisms would demonstrate that the same yeast rose among them as among the other sects: that the majority of Burned-over District laymen and some proportion of ministers would go along with radical religion.

In all the benevolent agitations, again as in Antimasonry, laymen played leading roles. The more dignified clergymen, at least, either stepped aside, turned conservative, or reluctantly let themselves be pushed to the fore in hope of keeping a degree of control. They learned perforce to meet the tastes of laymen in their preaching, if they wished to hold their pulpits. Perhaps the class alignment induced by Antimasonry was also abetted by its fellow excitements. The temperance crusade, for one, was reported to alienate generally "some of the oldest—wealthiest + most influential members of the church."

Possibly this kind of reaction occurred only in the country, however. City manufacturers and merchants were apt to discover in the temperance, Sunday school, and other movements dedicated to eradicating personal sins a very satisfactory hypothesis for renovating society without the necessity of foregoing profits in favor of better wages. The *Rochester Observer,* mouthpiece of Bissell and much of the Genesee Valley entrepreneurial community, thought the competition of Auburn Prison labor against mechanics' wages could best be handled by abolishing the prison. "Let all unite in promoting Sabbath Schools and Temperance Societies and in less than twenty years the thing is done." [22]

Like Antimasonry again, the benevolent movement controversies discouraged revivalism for the moment:

---

[22] Amos Brown, Moscow, Jan. 30, 1829, to Miles P. Squier, G. W. Elliot, Lenox, July 20, 1830, to Secretary Cushman, A.H.M.S. MSS; *Rochester Observer,* July 3, 1829.

the excitements . . . have been connected with unhappy divisions in the churches, and have thus led . . . to a decline of vital religion. . . . It requires comparatively little self-denial, to float onward with . . . public opinion. . . . When shall the burning zeal, the vigorous activities of the Church be visibly accompanied with the gentle virtues and the winning graces of the Spirit? [23]

But the aftereffect would be the opposite. Sunday-school pupils, temperance advocates, and Antimasons all had a training in religious enthusiasm which would make them easy targets in the next revival. Furthermore, much of the restraining opinion within the sects most addicted to sensational evangelism had been removed or silenced, and the now predominant groups were actively concerned to convert the world in a hurry. Indeed, as Orestes Brownson said, the benevolent movements had developed to evangelize the world. "But there is not the less danger . . . from the mistakes of conscience than from the violence of depravity." [24]

---

[23] *Western Recorder*, VII (Jan. 5, 1830), 3.
[24] *Gospel Advocate*, VII (May 2, 1829), 140.

Chapter 8. THE PROPHET

THE Mormon Church, having survived and grown in the last hundred years as did none of its companion novelties, interests the present generation far more than any other aspect of Burned-over District history. Yet its impact upon the region and period from which it sprang was extremely limited. The Saints made their first westward removal immediately upon founding the religion, when they numbered not more than a hundred persons. The obscurity and scarcity of local material on the subject reinforces the logical conclusion that few western New Yorkers could have been seriously aware of the episode. In this respect it contrasts strongly with the other omens of the day. In another way, however, Mormonism comes closer to being the true oracle than other developments in the inaugural years just before 1831. It was the first original product of the common circumstances which would breed a train of successors within the quarter century. It predicted what was to come, whereas the larger simultaneous excitements merely heated the cauldron from which future experiments would boil.

The Smith family arrived in western New York in 1816 when Joseph was ten years old. Fate had been rough on them in Vermont, where each of several different ventures and consequent removes left them poorer than the one before. The war years had been hard enough in the home state, but peace canceled the business of supplying the armed forces, or indulging in trade with the enemy across the border, which had helped sustain the local economy. The postwar slump which gradually spread over the nation was punctuated in the north country by the frigid summer of 1816. Vermont farmers started west in droves. The Smith family poverty doubtless reached the extreme among the emigrants, since for several generations both the Smith and Mack lines had been running to the visionary rather than to the acquisitive Yankee type.[1] Even so, the Smiths could in no way be considered uncommon in the westering horde. Like the bulk of their fellows, they sought a new start in the acres of New York just about to be enriched by the projected Erie Canal. Unwisely perhaps, again like many others, they shunned the rugged pioneering life demanded by the more primitive regions in Ohio or west of the Genesee in New York, in favor of a community of some age, respectability, and commercial prospects, where they would have a greater struggle to pay for their land.

Northward from Canandaigua, the rolling hills of the Finger Lakes section gradually descend to meet the drumlin-studded Ontario plain. Twelve miles takes one across the line between Ontario and Wayne counties to Palmyra, situated on the lower level among the glacial hills. Halfway between the two towns, nearly in the dead center of the richest soil area in western New York, lies the village of Manchester. All three villages and their immediate vicinities had been early settled and by 1820 had attained populations approximating sixty persons per square mile. From Palmyra north to the lake, habitations appeared less frequently, while a journey of thirty miles west or south would reach towns where little land had been cleared more than ten years.[2]

Canandaigua, the oldest town of the three and in fact one of the two oldest in western New York, had until the twenties enjoyed a dominant position in the region's economy. Here the stage route to Albany crossed the main route to the south, which from the days of the Iroquois had connected Irondequoit Bay, Canandaigua Lake, and the southward-facing valleys of the upper Susquehanna. Up to 1824 Rochester millers had to use pony express to reach the banks at this center. As a seat of culture, the Finger Lakes village retained its leadership even later. For years the country seat of great

---

1 Fawn M. Brodie, *No Man Knows My History: The Life of Joseph Smith, the Mormon Prophet* (New York, 1945), 1–5, 7–9.
2 See maps I and II.

landlords and their agents, it was for this section a sophisticated, aristocratic community with a strong Episcopal church. Even Presbyterians there maintained a conservative tone throughout the period. Its newspapers and schools had attained establishment and reputation. But with the approach of the canal the economic orientation of the three villages rapidly changed.

Palmyra for a time became the chief local mart. Limited use of the waterway began in 1822, and the same summer brought daily stage·and mail service connecting several canal towns with each other and with Canandaigua. By the following autumn the canal had opened to Rochester.[3] Palmyra and Manchester, unlike their southern neighbor, very nearly typified the region. Their folk came chiefly from Connecticut and Vermont. Younger and less culturally sophisticated, they had nevertheless enjoyed the services of evangelistic churches from their earliest days, as well as the schools and journals which always followed in rapid succession. Palmyra particularly would have a considerable bonanza in the early twenties and evince the social restlessness accompanying such rapid expansion. But before the end of that decade the village was destined to come quite suddenly to stability, with even a touch of the doldrums, after the canal had reached Buffalo and Rochester had seized local commercial leadership.[4]

Thus the Smiths came to no frontier or cultural backwash. Though the society they entered was more youthful, it was less isolated and provincial, more vigorous and cosmopolitan, than Vermont. It was reaching economic stability but remained on the upgrade, whereas rural Vermont had already started into decline.

Nor yet in religion was the younger area less experienced than the homeland. The Great Revival had come here at the turn of the century, just as to western New England. Seven of twelve primary centers of enthusiasm ranged from Palmyra southward. The crest of fervor following the War of 1812 noticeably affected towns sprinkled about the same neighborhood, and the pattern repeated, though less intensively, during the early twenties. So the area had been thoroughly indoctrinated in revivalistic religion

---

[3] *Palmyra Herald and Canal Advertiser,* July 17, 1822; *Western Farmer* (Palmyra), Summer, 1822, *passim; Wayne Sentinel* (Palmyra), Oct., Nov., 1823.

[4] Brodie, *No Man Knows,* 9–11.

throughout thirty years of its youth.[5] And Palmyra at least was old enough by the mid-twenties to exhibit the increased interest in community morals and spirituality which characteristically grew upon villages and countrysides of Yankee stamp as the problems of maturity replaced the struggle to live.[6]

In this richer clime the Smiths and their fellow Vermonters fared better than before. A shop in Palmyra and the labor at hire of father and sons swelled the family funds in two years sufficiently to permit initial payment on a hundred-acre farm practically astride the Palmyra-Manchester town line. It must have been a relatively inferior piece of land, else it would long since have been cleared. It seems to have been contracted for at the height of a speculative boomlet which a decade's time would demonstrate to have been based on false expectations. Evidence exists, in any case, to show that the family exerted considerable diligence and enterprise in hope of completing payment. Nevertheless, the farm had been foreclosed by 1830.[7]

Many companion emigrants, managing more wisely, made good in the Genesee country, some having brought with them at least enough money for the first deposit on a farm. A sizable minority found land values here inflated beyond their earning ability and were making for Michigan or Illinois about the time the Smiths were losing out. In April, 1829, a Manchester clergyman noted: "Many families are floating about . . . because in two or three months they expect to remove." [8] Every circumstance seems to invalidate the obviously prejudiced testimonials of unsympathetic neighbors (collected by one hostile individual whose style of composition stereotypes the language of numerous witnesses) that the

[5] Rev. James H. Hotchkin, *A History of the Purchase and Settlement of Western New York, and of the . . . Presbyterian Church in That Section* (New York, 1848), contains outline histories of each church in the denomination west of Madison County. Tabulated geographically, it provides a reliable guide to revival cycles and locations.

[6] *Western Farmer*, Feb. 27, 1822; *Palmyra Herald*, Jan. 15, 1823.

[7] John H. Evans, *Joseph Smith, An American Prophet* (New York, 1945), 30–32; Brodie, *No Man Knows*, 10, 11, 55. Land values ran from twenty to thirty-five dollars an acre by 1833, *Rochester Daily Advertiser*, May 15, 1833.

[8] Peter Kimball, Manchester, Oct. 5, 1829, to Absolom Peters, American Home Missionary Society Papers, Chicago Theological Seminary.

Smiths were either squatters or shiftless "frontier drifters." [9] Many an honest and industrious farmer followed their identical experience, pursued by bad luck or poor judgment, and sought a new fling at fortune farther west. No doubt the Smiths, like many of their fellows, wasted valuable time hunting gold at the proper turn of the moon. One of the potent sources of Joseph's local ill repute may well have been the jealousy of other persons who failed to discover golden plates in the glacial sands of the drumlins. [10]

The entire family was at least barely literate. Hyrum had attended a Vermont seminary, and Joseph had some part of a few years' schooling in Palmyra, possibly increased by brief attendance at Bainbridge in 1826. He had belonged to the young men's debating society in Palmyra. Though he read easily, his writing was at best halting and he attained only the rudiments of arithmetic. Probably the family budget had required his labor a good deal of the time when he might have been in school. [11] But this was rather the average than an unusual experience among the poorer Yankee migrants to western New York. Despite testimonials to the contrary, it must be concluded that neither Joseph nor any of his family was especially ignorant according to the standards of the place and time. Interest in things marvelous and supernatural they certainly had abundantly, but even this made them differ only in degree from their neighbors. After all, Joseph's peeping stone attracted loyal followers. The rest of the family, though perhaps not the prophet himself, behaved like others in attending services in revival seasons. Perhaps, as not infrequently happened, they shifted sectarian affiliation considerably as different denominations happened to lead the awakenings from time to time. Joseph, Senior, was by profession Methodist; and Lucy, the mother, and Hyrum, the elder brother, had most recently been Presbyterian when Joseph's thoughts began to turn toward religion. [12]

---

[9] Brodie, No Man Knows, accepts and prints these testimonials. See pp. 405–418.

[10] Western Farmer, Dec. 12, 1821; Vardis Fisher, Children of God: An American Epic (New York, 1939), 29, suggests this cause of antagonism.

[11] O. Turner, History of the Pioneer Settlement of Phelps and Gorham's Purchase, etc. (Rochester, 1852), cited in Evans, Smith, 32; Orson Pratt, Remarkable Visions, quoted by [Henry Mayhew], History of the Mormons, etc. (Auburn, 1853), 19 ff.; Palmyra Herald, Oct. 2, 1822; and Western Farmer, July 11, 18, 25, 1821.

[12] [Mayhew], Mormons, 36.

The whole Smith family seems to have been quite thoroughly typical of the westering Yankees in the Burned-over District. It seems entirely plausible, as his most recent biographer claims, that Joseph became a prophet in quite accidental fashion. Having risen above his own early experiments in necromancy, his imagination wandered into new realms. When he found others taking his new hobby seriously, he had to live up to expectations and spend the remainder of his short life learning to assume the consequent responsibilities. In so doing he improved and demonstrated his naturally dynamic character.[13] This was nothing more than happens to any man who enjoys the great responsibilities which fate thrusts upon him, though religious leadership demands somewhat rare personal qualities. It might have happened to almost anyone of Joseph's fellow Yankee migrants. The fundamental condition leading to the new faith was the credulity and spiritual yearning which made people anxious to follow a prophet, whoever he might be. In order to explain why Joseph developed into this role one must either utilize faith, traffic in a psychoanalysis which at such a distance from the event becomes highly imaginative, or descend to coincidence. Historical analysis profits little by any of these alternatives.

It should be added, however, that interest in Mormonism was no necessary indication either of extraordinary ignorance or of unusually febrile imaginings. Converts like Brigham Young, Heber Kimball, J. J. Strang, William Phelps, Sidney Rigdon, Orson Pratt, and Lorenzo Snow, to name only a few, had on the whole superior education for their times, and most of them proved to be as vigorously realistic pillars of the church as anyone might desire. The man who exercised primacy over these individuals approached some kind of genius, however it may have been inspired.

What was it, then, about Joseph Smith which satisfied the spiritual needs of his converts? Clearly it was no case of deliberate imposture, no consciously calculated set of devices to attain power over others. Joseph may have gathered some inklings from an imperfect knowledge of the Shakers or of the New Jerusalem on Keuka Lake, just as he did from Owenite communism by way of

---

[13] Brodie, *No Man Knows, passim.* Whitney R. Cross, "Mormonism in the 'Burned-over District,' " *New York History*, XXV (July, 1944), 326–338.

Sidney Rigdon at Kirtland, Ohio, but he did not premeditate a system for self-advancement patterned upon the observed success of Jemima Wilkinson or anyone else. This kind of hypothesis, like the one which claims that the *Book of Mormon* was copied from Solomon Spaulding's novel on the early Indian wars, is too transparently simple to explain the broad appeal of the new church. Such myths not only distort Joseph's character but also breed serious misconceptions of how any religious novelty is likely to arise. All the spiritual experiments of western New York were alike genuine growths, rooted in a heritage of moral intensity and blossoming in the heat of evangelistic fervor.

The question is better put this way. How did the Church of Latter-day Saints select and emphasize from its Burned-over District milieu those principles of religion and society which would patently attract persons bred in the same environment? First of all, it crystallized and provided an apparently authoritative formulation for what had perhaps been from the beginning the most prominent legend in the region's folklore. The story of a gigantic battle on the hill Cumorah, in which the superior pre-Indian civilization was exterminated, seems today both fantastic and remote from the realm of religion. It was not fantastic to a generation bred in the belief of such a civilization's existence; and neither American society generally nor that of western New York in particular had passed the stage wherein common myth might reinforce Biblical sanction of doctrine.[14]

The *Book of Mormon* also incorporated contemporary interests of the locality, supplementing the sense of familiarity to be gained from its historical approach. Walter F. Prince proved beyond dispute thirty years ago, by a rigorous examination of the proper names and other language in the volume, that even if no other evidence existed, it could have been composed only in western New York between 1826 and 1834, so markedly did it reflect Antimasonry and other issues of the day. Unfortunately, his work has been so neglected that the most recent historian of the movement had to demonstrate the proposition all over again, independently.[15]

---

[14] Brodie, *No Man Knows*, 34–49.

[15] Walter F. Prince, "Psychological Tests for the Authorship of the Book of

The prophet, moreover, for all his imagination, was, like the Yankees he led, in many respects an eminently practical man. He combined appeals to reason and self-interest with emotional attractions. The logic of his mythology and theology, specious though it seem to the Gentile of today, satisfied the inbred desire of Yorkers to achieve an orderly, intellectual formulation of their beliefs. Again, he expected all laymen to participate in the priesthood of the church. This democratic and flattering conception paralleled chronologically the developing controversies over clerical influence in most of the sects of western New York; and its reasonableness, like the Mormon approach to doctrine by argument rather than excitement, contrasted pleasantly with the flamboyant oratory of orthodoxy's revivals. And whereas the evangelists emphasized salvation from personal sins in preparation for the life to come, Joseph's ideas about earthly and heavenly society alike judged happiness more largely in terms of physical comfort and earthly abundance.[16] His degree of communism resurrected the strong sense of social obligation that all should have for each and each for all, which had been long declining in the Puritan tradition of old New England. Born Yankees troubled by the problems of security in a more individualistic society found this doctrine pleasing.

In theology, again, this practical emphasis appeared. Alexander Campbell very quickly discerned how accurately the *Book of Mormon* reflected "every error and almost every truth discussed in N. York for the last ten years." It presented a definitive answer indeed to every issue of orthodox evangelical religion:

infant baptism, ordination, the trinity, regeneration, repentance, justification, the fall of man, the atonement, transubstantiation, fasting, penance, church government, religious experience, the call to the ministry, the general resurrection, eternal punishment, who may baptize, and even the question of freemasonry, republican government, and the rights of man.[17]

Mormon," *American Journal of Psychology*, XXVII (July, 1917), 373-395, and "A Footnote: Authorship of the Book of Mormon," *American Journal of Psychology*, XXX (Oct., 1919), 427, 428; Brodie, *No Man Knows*, 59, 63 ff.

16 *Ibid.*, 99 ff.

17 Alexander Campbell, *Delusions: An Analysis of the Book of Mormon*, etc. (Boston, 1832), 13 and *passim*.

Especially did the Saints lay emphatic stress upon, and offer concrete instead of vague conceptions of, the very doctrines which thirty years of revivalism had made most intensely interesting to the folk of western New York. They incorporated literal interpretations of the Bible, made expectation of the millennium coincident with the prophet's career on earth, and provided a mode for fresh revelation direct from God. Above all, in the person of Joseph Smith they found living, intimately available embodiment of their entire faith. How much more effectively than the orthodox evangelists could they hammer home the consciousness of sin and the hope of regeneration which had been preached here since the first settlement of the region!

Mormonism has usually been described as a frontier religion. But study of the circumstances of its origin and its continuing appeal in the area which bred it suggests a different view. The church did not rise during the pioneering era of western New York. Its early recruits came from many sects, but invariably from the longest-settled neighborhoods of the region. Joseph's peregrinations during the period when he was pregnant with the new religion were always eastward, not westward, from his Manchester home. The first congregations of the church formed at Manchester, Fayette in Seneca County, and Colesville in Broome County.[18] These facts, together with the realization of Mormonism's dependence on current excitements and upon myths and doctrines built by the passage of time into the locality's very fabric, demonstrate that the Church of the Saints was not a frontier phenomenon in origin.

Nor did it expand through an appeal to frontiersmen. The far greater gathering of converts from this area came during the region's riper maturity, after Zion itself had removed to the West. And the recruits enlisted here and elsewhere in the East by returning missionaries far outnumbered those gained in areas of the Middle West where Mormon headquarters chanced from time to time to be located. These propositions could best be supported by the church's publication of missionary journals, if they exist in the official archives. Even without that evidence, however, they can be adequately documented from scattered references of orthodox

---

18 See map XIX.

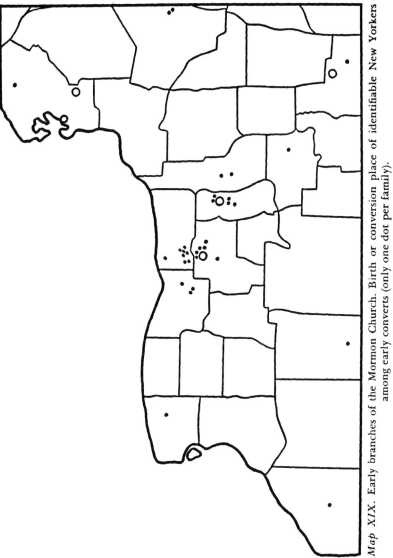

Map XIX. Early branches of the Mormon Church. Birth or conversion place of identifiable New Yorkers among early converts (only one dot per family).

sources to Mormon proselytizing, and from an analysis of the nativity figures in the Utah Territorial Census of 1860.

Whether particularly successful missionary tours are indicated by the concentration in certain years of occasional remarks by others on the Mormon conversions, or whether coincidence is responsible, the notices discovered focus upon 1832 and 1841. During earlier years Mormons had "made considerable inroads in the southern part" of the town of Borodino, whose people, according to the Presbyterian minister, had been "wafted and bemused with *every wind of doctrine,* till they neither know nor care what is truth, or what is error." In northern Allegany County, "A Mormon Preacher came along" carrying "a solemn visage and nearly persuaded some over to his delusion." In the same year Alexander Campbell's strictures on the new faith were republished by Joshua Himes at Boston, because two Mormons already had fifteen converts from that city.[19] Early the following summer missionaries in the middle Genesee Valley were reported to have collected fifty recruits by making use of the northern lights to scare the superstitious. A few Mormons helped to turn West Otto, in Cattaraugus County, against Presbyterian doctrine in 1835. The *Baptist Register* of Utica began publishing occasional exposures of Mormonism in 1839, intensifying its interest during the following two years. Explanation came forth in February of '41. "Mormon emmissaries are now circulating in various directions through the State . . . and in some instances [are] surprisingly successful." The Methodist *Zion's Watchman* in the same year commenced to present anti-Mormon material in some quantity. Occasional press notices emanated from Rochester throughout the forties. One of John Humphrey Noyes's supporters recommended that he visit Utica, where the correspondent and forty-four others had supported a Mormon Church in 1841. The same year a returned missionary visiting friends in Low Hampton requested permission to attend William Miller's preaching.[20]

---

[19] B. B. Drake, Borodino, Aug. 27, 1832, to Secretary Hoyt, Horace Galpin, Centerville, Nov. 3, 1832, to Absolom Peters, A.H.M.S. MSS; Campbell, *Delusions,* 3, 4.

[20] *Evangelical Magazine and Gospel Advocate* (Utica), IV (July 13, 1833), 220; Simeon Peck, West Otto, Aug. 5, 1835, to Secretary Murray, A.H.M.S. MSS; *Baptist Register* (Utica), XVI (May 17, 1839) 54 and ff., XVIII (Feb. 19, 1841), 6; *Zion's Watch-*

But what degree of success did this proselytizing achieve, and how did it compare with similar efforts farther west? In 1860, when many original New York converts who had been adults in 1830 must have died, the natives of this state in Utah Territory numbered fewer only than those from Illinois. Iowa, Ohio, Pennsylvania, and Missouri followed in order. The manuscript of the census shows that the numbers from Iowa, Illinois, and Missouri were of such an age range that they must have been mainly the children of the fertile members transplanted from the East. While it is thus clear that few adults joined in the Middle West, many whose nativity was in New England or Pennsylvania had removed once and resided in New York at the time of their conversion. No exact analysis is possible, but it is clear that many more adherents came from the East than from the West, and probably more of them from New York than from any other state. It may not be improper to imagine that the bulk of these hailed from the same Burned-over District which in these very years provided so extensive a personnel for a host of other religious experiments.[21]

To discover when the conversions in the region occurred is again difficult, but basis for an estimate is found by analyzing age groups among the New York-born in Utah in 1860. Of 923 persons so counted, 221 were over 45 and might have been original members, though many presumably emigrated and joined later farther west or came under the influence of the Mormon itinerants who combed this region after 1831. The remainder under 45 could have been children of original members. But since only a hundred persons in all removed to Kirtland, Ohio, in the first hegira, the greater number must have been later converts or their children. Persons under 25, and families with a member in this age group born in this state, could scarcely have emigrated before 1835. The number in this

---

man (New York), VI (1841), *passim;* Blake McKelvey, *Rochester: The Water-Power City, 1812–1854* (Cambridge, Mass., 1945), 288 and notes; *Perfectionist* (Putney, Vt.), I (Feb. 15, 1843), 1; J. W. Sawyer, Shaftsbury, Vt., Nov. 2, 1841, to William Miller, William Miller Papers, Aurora College Library.

   21 Joseph C. G. Kennedy, Superintendent, *Population of the United States in 1860: Compiled from the Original Returns of the Eighth Census, etc.* (4 vols.; Washington, 1864), I, 578. Nativities in Utah are: Illinois, 1796; New York, 1744; Iowa, 1551; Ohio, 884; Pennsylvania, 862; Missouri, 726; Massachusetts, 523; Vermont, 326; Connecticut, 232; etc.

category totals 446 out of the 923 counted, or more than 50 per cent.[22]

It seems conservative to estimate that of Mormons brought into the church from the Burned-over District at least three-fourths must have been gathered by returning itinerants between 1831 and the early fifties. Yankee groups in Ohio, Pennsylvania, and New England itself responded similarly, but less intensively, and after 1850 a substantial portion of new members came from England and Scandinavia. Obviously, then, Mormonism should not be called a frontier religion in terms of the persons it appealed to, any more than it should in terms of its origin.

To be sure the church existed generally on the frontier and kept moving westward with the tide of settlement. It also carried into the West a number of ideas characteristic of the Burned-over District. Its location was determined by the fact that the evangelistic-mindedness from which it developed in the beginning, and which constantly fed it with members, had little tolerance for such an unorthodox offspring, and drove the Saints by its persecution along their westering course. But neither the organization of the church, nor its personnel, nor its doctrines were frontier products. All belonged rather to that Yankee, rural, emotionalized, and rapidly maturing culture which characterized western New York so markedly in the second quarter of the nineteenth century.

---

[22] "8th Census, Utah, Vol. I, Miscellaneous Territories," Microfilm, Bureau of Census. MS is written in a hand which makes U.T. and N.Y. at times indistinguishable. The number counted represents those which could be classified.

Chapter 9. THE EVANGELIST

BIRTH in Connecticut and a youth spent on the shores of Lake Ontario identified Charles Finney with the majority of his local contemporaries. Education in Connecticut and New Jersey academies, a stretch of school teaching and an apprenticeship at law marked him for leadership. Only slightly above medium height, he had a somewhat receding chin and manners "bordering on the rough and blunt" which made his first appearance unprepossessing. But a "guileless, honest, frank heart," a friendly, informal approach to people, his "large and prominent blue eyes" ("never was a man whose soul looked out through his face as his did"), and a degree of self-confidence usually but not always just short of arrogance gave him commanding influence wherever he went.[1]

At the age of twenty-nine, he had in the year 1821 served four years in Benjamin Wright's law office at Adams, an unconverted, and according to his own recollection, a worldly, sinful man. But the minister who introduced him into his new career remembered that "he had a respect for good people, and the institutions of religion." Asked why he resisted conversion, he replied, "It would

---

[1] Charles G. Finney, *Autobiography of Charles Grandison Finney* (New York, 1876), 4–7; G. Frederick Wright, *Charles Grandison Finney* (Boston, 1891), 5–37; George W. Gale, "Autobiography of George W. Gale," (MS, 1853), II, 45; Theodore Weld, in Charles Beecher, ed., *Autobiography, Correspondence, etc. of Lyman Beecher, D.D.* (2 vols.; New York, 1863), II, 311; Sidney E. Mead, *Nathaniel William Taylor . . . Connecticut Liberal* (Chicago, 1942), 203; Charles Grandison Finney Papers, Oberlin College Library, *passim.*

hardly be consistent with the profession he was to follow." Nevertheless, he led the choir in George W. Gale's Presbyterian Church. Added to his own sense of guilt, his fiancée was praying for him, and Gale and Jedediah Burchard had focused attention upon him as the "one man who stood in the way of the conversion of many." [2] By his own testimony, Finney began his more intense religious concern when he undertook to study the Bible as an introduction to Hebraic law. Such circumstances neither question the honesty nor belittle the virility of his religious experience. He himself realized that the Holy Ghost appeared from within "the philosophy or workings of my own mind, as revealed in consciousness." [3] Modern psychology can say little more to open Finney's regeneration to historical analysis.

After an interval of some eighteen months' soul-searching, he undertook his theological studies under Gale's tutelage and began occasional missionary tours into the "Burnt districts" to the north. Graceful in motion, skilled in vocal music, with a voice of extraordinary clarity, tone, and ranges of power and pitch, he spoke without mannerisms in concise, familiar figures. Having been not only a lawyer but also an accomplished horseman, marksman, and sailor, he could utilize parables meaningful to common folk. Ordained on July 1, 1824, he continued to tour northern Jefferson County, on his second appointment as agent for the Utica Female Missionary Society. Throughout the hamlets of that remote hinterland, multitudes fell before the Lord's power. He and his teammate, Daniel Nash, spent "from 3 to 4 hours a day" in prayer, living for the most part "directly on the providence of God for the supply of their temporal wants," and using their full liberty "to go where the Spirit of God directs them," for the best part of two years.

Their methods were more extreme than Finney remembered them to be in his autobiography. A Universalist minster quoted at the moment of origin the evangelist's reference to himself: *"That I have no more religion than your horse; that I am the wickedest man in all this country; that I do not believe what I preach; and that I told you I did not believe what I preached,"* which virulence he could explain only by supposing Finney might be "subject to par-

---

[2] Gale, "Autobiography," II, 25, 39, 45.

[3] Finney, *Autobiography*, 54.

oxisms [sic]of insanity." [4] Late in 1825, during a visit to Gale, who had retired at Western just north of Rome, the now-experienced Boanerges began his invasion of the upper Mohawk Valley.

Rome ignited from Western, and "the explosion of Rome . . . scattered the fire over all this region of country," sending sparks to Utica, Boonville, Verona, and many other towns. Nash knew "not where to go, or what to do," and Finney felt himself "pulled 40 ways at once." The excitement retained high pitch even into the mid-summer of 1826. "Never before . . . [was] such a spirit of agonizing prayer among Christians as of late. . . ." Only in the fall of 1829 could the "moment of delirium" in Utica be pronounced finally passed. Perhaps three thousand experienced conversion, half of them joining Presbyterian churches, the rest going with the Methodists or Baptists. The fame of the awakening spread over the Northeast and promptly made Finney a figure of national importance.[5]

Every favorable circumstance had conspired to the itinerant's advantage, and he was a man who could seize fleeting opportunities and make them serve his purposes. The dead of winter had closed the canal, enforced leisure upon overworked farmers, and left villagers' spirits lagging in tedious boredom after that booming autumn which had witnessed the great celebration over DeWitt Clinton's ditch. The area had been bred in revivalism and was already noted for strong evangelical interests. A population of under eight thousand in Utica had perhaps been spending about seventy thousand dollars a year for churchly concerns.[6] Communities now kept in closer touch with each other than in pioneering days, and no

---

[4] Finney, *Autobiography*, 61, 77–140; Commissions, March 17, June 29, 1824, Finney MSS; John Fine, Ogdensburg, Feb. 11, 1826, to Absolom Peters, American Home Missionary Society Papers, Chicago Theological Seminary; *Herald of Salvation* (Watertown), II (Aug. 28, 1824), 102, 103.

[5] Daniel Nash and Charles G. Finney, Western, Feb. 3, 1826, to John Fine (enclosure to Absolom Peters), Samuel Sweezey, Florence, April 24, 1826, to Absolom Peters, A.H.M.S. MSS; *Gospel Advocate* (Utica), VII (Nov. 14, 1829), 360; Gale, "Autobiography," III, 25 ff.; Finney, *Autobiography*, 140–183; *A Narrative of the Revival of Religion . . . in the Year 1826* (Utica, 1826); J. Parker, Auburn, March 7, 1826, to Andover Society of Inquiry, Society of Inquiry Papers, Newton Theological Seminary; William R. Weeks, *Pastoral Letter . . . of the Oneida Association*, etc. (Utica, 1827), and *A Letter on Protracted Meetings* (Utica, 1827).

[6] *Gospel Advocate*, VII (Nov. 14, 1829), 360.

good Yankee could see his own church dozing in formalism while another added members. The local clergymen joined in Finney's train; whatever their reservations, the pressure of parishioners' demands could no more be resisted than a cyclone. One minister who dared protest soon left his charge for more comfortable quarters, but others suffered in silence.

Calls for the evangelist's services flooded in from all sides as the news spread, and for four years he answered the most pressing of them. Interspersing return visits to the Utica neighborhood (his wife's home was in adjacent Whitesboro), he toured widely, touching at Auburn, Troy, Little Falls, Wilmington, Philadelphia, Reading, Lancaster, New York City, and intermediate points. In September, 1830, he moved to Rochester, where the more famous and influential of his two most sensational campaigns occupied the next six months.

Rochester proved to be even more ripe for the sickle than had Utica and Rome five years before. The canal boom had slackened for two years, Antimasonry had yielded to a postfever state, and so also had the Sabbatarian crusade. Surviving animosities had the town's three Presbyterian churches embroiled in a bitter quarrel, but all sides were ready to accept Finney as arbitrator and counted on him to resurrect the vital piety so lacking in recent seasons. The year just passed had witnessed Sam Patch's death jump over the Genesee Falls, and a four months' search for the body in the lower river. Elder Bissell had lectured the Sunday school on the affair, holding that "all who had, by their presence or in any other way, induced that man to jump over the falls, were accessary . . . and would be accounted murderers in the sight of God."[7] Sam had probably been drunk (he had with no difficulty previously leapt both the Genesee and Niagara Falls), and a fillip for temperance sentiment accompanied the generally chastened feelings permeating the village throughout 1830.

As he had done on the Mohawk, Finney held forth during the winter season, when commerce ebbed and ceased while an apathetic but penitent Yankee community contemplated its past and present sins. He had apparently promised to make Buffalo the next stop,

---

[7] Blake McKelvey, *Rochester: The Water-Power City, 1812–1854* (Cambridge, Mass., 1945), 188–190; Mary B. A. King, *Looking Backward* (New York, 1870), 117.

and in February his correspondents there urged him to come "before the navigation opens," since people had "nothing to do now but to attend to preaching or pleasure." [8] His better judgment, however, led him to capitalize more thoroughly on the same circumstances in the place where he was already doing famously.

No more impressive revival has occurred in American history. Sectarianism was forgotten and all churches gathered in their multitudes. The Presbyterians alone added six hundred in the village. Finney took Dirck Lansing's advice from Utica to "Run away" frequently into the environs "+ then come back + fire again." When in town he preached thrice on Sundays and as many times during the week. The First Church roof had been weak but unrepaired for two years; when it partially collapsed over a particularly jammed meeting in December with injury to no one, the apparently divine intervention aided the cause. Finney's now-polished style held the people entranced. When he described a sinner's slide to perdition, tracing his course from ceiling to floor with outstretched finger, "half his hearers . . . would rise unconsciously to their feet to see him descend into the pit below." [9]

But the exceptional feature was the phenomenal dignity of this awakening. No agonizing souls fell in the aisles, no raptured ones shouted hallelujahs. Rather, despite his doses of hell-fire, the great evangelist, "in an unclerical suit of gray," acted "like a lawyer arguing . . . before a court and jury," talking precisely, logically, but with wit, verve, and informality. Lawyers, real-estate magnates, millers, manufacturers, and commercial tycoons led the parade of the regenerated. The theatre became a livery stable. Taverns closed. An Institute of Practical Education, modeled on Gale's school at Whitesboro, planned to train the forty young converts heading for the ministry while they worked to support themselves.[10]

More remarkable yet was the way the fire threw off sparks. More than ninety letters directed to Finney during his sojourn have sur-

---

[8] Edward Coming, Feb. 9, and Busby Torrey, Feb. 28, 1831, Buffalo, to Finney, Finney MSS.

[9] *Reminiscences of Rev. Charles G. Finney*, etc. (Oberlin, O., 1876), 7–15; King, *Looking Backward*, 141; Finney, *Autobiography*, 288–299, 366; D. C. Lansing, Utica, Sept. 20, 1830, to Finney, Finney MSS; *Rochester Observer*, I (May 16, 1828), 79; McKelvey, *Rochester*, 191; Henry B. Stanton, *Random Recollections* (New York, 1887), 42.

[10] Stanton, *Recollections*, 40–42; *New York Evangelist*, II (Aug. 13, 1831), 287.

vived to show that communities from Ohio to Boston begged for his services. Delegates came in person to view the marvel and engage its director. Former enemies ranked large among the petitioners, some writing enthusiastically in secret lest former strictures rebound upon them, others quite obviously yielding reluctantly to lay pressure, and still others admitting their fault openly.[11] Even Auburn Seminary dallied with the notion of a short course to stave off the competition of the revivalistic training schools springing up at Troy, Whitesboro, and Rochester. Between seven and ten thousand converts in this state alone came from the sympathetic awakenings which spread in concentric waves. Finney later quoted Lyman Beecher's testimony that a hundred thousand in the nation made religious affiliations within a year, an event "unparalleled in the history of the church." Everywhere, "a spirit of zeal and boldness . . . made the addition of numbers a matter of far less consequence, than the increased energy . . . infused into Christian character and exertion." [12]

Finney went on to Buffalo, Boston, and New York, making his headquarters in the metropolis until his removal to Oberlin in 1835. His sermons, published in the *New York Evangelist* and utilizing his already made fame, boosted that paper's circulation immensely and sold widely in book form. One volume alone, he recollected, reached twelve thousand copies here and eighty thousand in England and eventually achieved translation into French, Welsh, and German. From Oberlin he continued to take winter leaves of absence for evangelistic tours, often through western New York, but no such explosion again followed in his wake, here or elsewhere. His dynamic impact upon the Burned-over District and equally on the country at large, though it long survived, came primarily from the two great campaigns of 1826 and 1831, more particularly from the latter. To be sure he helped train a generation of clergymen and educators at Oberlin, who spread over the West and, during Reconstruction, into the South;[13] but such a

---

[11] See map XX.

[12] J. Hopkins, Auburn, Nov. 19, Dec. 13, 1830, Feb. 19, 1831, to Finney, Finney MSS; *Western Recorder* (Utica), VIII (May 24, 1831), 83; Finney, *Autobiography*, 301; *Rochester Observer*, VI (Oct. 6, 1832), 40.

[13] Finney, *Autobiography*, 330, 331; Robert S. Fletcher, *A History of Oberlin College . . . through the Civil War* (2 vols.; Oberlin, O., 1943), *passim.*

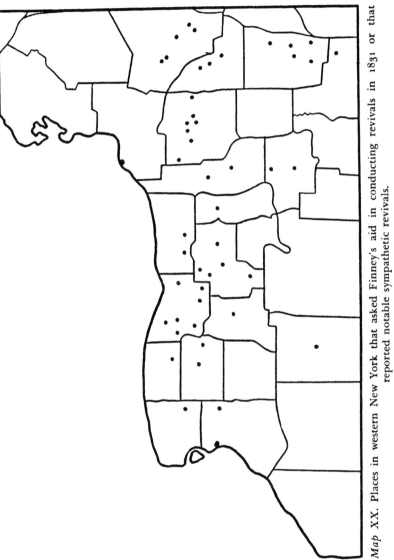

Map XX. Places in western New York that asked Finney's aid in conducting revivals in 1831 or that reported notable sympathetic revivals.

professorial influence is hard to analyze in specific terms, and in any case could scarcely equal the direct effect on a broad public of his early revivals.

Charles Finney has seemed to some historians, as to many of his contemporaries, to be one of those rare individuals who of their own unaided force may on occasion significantly transform the destines of masses of people. His influence was indeed extraordinary. His example probably contributed more to the complexion of ensuing events than did any of the other coincident phenomena which introduced the distinctive phase of Burned-over District history. Yet all the portents of the time rested on deeply imbedded traditions and broadly felt social trends. Furthermore, the thesis which makes him the original and nearly exclusive cause of all that followed attributes the effectiveness of his early revivals to a distinctive and novel theology.[14] In fact, not only was his doctrine at this time by no means distinctive or original, but it is fair to question whether he had at the beginning anything whatsoever which deserves the title of a theology. Adequate examination of the subject must refuse to take him at his own evaluation or to read back into his early ministry notions developed in the course of a lifetime. Like other men, he gathered his education as he lived. He was the creature of his environment and inheritance, and his ideas matured gradually as he learned from other men and from his own experience.

The evangelist himself recollected in the 1870's that he had refused a theological scholarship at Princeton because he perceived even then that orthodox preparation rendered preachers ineffective. But George W. Gale, whose memory played fewer tricks on him, recorded some twenty years earlier that he tried and failed to obtain a scholarship for Finney at Andover, Princeton, and Auburn. Furthermore, "His peculiar views, adopted since he has been at Oberlin, were no part of his theology at that time, and for a number of years afterward." His initial studies therefore began in Gale's library under supervision of the local presbytery.[15]

At the time, however, Finney was a grown man, accustomed to study and independent judgment. He probably learned more from

---

[14] Gilbert H. Barnes, *The Antislavery Impulse, 1830–1844* (New York, 1933).
[15] Finney, *Autobiography*, 45, 51; Gale, "Autobiography," II, 47, 48.

Gale than he ever chose to admit, but he evidently submitted to no systematic guidance in reading or thinking. He spent much of his time on his knees over the Bible. "At first I found myself unable to receive his [Gale's] peculiar views; and then gradually formed views of my own . . . which appeared to me . . . unequivocally taught in the Bible." Often too, he "spread the subject before God, and soon made up my mind what to do." When presbytery examined him for ordination he did not even know the Confession of Faith. He passed unanimously, not upon his learning but upon his already handsome reputation for conducting revivals.[16] In fact, much of his training period had been spent campaigning instead of studying, and his only basis for doctrinal conflict with Gale was his experience with what worked in creating conversions.

No more than Nathaniel Taylor and Lyman Beecher, who earlier made the same adjustments of New England theology which Finney happened upon, did he consciously emulate Methodism or other Arminian thought. All alike merely studied the theologians (Finney in most summary fashion for the present) and made refinements where they seemed illogical, obtuse, or erroneous. This process of checking established notions against one's own reason and sense of right made the result conform to the needs of the society which produced the thinker. Finney did not deliberately attempt to make Presbyterianism palatable to the rising common folk, but his conclusions did just that. All he had to do was to insist "that the sinner's cannot is his 'will not,' " and the remaining determinism in the already thoroughly watered-down Calvinism of his day disappeared.[17] Taylor had put it in more refined terms: the "certainty" that man would sin left him "with power to the contrary." [18] The influence of Taylor and Beecher, though perhaps not yet widely spread among laymen, had been gradually penetrating upstate New York for several years. No discernible distinction is to be made between their point of view and Finney's until the late thirties and early forties, when several Oberlin professors together pushed farther toward perfectionism in a system they called the "Doctrine

---

[16] Finney, *Autobiography*, 51, 52, 54, 304; Wright, *Finney*, 23; W. Platt, Adams, June 22, 1824, to Finney, Finney MSS.

[17] Finney, *Autobiography*, 307.

[18] Mead, *Taylor*, 189.

of Sanctification." Only two pamphlets and one book by the New Yorker appear to predate his Oberlin theology. One is an exercise on human ability which could as well have come from anyone of a score of New Haven apostles; the second, a violent castigation of "cold" clergymen; and the third, a treatise on techniques for engineering revivals.[19]

But no individual or school of thought could equal experience, as Finney's teacher. His doctrine, in fact, grew out of actions which met the pragmatic test; success could be measured only in numbers of converts and in the apparent intensity of their convictions. Thus it was that Finney's chief contribution in the New York campaigns was not a theology but a set of practices. These devices met effectively the demand for larger revivals, and served to popularize and vitalize the New Haven theology. The "new measures" which first achieved fame in the great "Western Revival" of 1826 accumulated in the evangelist's repertoire during his first tours in the north country. Jedediah Burchard preached in the same territory and may have provided a link between New Haven and new measures. But Finney's constant companion throughout these years was Daniel Nash.

If Charles Finney was a "portent," Father Nash was a saint. His intimacy with the greater man was closer for several years than that of any other person before the Oberlin period. Elderly, humble, and unschooled ("a plain, good man, but not much of a preacher," Gale remembered), Nash was wise in the folkways of the hinterland and by no means the crotchety, ignorant eccentric Finney later made him out to be. Extensively self-educated, he knew the works of Jonathan Edwards and quoted from Pope. He later wrote a popular series of articles for the *New York Evangelist,* and assisted the editor of the *Western Recorder* at Utica. He had ministered to a church at Cohocton in the southern tier about 1820, but apparently before as well as after that date had stumped the Black River country. In 1824 he served a congregation of poverty-stricken squatters in the town of Orleans between excursions afield.[20] Prob-

---

[19] Charles G. Finney, *Sinners Bound to Change Their Own Hearts* (New York, 1834); *A Sermon Preached . . . from Amos III, 3: Can Two Walk Together Except They Be Agreed?* (Philadelphia, 1827); *Lectures on Revivals of Religion* (2d ed.; New York, 1835).

[20] Rev. James A. Miller, *The History of the Presbytery of Steuben,* etc. (Angelica,

ably his prayers for the conversion of individuals did somewhat offend, since his deafness made him shout so they could be heard a half mile away; but no other letters written to Finney during the New York campaigns compare with his in vigorous crisp simplicity of style and in the evidence they reveal of constant agonizing self-humiliation in the service of his God and fellow men. Asa Mahan, who had direct contact with both the Utica and Rochester revivals, believed in retrospect "that the world now feels, and ever will feel, the influence of that holy man, who was at last found in his closet, on his knees dead before God. . . ."[21]

Charles Finney was no man's slavish disciple; in fact he apparently led Nash himself to "a sort of new conversion."[22] He probably sensed the ease with which a less humble person could be led astray by so supreme a belief in specific prayer as the old man held. And the new measures could scarcely be any more exclusively attributed to Nash than to Finney. Essentially, they rose from experience. But the likelihood is that Finney learned more from this old veteran of the backwoods than he taught in return. Father Nash served as lieutenant and interpreter of experience, the chief instructor.

While Nash lived, Finney received such warnings against his growing pride as none other dared voice and apparently made the criticism mutual. He could profitably have continued to learn at least from the humility of his early mentor. ("I know, very well, that much ballast is needed to keep me steady, taken from the dung-hill, as I was, + sailing before such a wind as we have done.")[23] But he was growing out of his early crudities and hobnobbing with the great men of the country, and he chose not to be embarrassed by his old friend's presence. Never after 1827 did Nash accompany him. The arrangement seems to have been deliberate. The aged devotee felt the affront but nevertheless continued to lend his prayers and counsel from afar. ("I wish I could see you one hour—

1897), 59; New York Evangelist, IV (July 20, 1833), 115; Gale, "Autobiography," III, 43; Daniel Nash, Utica, Feb. 2, 1825, with P.S. by S. C. Aikin, to Executive Committee, Domestic Missionary Society of New York, A.H.M.S. MSS.

21 Asa Mahan, Autobiography: Intellectual, Moral and Spiritual (London, 1882), 226, 227.

22 Gale, "Autobiography," III, 43.

23 Daniel Nash, Denmark, March 12, 1830, to Finney, Finney MSS. ·

then pray with you another. . . . I have neither guide, nor assistant, this side heaven. That, however, is sometimes, much nearer to me than Philadelphia . . ."). [24]

Historians have removed from its original context and perpetuated a misleading use of the phrase "Finney's Holy Band." A crowd of young men were drawn by the magnet of the Oneida County awakening, some of them new converts who had to be trained before their ministry, more of them already-ordained preachers who could lend an immediate hand. The bands were differently constituted in each local revival and never had more than the most shadowy kind of casual unity. All had similar interests with Finney and Nash and learned to use the measures which the revival made famous, but at no time during either upstate campaign was there a distinctive Finney "school" in the doctrinal sense. As far as practices are concerned, George Gale testified that the young followers aped the techniques "more especially of the Rev. Mr. Nash." And while Finney was wandering far afield, these itinerants continued to beat up and down the hills and vales of the Burned-over District, accompanied by the ubiquitous prayers and nearly as omnipresent person and counsel of the elderly backwoods saint. Practically without exception, the evangelists who were soon to carry sensational revivalism over into heterodox expressions had been longer and more intimately associated with the older man. [25]

The revival which spread from Western in 1826 had a very different style from that in Rochester five years later. On the earlier occasion Finney and his mentor had come fresh from the north country, where dramatic showmanship and violent threats of damnation sufficed to start a tremor, and where the abnormal appetite of the populace for excitement led contagion to continue the process. No evidence appears in contemporary accounts to indicate any marked emphasis on social attitudes in this campaign. The extreme sensationalism mastered in the first tours was what captivated the upper Mohawk area. Oneida Presbytery disliked much of the Finney technique, "but God was with him," and their hands were tied.

---

[24] Daniel Nash, Albia, Oct. 27, 1828, to Finney, Finney MSS.

[25] Barnes, *Antislavery Impulse*, 204 and *passim*, helped to give currency to the phrase. King, *Looking Backward*, 119, 120, shows the original connotation. Composition of the bands in both revivals appears clearly in study of the Finney MSS.

Gale later questioned "whether we did our whole duty in this matter. Evils that ensued . . . might have been prevented," even though they came "more from young men who attempted to follow Mr. Finney's lead, but who went much farther in the wrong direction than he did." [26]

Beyond the immediate area of infection, however, people inclined to look askance at such sensationalism. Its enthusiasm, as in the Great Awakening whose excesses better-educated men had learned about, implied that excitement must necessarily accompany vital religion. Dignified clergymen, whatever their theology, objected to being called antichristian merely because they hesitated to act like common ranters. Opposition began to rise during Finney's visits to Auburn and Troy, following his Utica sojourn. In New England, meantime, it gathered furiously, coming to a head at the New Lebanon Conference of July, 1827.[27]

Prepared by preliminary negotiations between Lyman Beecher and Nathaniel Beman of Troy (the latter initiated the proposal), the meeting aimed to heal the breach between the groups in New England and New York who had no doctrinal quarrel, and thus to present a solid front against the more strict Calvinists on one hand and the rising threat of Universalism and Unitarianism on the other. Gale and Beman, Gillet of Rome, Lansing of Auburn, and Frost of Whitesboro came to uphold Finney, while President Humphrey of Amherst, Jonathan Edwards of Andover, Lyman Beecher, and Asahel Nettleton, the famed evangelist of the Great Revival in 1800, led the New England group. Beecher came ready to compromise, as did most of the westerners. That there was no essential conflict of principles is demonstrated by one resolution which attained unanimous approval: "The idea that God ordinarily works independently of human instrumentality, or without reference to the adaption of means to ends, is unscriptural."

But Nettleton, too old to remember accurately his own earlier

---

[26] Gale, "Autobiography," IV, 2–5.

[27] *Letters of the Rev. Dr. Beecher and Rev. Mr. Nettleton, on the New Measures in Conducting Revivals of Religion* (New York, 1828); Finney, *Autobiography*, 192–201; J. Brockway, *A Delineation . . . of a Revival . . . in Troy*, etc. (Troy, 1827), and *A Brief Account . . . of the Divisions in the . . . Presbyterian Church . . . in Troy*, etc. (Troy, 1827).

methods, and either touched by jealousy or already adrift in the conservative direction, was intransigent, and Finney utterly refused to bend.[28] The session ended in conflict but paved the way for future settlement. Nettleton soon parted company with Beecher and later opened a correspondence with the orthodox Presbyterians at Princeton in which he blamed all the developments of the West on Nathaniel Taylor's theology. Soon he urged the Princetonians to adopt a creedal test for all New England ministers taking pastorates farther west. Beecher and Finney, however, came to complete agreement in Philadelphia before the year was out, and not many years later Finney came to Boston at Beecher's urgent request and with his total co-operation.[29]

If Beecher in a degree capitulated, Finney on his part was evolving toward more circumspect behavior. Accord with the New Englander was only one, and not the first, step. He admitted no errors, announced no new policy, and in fact may even have been unaware of the transformation. Learning always from experience, he merely judged with broader data and let his action conform to the wiser thinking. Aiken believed he toned down after first reading Jonathan Edwards in Utica. As he moved from Oneida County he threw off his ties with Father Nash and found more critical audiences. In Auburn and Troy, substantial citizens obstructed his work whenever it violated propriety. Such opposition to his methods dissipated the fundamental agreement on ends at New Lebanon. A conference of December, 1827, brought him and his upstate companions into session with the leading clergy and laymen of New York City and paved the way for another visit in 1829.[30]

Meanwhile, the Oneida pastors tried to exercise the moderating influence they had been unable to exert in the first flush of local excitement. Moses Gillet warned Finney against "calling down fire" on cold ministers and professors. Gale cautioned him against

---

[28] Barnes, *Antislavery Impulse*, 8, 9, misinterpreted the conference in such a way as to misconstrue relations between Finney and Beecher henceforward. I have relied mainly on Fletcher, *Oberlin*, I, 159-166; *Christian Examiner and Theological Review* (Boston), IV (July, Aug., 1827), 360; Beecher, *Autobiography*, II, 96-106 and notes; and particularly, Gale, "Autobiography," IV, 2-4.

[29] Asahel Nettleton, E. Hampton, L.I., Aug. 11, 21, Sept. 10, 1835, to Samuel Miller, Samuel Miller Papers, Princeton University Library; Fletcher, *Oberlin*, I, 30.

[30] Fletcher, *Oberlin*, I, 26, 27.

overelation at the New Lebanon victory. A Hamilton professor of doubtful literacy risked stronger words. "Bro. Finney when you go among strangers dont talk too much about yourself. They have an idea that you are an self sufficient an Egotist. + this confirms them—Restrain too your natural vivacity + cheerfulness—it sometimes amount to levity." Theodore Weld thought revivals had become so commonplace with him "as scarcely to throw [on?] you the best tinge of solemnity . . . dip not your pen in the gall of sarcasm, but dip it in tears and write with a trembling heart. . . ." [81]

At the same time, other letters from upstate indicated that in less skilled hands, under Nash's guidance, things done in emulation of the 1826 revival were running toward excess. Two direct witnesses testified that under such influences Finney's own techniques progressively moderated.[32]

The next to last stage in this evolution occurred in New York City. The great philanthropists surrounding the Tappan brothers had been directed in their road to charitable activities under the influence of Nathaniel Taylor, and Finney may even have met his doctrinal parent on one of his early visits. This circle had been driving the "Great Eight" benevolent societies for some years. Here were men who raised eyebrows at the paroxysms of excitement which passed for conversion in Jefferson and Oneida counties. Saintliness to them meant rather humanitarian enterprise. They drew the evangelist to them, for his vigorous methods could add vitality and zeal to their own already booming crusades. Finney, in turn, began to realize that anxiety for one's soul, the preliminary state to conversion, might be engendered even more effectively by dwelling upon the specific sins of men in society than by extravagant language and heated denunciations. The reform movements provided an established set of immediate objectives whose progressive realization could be counted steps toward the millennium. Here was an ideological content, then, fitted to accompany the sobered

---

[81] Harriet and Moses Gillet, Rome, Feb. 28, 1827, G. W. Gale, Greenbush, July 28, 1827, H. H. Kellog, Sheffield, Mass., July 29, 1827, and T. Weld, Fabius, April 22, 1828, to Finney, Finney MSS.

[32] G. W. Gale, Whitesboro, March 4, 1827, and H. Norton, Augusta, Feb. 19, 1827, to Finney, Finney MSS; Gale, "Autobiography," IV, 4; William R. Weeks, *The Pilgrim's Progress in the Nineteenth Century* (New York, 1848).

measures of the Western Revival. The alliance was by no means new, for it had been approaching since the Great Revival of 1800. But in the thoroughness with which the lawyer-turned-minister explored the combination it acquired dynamics of new proportions.

The consolidation of forces, however, did not spring full-grown over night; Finney's New York visits of 1827 and 1829 prepared the way. Protracted negotiations with the A.H.M.S. preceded formation of the first "Free Church" of New York, which was to be devoted to more vigorous revivalism in the metropolis. Joel Parker of Rochester, hitherto unconnected with the great itinerant, was called to its pastorate. It may have been Parker who first suggested installing Finney himself in a second similar church. "It might make me more of a Finney-ite and him more of a Parker-ite. . . ." The evangelist's invitation to the charge came only in 1832, after he had more thoroughly demonstrated his change of technique.[33]

The intervening years saw this change proceed apace. The young man bred in the isolated country east of Lake Ontario found city ways and an association with the wealthy and learned far more to his taste than the rigorous life of a rural itinerant. Seeking some leisure a few years later, he wrote his wife, "I suppose we might get a house in Rome but I hate a village. . . ." [34] He justified his transformation by a new theory of evangelism which broke with his earlier habits and as well with the ideas of his closest friends in the home region.

Whereas souls everywhere were in need of salvation, the folk of the metropolis seemed more needy than the farmers of the country-side. New York drew people from every quarter, and one might influence a vast territory by working there. Much indeed was there to recommend this view probably urged upon him by the Tappan

---

[33] Fletcher, *Oberlin*, I, 28; Finney, *Autobiography*, 318, 319; letter of Lewis Tappan in *New York Evangelist*, VI (Feb. 21, 1835), 29; Committee, Association of Gentlemen, New York, June 14, 1830, to Absolom Peters, William Green, Jr., and Lewis Tappan, New York, March 29, 1833, to Peters and C. Hall, A.H.M.S. MSS; Joel Parker to Josiah Bissell (enclosure in Tappan to Bissell, for Finney), New York, Feb. 2, 1831, Lewis Tappan Papers, Library of Congress. Contrast interpretation of Barnes, *Antislavery Impulse*, 21 ff.; the Tappan crowd had to quiet opposition among the clergy before Finney could be invited with assurance of full support. Tappan and Matthews, New York, March 17, 1831, to Finney, Finney MSS.

[34] Charles Finney, New York, Nov. 10, 1834, to Mrs. Finney, Finney MSS.

brothers. It conformed with coming trends in American society. Within their more limited upstate range, his stands at Utica and Rochester did serve to infect whole districts. But applied to New York by Finney at this time, the change of base was mistaken in one particular: the man would never fit the milieu of the metropolis as he did that of the Burned-over District. His own constantly sanguine view of all his activities never allowed him to realize any difference of proportion in his various successes. He never could recognize that any circumstances—at least of earthly origin—beyond his personal magnetism had ever operated on the growth of his fame.

Weld and Gale knew full well how much his more phenomenal achievements rested upon that susceptibility which so peculiarly characterized western New York. Gale feared he would, like others, "undergo a good deal of change" and let "revival spirit . . . evaporate." Weld wrote him to "Kindle *back fires* BACK FIRES BACK FIRES" against the metropolis. He wanted him to stay in western New York where "every blow you strike . . . is a blow on the head. . . . Once get that region thoroughly soaked and all hell cant wring it dry you know." Even Parker, perhaps with a double meaning, wrote, "An extensive work in that region will . . . open a more effectual door for revival in this city than there has been before." [35]

When knowledge spread of Finney's determination to go to New York as soon as the metropolis would receive him, protests multiplied. One follower queried, "How many Evangelists have been shorn of their strength in cities?" Dirck Lansing asked him to come for consultation, as he was "awfully convinced that you have never accomplished the amount of good you might have . . . by the same labor . . . had it been a little differently directed." Others noted that his preaching was losing the "soul stirring appeals to the heart . . . which . . . once brought so many sinners down at the feet of Jesus"; that "your preaching a few years ago, was better . . . you reason more than formerly." [36]

---

[35] G. W. Gale, Whitesboro, Jan. 24, 1830, Joel Parker, New York, Nov. 11, 1830, to Finney, Finney MSS; Weld to Finney, March 2, 1831, in G. H. Barnes and D. L. Dumond, eds., *Letters of Theodore Dwight Weld, Angelina Grimké Weld, and Sarah Grimké, 1822–1844* (2 vols.; New York, 1934), I, 40.

[36] N. C. Saxton, Albany, June 25, 1832, D. C. Lansing, Utica, April 23, 1831, E. W.

In abandoning lurid sensationalism for the reformer's mantle, Finney traveled in company with the leading progressives in Plan of Union territory. His eminence lay not so much in what he did as in the striking way he had of doing it. The wedding of humanitarian movements and revivalism followed upon a lengthy betrothal as naturally as the marriage of any affianced couple. Tendencies deeply rooted in the age contributed to their growing congeniality. Jacksonian Democracy, whose marked worldliness and hints of outright infidelity pointed out the necessity for spiritual and moral progress, drove them into each others' arms. It also highlighted the power to be gained from a concerted influence upon the rising common folk. A similar marriage of sister and brother in England supplied precedent. The rampant optimism of the period was the cupid who whispered that this ceremony would consummate happiness for all in the approaching millennium. Such a union could blot out every remaining sin which stood between man and perfection.

The bans of marriage had been read in New York, but the nuptials were performed in Rochester. Charles Grandison Finney, probably aware of critical eyes in Gotham and of the preferment to be gained there if the ceremony went smoothly, was the minister. The wedding chapel, the audience, and the pastor alike perfectly suited the tastes of bride and groom, and the occasion passed off in such admirably happy fashion that it augured well for a long prosperity and a healthy increase.

The Rochester revival marked the maturity, indeed the climax, of Finney's measures. It also, for the first time in such frank and dramatic style, combined purely personal religion with a reform crusade of definitely social nature. Intemperance was here made the symbol of the sinner's descent into hell, and the pledge became the token of the new life. Similarly, Theodore Weld's coincident quest for funds for Gale's Oneida Institute was "an impulse to a system of education that is to introduce the Millennium. . . . If you and I live 20 years longer, or half of that, we shall see it." [37]

Contemporaries demonstrated unusual acumen in realizing just

Clarke, Hadlyme, Conn., May 23, 1832, and H. H. Norton, New York, March 19, 1832, to Finney, Finney MSS.

[37] G. W. Gale, Whitesboro, Jan. 29, 1831 [misdated 1830], to Finney, Finney MSS.

what had happened. The *Rochester Observer* noted that temperance "was then a 'new measure' for the promotion of revivals," and the *New York Evangelist* circulated the presbytery report "that the Temperance Reformation and Revivals of Religion have a peculiarly intimate relation and bearing upon each other. . . ." The Baptists also rejoiced. "The glorious cause of temperance, and religion . . . march with correspondent steps, onward to perfection. . . ."[38]

Thus did Charles Finney grow out of and soon outgrow his environment. He was as much the product as the producer of religious emotionalism. And significant as was his role, he bears neither credit nor blame, exclusively, for what followed.

---

[38] *Rochester Observer*, VI (Dec. 15, 1832), 50; *New York Evangelist*, II (Aug. 20, 1831), 292; *Baptist Register* (Utica), VII (Jan. 31, 1831), 189, 190.

BOOK IV

Genesis of Ultraism:
1826-1837

Yet who knows but the institution of a new order of labourers in the great Spiritual vineyard, is to prove the signal for the outpouring of such blessings as have been hitherto unparalleled in the history of our American Israel.—Western Recorder, II (MARCH 22, 1825), 46

Chapter 10. NEW MEASURES

THE resurgence of revival religion, swelling since 1800, was in
the Burned-over District prepared for its climactic stage by
the excitements of the twenties. Enthusiasm rose to its peak in the
middle years of the next decade. The stage of religious emotionalism immediately preceding heterodoxy was that which contemporaries called ultraism. An amorphous thing in an intellectual sense,
it can scarcely be considered a system of belief. It is better described
as a combination of activities, personalities, and attitudes creating
a condition of society which could foster experimental doctrines.

The distinctive activities of the period were the "New Measures"
of the Finney revivals. These devices formed a far more comprehensive set of innovations than the New Englanders suspected
when they attacked them at the New Lebanon Conference. Permeating every department of the ministerial function, they became
more democratic as they became more effective.

Preaching was more direct. Finney well knew that "the impas-
sioned utterance of a common exhorter" could move congregations when "splendid exhibitions of rhetoric" could not.[1] He
advised that language be simple, sentences short and cogent, the
manner colloquial, and repetition frequent. The minister should
not let his audience off by discussing sinners in the third person
but should heighten their own awareness by saying "you." He tried

---

[1] Charles G. Finney, *Autobiography of Charles Grandison Finney* (New York,
1876), 91.

always to pick a text for a particular assembly and used it to build among his hearers a "present obligation." Illustrations were parables derived from the common habits of farmers, mechanics, and housewives. Above all, sermons must be extemporaneous. The folk of the north country, at least, had been prejudiced against prepared discourses for years. Writing also occupied time better used for more preaching, while the speaker could better utilize his hearers' reactions when not bound to a manuscript. "We must have exciting, powerful preaching, or the devil will have the people, except what the Methodists can save." [2]

While this kind of advice was in most respects unexceptionable if utilized by a person of some natural dignity, others who followed the great evangelist abused its spirit, whether he himself did so or not. Adapting texts to the need of the hour cultivated a taste for the sensational. Sermons took such titles as "The Carnal Mind is Enmity Against God," "The Wages of Sin Is Death," and "Can Two Walk Together Except They Be Agreed"—the last a stinging denunciation of "cold" clergymen. At least in his earlier campaigns Finney castigated as impious all educated divines, indeed all who in any way differed with him. The "preaching . . . [aimed] *most directly over against wrong hearts* . . . [was] nearest right." Invective easily came to predominate in attacks on clergy and laymen alike. Finney himself, apparently relatively and certainly increasingly urbane, used terms like "shake them off their seats," "shake them over hell," "Lord wake up these stupid sleeping ministers; [else] . . . they will wake in hell," "smite them this night." The master had too a caustic, grim kind of wit which his friends warned him to hold in leash, and which may have been imitated with poor success by his followers. [3]

An evangelist's sermons, when they did not directly call down

---

[2] Charles G. Finney, *Lectures on Revivals of Religion* (2d ed.; New York, 1835), 184-204, 252, 253; *Autobiography*, 81, 83, 91; George W. Gale, "Autobiography of George W. Gale," (MS, 1853), I, 95.

[3] Finney, *Autobiography*, 160; *Reminiscences of Rev. Charles G. Finney, Speeches and Sketches . . . at Oberlin*, etc. (Oberlin, O., 1876), 11, Charles G. Finney, *A Sermon Preached in the Presbyterian Church at Troy . . . from Amos III, 3: Can Two Walk Together Except They Be Agreed?* (Philadelphia, 1827), 12; Ephraim Perkins, *A "Bunker Hill" Contest, A.D. 1826*, etc. (Utica, 1826), 6; J. Brockway, *A Delineation of . . . a Revival . . . in Troy*, etc. (Troy, 1827), 25; Nathaniel S. S. Beman, Troy, Oct. 23, 1829, to Finney, Charles Grandison Finney Papers, Oberlin College Library.

fire or merely advocate his own peculiar system and qualifications, might occasionally approach a theological discourse, though not in any sectarian sense. The practices of the revivalist dulled nice distinctions between denominations and confused logical lines of thought. But a short period of conviction and a sudden conversion had to be emphasized if the new measures were to become effective.

Pulpit manners matched the burden of the address. The imitator of Finney and Nash "must throw himself back and forward just as far as they did; and must if strong enough, smite as hard upon his chair, besides imitating their wonderful drawl and familiarity with God." Hand clapping, wild gesticulation, and the shift of voice from shout to whisper added visual and auditory sensation to a theatrical performance. The evangelist had time to study manners, since a small stock of sermons could be frequently repeated in his cruising routine. In these few stalwart outlines he could hold to bold generalization and sweeping coverage, whereas the settled clergyman had constantly to develop smaller points with less dramatic purport if he would avoid undue repetition.[4]

The more sensational kind of preaching, moreover, tended to establish among listeners a standard for all ministers. When one of Finney's colleagues reported concerning a local pastor, "We have got the old man halter broke he will lead quite well now," he was merely describing with unusual frankness a common occurrence. Popular demand, whetted by constant revivals, invited ever-more-novel departures. Finney's relatively sane popularizing tendency grew among his emulators into a mania. More than one itinerant may have claimed to be *"recipient and channel of a sensible divine emanation, which he caused to pass from him by a perceptible influence,* as electricity passes from one body to another."[5] From such a point it would be only a short step to eccentricities of doctrine.

If preaching moved the multitudes, prayer remained the vital feature of the new measures. In Sunday meeting, the evangelist reported to God his auditors' behavior much in the style of his

---

[4] Brockway, *Revival in Troy,* 57; Russell Streeter, *Mirror of Calvinist Fanaticism, or Jedediah Burchard & Co.,* etc. (2d ed.; Woodstock, Vt., 1835), 17; *The Life and Times of Rev. George Peck, D.D., Written by Himself* (New York, 1874), 123.

[5] William Clark, Cooperstown, Nov. 17, 1830, to Finney, Finney MSS; [Sylvester Eaton], *Burchardism vs. Christianity* (Poughkeepsie, 1837), 7.

sermon. But during the week as well, from morn 'till eve and on occasion into another dawn, the itinerant and his lay supporters implored Heaven to save the community. They prayed as individuals, in small bands, and in publicly appointed sessions dedicated to the purpose.

A daily sunrise gathering of a few pious souls enabled the leaders of the revival to preserve a certain intimacy and to direct the course of the day's events. Charles Stuart and Theodore Weld had such a regular period of devotions before either of them had ever heard of Charles Finney.[6] Often the "agonizing supplication" of "a little band of sisters," so organized, started off a local awakening. Especially were such devotions powerful incitements to conversion when the women compacted to spend "a certain portion of time each day in praying for their unconverted husbands," meanwhile no doubt withholding their affections in preparation for the joyous day. The same "praying circle" or "holy band," or a number of them, often gravitated about the village through the day, seeking subjects among acquaintances and neighbors. They also served as monitorial assistants in larger assemblies, questioning and advising those who had become anxious for salvation.[7]

Formal prayer meetings followed usually in the evening. These, too, often preceded the awakening and urged its arrival. Once the spasm had commenced, elaborate precautions were aimed at preventing untoward incidents and at sharpening and deepening fervor. Finney advised that meetings be held often enough to let every male and female express himself regularly. The impenitent, if they did not come voluntarily, should be inveigled to attend, and the congregation should "pray that they may be converted *there.*" Groaning, to which the eastern conservatives objected, should not be artificial, but there was "such a thing as being in a state of mind, in which there is but one way to keep from groan-

---

[6] Charles Stuart, New York, Jan. 10, 1826, to Theodore Weld, Theodore Dwight Weld Papers, William L. Clements Library, University of Michigan.

[7] Stephen Porter, Castleton, March 14, 1831, and Richard Dunning, North Penfield, March 20, 1830, to Miles P. Squier, American Home Missionary Society Papers, Chicago Theological Seminary; Finney, *Autobiography*, 171; *A Narrative of the Revival of Religion . . . in the year 1826* (Utica, 1826), 12, 13; [Orville Dewey], *Letters of an English Traveller to His Friend in England on the "Revival of Religion" in America* (Boston, 1828), 109.

ing; and that is, by resisting the Holy Ghost." All who wished to pray aloud should be called on, the most spiritual first to set the tone for the rest; but fanatics, hypocrites, or persons too inarticulate to impress people of good taste would have to be discouraged. A long hiatus, which might otherwise chill ardor, could be designated as a period of private, silent supplication. Meetings ought not to be too long extended, and should take place in comfortable but not luxurious surroundings, with children and dogs left at home.[8]

There had been women preachers in western New York among Christians, Free Baptists, and Friends from an early date. They had taken an equal part in all meetings among Methodists, at least by 1812. They united only in audible congregational responses in the Episcopal Church but had full liberty among Baptists in all meetings except formal public Sunday services. Even in Presbyterian churches they had apparently long been accustomed to praying aloud in weekday meetings when they felt any urge to do so.[9] This was by no means strange. Women composed the great majority of members in all churches. They dominated revivals and praying circles, pressing husbands, fathers, and sons toward conversion and facilitating every move of the evangelist. One witness believed that "in *all instances,* where they were most active, revivals were most powerful." No evidence has appeared to support the notion that either Charles Finney or Theodore Weld made any bold innovation in allowing feminine prayers in "promiscuous assemblies." No one in Oneida County thought the matter worthy of mention until the practice had to be defended before the shocked New Englanders at New Lebanon.[10]

This eastern opposition probably sprang mainly from Nettleton's hidebound conservatism. Yet a man as keen as Lyman Beecher may have foreseen the extent to which women, once encouraged, might make difficulties for clergymen. They were on the whole

---

[8] Finney, *Revival Lectures,* 95, 117, 124–127, 220 ff.

[9] Peck, *Life,* 29; *Gospel Luminary* (West Bloomfield), II (Aug., 1826), 196, III (June, 1827), 141; *Gospel Advocate* (Auburn), V (June 2, 1827), 175; *Baptist Register* (Utica), II (April 29, 1825), 34, IV (July 20, 1827, Feb. 1, 1828), 83, 194.

[10] Charles Hall, Utica, Dec. 17, 1830, to Absolom Peters, A.H.M.S. MSS; Gilbert H. Barnes, *The Antislavery Impulse, 1830–1844* (New York, 1933), 12, attributes the innovation to Weld. In contrast, note Finney, *Autobiography,* 178.

less educated, more superstitious, and more zealous than the men. Their equal participation in evening meetings introduced potential dangers when those sessions grew excited and prolonged. One contemporary noted that the night watches wherein "*brothers* and *sisters* have *prayed together*" were "signally blessed. . . . Here Christians have been compelled to remain in some instances agonizing in prayer, till almost the break of day. . . ." Finney himself reported to George W. Gale how "Brother Gillet was frightened" in Rome in 1826. "After the meeting some of the young people wrung their hands and fell upon each other's necks. We had to send them home." [11]

The practice of having women praying with men in "small circles" for the conversion of individuals was apparently new in the Western Revival but henceforth widely adopted. John Frost, at first taken aback at the idea, concluded that these very petitions "heard, till the little band of suppliants were bathed in tears around the mercy seat," were the most effective he had ever encountered. One critic of Jedediah Burchard's campaigns believed that the women so engaged under his wife's guidance "found the foibles of a depraved nature were leaving them . . . they were nearly perfect." [12]

Equal participation of women had in itself little to do with the nature of the new measures, but the superior feminine susceptibility provides significant documentation on the nature of the revival impulse. Moreover, the freer reign for exuberant emotionalism which all the measures provided, when fully shared by women, could permit some of the more amazing expressions of ardor to rise out of the temptation to confuse heavenly and earthly love.

The new measures probably made for an increased prevalence of prayer, but the more significant departure was a qualitative one. From the Western Revival on, all devotions in a season of awakening utilized "the new system of particularity." It became an offense against true religion to ask of God any vague request. Each entreaty must be for a precise object, one revealed in the Bible as the will of God. It must be offered from the proper motive—desire for

[11] *Narrative Oneida Revival*, 30; Gale, "Autobiography," 32.
[12] *Western Recorder* (Utica), III (Aug. 15, 1826), 130; [Eaton], *Burchardism*, 14.

the Lord's supreme glory—not for any selfish purpose, and it must be delivered in absolute faith of immediate and direct accomplishment. Congregational prayers had to indicate complete unison of feeling; should the expected result not be forthcoming, failure gave final proof that someone in the assembly had been out of accord. Under such assumptions, prayers became high-leverage presses for enforcing community opinion upon stubbornly impenitent consciences. At the same time, they fortified sympathizers in their confidence of special powers, since the perfect alibi was ready-created for any apparently adverse result.[13]

This "prayer of faith" seems to be traceable—in so far as any of the measures stemmed from individual invention—to Father Nash, who was reputed to practice his powers by praying his horse into an adjacent pasture.[14] It was the prayer of faith which came into constant use to single out unrepentant sinners, to invoke revivals, to castigate indifferent ministers. In utilizing this device, the holy bands earned their notoriety for conducting "private devotions, in a manner so loud and boisterous, as to disturb the inhabitants . . . and arrest the attention of travellers as they passed in the streets." Charles Finney on more than one occasion started the first tremor by analyzing the more orthodox prayers of a shocked assembly, and condemning their "mockery of God." [15] Finney, himself, of course evolved toward more sober practices after the Oneida campaign. His remarkable psychological perception had probably discerned from the first that the prayer of faith did its work within the individual mind. But more literal-minded evangelists apparently attributed the device's power to its influence upon the God above, rather than upon that portion of Deity grown in each human being.

Daniel Nash, at least, believed that "very few . . . know much about praying"; little as he himself confessed to know, he said, "I do not find anybody that knows how to teach me on that subject." He discovered one of his greatest stimuli to "action prayer" in his

---

[13] Finney, *Revival Lectures*, 26, 27, 45–50; Brockway, *Revival in Troy*, 16, 17, 29, 53.

[14] Perkins, *"Bunker Hill" Contest*, 65.

[15] Gamaliel S. Olds and Richard S. Corning, *Review of a Narrative by John Keep* (Syracuse, 1833), 6; Finney, *Autobiography*, 147, 167; Brockway, *Revival in Troy*, 23–25.

views of the Bible prophecies. Just four months before his death, he was checking his interpretation of prophecy in the works of Jonathan Edwards, to find, surprisingly, "that Edwards + I view the subject nearly in the same light." Nash always prayed himself into a fervid state before reading and quite possibly exaggerated the similarity. He may even have been approximating the similar and contemporary researches of William Miller. At any rate, his assurance of a prior claim on God's attention by way of prayer was related to his prophetic urge. The scouring of the Burned-over District by Nash and his closest colleagues undoubtedly served in some measure to pave the way for an extreme sensitivity to the question of a judgment day in 1843.[16]

As thoroughly ingrained in the religion of the past as preaching and praying, pastoral visiting likewise suffered new adaptations for revival usage and became one of the potent measures in evangelistic routine. Whereas the settled pastor had called only on his own flock and enjoyed ordinary sociability during his visits, the itinerant and any minister following his sojourn must visit every house and forego pleasure for constant exhortation. With the aid of the holy bands, the gap between morning devotions and evening meetings was thus usefully occupied. Ordinarily this exercise most affected housewives, as the husbands would be at work, but Finney believed that merchants should be prepared "to lock up there [sic] stores for six months" in aid of a revival. He himself seems seldom if ever to have demanded more than the readiness to do so, but Burchard boasted of closing down every enterprise during his stands. In the visiting routine the prayer of faith found its greatest potency, as minister, assistants, and converted members of the family knelt together about the unregenerate ones and bore home their awful plight. The sick and dying were saved when possible and rendered into horrible examples when beyond rescue. Parents learned their own sin if children were not hourly urged to repentance.[17]

An occasional individual might escape both the house-to-house canvass and the public meeting, but he could scarcely dodge en-

---

16 Daniel Nash, Verona, Nov. 26, 27, 1831, to Finney, Finney MSS.

17 Finney, *Revival Lectures*, 30; Streeter, *Mirror*, 68; *Narrative Oneida Revival*, 16, 26; [Dewey], *Letters on Revival*, 18, 56; William Clark, Cooperstown, Jan. 26, 1830, to Finney, and Sarah Brayton, Western, May 6, 1829, to Mrs. Finney, Finney MSS.

counters on the street or at work. "Christians . . . [were] bound to warn sinners" whether husband, wife, children, partners, or mere acquaintances. The evangelist himself accosted passers-by and warned the impenitent, "You are an enemy to the King," "You are going right to the pit," "There is not a fiend in hell, nor out of hell, so bad as you are." [18] Such measures must have forced many a reluctant soul into silent acquiescence, while among enthusiasts they surely compounded excitement.

All the devices mentioned so far were tools for rousing a community-wide anxiety over the inhabitants' spiritual state. From this intermediate stage, under proper guidance, developed the new conviction which was the evangelist's final goal. Time and usage developed just as effective tools for this later part of the revival process.

Inquiry meetings and anxious seats came as a natural result of efforts at mass conversion. At first, interested persons merely gathered at the end of the service to secure ministerial counsel. Later, separate sessions in a basement room or a private house met concurrently with prayer meetings or in the mid-morning. Finally the "anxious bench" was instituted, on which the seekers gathered in front of the congregation. This evolution can be clearly discerned in Finney's *Autobiography* as such practices rose out of circumstances and grew with experience.

Set apart on the one hand from the regenerate, and on the other from the unconverted, indifferent, and curious, the anxious ones became subjects for unlimited and merciless exhortation. Their pride had been cast off by the act of coming forward. All alike were pleading, abject sinners. All that remained was to become sufficiently penitent for the automatically operant Holy Spirit to descend and signalize the start of the new life. Conveniently, the recently more liberalized Calvinist theology and the Arminian doctrine alike avowed that the individual's expression of a new intent was identical with the miraculous inward change of sudden conversion. Managed by a Finney, such a process might be sober, restrained, and highly impressive. But it could also become a relentless mechanism forcing the person to say he was converted, and to

---

[18] Finney, *Revival Lectures*, 133; William R. Weeks, *The Pilgrim's Progress in the Nineteenth Century* (New York, 1848), 234.

imagine the corresponding inner transformation. With a reputation for wholesale success to be maintained and a community expectation to be met, the ordinary itinerant may have roused more excitement than piety and mistaken the outward sign for the inward change.

A series of less notorious measures varied to fit local conditions and individual habits. All "peculiar and alarming events" could be turned to use. Rumors, dreams, and visions went hand in glove with religious excitement. Fast days focused attention upon sin. Cholera epidemics occasioned special activities. Funeral sermons provided opportunity to draw a moral from errant behavior. Upon clerical suggestion parties gave way to revulsions of guilt. The conversion of a supposedly skeptical schoolmaster might bring about action for a whole body of students. Children might on occasion be drawn from school to pray with the evangelist's wife. More than once some incident opened factory doors while work yielded place to worship. Certain itinerants specialized in a sensational entry, which could be managed by imposing "a gross insult . . . on some individual who enjoyed the public confidence," or by maneuvering to be ejected bodily from the home of a bitter enemy of revivals. Universalist-baiting served the same purpose. One evangelist left town (expecting to be recalled when the measure had taken effect) because a church listened to a returned missionary from Hawaii, who "tickled the ears of a large audience by historical facts and anecdotes . . . upon the Sabbath" when all should have been "distressed for Sinners." [19]

Such devices were deliberately adopted, because experience showed that they worked. Their use does not itself prove that the perpetrators were hypocrites or scoundrels. People had come to expect this kind of thing and rewarded the ingenuity which provided new sensations. All the devices to "get up" a revival were

---

[19] Finney, *Revival Lectures*, 25; *Autobiography*, 166, 183, 206, 292; [Dewey], *Letters on Revival*, 20, 59, 70; *Narrative Oneida Revival*, 14, 20, 33; Streeter, *Mirror*, 10, 67; Sylvester Eaton to Edward Hooker, Feb. 2, 1837, Edward Hooker Collection of Letters on Burchardism, Congregational House Library; Laura Fish, Clinton, Aug. 6, [1826], to Mrs. Finney, and M. Brayton, Western, to Finney, James Boyle, Little Falls, May 12, 1867, to Finney, and M. S. Wright, Rome, Feb. 28, 1828, to Mrs. Finney, Finney MSS; [George Rogers], *Memoranda of the Experience, Labors and Travels of a Universalist Preacher* (n.p., 1846), 105; Perkins, *"Bunker Hill" Contest*, 51.

frankly admitted, accompanied in every case by apparently sincere statements that all came from God. The contradiction did not become apparent to either lay or clerical minds tuned to the evangelistic mood. As Nathaniel Beman succinctly expressed the proposition, "I hope we look to God, but we must have means." [20]

Within the season of awakenings it gradually became habitual to designate a shorter period, at first three or four days but later thirty or more, in which all energies would be especially concentrated. Neighboring ministers gathered for the time, an evangelist came if he was not already on the scene, and often several sects co-operated in the venture. This village counterpart of the camp meeting, called the "protracted meeting," encompassed all the characteristics of the new measures. It came to flourish first in the Burned-over District revivals of 1830, and in the Presbyterian Church, merely because the excitement commenced there and because it proved a convenient vehicle for that particular society. Spread throughout and beyond the region in the two or three years after the Rochester Revival, it became a fixture of the evangelistic sects for at least twenty years.[21]

The protracted meeting may have led church members to an exaggerated dependence upon revivalistic measures, since its operation might "do their work for them." It certainly played up the itinerant to the disadvantage of the settled minister, for it helped establish the notion that special efforts under a person of particular talents would create a keener spirituality than the ordinary course of events could achieve. Its rapid spread after 1830 made many a person echo the thoughts of a Lockport clergyman: "by the by— before the millenium [sic] comes will not Christians hold 365-day-meetings every year? How many such meetings would it require to be held before the world should be converted?" Another enthusiast, proposing a six-man touring team for perpetual sessions in rural regions, thought that "the great State of New York" brought "over on the Lords side . . . would turn the scale and

[20] N. S. S. Beman, Troy, Sept. 23, 1826, to Finney, Finney MSS.

[21] Rev. James H. Hotchkin, *A History of the Purchase and Settlement of Western New York, and of the . . . Presbyterian Church in That Section* (New York, 1848), 163–167; William Mitchell, "An Enquiry into the Utility of Modern Evangelists, and Their Measures," *Literary and Theological Review* (Andover, Mass.), II (Sept., 1835), 498, 499.

convert the world." [22] Concentrated use of all the new techniques familiarized those maneuvers much as modern juke boxes quickly kill a new tune. The revival engineers had to exercise increasing ingenuity to find even more sensational means to replace those worn out by overuse. In all of these ways the protracted meeting, though only a form within which the measures operated, helped the measures themselves grow ever more intense, until the increasing zeal, boiled up inside of orthodoxy, overflowed into heresy.

[22] William R. Weeks, *A Letter on Protracted Meetings,* etc. (Utica, 1832), 7; William F. Curry, Lockport, Feb. 1, 1831, and Moses Hunter, New Lebanon, June 7, 1828, to Finney, Finney MSS.

Chapter 11. NEW MEN

PROTRACTED meetings and the entire system of measures they utilized came after 1830 to depend increasingly upon the services of a traveling clergyman who made a profession of revivals. Charles Finney served as chief immediate example for the type, though precedents for such itineracy might be discovered in the Methodist circuit plan and in the frontier habits of many other sects, and dated both from the Great Revival of 1800 and the Great Awakening sixty years earlier. The touring preacher was as much the product of prevailing religious zeal as its instigator. Like his measures, he assisted the translation of rising enthusiasm into ultraism.

The post-Finney evangelists were as numerous as they are now obscure. The variant behavior of those who can be traced with some success suggests that they comprised an assortment of individualities rather than a type. They did, however, utilize common methods and labor under similar conditions, and a few generalizations can be drawn about the group as a whole.

First of all, whatever their education, these itinerants could scarcely be intellectuals or original thinkers. Their success lay in ability to meet the folk on their own terms and to save souls fundamentally in the manner to which people had become accustomed. Their leadership in reaching toward doctrinal novelties, if indeed it should be called leadership, was of the unintentional, unconscious sort, arising because methods which they found convenient and rendered habitual might require an explanation after the fact. Most of the group had little formal education, since their zeal for saving the world quickly led them into action without even the preparation considered adequate for most settled clergymen. They had less in common with orthodox clerics than with the laymen who so often imposed them upon an established ministry.

With a position especially hallowed in public esteem, the evangelist had something like the prestige of an ex-general in politics. His reputation had been automatically made and traveled ahead of him. He required no pre-eminent abilities or extraordinary saintliness, though the burden of proof rests on those who claim insincerity in any one of the lot. But the temptations and dangers natural to the profession submitted his character to unusually rigorous testing. Worked usually beyond his physical capacity, he was more than other men subject to nervous exhaustion, pneumonia, or tuberculosis. It was "as if Satan had come . . . urging on a good work, but pushing it so hard as to destroy the labourers by overaction." Scarcely one escaped some moment when either his lungs let blood or in some other fashion he approached collapse.[1]

In such an often-weakened condition, he was forever surrounded by flattering admirers and might consequently scarcely escape a degree of overconfidence and self-righteousness. Honored though he was, the curious and intimate society of the rural village scrutinized his every move and mannerism. His wife and family, if he had any, must usually be left behind; yet circumstances threw him constantly with a majority of feminine associates: zealous, excited women who looked to him for spiritual guidance and hovered about him as the immediate representative of that heavenly piety they so thirsted to attain. On occasion such distraught and fawning females attempted to prove their sanctification by intimacies which showered upon the preacher tokens of a love supposedly, but not always completely, cleansed of earthly attributes. John Humphrey Noyes found a rational, scriptural solution for this problem, but at

---

[1] Calvin Colton, *Thoughts on the Religious State of the Country*, etc. (New York, 1836), 40; Charles G. Finney, *Autobiography of Charles Grandison Finney* (New York, 1876), 80; N. S. S. Beman, Troy, Sept. 25, 1826, to Finney, Charles Grandison Finney Papers, Oberlin College Library.

least thirty settled clergymen became its victims within four years.[2] The itinerants, who were no more saintly and faced the condition in a degree highly intensified by revivals, did well to fall from grace as infrequently as they seem to have done.

Certain of the evangelists suffered charges that their motivation lay in promise of fiscal gain. Some did indeed receive larger rewards than stationed pastors. Both Finney and Burchard apparently had reasonably well-established rates which, if they were constantly busy, would net them an annuity handsome for those days. But payment often failed to materialize, and no one seems to have accumulated a fortune. Since most of the crowd probably gained not even a competence at the trade, a depth of genuine zeal is the apparent motivation in almost every case which can be observed.

Some of the Burned-over District revivalists at times secured the support of a specially organized co-operative philanthropy. The Oneida Evangelical Society, later known as the Central Evangelical Association, took form in the Western Revivals. It apparently pooled the receipts of member itinerants with contributions dedicated to the purpose by Utica capitalists and attempted to pay each co-operating preacher a salary of six hundred dollars. Finney may possibly have provided its main funds for several years. Father Nash, Horatio Foote, Jedediah Burchard, Herman Norton, Nathaniel Smith, Augustus Littlejohn, Luther Myrick, and Daniel Nash, Jr., received some aid from it at different times during a period of nearly ten years.[3]

Men who fitted themselves more or less consistently into this mode of life—multitudinous little men, whose insignificance, poverty, roving habits, and shifting careers practically defy analysis —personified and created ultraism. The special labors of a Finney in sanctification, a Weld in abolition, or a Miller in premillennialism cannot adequately be appreciated without realizing the dependence of all three upon each other, and more emphatically upon the veritable host of evangelists who swarmed over Yankeedom, old

---

2 Theodore Weld to Lewis Tappan, Feb. 6, 1844, in G. H. Barnes and D. L. Dumond, eds., *Letters of Theodore Dwight Weld, Angelina Grimké Weld, and Sarah Grimké, 1822–1844* (2 vols.; New York, 1934), II, 994.

3 A. B. Johnson, Utica, Dec. 5, 1826, Oct. 23, 1827, to Finney, Finney MSS; Rev. James H. Hotchkin, *A History of the Purchase and Settlement of Western New York and of the . . . Presbyterian Church in That Section* (New York, 1848), 173.

and new, preaching every shade of gospel, heresy, and reform to a people who for a generation had been saturated with spiritual and moral intensity.

The impulse to eccentricity and radicalism was thus broadly and deeply planted. The few of these men whose careers can be patched together must stand, presumably representative, for all. The effect of the few, however, should be many times multiplied in imagination to approximate the total impact of the profession.

Jedediah Burchard probably ranked next to Charles Finney in the Burned-over District's favor. Like his greater colleague, he came from Connecticut as a child, growing up in central New York. After failing in business at Albany, he retired to Sackets Harbor, studied under direction of George W. Gale at Adams, again like his younger confederate, and attained tentative license in 1822 from the local Congregational Association. After two more years crowded with revivals and some more study, he satisfied the Watertown Presbytery and received ordination as an evangelist. The three succeeding years found him touring from a station at Sackets Harbor and Cape Vincent, with A.H.M.S. support. An intimate of Gale's for several years, he may have provided Finney a model in the use of revivalistic measures. Gale remembered that he had "correct views of the doctrines of the Gospel," and "uncommon tact at reaching the conscience of sinners," though he was inadequately educated and too impulsive to profit from instruction.

After Finney's departure from Oneida County Burchard took a pastorate in Utica, but during the widespread awakenings of 1831 he retired again to the north. A three months' revival at Rome in 1832 brought him back into circulation, and for the next two years he swung westward on a prolonged series of protracted meetings centered upon Homer, Binghamton, Ithaca, Auburn, Rochester, Bergen, and Buffalo. Then he invaded western New England and reached New York City in 1837. Five years later he again appeared at Rochester, operating separately from Charles Finney, who happened to be there at the same time. Since their two paths crossed at no other point, and since Finney often expressed privately, but refused to publish, strictures on Burchard's character, there may be grounds for one contemporary opinion that Finney owed a large and unacknowledged debt to the older man and that

Burchard harbored jealousy on this account. Jedediah finally left the ministry, presumably to improve his financial status, and died at Adams, New York, in 1864.[4]

At one time this accomplished Boanerges enjoyed the full confidence of Oneida Presbytery, but in the thirties either he grew more extreme or they grew more conservative. Charges that he was an alcoholic, a drug fiend, and even an occasional mental case may or may not have been justified, but he was obviously impulsive and shallow. He seems to have planned his methods on the explicit assumption "that not more than one person in twenty could think," and to have made a point of the most exciting measures, stimulating the confusion of multiple prayer and all-night sessions. Clergymen always objected to him, but protest was futile. "Nobody believed that the fire would burn, until it singed them." Innocent alike of either conscious heresy or any coherent doctrine, he greatly enhanced the taste for exhibitionism and helped increase aptitude for emotional exercises.[5]

The man next in influence after Finney, Nash, and Burchard was by contrast a serious if vacillating thinker, apparently adequately educated and genuinely able. James Boyle's career, like that of Orestes Brownson, constitutes a veritable "pilgrim's progress," [6] but in the opposite direction. Born a Catholic in upper Ontario, he became first a Methodist minister and worked five years mainly in western New York, Ohio, Michigan, and Canada. He married Laura Putnam of Rochester in August, 1825, took a Presbyterian A.H.M.S. station at the present village of Watkins

---

[4] P[hilemon] T. Fowler, *Historical Sketch of Presbyterianism . . . of Central New York* (Utica, 1877), 278 ff.; George W. Gale, "Autobiography of George W. Gale," (MS, 1853), II, 29–35, *passim*; William R. Weeks, *The Pilgrim's Progress in the Nineteenth Century* (New York, 1848), 268; the Finney MSS; the Hooker Letters on Burchardism, Congregational House Library; Russell Streeter, *Mirror of Calvinist Fanaticism, or Jedediah Burchard & Co. . . . in Woodstock, Vermont* (2nd ed.; Woodstock, Vt., 1835), 78.

[5] Gamaliel S. Olds and Richard S. Corning, *Review of a Narrative by Rev. John Keep* (Syracuse, 1833), 4; Moses Gillet, Rome, Feb. 21, 1832, to Finney, Finney MSS; James Richards, Auburn, Feb. 20, 1836, to Hooker, Hooker MSS; C. G. Eastman, ed., *Sermons, Addresses & Exhortations, by Rev. Jedediah Burchard*, etc. (Burlington, Vt., 1836).

[6] Arthur M. Schlesinger, Jr., *Orestes A. Brownson: A Pilgrim's Progress* (Boston, 1939).

Glen early the next year, became an evangelist with Oneida Presbytery in 1827, and then returned to the Watkins Glen station, again on Missionary Society funds, for three more years. He first made himself known to Charles Finney in April, 1827, but it cannot be conclusively demonstrated that the two ever met, despite a considerable correspondence. The summer before Finney's visit to Rochester, Boyle removed to Marion, Newark, and Palmyra, just east of the Genesee town, commencing to hold large revivals before Finney's started. From a base here shared with Daniel Nash, Boyle occupied the next two years touring the Genesee country southward as far as the Cohocton Valley. His favorite son he named for Theodore Weld, and his intimacy with Nash and the Weld brothers seems to have been far greater than with Finney.[7]

The winter of 1832 took him to New England and, at John Humphrey Noyes's instigation, to the Free Church pastorate in New Haven a year later. There Lewis Tappan heard him and wished to move him to New York. During 1834 Noyes and Boyle trod the heretic's path together and the next spring began publishing the first *Perfectionist*. But within a few months the two parted company, Noyes initiating matrimonial theories which Boyle disliked, and Boyle drifting toward the sentiments of Theophilus Gates, the Philadelphia "Battle-Axe," who had contributed to the paper. By the spring of 1836, Boyle had renounced holiness and taken employment in a Newark, New Jersey, machine shop. Two years later he turned up in Cincinnati corresponding with William Lloyd Garrison and for three more years seems to have been an agent for the Ohio Antislavery Society. In 1842 he lectured in New England on socialism and soon joined the Northampton Fourierist community. Later yet he interested himself in Swedenborgianism and became an associate of Professor George Bush and Andrew Jackson Davis in faith-healing enterprises in New York City.[8]

---

[7] Notation from *Rochester Telegraph*, Aug. 23, 1825, card index to Rochester newspapers, City Historian's Office; six letters in Finney MSS, 1827–1831; James Boyle, Havanna, Aug. 22, 1826, Veteran, April 27, 1828, Nov. 23, 1829, Marion, Nov. 6, 1830, Newark, Feb. 21, 1831, and Elders, Church of Veteran, Jan. 24, 1829, Richard Dunning, N. Penfield, July 1, 1830, to Miles P. Squier, American Home Missionary Society Papers, Chicago Theological Seminary.

[8] George W. Noyes, ed., *Religious Experience of John Humphrey Noyes, Founder*

Innocently and sincerely seeking a finer spirituality within orthodoxy by the use of revival techniques, Boyle undoubtedly carried to more logical conclusions the prayer of faith and the prophetic urge of his closest mentor, Father Nash. In engineering protracted meetings he may have encouraged belief in special communion with God, tending toward the antinomian perfectionism he so soon espoused. Upon his departure from the village of Cohocton, one Mrs. Conn took up his mantle, to emerge in 1837 a full-fledged prophetess. Banished from her home community, she migrated to Wyoming County and gathered a few followers before her disappearance into oblivion. Boyle also seems to have been acquainted with several leaders of what soon came to be perfectionist cults scattered through the Finger Lakes region, groups which drifted in time into John Humphrey Noyes's Oneida Community.[9]

James Boyle provides a sample of itinerant character which by chance illustrates at different stages a number of the alternative outgrowths of ultraism, only one or two of which would be pursued in the majority of lifetimes. Luther Myrick similarly shows several successive turns the revival-born impulse might follow. He may have been a convert in the Western Revivals but upon his first ministerial appearance in Oneida County, in February, 1827, seems to have been a stranger to Charles Finney. Oneida Presbytery soon ordained him as an evangelist, and after some touring in that area he took a pastorate at Warren, near Lake Champlain, during the year 1829. The next year he returned to a station at Verona and later seems to have been settled at Jamesville, Manlius, and Cazenovia. At all times, he appears to have traveled about considerably in the vicinity of his charges, so that between 1830 and 1834 he covered quite systematically an area reaching from Cayuga Lake to the Black River Valley. Oneida Presbytery tried and discharged him in the latter year. After an unsuccessful attempt to gain admittance to the Black River Congregational Association, he

---

of Oneida Community (New York, 1923), 59, 116, 155, 253; Lewis Tappan, New York, June 9, July 10, 1833, to Finney, Finney MSS; *Union Herald* (Cazenovia), VI (June 3, 1841), 22; John H. Noyes, *History of American Socialisms* (Philadelphia, 1870), 277, 537–550.

9 Noyes, *Religious Experience*, 189–192, 209, 210.

organized his own unrecognized, competing society. This in turn became the skeleton of his project for a Union church two years later.[10]

Though Myrick trespassed on his limited acquaintance with Finney and sought defense from him in trouble, his closest association was with Father Nash. More than any other single man he seems to have been Nash's heir. It was at Verona, in Myrick's care, that the old man died; and there Daniel, Junior, undertook clerical training in the local church. This extremist had also a degree of intimacy with a small group excommunicated in Albany in 1830, some of whose members similarly influenced John Noyes in New Haven. Likewise, he joined with Burchard, Augustus Littlejohn, and the Baptist Elder Knapp in several supremely sensational revival campaigns. It was one of these in Oswego which converted Gerrit Smith's eccentric brother Peter, and the evangelist thenceforward maintained close affiliation with the wealthy landlord of Peterboro.[11]

Myrick apparently from the first went all out for enthusiasm. In 1827, one of his fellow clergymen, returning to a prayer meeting at eleven in the evening, "found the house in great confusion, some exhorting sinners, some on the floor making . . . distressing noises. While others were praying very *loud* all over the room at the same time." It went on until two o'clock. Perhaps thirty congregations in Onondaga, Cayuga, Cortland, Madison and Oneida counties suffered quarrels and schisms during the early thirties as a result of his incipient perfectionism, spreading contagiously in the region.[12] From the same area came the bulk of the membership

---

10 Samuel Moss, Augusta, Feb. 13, 1827, George W. Gale, Whitesboro, March 11, 1827, to Finney, Finney MSS; Luther Myrick, Warren, Sept. 2, 1830, to Absolom Peters, A.H.M.S. MSS; *New York Evangelist,* V (July 12, 1834), 110.

11 Luther Myrick, Verona, Jan. 20, 1832, Jamesville, Sept. 3, 1832, Jan. 10, 1833, Manlius, July 15, 27, Sept. 19, Oct. 4, 1833, Lenox, Oct. 1, 1834, to Finney, George Spaulding, Daniel Nash, D. C. Lansing, J. Hopkins and J. Spencer to Finney, 1827–1833, Finney MSS; Ralph V. Harlow, *Gerrit Smith, Philanthropist and Reformer* (New York, 1939), 54; Myrick to Smith, Sept. 28, 1836, Jan. 30, May 12, 1841, Gerrit Smith Papers, Syracuse University Library.

12 George Spaulding, Augusta, Feb. 16, 1827, to Finney, Finney MSS; Hotchkin, *Western New York, passim;* reports to American Home Missionary Society from Chittenango, Cicero, Cincinnatus, De Ruyter, East Genoa, Florence, Norwich, Oneida, and South Onondaga, 1832–1835, A.H.M.S. MSS.

of Oneida Community as well as numerous Adventists to answer Father Miller's call in 1843.

Like Boyle, Myrick gives evidence of some intelligence. He claimed, perhaps correctly, that he represented the early measures and beliefs of Charles Finney from which others were backsliding. He took in advance of his claimed mentor two steps to which the greater man was eventually led: he departed the Presbyterian Church in the Congregational direction, and he espoused a brand of perfectionist doctrine. Thus Myrick could qualify as leader rather than follower of Finney. Apparently a really strong personality, he led a number of the area's clergymen through his management of the Oneida Evangelical Association. Developing from his perfectionist phase in the mid-thirties, he carried his followers into antislavery agitation and finally to his eventual position that radicals of all sects belonged together in one sinless church.[13]

Far slighter in stature than Boyle and Myrick was an eccentric, ignorant itinerant named Augustus Littlejohn. A native of Haight, Allegany County, as a young unskilled laborer he improved his gift of eloquence for the entertainment of fellow workers. He practiced as a local exhorter for several years before the older ministers of Angelica Presbytery yielded to popular pressure and licensed him as an evangelist in 1829. Thereupon he promptly headed for the richer field of Oneida County, where he circulated for three or four years. Observers were amazed at the success of this "feeble instrument," and found their faith enhanced when "not by might nor power; but by the spirit of the Lord sinners are brought to submit." Working with Myrick and Knapp in central New York, Littlejohn probably acquired techniques to carry back to his home area. Returning late in 1833, for eight succeeding years he toured fairly continuously over the region west of the Genesee River, at times in team with a fellow worker named Samuel W. May. The clergy seemed constantly skeptical of his utility, but "Such was the current of feeling . . . that nothing would satisfy but for Messrs. Littlejohn and May to come." [14]

---

13 See later, pp. 279 ff.

14 Rev. James A. Miller, *The History of the Presbytery of Steuben*, etc. (Angelica, 1897), 15 ff.; M. Brayton, Utica, Nov. 18, Dec. 16, 1829, to Finney, B. N. Johnson, Rome, April 13, 1830, William Clark, Cooperstown, April 25, 1831, Oneonta, Dec.

Increasingly bitter complaints from neighboring presbyteries drifted to the Angelica organization during the late thirties, but Littlejohn's own group was so impressed with his labors as to elect him moderator. Before long his wife began to voice her discontent, and "common fame" amassed charges against him. Finally clerical efforts to hush rumors and avoid the disillusionment of his fall completely failed. His trial, dragging through the early months of 1841, produced sworn testimony from the victims and their families which established five different cases of attempted or successful seduction within three years. The testimony is sufficiently descriptive to show how the unusual position of an evangelist in popular esteem permitted one "under the pretence of uncommon sanctity . . . to accomplish his base designs." The woman in each case was "called into his room, to brush his hair" or "bathe his head with camphor." In this holy intimacy he confessed "he did not believe his wife to be a woman," "laid his hand upon her private parts, proposed to examine her . . . [and if resisted] told her that she had sinned against the Holy Ghost, or words to that effect." [15]

A man of Littlejohn's caliber could hardly engineer important doctrinal departures, but his unregulated zeal did attract crowds and raise the general level of excitement. Miscellaneous "laxness . . . fanaticism and . . . irregularities" may well have followed in his train. [16]

Horatio Foote, alone of the more notable itinerants of the period, might with some accuracy be called a Finney apostle, but not a convert, since he had been preaching at Kingston, Ontario, before Finney's own conversion. He accompanied the leader, however, during the Oneida and Troy campaigns, along with Father Nash, substituted for them on occasion, and supplemented their efforts on independent circuits in the two neighborhoods. In 1829 he took a station at Champlain, New York, where he remained for eight years, making extensive tours at least two of which were prolonged excursions into western New England. [17]

14, 1833, to Finney, and Cynthia Brayton, Western, Jan. 15, 1830, to Mrs. Finney, Finney MSS; Abel Caldwell, Hunt's Hollow, June 14, 1834, to Miles P. Squier, A.H.M.S. MSS.

15 MS records of Angelica Presbytery, 360, 363, 367, and *passim*.

16 Hotchkin, *Western New York*, 171, 172.

17 Finney, *Autobiography*, 204; "Memorandum on Foote," Hooker MSS; M. Bray-

The quality of his letters confirms an accusation that the reputed power of his sermons stemmed from his extensive borrowing from Finney. He may have had connections with the Albany perfectionist cult and helped to spread their notions both to his temporary neighbor Myrick and to Massachusetts. In any case, he attracted throngs and built a considerable reputation. His career in these parts ended in 1837, when his presbytery renounced him after he seduced a girl taken into his home to rear.[18] He fled westward and apparently re-established himself, as he appears in presbytery reports as late as 1854.

Among the men who worked with Finney in the Western Revivals and continued to circulate in this region were Nathaniel Smith and Herman Norton. Smith seems to have been an illogical and superficial individual, operating from Madison County to the St. Lawrence Valley for two years after 1828.[19] Norton cut a larger figure: a Hamilton College graduate, with a popularity nearly equal to Finney's in the opening campaigns, he soon filled one of the Tappans' Free Church pulpits in New York. Later, after a sojourn in Ohio, he became in 1843 secretary of the nativist American Protestant Society.[20]

A man who seems never to have been closely allied with the Oberlin evangelist, but who corresponded with and borrowed sermon skeletons from him, was Edward Kirk. He toured fairly extensively from his station at Albany, holding great revivals in Jefferson County in 1834 and in Boston in 1842. He also ran an evangelists' training school for a time, which bred the Albany perfectionists.[21] Another itinerant, Charles Stuart, long a pious man and one of the original influences upon the abolitionist expression of the evangelical movement, was captivated by the Finney

---

ton, Abby Bullock, H. B. Pierrepont, Horatio Foote (3) to Finney, Finney MSS, 1827–1832; *New York Evangelist*, II (Oct. 8, 1831), 318, IV (July 27, 1833), 129.

[18] P. Bailey, Hebron, May 10, 1843, to Hooker, Hooker MSS.

[19] N. S. Smith, Utica, March 25, 1828, Morrisville, Dec. 10, 1830, and Daniel Nash, Denmark, March 12, 1830, to Finney, Finney MSS.

[20] Barnes and Dumond, *Weld-Grimké Letters*, I, 18, note 9; H. Norton and Mrs. Norton, Whitesboro, April 30, 1827, G. W. Gale, Whitesboro, Sept. 6, 8, 1827, Samuel Moss, Augusta, Feb. 6, 1827, to Finney, Finney MSS.

[21] Zebulon R. Shipherd, Albany, Dec. 24, 1827, E. N. Kirk, Albany, Nov. 23, 1830, to Finney, Finney MSS; Theodore Weld to Finney, March 2, [1831?], in Barnes and Dumond, *Weld-Grimké Letters*, I, 40, 41.

personality and himself undertook a few tours in Oneida County after Finney's departure.[22]

One more man of Presbyterian origins whose importance can only be guessed from imperfect fragments of information demands mention. Charles H. Weld, Theodore's older brother, graduated from Yale in 1822 and from Andover four years later. He became a licensed evangelist under Oneida Presbytery in 1828 and two years later traveled for the Bible Society in Mississippi. Some kind of breakdown followed, for the early thirties found him recuperating at his father's home in Apulia, New York. During this interval he espoused perfectionism and made some acquaintance with several of the cults in central New York. He may well, as he claimed, have "exercised a paternal supervision over Finney, Boyle, Lansing, his brother Theodore, and others." More certainly he assisted John Noyes, both in evolving his own doctrines and in cultivating the New York groups of similar inclinations.[23]

Although the sensational evangelism of the period rose and developed primarily in the Presbyterian Church, it rapidly crossed denominational lines. The greatest Baptist itinerant frankly admitted his indebtedness to the Presbyterians before him and worked with some of them in his first campaigns. Jacob Knapp was ordained in September, 1824, after graduation from Hamilton Seminary, where his commencement oration had been entitled "On the Advent of the Messiah." Stationed first in Otsego County and later at Watertown, where he farmed to help support himself, he commenced his itineracy in 1832 and continued to gravitate throughout the Burned-over District for about seven years. During the forties his fame spread farther afield, whereupon he followed it. Like Finney, but more persistently, he made himself an urban evangelist in his middle years, visiting Rochester, Syracuse, Baltimore, Boston, Washington, and other cities. No more pleasing to the regular ministry of his church than were the Presbyterian

---

[22] Charles Stuart, New York, Aug. 7, 1828, to Theodore Weld, Theodore Dwight Weld Papers, William L. Clements Library, University of Michigan; Sarah Brayton, Rome, Feb., 1828, to Mrs. Finney, Finney MSS.

[23] Noyes, *Religious Experience*, 126, 127, 133; Charles Stuart to Weld, Aug. 5, 1834, in Barnes and Dumond, *Weld-Grimké Letters*, I, 164; Cornelius and Ludovicus Weld [and Mrs. Weld, unsigned], Apulia, Sept. 2, 1822, to Theodore Weld, Weld MSS; Charles Weld, Hallowell, Me., April 9, 1829, to Finney, Finney MSS.

itinerants to theirs, his relations with the dignitaries of Hamilton where he made his home through the late thirties were constantly unpleasant. An investigation of his finances by a local committee about 1843 totally cleared him of guilt, according to his own report, but he immediately left the region to continue his career in Illinois.[24]

Knapp's ideas and practices cannot be differentiated from those of his Presbyterian colleagues. He believed certain men had "peculiar unction," which if inadequately utilized would let "the mass . . . soon be drowned in perdition." He also held that "the Evangelist may sometimes be compelled to violate ecclesiastical order and ministerial courtesy," since "courtesy would require him to honor the unfaithful at the expense of souls." The greatest preaching he ever heard came from the lips of a Presbyterian minister crazed by revival engineering, at the times when he bordered "on the verge of insanity." [25]

Such samples of the itineracy demonstrate its complex nature, as well as the intensity of revival religion as it mounted to a climax in the Burned-over District. Itinerants symbolized, incited, and directed the roused emotions of the day. The institution was furthermore a model ready for adaptation to the crusades which would follow from ultraism. In fact, most of the individual evangelists themselves dispersed into the various consequent movements.

---

[24] *Baptist Register* (Utica), I (June 11, Sept. 10, 1824), 135, 239; Jacob Knapp, *Autobiography of Elder Jacob Knapp,* etc. (New York, 1868), xi, xx–xxiii, 25–94, *passim;* Jacob Knapp, Rochester, March 27, 1839, to William Colgate, Samuel Colgate Memorial Baptist Library, Colgate University.

[25] Jacob Knapp, "Evangelism," *The Evangelical Harp . . . Designed for Revivals of Religion,* etc. (Utica, 1845), 195, 197, 199; Knapp, *Autobiography,* 77.

Chapter 12. NEW IDEAS

THE new measures and new men of the early thirties helped to propagate increasingly radical religious beliefs, doctrines which were the essence of ultraism. These intellectual attitudes controlled the enthusiastic activities of the thirties, dictated collapse and alteration at the end of the decade, and likewise predetermined the character of operations in the forties. Careful analysis of these ideas becomes therefore the primary necessity for an understanding of Burned-over District history.

The ultraist state of mind rose from an implicit, even occasionally an explicit, reliance upon the direct guidance of the Holy Ghost. Traditional orthodoxy fostered the belief by attributing revival conversions to this supernatural agency. The aim of the most circumspect clergyman was *"to be rightly impressed with the importance of doing all we can, + at the same time to feel that we are nothing + that all must be done by the word + Spirit of God. . . ."* [1] Conservatives in the region championed extemporaneous preaching on similar grounds. The pastor delivering an unprepared sermon was guided "by the Spirit's energy" to speak "the truth in the demonstration of its might." [2]

Inspiration, of course, could easily be confused with thoroughly human impulses, but it provided the perfect rationalization to

---

[1] Moses Gillet, Rome, Oct. 26, 1829, to Charles G. Finney, Charles Grandison Finney Papers, Oberlin College Library.

[2] *Baptist Register* (Utica), III (June 23, 1826), 67.

explain any given course of action. One reliable witness believed that if "the idea of anything extraordinary and preternatural" were removed from revival phenomena, "three quarters of that which supports them in the public mind would be taken away also." [3] The established ministers dared not attempt the correction of irregularities lest they serve "the purpose of the adversary of souls to spoil every good thing." [4] Even in more sophisticated minds which shunned the outright miracle, the same assumption of divine purpose could in more subtle fashion be made to justify whatever action one might choose to take. Charles Finney, for instance, believed "no doctrine . . . more dangerous" than that revivals were miraculous, but perceived an inner as well as an outer revelation, which "God had made in each human soul." Working internally, "the spirit has power to arouse the conscience and make it pierce like an arrow. . . ." [5]

This basic assumption of direct divine interposition in individual concerns gave peculiar energy and direction to other assumptions held by religious radicals in common with the rest of their contemporaries. The dogma of American democracy, vigorously rising in Jacksonian days, contained a supreme optimism, a belief in the ultimate perfection of society through progressive improvement in humankind. Church folk shared this conviction in a qualified form. They believed progress to be attainable by human effort and practically inevitable; but they derived from their Calvinist traditions an equally powerful suspicion that the natural tendency, unaided by willful diligence, was toward degeneracy. [6]

The tried methods of the past had failed to move man very far toward Utopia, so new kinds of energy must be applied to the enterprise. Still, truth was a fixed, permanent entity which all minds must, by their very nature, understand whenever it should be properly presented. Hence, the energies spent on attaining perfection should be applied primarily not to arouse direct action but

---

[3] [Orville Dewey], *Letters of an English Traveller to His Friend in England on the "Revival of Religion" in America* (Boston, 1828), 30.

[4] *Western Recorder* (Utica), VIII (July 5, 1831), 105.

[5] Charles G. Finney, *Lectures on Revivals of Religion* (2nd ed.; New York, 1835), 12; *Sermons on Gospel Themes* (delivered 1845 ff., Oberlin, O., 1876), 231–244, 252.

[6] Ralph V. Harlow, *Gerrit Smith, Philanthropist and Reformer* (New York, 1939), 100 ff.; *Oberlin Evangelist*, V (Aug. 2, 1843), 126.

to create "the mild and safe influence of a reformed and enlightened public sentiment."[7] "Convince a man [that] what you propose is really good, make his mind perceive that it is truly desirable, and you enlist all his powers to accomplish it." This reliance on man's reasonableness was a part, too, of the general faith of the era. But whereas some persons of skeptical leanings had begun to discover "an army of appetites and passions which overwhelm the reason . . . and carry it away captive,"[8] religious folk inclined to believe that only man's deliberate perversity stood in his way. The answer to perversity, of course, was regeneration.

The conversion of masses of individuals was proceeding so rapidly by 1830, moreover, that it became easy for the moment to overlook or minimize the great obstacles which his sinful original nature placed in man's path toward perfection; easy to believe also that the willful kind of perversity which made some men refuse to follow truth even when it had been clarified for them must soon be extinguished by advancing revivalism. Orthodox Protestantism had long been developing a strong millennial tone. The degree to which society in the United States had become homogeneously Christian (evangelical Protestant) helped to fulfill the Bible prophecy of premillennial unanimity of belief. Removal of ignorance and delusion by the progress of the benevolent movements in the last fifteen years enhanced the sense of consummation. Finally, the increasing number and magnitude of revivals heightened interest in the Second Coming, while they themselves fed on this same nourishing concern.

Some people thought as early as 1825 that the millennium was approaching. Four years later, the most conservative reckoning placed its advent at between fifty and two hundred years' distance. The phenomenal awakening of 1831 convinced multitudes the day must be quite near. John Noyes long remembered that year, how his "heart was fixed on the millennium, and I resolved to live or die for it." In retrospect he believed that "in 1831, the whole orthodox church was in a state of ebullition . . . [having] a fit of

---

7 *New York Evangelist*, V (Jan. 4, 1834), 2.
8 *Gospel Advocate* (Auburn), VII (Jan. 24, 1829), 17–20.

expectation as enthusiastic and almost as fanatical as the Millerites." [9]

People closer to the center of the excitement became even more attuned to great expectations. A Miss Seely at Oswego waited in January, 1831, momentarily expecting "to hear the cry *'Behold the bridegroom cometh.'*" In the same month the *Baptist Register* stated, "The sky, to mere mortal vision, never looked more dark and terrific; but to the eye of faith, the lustre of millennial glory beams behind the darkness. Messiah is travelling in . . . the storm. . . ." [10]

Such concern continued to grow, at least in some quarters, as fervent revivalism ran its course through the decade. The prophetic gifts of old Father Nash and his disciples accorded perfectly with the views of those laymen who were properly aroused. By 1837 it had become habitual for Christians to interpret "everything that deeply engages public attention" as a symbol of "Messiah's kingdom." [11] Even though refusing to accept the details of William Miller's calculations, the more enthusiastic segments of orthodoxy in 1841 were "laying out our plans upon this basis: THE MILLENNIUM IS AT HAND." [12]

Just what would happen at the Advent, and whether the thousand years' heaven on earth would precede or follow judgment day, were by no means universally agreed, but all varieties of the belief lent a severely pressing urgency to the inspired campaigns carried on in the Lord's name. Radical in divergence from orthodox doctrine on account of its assumed guidance by the Holy Ghost, ultraism was also radical in the sense of haste to accomplish great changes, because it was the harbinger of the millennium.

What manner of minds were these which could fuse the disparate concepts of original sin and human perfectibility; which had such high confidence that a special Providence motivated their each and every act; which contemplated an all-powerful God Who had long since appointed the judgment day and yet felt themselves pressed

---

[9] John H. Noyes, *Confessions of John H. Noyes,* etc. (Oneida Reserve, 1849), 2; *Spiritual Magazine* (Oneida), II (Aug. 5, 1848), 193.

[10] J. T. Marshall, Oswego, Jan. 6, 1831, to Finney, Finney MSS; *Baptist Register,* VII (Jan. 7, 1831), 182.

[11] *Baptist Register,* XIV (June 23, 1837), 74.

[12] *Oberlin Evangelist,* III (June 23, 1841), 101.

to assist Him in bringing it to pass; which accomplished all these marvels practically without conscious intellectual effort and believed all these conclusions to be self-evident, without need of apology?

The minority of western New Yorkers who indulged in isms apparently ranged far from the bottom of the scale in schooling as well as in social standing, but seldom did any of the religious radicals exhibit profound understanding or trespass upon the threshold of critical thought. For the most part they accepted the leadership of the itinerant evangelists, men of their own class and order of talents, without superior intellect or learning. Theological training, in fact, might be more a liability than an asset to such persons, for revivalism tended quite definitely to substitute emotion for reason and enthusiasm for knowledge. The ultraist party wanted the notion "that religious impressions are unfavorable to the progress of study . . . forever to be discarded," so there might be *"constant* revivals" in the schools. Charles Finney, most intellectually inclined of all the evangelists, thought it "all a farce to suppose that a literary ministry can convert the world"; "a *Holy* ministry . . . would be far more important." Many would have agreed that "success in saving souls is evidence that a man understands the gospel, and . . . that he has common sense. . . . This requires great wisdom. And the minister who does it, shows that he is wise." [13]

Assuredly it was an uncritical generation which so defined wisdom. Most people, like Gerrit Smith, probably "fell easily and thoughtlessly into the common modes of religious terminology . . . as a matter of course." [14] Loving excitement and action, they flocked to any standard which promised progress and somewhat suspected the genuineness of their fervor if they failed to become absorbed heart and soul in the undertaking. They lacked, in the view of one seasoned observer, *"discriminative judgment,* and . . . that *common sense,* which may be defined, as *the right application of general principles to particular causes."* They looked "at part of a subject, not at the whole, or . . . as isolated, and not in its

---

[13] *Western Recorder,* VIII (May 10, 1831), 75; Charles G. Finney, *Lectures to Professing Christians* (New York, 1837), 106, and *Revival Lectures,* 109, 170, 172.

[14] Harlow, *Smith,* 193.

multiform relations, in its immediate effects, not in its remote consequences." Adopting a correct principle, they rode it to excess, and applied it to all cases without exception.[15] At times, persons acknowledged insane were even sought after for leadership into higher inspiration. Minds of considerable stability in other respects seem to have sought good results from measures repugnant to their tastes and to have taken the means to be sacred upon the first appearance of superficial benefits.

Balanced judgment these folk seemed entirely to lack. Yet in their circumstances little else could be expected. Cause and effect in their eyes related to each other only by way of a supernatural connection, seldom short-circuited by any sense of coherence through the natural laws of the physical universe. Truth was an abstraction and religion a "paroxysm" detached from daily life. Conviction superseded knowledge and logic developed from the axioms of conviction rather than from observation of fact. Generalizations made themselves up from fragments, quickly and simply, without any considerable perspective. No evolutionary concept suggested growth by gradual stages. Expediency, a respectable word to moderns accustomed to weighing probabilities, was then disreputable. It carried a strong connotation of lack of principle and could be viewed by the righteous only with disdainful horror. Yet the religious-minded of the day conformed with others in a disposal to experiment with innovations and indeed considered it a virtual necessity "to receive the rays of truth from every quarter . . . changing our views and language and practice as often and as fast, as we can obtain further information." [16]

When cosmic and insignificant events alike appeared to occur spontaneously without precedent or earthly causation, sensitive people must have lived in an atmosphere of constant provocation. Should one be steadfast in faith and feel secure in his salvation, he must with joyous zeal prepare to observe and understand God's every unforeseen handiwork, while he outwardly demonstrated his sanctity by sympathetic behavior. Such motivation could drive a

---

15 [Leonard Woods, Jr., ed.], "On Radicalism," *Literary and Theological Review* (New York), II (Sept., 1837), 523.

16 Charles G. Finney, *Lectures on Systematic Theology* (James H. Fairchild, ed., Oberlin, O., 1878, copyright 1846), xii.

person to energetic affirmations of very extreme positions. In such a frame of mind, for instance, Mary Cragin reported to John Noyes her spouse's conversion to his doctrine: "My dear husband one week since, entered the kingdom. . . . Bless the Lord, on the first of December he will be without money and without business. How this rejoices me. We shall stand still and see the Lord provide." [17]

But perhaps an even stronger motivation, and certainly the more common one, came from the opposite kind of provocation. The great majority of enthusiasts, no matter how frequent their rededication or how nearly secure they might feel about their own destination, preserved at least some remnant of the Puritan doctrine of imperfect sanctification. The ultraist professors underwent "great heart-searchings" continually. Many were the chronicles "of doubt and fear and dread, of struggling with my own convictions and the frequent triumphs of my own depraved nature." Theodore Weld characteristically reported to Finney his "slow headway beating up against the wind and tide of my wicked heart," and asked of Finney himself, "Are you digging your way *deeper* and *deeper* into the dust?" In fact, the more "spiritual Christians" had the greater battle with Satan, who knew their vast injury to himself and tempted them as they had never been tempted before regeneration.[18] Even the staunch and stolid soul who could assume his own sanctity, without either incitement to zealous action or neurotic introspection, gathered incentive to labor for a cause from the common conviction that his own destiny, with that of the world, depended upon human labor to fulfill Heavenly designs.

Motivated thus from all sides to intensive activity, convinced of the immediate urgency of all they did because of the dawning millennium, and favored only with rootless mentalities, the ultraists in their perpetual excitement were bound to become victims of caprice. The slightest coincidental zephyr might shift a person

---

[17] Mary E. Cragin, New York, Nov. 22, 1839, to Noyes, in *Witness* (Putney, Vt.), I (Jan. 3, 1840), 11.

[18] *A Narrative of the Revival of Religion . . . in the Year 1826* (Utica, 1826), 38; Diaries of John L. Lewis, Jr., VI, March 30, 1836, MS at Penn Yan Public Library; Theodore Weld to Charles Finney, April 22, 1828, G. H. Barnes and D. L. Dumond, eds., *Letters of Theodore Dwight Weld, Angelina Grimké Weld, and Sarah Grimké, 1822–1844* (2 vols.; New York, 1934), I, 14 ff.; Finney, *Revival Lectures,* 107.

from one tack of thought to another, changing his particular concentrated interest to a wholly new course in a moment.

Turn as they might from one crusade to another, however, most
revivalists and reformers of similar mind were consistent in one
thing: they ground only one axe at a time. Their whole set of
attitudes conspired to make them feel that some one cause constituted the single path, the great panacea, for man's forward march.
Their immediate aim, change as it might from time to time, was
always an exclusive one, narrowing progressively with increased
concentration.[19]

Such a fervent, unregulated disposition, loosed for action, became perhaps more often unpleasant than delightful to behold.
The man who trusted in his own commission as the Creator's agent
could have little tolerance for variant opinion. "For why should
a good man stop, who knows certainly that he is right exactly, and
that all men are wrong in proportion as they differ from him?"
He made a profession of asserting his superiority, either directly
by brother-keeping or in less agreeable fashion by "instilling into
the minds of others a persuasion of . . . [his] pre-eminent goodness" by "rebuking all manner of wrong" in feigned humility. He
expected to be regarded as eccentric and considered the world's
bludgeons a badge of honor.[20]

With the world to save and time short, the indifferent, cautious,
or merely less than supremely zealous person seemed to the ultraist
a very poor specimen of humanity. Indeed, he appeared to be a
more obnoxious and deliberate sinner than the outright offender
who probably knew less of what was right. There was "no neutral
ground" where the Christian could "plant his foot." Reluctance
or hesitation on one score, moreover, the radical understood to
be a generic, not a specific, attitude. Opposition to antislavery agitation, for instance, was "wickedness . . . marshalling its forces
against *all* pure, thoroughgoing + radical reform, + therefore
against *each specific instance* of such reform. . . ." Charles Finney

---

[19] William B. Sprague, *Religious Ultraism* (Albany, 1835), 7, 28; Harlow, *Smith*,
72; Ezekiel Bacon, *Recollections of Fifty Years Since* (Utica, 1843), 27–30.

[20] *Letters of the Rev. Dr. Beecher and Rev. Mr. Nettleton, on the New Measures
in Conducting Revivals of Religion* (New York, 1828), 93; [Woods], "Radicalism,"
532; Finney, *Revival Lectures*, 104, 105.

put the proposition in equally definite words: "The individual who will indulge in any one sin, does not abstain from any sin because it is sin." [21] This reasoning, which could transform into a strong Satanic resemblance any thoughtful, considerate individual, however pious, indicates the high conceit of the enthusiast in passing judgment on his fellow men. It also suggests why ultraist endeavors were destined to diminish in breadth of appeal the farther they advanced.

Another characteristic of the radical religious mind perhaps exerted a still greater limitation. An inherent paradox inhabited the center of ultraism. Inspiration came to individuals, and each person charted his own course. Disregarding any established authority or institution, ultraists concerned themselves with single souls, their own and others', their standards of piety and morality absolutely fixed by personal holiness. But their objectives—rooting out sin, converting the world, and bringing forth the millennium —could be approached only by concerted energies. Organization must be the watchword of reform. An organization demanded some conventionality of standard, some conformity of inspiration.

In fact if not in theory, what strength the various ultraist associations gathered unto themselves originated substantially in that "excessive regard to opinion," which Harriet Martineau labeled "the great fault in American morals." Within minority communities of zealots there existed a rivalry in attaining saintliness according to a radical formula; and in parts of the Burned-over District at frequent intervals the *"esprit du corps* of a great religious excitement" produced "the force of example . . . the power of habit . . . the pride of consistency" to hasten large numbers of people together along a single course of extremism.[22] But the farther along the path the crowd went, the more it suffered the disorganizing influence of the discordant individual inspirations which inevitably accompanied rising enthusiasm.

Utraism induced distinctive concepts of polity and sociology as

---

21 *Western Recorder,* VI (April 28, 1829), 66; Amos Phelps, Buffalo, Oct. 2, 1835, to Gerrit Smith, Gerrit Smith Papers, Syracuse University Library; Finney, *Lectures to Christians,* 137.

22 Harriet Martineau, *Society in America* (3 vols.; London, 1837), III, 256; [Dewey], *Letters on Revival,* 121; Sprague, *Ultraism,* 16.

well as a cosmology and a personality. Though unconverted man would of his own accord degenerate in sinfulness, God in His bounty had granted government to enforce the moral law: government adapted to man's improving condition. Monarchy was a primitive form, democracy an advanced one, and anarchy the ultimate, to come with the millennium. The great superiority of American democracy over earlier political systems constituted indeed one of the heralds of an early Advent. Democracy's equality of right and opportunity symbolized the common level of all men before the judgment seat and foreshadowed the finer justice of millenarian anarchism.

But the good fortunes of Americans came as an unmerited token of Heavenly favor, not as a reward for virtue attained. Continuance and increase of such bliss depended upon the preservation of the moral law and the advancement of religion. Even the American was yet a weakling, sustained only by the church. Thus ultraists could justify proposing a Christian Party in politics, and take upon themselves as converted men full responsibility for dictating to lesser fellow beings, in a fashion which to skeptical folk might seem the very perversion of democracy.

Exactly because men remained so feeble in morality and intellect (as the entire sequence of nonreligious events often seemed to demonstrate), God had fortified His political philanthropies with another great gift. He had shown His earthly agents how man's enervated, excitable state could be utilized to fulfill His prophecies quickly. The revival fervor was unfortunately still somewhat spasmodic; but as the end of time approached it would become perpetual, reducing the unregenerate to nought and keeping the saved under constant re-examination and conversion as a safeguard against backsliding.[23]

His preoccupation with sin served the ultraist for a sociology. Worldly concepts of morality could often be satisfied with partial moves and less than perfect aims; so the most utterly circumspect goodness of the skeptic entitled him to no consideration in heaven.

---

[23] Sprague, *Ultraism*, 5; Finney, *Systematic Theology*, 222 ff.; Robert S. Fletcher, *A History of Oberlin College . . . through the Civil War* (2 vols.; Oberlin, O., 1943), II, 732; [Dewey], *Letters on Revival*, 133; Finney, *Gospel Themes*, 250, 251, and *Revival Lectures*, 9–11, 251, 262.

Sin had a different scale of measurement. Since any deviation, however slight, might lead to greater ones, since wrong was a specific quality, regardless of quantity, and since an offense against the infinite good automatically became itself infinite, any departure whatsoever from divine rule constituted an absolutely enormous crime. In case of any question, the saint must shun the doubtful act; if he failed to reprove others' faults, their guilt became his also.[24]

Once any item of social behavior came to be classified as a sin, it thus lay open to the complete operation of the most radical conceptions. It was the function of Burned-over District ultraism to expand the category of sin far beyond its accustomed limits.

Ultraism was, it seems, a thoroughly remarkable phenomenon. It came very close, in fact, to being an impossible state of mind. Its existence could be only momentary, for its nature prohibited concerted and prolonged agreement by any considerable group of persons. It could be achieved only at the exact climax of religious zeal, before inherent discords loosed the fervor it contained into a multitude of various channels. But its short life in the middle-thirties encompassed numerous manifestations and was the precedent condition to all the ensuing crusades.

---

[24] Harlow, *Smith*, 90; [Dewey], *Letters on Revival*, 123 ff.; Finney, *Lectures to Christians*, 29–37, 44, 57–62, 138.

BOOK V

Harvest: 1830-1845

There is nothing to which the minds of good men, when once passed the bounds of sound discretion, and launched on the ocean of feeling and experiment, may not come . . . nothing so terrible and unmanageable as the fire and whirlwind of human passion, when once kindled by misguided zeal. . . . For, in every church, there is wood, hay, and stubble which will be sure to take fire on the wrong side. . . . New-England of the West shall be burnt over . . . as in some parts of New-England it was done 80 years ago.—LYMAN BEECHER TO NATHANIEL BEMAN, Letters of Beecher and Nettleton (1828), 96–98

Chapter 13. A MORAL REFORMATION

THE temperance movement was larger in every dimension than Burned-over District ultraism. It began much earlier and has not yet ended. During the 1830's it attained national scope in far more genuine manner than did most other reforms of the day, while in western New York alone it commanded support grounded on a range of motives extending well beyond the field of radical religion. Yet in the one decade the larger crusade yielded to the more limited phenomenon and for the time assumed the style of ultraism. At this stage, and for this very reason, the suppression of alcoholic beverages became a more vital and exclusive concern with its proponents than at any other time. During the same moment, also, the campaign both gained its widest following in upstate New York and accepted a larger proportion of direction and management from that region than from any other. And having imbibed the ultraist draught, the temperance movement, like its companion radicalisms, suffered the morning-after consequences.

The prolonged affiliation between temperance and revival religion which preceded their final union in the Rochester awakening of 1831 had already made drunkenness a severe obstacle to a Christian reputation. During the next few years the growing enthusiasm altered the prevalent attitude in two ways: use of intoxicants became a sin instead of a mere departure from decency and expediency, and the existence of intemperance in American society came to be considered the major hindrance to that revival of spirituality which was to introduce the early millennium. The one consideration made the regenerate soul fear for himself, lest in some ill-considered ramification of daily living he participate indirectly in evil. On the second score, would-be saints felt an intensified concern for the habits of the unregenerate, lest God abandon or postpone the Advent. These two co-ordinate propositions drove their advocates to fantastically absolute views.[1]

Wine, beer, and cider, moderately used, did not intoxicate and had until now not been included in the pledge. But temperance societies which devoted monthly meetings to discussing whether anything could restrain "the depravity of man, except the sanctions of the Holy Scriptures," must needs take a different stand. Some men failed to partake moderately of these lighter beverages, and he who did "anything whereby thy brother stumbleth" [2] was culpable. Further, if alcohol was a specifically sinful compound, the slighter quantity could not change the fundamental nature. The most trifling departure from righteousness would be infinite on judgment day and in the meantime would encourage progressively wider deviations into error. By the same reasoning, if alcohol was evil because it frustrated the Lord's design for the human body, other drugs like tea, coffee, and tobacco must be equally wrong.

Well might the true saint ask of one less rigorously logical, "Do you drink wine, yet, my dear Sir? And has it not hurt you, + our cause? To stop the mouth of our Enemies, + for my own good, I left off using Tobacco nearly a year ago, after chewing between 45 + 50 years." Josiah Bissell, the Pioneer Line ultraist, had even before the 1831 revival "got beyond Temperance to the Cold Water Society—no Tea, Coffee or any other slops." Charles Finney, though never himself the most radical of reformers, complained that "five times" as much money went for these various intemperances as "for every effort to save the world." He and many others agreed with the New York Evangelist that such devotion to principle constituted "a triumph of conscience over the lower desires" and expected to see "revivals follow in the train of every great strug-

---

1 *Temperance Manual for 1836*, 9, and *Temperance Recorder*, March 6, 1832, quoted by John A. Krout, *The Origins of Prohibition* (New York, 1925), 114, 115, 119.

2 *Rochester Daily Advertiser*, Dec. 31, 1832; Charles G. Finney, *Lectures to Professing Christians* (New York, 1837), 29.

gle by which conscience gains a triumph over passion, and truth becomes ascendant." [3]

The ultraist might himself never touch even wine, except at Communion, and yet sin because he manufactured or sold liquors, rented to a grog shop, or marketed his crops without knowing their destination. Western New York farmers soon learned "the immorality of furnishing grain," grapes, and apples for the liquor trade. One might err again by trading with a store, inn, or canal line, or by attending public occasions which encouraged debauchery. One should reprove associates who came "under the influence." Women particularly could exert their virtuous powers by refusing the attentions of men who proved to be less than circumspect. [4]

These radical prohibitionist concepts spread through the Burned-over District speedily during the early thirties, and just after the middle of the decade they captured the national temperance organization also. Itinerant preachers utilized the various sins of intemperance as excuses for protracted meetings, and lecturers who centered upon social rather than religious reform utilized the same techniques with much the same ideological content. From both camps came leaders and followers who increasingly focused on the alcoholic question as the greatest, if not the single vital one of the day. Losing sight of others, they magnified this one objective until it assumed in their minds exclusive proportions.

For the time, ultraist temperance campaigning produced results commensurate with the zeal devoted to it. Arthur Tappan's conditional philanthropy hastened Presbyterian churches into line: he offered congregations under A.H.M.S. supervision twenty-five dollars each, up to a thousand-dollar total, for adopting "the temperance principle in the admission of persons to the communion," and similar amounts to congregations which in addition "made the use, traffic, or manufacture of ardent spirits . . . a

---

[3] Ebenezer Watson, Albany, Aug. 8, 1835, and Joseph Speed, Caroline, Jan. 25, 1832, to Gerrit Smith, Gerrit Smith Papers, Syracuse University Library; Bissell to Smith, April 28, 1830, quoted by Ralph V. Harlow, *Gerrit Smith, Philanthropist and Reformer* (New York, 1939), 72; Charles G. Finney, *Lectures on Revivals of Religion* (2nd ed., New York, 1835), 386; *New York Evangelist*, V (Jan. 11, 1834), 6.

[4] Krout, *Prohibition*, 116, 132, 145 ff., 215; Finney, *Lectures to Christians*, 37; Isaac K. Brownson, Fenner, March 24, 1834, to Gerrit Smith, Gerrit Smith MSS.

subject of discipline." At least three townships under the eye of A.H.M.S. pastors drove all manufacturers and handlers of liquor beyond their limits. Presumably many churches, like the one in Naples, passed strong resolutions against intemperance, promising to exert "all our influence to restrain others from a habit so pernicious." More slowly and in more moderate fashion on the whole, the Methodist conferences and Baptist associations took similar action.[5]

Propaganda for the cause flourished. The New York State Temperance Society, whose affiliates predominated in the Yankee counties of the western area, printed twelve million copies of tracts and periodicals by 1838, selling enough of them to make more than two-thirds of its expenses. The religious, literary, and agricultural journals co-operated, and more than one of them probably showed the true ultraist spirit by denying the presentation of divergent opinions. On moral questions only the "right" ought to be published. At least one grand jury added to the religious motivation of the campaign by blaming most of the cases on its docket to the evil fluid. The cholera epidemic of 1832 also furnished a capital argument, both on grounds of health and as a Heavenly visitation upon sinful communities. In a few localities attempts were made to elect boards of excise or trustees which would refuse to license dealers. By 1833 the state society could boast over 700 affiliates (50 per cent of the groups in the country), 12 signers of the pledge for every 100 citizens, 1200 nonalcoholic stores, and the closing of 133 out of 292 distilleries which had operated in 1830.[6]

Ultraists were so sanguine that their figures are justly suspect. It also seems quite possible, as opponents charged, that the reduced

[5] Arthur Tappan, New York, Jan. 2, 1832 (unaddressed), Hiram Smith, Marcellus, April 1, 1833, James H. Hotchkin, Wheeler, July 8, 1833. and Isaac Flagler, Chapinsville, Feb. 1, 1834, to regional Secretarys Crane and Squier, American Home Missionary Society Papers, Chicago Theological Seminary; entry for Jan. 20, 1830, "Record Book of Naples Presbyterian Church, 1815–1837," MS at Ontario County Historical Society; *Zion's Watchman* (New York), I (Nov. 2, 1836), 44; *Minutes of the Twenty-Second Anniversary of the Madison Baptist Association*, etc. (Utica, 1830), 9.

[6] Krout, *Prohibition*, 225, 232; *Rochester Daily Advertiser*, Dec. 10, 1831; *Rochester Observer*, VI (Feb. 22, 1832), 8; Lyman Manley, Ontario, March 22, 1834 (unaddressed), A.H.M.S. MSS; John A. Krout, "The Genesis and Development of the Early Temperance Movement in New York State," *New York State Historical Association Quarterly Journal*, IV (April, 1923), 91.

consumption of alcohol had been accomplished mainly by the abstinence of the already temperate, while hard drinkers, driven to stealthy habits, increased their consumption. One A.H.M.S. report almost suggested as much, noting that the local association had been effective "in reforming many *Temperate* families + . . . is already exerting an influence on some of the intemperate." [7]

Even allowing for such reservations, however, the record indicates a thoroughly creditable, even a remarkable, accomplishment, once validity of the purpose is granted. Ultraism, working upon properly conditioned people, could definitely achieve results. No doubt the superior success of local New York and New England groups working on radical principles contributed to the adoption by the American Temperance Union of the teetotalist pledge. After 1836, instead of "total abstinence from intoxicating beverages," the platform read, "total abstinence from all that can intoxicate." [8]

But however successful it seemed in the mid-thirties, ultraist temperance was not destined to endure. The panic of 1837 hit the fortunes of its great philanthropists; and the ensuing depression, by puncturing the easy optimism of the preceding years, helped to introduce different methods of procedure. More serious, in all probability, were the multiplying challenges to the increasing radicalism of the reformers. Need honestly temperate men who aided the cause with money and influence but liked their beer and wine, be excommunicated as unregenerate sinners? Could the purpose be accomplished in any case without legal prohibition? If not, how could proper Christians preserve the purity of their aims in the turmoil of party politics? Should women join and participate in men's societies? Must churches press this item of reform so consistently as to interfere with accustomed religious interests? Only small groups could preserve unanimity on these fundamental issues, and within three or four years of its peak, evangelistic temperance had disintegrated into a variety of factional quarrels.

The teetotalist pledge of 1836 alienated approximately 40 per cent of the state membership, many of them wealthy supporters. The remainder continued to argue the merits of that step more fervently than they pushed the crusade. In addition, many leaders

---

[7] John C. Morgan, Naples, Oct. 10, 1828, to Miles P. Squier, A.H.M.S. MSS.

[8] *Permanent Temperance Documents,* II, 25, quoted by Krout, *Prohibition,* 156.

bred to "one-ideaism" in temperance had now gone over to other reforms. Again, by 1838 most of the societies had turned to petitioning the legislature and, except for the brief flurry of Washingtonianism in the early forties, political action became the prevailing custom in the following decades. Some men had so adequately identified this one cause with their religious belief that it seemed the height of piety "to procure legislative help to finish up the . . . reformation." But many found political action inconsistent with their faith, and others feared with some justice that the one idea would become confused and compromised when it entered politics.[9]

The greatest divider seems to have been the argument over Communion wine. In true ultraist fashion the radicals attempted to reach the logical end, the absolute truth, of their position. Having declared that "all use of spirits is sin," they had for consistency's sake to condemn the alcoholic beverage of the Eucharist. The reformers' attempted dictation to the churches naturally roused resentment. Worse yet, the principle violated Scripture itself! The *New York Evangelist* sponsored the change, and the Free Baptists in 1841 adopted a denominational resolution against wine, but regular Baptists and most Presbyterians, even including Lewis Tappan, were shocked at this contradiction of the Bible. Those who, like Gerrit Smith, argued that, since they knew more about the evils of alcohol than did Jesus, they would sin in following His practice, had set foot on the road to skepticism. One of the sanest observers of the period thought no one could tell how far temperance might have advanced "had not the ultraism on the wine question, and the impious invasion of the eucharist produced lamentable discords"[10] which could never be resolved.

The Burned-over District's interest in temperance had been so deeply imbedded in the thirties that the area continued a degree

---

[9] Krout, *Prohibition*, 160–163, 169–175; Seth M. Gates, LeRoy, Aug. 28, 1839, to Gerrit Smith, Gerrit Smith MSS.

[10] [Leonard Woods, Jr., ed.], "On Radicalism," *Literary and Theological Review* (New York), II (Sept., 1837), 524; *New York Evangelist*, VI (Aug. 22, 1835), 224; *Minutes of the General Conference of the Freewill Baptist Connection*, etc. (Dover, N.H., 1859), 187; William B. Sprague, Albany, May 14, 1842, to Samuel Miller, Samuel Miller Papers, Princeton University Library; *Baptist Register* (Utica), XVI (Dec. 13, 1839), 174; Harlow, *Smith*, 78; *Baptist Register*, XVII (March 13, 1840), 18.

of leadership in the legal experiments of the forties and fifties. After 1840, however, the subject ceased to be a religious issue.

Like the temperance reform, the antislavery movement permeated broad segments and areas in American society, and persisted from pre-Revolutionary times until the thirteenth amendment accomplished its objective. But the intensified demand for immediate emancipation, which drove North and South apart and prepared them to come to blows, arose in the 1830's as a manifestation of religious ultraism. This demand could scarcely be called dangerous until it entered politics in the following decade, but the religious phase created its strength, sharpened sectional hostility, and pushed the issue into the political arena. The Burned-over District seized leadership in the abolition crusade, and the consequent influence of this region upon the enlarged antislavery agitation of the forties and fifties and upon the Civil War itself, constitutes the most important single contribution of western New York's enthusiastic mood to the main currents of national history.

Intent upon the eradication of evil and launched in radical ways, Burned-over District folk could be expected to join zealously in any campaign against sin, wherein a victory might launch the millennium. Their particular function would be not to give birth to an idea, but to invigorate it upon importation. The notion of presenting the slavery question in this guise grew gradually from several practically independent inspirations which seem to have reached the section almost simultaneously from the outside.

The first issue of William Lloyd Garrison's *Liberator* arrived at the office of the *Rochester Observer* before January 13, 1831, during Finney's revival. By March the Rochester paper reflected sympathy with the Boston publication. Presumably, the inflammatory journal had been sent also to the other reform magazines of the region. Within the same year, William Goodell introduced Benjamin Lundy to Gerrit Smith for consultation on the "important objects of his present tour in this state." Goodell himself, soon to become a leading agitator in the Utica neighborhood, had known Lundy intimately for four years. Captain Charles Stuart had probably been an immediate emancipationist for some time, although whether he was on this question a disciple of Lundy and Garrison or had the idea before he knew them, is a moot point. In any case, in 1829 he left this country for nearly five years. The Tappan brothers and their associates in New York City had long been concerned about slavery but shifted to immediatism in 1831. William Goodell believed in retrospect that Garrison and the Tappan brothers should divide credit for the origin of "The Antislavery Impulse." [11]

Lundy, Garrison, George Bourne, and William Goodell had traceable roots in the earlier native antislavery movement. Probably the stronger influence on the New York philanthropists came from the example of contemporaneous British debates on emancipation in the West Indies, expressed no doubt through these same men, but probably more persuasively by Stuart, through his spokesman, Theodore Weld. Captain Stuart, a retired British officer, had been supporting Weld at Hamilton College before the Oneida Revival. The older man was a school principal and Bible agent; the younger, a devout descendant from several generations of New England divines, who had toured the South on religious lecture missions in the early twenties. Their piety is attested by their daily sunrise "heart meeting," in which each prayed for the other. Both were accomplished religious "activists" before 1826, at a time when Finney himself had shown no such tendency. But both luxuriated in new conversions under his guidance and gained new methods and novel heights of moral tension from the experience.[12]

After Stuart's departure to join in the emancipation struggle of his home country, he continued to correspond with Weld, sending him the current British antislavery literature. Theodore meanwhile transferred from Hamilton to the more devout atmosphere

---

11 Robert S. Fletcher, *A History of Oberlin College . . . through the Civil War* (2 vols.; Oberlin, O., 1943), I, 143; William Goodell, New York, Nov. 24, 1831, and Elliot Cresson, London, Aug. 15, 1831, to Gerrit Smith, Gerrit Smith MSS; Gilbert H. Barnes, *The Antislavery Impulse, 1830–1844* (New York, 1933), 33 ff.; *Christian Investigator* (Honeoye), II (Feb., 1844), 2.

12 Charles Stuart, Clinton, May 10, 1825, New York, Nov. 16, Dec. 7, 1825, Jan. 10, 1826, to Theodore Weld, the Theodore Dwight Weld Papers, W. L. Clements Library, University of Michigan; G. H. Barnes and D. L. Dumond, eds., *Letters of Theodore Dwight Weld, Angelina Grimké Weld, and Sarah Grimké, 1822–1844* (2 vols.; New York, 1934), I, xix–xxv, 5, 7, 9; Charles G. Finney, *Autobiography of Charles Grandison Finney* (New York, 1876), 184–188; Charles Beecher, ed., *Autobiography, Correspondence, etc. of Lyman Beecher, D.D.* (2 vols.; New York, 1863), II, 310–314.

of Oneida Institute and during vacations lectured far and wide upon temperance and manual labor schools. His personal loyalties came under test in this period, since he was pressed by Stuart not to interrupt his studies, by Gale to help raise funds for the institute, and by Finney to assist in the Rochester Revival. Finney's claim upon him proved the weakest of the three.[13] As time went on, moreover, despite an intense admiration for his "Dear Father in Christ," Weld found himself at odds with Finney on point after point. He named his first son for Charles Stuart. One acquainted with the extravagantly pious language of the day cannot but be inclined to minimize the meaning of his reverential words to Finney as indications of a primary attachment, and to minimize likewise the significance of his reconversion by the great itinerant. His behavior changed little in direct consequence. If he must be labeled a disciple, Charles Stuart was the man to whom he bore virtually exclusive apostleship.

With Henry B. Stanton and other Oneida men, Theodore removed in 1833 to Lane Seminary in Cincinnati, the better to shake the great valley of the West for Christian purposes, at a time when Finney thought the key to the West lay in New York. But before going he attended the discussion called by the Tappans to prepare for a national antislavery society on the principle of immediate emancipation. He became one of the first four agents of the American Antislavery Society upon its foundation, converted the Lane "rebels" to the cause, lectured during the next two years in the Middle West on the sin of slavery, and selected, coached and dispatched the seventy itinerants who during 1836 and 1837 brought the ultraist phase of abolition to its climax.[14]

The famous seventy—"he-goat men . . . butting everything in the line of their march" and "made up of vinegar, aqua fortis, and oil of vitriol, with brimstone, saltpetre and charcoal, to explode and scatter the corrosive matter"—[15] were almost certainly the

---

[13] Barnes and Dumond, *Weld-Grimké Letters*, I, 22; M. Brayton, Utica, Nov. 12, 1830, Daniel Nash, Palmyra, Jan. 22, April 1, 1831, George W. Gale, Whitesboro, Dec. 3, 16, 1830, to Charles G. Finney, Laura Boyle, Palmyra, June 11, 1831, to Mrs. Finney, Charles Grandison Finney Papers, Oberlin College Library.

[14] Barnes, *Antislavery Impulse, passim*.

[15] Lyman Beecher, Lane Seminary, July 15, 1835, to William Beecher, Beecher, *Autobiography*, II, 345.

major concerted force in the abolition crusade, but their most sensational results occurred in regions like western New England, the Ohio Western Reserve, and the Burned-over District, where ultraism already flourished and where spontaneous feeling on the subject of slavery had been developing in more spasmodic fashion ever since the inception of immediatism in 1831.

The issue received considerable attention about Utica in 1833. The next year a correspondent could assure Absolom Peters that knowledge in that neighborhood of collusion in slavery by A.H.M.S. representatives in Missouri "will be disastrous on your funds." The *Rochester Observer,* in the meantime, wished Garrison success with his third year of publication. Several local societies were functioning at least a year before the national organization put any men in the field. The Tappan crowd, advised by Weld and Elizur Wright, were even then pressed beyond their own will in getting the crusade under way. Wright confessed that his "plan was, not to start the National Car till we had got our team *harnessed*. But Garrison and the New Englanders prevailed . . . and now we are trying to 'tackle' while it is in motion." Beriah Green, converted first by Garrison and second by Weld, assumed leadership of Oneida Institute the next year and failed to become one of the first agents only because he was already "carrying away the religious influence of that region." [16]

Charles Stuart, returning from England in 1834, toured northern and western New York late in the year for the national society, with evident success. On repeating his circuit the next year, he began working on Gerrit Smith, until then a staunch colonizationist. Chiding him for calling the Lane rebels "boys," he wrote, "Perhaps you may some day experience the glorious grasp of their intellect . . . + rejoice in the holy fire of their hearts." Smith's difficulty was "substituting" his own "idea of what the Saints *ought to be,* for what *it is!*" The executive committee in New York realized how the upstate was turning its way, hunted for more agents to canvass the section, and urged Weld to abandon the West for this mo-

---

16 L. H. Noss, Utica, Oct. 14, 1834, to Absolom Peters, A.H.M.S. MSS; *Rochester Observer,* VII (Jan. 12, 1833), 2; Elizur Wright, Brooklyn, Sept. 19, 1834, to Beriah Green, Elizur Wright, New York, March 3, 1834, to Anson Phelps, Elizur Wright Papers, Library of Congress; Fletcher, *Oberlin,* I, 144, 174.

ment, in which "a great effort . . . will give us the moral power of the State." [17]

By the time Weld consented to come East, indeed, at least 200 local auxiliaries had formed in New York, while the Genesee Congregational Consociation, the Holland Purchase and Genesee Baptist Associations, the state Freewill Baptist Convention, and possibly other religious groups had gone on record to label slavery a sin.[18] The *Emancipator* from New York, the *Rights of Man* from Rochester, the *American Citizen* from Warsaw, the *Friend of Man* from Utica, devoted exclusively to the one idea; and the *New York Evangelist,* the *Union Herald* of Cazenovia, and *Zion's Watchman* from New York strongly oriented in this direction; all these had commenced agitation in the Burned-over District before the middle of 1836, when Weld's own campaign in the region began to produce heightened results.

The most dramatic episode before the master abolitionist's own tour and before the appointment of most of the seventy disciples was probably the Utica Convention of October, 1835, called by Alvan Stewart, and endorsed by leading men scattered over the upstate region. Six hundred representatives came to found the first and ever most active state society. Mobbed in the city, the meeting adjourned to Peterboro, where Gerrit Smith, even more tender on the right to discuss radical issues than upon the possible sin of slavery, finally capitulated to immediatism.[19]

Nor was Smith unique in his reaction. Neighboring farmers, "being greatly excited against the mobites," volunteered their wagons to transport the exiled delegates to their rural retreat. Charles Stuart believed "the agricultural population, that is, the heart and nerve of People" needed only information to join up; [20] but even

---

[17] Charles Stuart to Theodore Weld, Aug. 5, 1834, Jan. 20, 1835, Barnes and Dumond, *Weld-Grimke Letters,* I, 165, 200; Charles Stuart, New York, Jan. 20, May 7, 1835, to Gerrit Smith, Gerrit Smith MSS; Elizur Wright to Theodore Weld, Nov. 5, 1835, Barnes and Dumond, *Weld-Grimké Letters,* I, 241.

[18] Fletcher, *Oberlin,* I, 143; *Minutes, Freewill Baptist Conference,* 123; *New York Evangelist,* V (Aug. 2, 1834), 122, VI (Oct. 17, 1835), 259; *Minutes of the Tenth Session of the Genesee Baptist Association,* etc. (Batavia, 1834), 8; *Minutes of the Nineteenth Anniversary of the Holland Purchase Baptist Association,* etc. (Buffalo, 1834), 7.

[19] Harlow, *Smith,* 116–121; *Baptist Register,* XI (Jan. 16, May 1, 1835), 42, 190 ff.

[20] James Birney to Charles Hammond, Nov. 14, 1835, Charles Stuart to James

in the cotton-manufacturing city it is more than likely that the mob provided the first basis for broad popular approval of abolition. Upon the question of abridging freedom of speech, assembly, and petition, ultraist reformers gained strength from fusion with the basic impulses of democratic society.

Theodore Weld, assuredly "one of the most astonishing men of the age," spent the spring and summer of 1836 earning in Burned-over District cities his reputation as the "most mobbed man in the United States." In Utica and Rochester, both already citadels of ultraism, he made great conquests; but no city proved in future years as strong in abolition sentiment as rural areas. The "thousands" who flocked to pledge their belief that bondage constituted a sin immediately to be wiped out probably in the main gathered to the standard rather because of agrarian sympathy with the difficult urban campaign, than because of direct conversion by the great abolitionist. Weld's succession of sieges in the main-line towns was probably the most effective single attack on the region, but the rural impulse was broader and deeper than the shadow of a single man, whatever his stature. Its growth came as well from the labors of the seventy, some of whom had learned some of their lessons at other schools than Weld's.

The earliest leaders in the region hailed largely from the same Presbyterian groups which had dominated in previous isms. Although some few Baptist Associations and most Free Baptists had espoused the cause at the start, the bulk of the other sects had until 1836 failed to catch fire from the new blaze. To broaden this religious crusade and make secure its foundations, someone must prove its interdenominational scope, and neither Weld nor those of the seventy connected with Lane Seminary could perform the task. In fact, a considerable shift of sectarian support took place in the middle thirties. Although New England Congregationalists shunned radicalism, the Plan of Union churches of New York had to revert to their original Congregational affiliation to escape the growing conservatism of the Presbyterians. At the same time, agitation begun in the dissenting churches of New England moved westward to center in the Baptist and Methodist groups of western New York.

Birney, Feb., 1836, Dwight L. Dumond, ed., *Letters of James Gillespie Birney, 1831–1857* (2 vols.; New York, 1938), I, 271, 361.

Orson Murray, Orange Scott, LaRoy Sunderland, and George Storrs, who had received their schooling from Garrison but deserted him when he abandoned orthodox religion, became members of Weld's seventy. With some help from others they had built by the end of 1835 a strong sentiment in the Methodist and Baptist communions of hill-country New England. Early the next year Storrs and Sunderland started *Zion's Watchman* in New York City and, with Orange Scott and Luther Lee, a native central New Yorker, commenced periodic tours through the Burned-over District. Mainly upon the support of this region the paper's circulation rose in four years to become the largest among Methodist journals. From an extremely solid conservatism in 1836, when no New Yorker voted for abolitionist resolves in the General Conference and the state convention required that no elder be elected until pledged "to refrain from agitating the church" over slavery, the Methodists had a considerable distance to travel; and the ultraist type of religion-inspired abolition reached its climax in this church only in the mid-forties, some time after the earlier converts had changed their style of attack.[21]

The development of the agitation among Baptists cannot be so clearly discerned, but seems similar. Local congregations and district associations had large degrees of independence; as has been seen, some of them early and zealously hoisted the abolition banner. Baptist churches could often be obtained for meetings when both Presbyterian and Methodist excluded antislavery lecturers. Elon Galusha, one of the leading clergymen in the western section, was preaching the sin of slavery before the national agents took the field. But the *Baptist Register* and the influential core of the church's state councils at Hamilton Seminary solidly and consistently resisted the tendency to make the issue a churchly concern, and this stand gained more than fragmentary support even in the more agitated western associations. As late as 1841, the *Register* could

---

[21] David M. Ludlum, *Social Ferment in Vermont, 1791–1850* (New York, 1939), 156–163; Lucius C. Matlack, *The Antislavery Struggle and Triumph in the Methodist Church* (New York, 1881), 85–98; *The History of American Slavery and Methodism, from 1780 to 1849*, etc. (New York, 1849), 98–105; *Zion's Watchman*, I (Nov. 9, 1836), 178, V (March 14, Sept. 12, 1840), 42, 147; Charles B. Swaney, *Episcopal Methodism and Slavery*, etc. (Boston, 1926), 49, 59, 76–87; *Friend of Man* (Utica), I (July 28, 1836), 22.

warn against holding an antislavery convention with the August anniversary sessions at Hamilton. "Let the decrepitude of the Oneida Institute, and the heresy which reigns in Oberlin, bid them beware how they seek to make our own Seminary a school for reformers." [22]

Yet the tide rose. Elon Galusha called an interdenominational convention at Warsaw in February, 1841, to resolve against slaveholding churches. At this convention Galusha and other westerners with the support of Jacob Knapp prevailed on the question of a denominational meeting that August. Claiming a majority of churches and ministers in the state, the Baptist abolitionists were conceded by Presbyterians to be "taking the lead in the anti-slavery enterprise." The convention adopted a totally ultraist position, condemned the *Baptist Register* and all others who acknowledged evil without taking action, and concluded that "the abolition cause . . . must prevail before the halcyon day of millenial [sic] glory can dawn upon the world." [23] For at least four more years, the common folk of the denomination continued to augment the increasing horde of immediatists.

But however long the ultraist mood was prolonged by the cultural lag of some groups, it carried the seeds of its own destruction in abolition as in temperance. The height of fervor, whenever the various segments of the movement attained it, could never last more than a year or two. After 1837 the disintegration of this phase of antislavery agitation proceeded rapidly. What more could be done, after all, by religious enthusiasm than to record a mass conviction of the sinfulness of slavery and urge its remedy at the earliest moment? One could, and many did, renounce the United States government, criticize its constitution, or break its laws by stealing and transporting slaves to freedom. But such methods raised resentment in South and North alike and only made emancipation more difficult, while few in any case had a taste for a radicalism as extreme

---

[22] *Zion's Watchman*, II (March 11, 1837), 37; Mary B. Putnam, *The Baptists and Slavery, 1840–1845* (Ann Arbor, Mich., 1913), 24, 30, 31; *Baptist Register*, II (Nov. 4, 1825), 145, X (Oct. 11, 1833), 134, XI (Sept. 11, 1835), 119, XVIII (July 30, 1841), 97, XIX (Dec. 30, 1842), 186; *Minutes of the Seventh Anniversary of the Monroe Baptist Association* (Rochester, 1834), 7.

[23] *Friend of Man*, VI (Nov. 9, 1841), 7; *Baptist Register*, XVIII (July 9, Aug. 27, Sept. 3, 1841), 86, 114, 118.

in action as so many admired in words. One could, and many did, denounce affiliation in any form with the evil institution, to save himself from collusion in sin. But such a course would hew great clefts in religious organizations and disrupt the revivalism which foretold millennial glory.

The majority, of course, moved by way of the petition campaign to interrogation of candidates and thence to party organization; but Weld himself and many followers could not accept "organizations . . . for the removal of *single* FORMS of *wrong*" which "leave untouched the *principle* from which they spring." The Garrisonian school felt that association with a sinful government was worse than the distant location of the original evil. Charles Finney, though he avidly preached the sin of slavery, had from the start tried to persuade Weld and his agents to subordinate abolition to revivalism, thereby earning the secret suspicion of the more zealous one-idea men. "If every preacher . . . were to take the course he does, when would there be time . . . for sounding the trumpet of jubilee? . . . you must not . . . sound a note, lest the noise should disturb the meditations of anxious sinners!" In Finney's view, outright denunciation of slavery in exclusive fashion would only "roll a wave of blood over the land." [24]

Among such differences of opinion the spirit of united religious enthusiasm of the mid-thirties disappeared. During the early forties, while religious sentiment among common folk still rose, the leadership of the movement floundered through a period of re-organization, to emerge in the middle of the decade with the political crusade which led to Civil War. Paradoxically, the eastern Garrisonians, who had early departed orthodoxy and championed emancipation as an exclusive cause, drifted away from the notion of direct action into an extreme sin-consciousness, refused to interest themselves in party politics, and dissipated their reforming zeal in a host of only distantly associated objectives. But the evangelicals, who had first seen the cause as one step toward the millennium and had gathered their intensity from revivalism, evolved toward

---

[24] Weld to Lewis Tappan, May 2, 1844, Barnes and Dumond, *Weld-Grimké Letters*, II, 1005; Elizur Wright, New York, March 7, 1835, to Beriah Green, Wright MSS; a very similar letter, Lewis Tappan to Finney, Dec. 24, 1843, Lewis Tappan Papers, Library of Congress; Finney to Weld, in Barnes, *Antislavery Impulse*, 162.

direct action on the one issue alone, by whatever political methods were required to achieve it.

The hang-over which followed the affiliation of antislavery with religious enthusiasm seemed for a time to destroy the movement, but beneath the surface manifestations the impulse strongly survived. No other section of the country would throughout the years before the Civil War prove to be so thoroughly and constantly sensitive to antislavery agitations. As the major issue of the century, furthermore, this crusade attracted more attention than others, and left more abundant traces to be scrutinized. It provides the most adequate test of the geographical distribution of religious fervor in western New York.

Political indexes must be used cautiously, for more abolitionists voted for the "Conscience" Whigs and "Barnburner" Democrats during the early forties than for the Liberty Party, while Gerrit Smith's land distributions may have artificially stimulated third-party polls in a few counties. But a combination of political and religious indications can be considered broadly reliable. Maps based on these factors clearly demonstrate that such enthusiasm was rural, although neighborhoods still scarcely beyond frontier conditions maintained relative indifference, and that antislavery conviction coincided closely with Yankee derivation, social maturity, superior education, and at least average prosperity.[25] The same pattern applies also to the less thoroughly ascertainable distribution of revivalism, Antimasonry, temperance, Adventism, perfectionism, and spiritualism, and to most of the minor ultraisms as well.

Abolition and temperance, though the largest and most noteworthy, were not the only social causes which revival religion espoused in the period of its climactic enthusiasm. Female Moral Reform, for example, rose to the status of a crusade against sin, under the guidance of John R. McDowall, an orthodox, Princetonian, Presbyterian clergyman in New York City. It immediately enlisted the sympathies of upstate ultraists, who for a time monopolized the movement. But after a career of a few years as a radical

[25] See maps XXI and XXII.

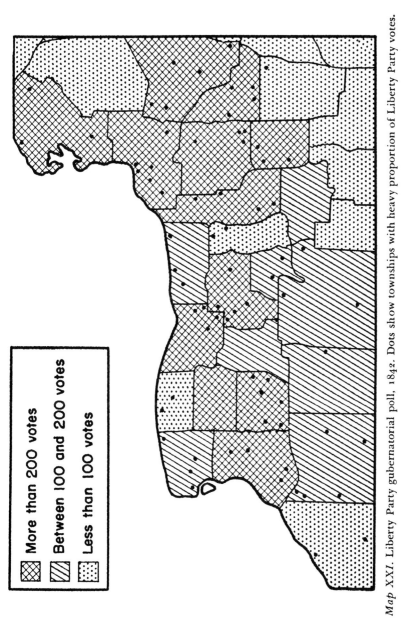

Map XXI. Liberty Party gubernatorial poll, 1842. Dots show townships with heavy proportion of Liberty Party votes.

Legend:
- ⊠ More than 200 votes
- ⊘ Between 100 and 200 votes
- ⋮ Less than 100 votes

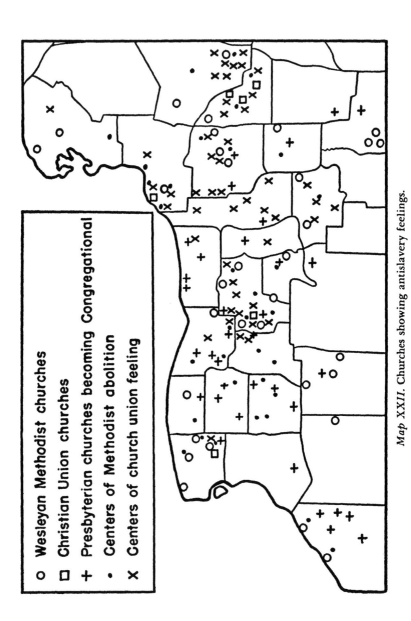

○ Wesleyan Methodist churches

□ Christian Union churches

+ Presbyterian churches becoming Congregational

• Centers of Methodist abolition

× Centers of church union feeling

Map XXII. Churches showing antislavery feelings.

ism it came upon a period of readjustment and underwent a comprehensive restyling.

McDowall apparently began with a reasonable approach to his problem. His New York Magdalen Society of the beginning of the decade seems to have aimed at rescuing fallen women and restoring them to social usefulness, but when his supporters "saw *no* fruits of our labors" and believed that "the same amount of effort applied *as a preventive*" would do more good, he turned gradually to other methods.[26] The first issues of *McDowall's Journal* in 1833 still recognized as primary causes of prostitution the low wages of seamstresses and the unstable employment of domestics and pleaded for asylums for wayward women. But either of his own accord, or in keeping with the mood of those who would lend aid, he now wrote that "public evil can be removed only by the public" and aimed chiefly at stimulating conviction among the righteous by sensational publicity. Occasional raids on brothels and constant lurid description of low life in Gotham served this purpose all too well for a generation imbued with the notion that sex should be discussed only with great delicacy. By "adopting the same means for checking vice, which the vicious use to spread it," his journal may, as conservatives charged, have served "as a sort of printed dictionary to all the bad houses in town." [27] At any rate, the New York Female Benevolent Society, established in 1833, felt it necessary to proclaim its independence of McDowall.

The founder's paper nevertheless stimulated the formation of upstate auxiliaries and led the next year to establishment of a national benevolent order, "The American Society for promoting the Observance of the 7th Commandment," which prevailed through the ultraist phase of the crusade. Dirck Lansing and McDowall, writing to offer Weld their secretaryship and agency, well stated the organization's attitude:

We have no doubt that the evil against which our efforts are and are to be directed, is one of Satan's strong holds. The enimy [sic] already begins to rave and foam; and many Christians . . . under the influence

[26] Arthur Tappan, letter to *New York Evangelist*, IV (Feb. 2, 1833), 14.

[27] *McDowall's Journal* (New York), I (Jan., March, 1833), 1, 17; "Moral Reform Societies," *Literary and Theological Review*, III (Dec., 1836), 614; Robert H. Collyer, *Lights and Shadows of American Life* (Boston [1844?]), 8.

of false delicacy, are encouraging him to roar louder. Very few know the awful and soul sickening extent of the evil . . . in this wonderful department of satan's empire, where this arch deceiver works to brutify our nature, and to damn the soul.[28]

In this ultraist stage moral reform appealed most strongly to the Burned-over District. Societies sprang up all over the region during 1833. Within two years the synods of Utica and Genesee, the Genesee Congregational Consocation, and even the *Baptist Register* had endorsed the movement, while the conservative theological seminaries at Auburn and Hamilton both made contributions. In two typical issues of *McDowall's Journal,* thirty-five letters appeared from western New York, against fifty from the entire balance of the country. McDowall himself came on tour in 1836 and gained a strongly favorable resolution from the Monroe Baptist Association which was at the time too conservative to approve abolition. By 1837, when the organization, now called the New York Female Moral Reform Association, had 250 auxiliaries and 15,000 members, this state alone contained 138 of the local groups.[29]

Only two years later, however, the ultraist phase had passed, and the reconstituted American Female Moral Reform Society, with a conservative and proper magazine, turned to studying girls' education, issuing vapid moral tracts on the preservation of innocence and campaigning for state laws to punish crimes against chastity. After the passage of three more years, the changed movement had overcome its postultraist slump and doubled the number of affiliate local groups of the previous peak year, 1837.[30]

The changing complexion of the movement during the late thirties and early forties came in part from new leadership. Extreme concentration upon a single evil ever warped thoughts in new directions; thus intensive concern with chastity led men to consider the possibility of finer kinds of holiness wherein release might be found from the temptations of sex. A series of leading lights in

---

[28] *New York Evangelist,* V (Feb. 22, 1834), 32; D. C. Lansing and J. R. McDowall to Theodore Weld, March 29, 1834, Barnes and Dumond, *Weld-Grimké Letters,* I, 136.

[29] *McDowall's Journal,* I, *passim; Rochester Daily Advertiser,* Nov. 9, 1833; *Baptist Register,* IX (Dec. 7, 1832), 166; *New York Evangelist,* V (June 14, 1834), 95, VI (Sept. 26, 1835), 245; *Minutes, Monroe Baptist Association,* (1835), 7; Fletcher, *Oberlin,* I, 298.

[30] Fletcher, *Oberlin,* I, 296 ff.; *Oberlin Evangelist,* III (Nov. 24, 1841), 189, IV (Nov. 23, 1842), 191, V (Aug. 30, Oct. 25, 1843), 143, 174.

moral reform trod various paths to different styles of perfectionism and each time had to be replaced by more orthodox and conservative individuals. Mrs. William Green, a cofounder of the New
York society, strayed from orthodoxy in 1837, and two years later
George and Mary Cragin likewise erred. All eventually joined
Noyes's venture in holiness. One prominent Oberlin member, the
editor of the *Evangelist,* became so confused as to involve himself
in a seduction. Two successive moral-reform "editresses" in the
early forties adopted views of sanctification of the Oberlin variety
which brought about their expulsion from the organization.[31]

Moral reform and most of the other isms wrapped up in ultraism
during the thirties attained mainly rural support in the Burned-
over District. "The Protestant Crusade" against Catholicism, by
contrast, was more largely urban. Suspicion and dislike of the
Roman Church lay deeply imbedded in traditional Protestantism,
and the awakened intensity of millennium-seeking fervor could
easily transform this passive attitude into an active condition.
Western New York had a constantly hostile bearing toward Catholics and observed with consistent interest the relative progress of
Catholic and Protestant proselytizing throughout the world.

From the late twenties into the mid-thirties the *Western Recorder,* the *Rochester Observer,* and the *Baptist Register* carried a
swelling volume of notices and articles devoted to the threat of
Catholicism. All of them, with the *New York Evangelist,* endorsed
George Bourne's *Protestant* upon its appearance in New York City
in 1830. So also did Oneida, Onondaga, and Ontario presbyteries,
Nathaniel Beman, Charles Finney, and Joshua Leavitt.[32] Finney,
Weld, and Gale probably had mingled with their interest in converting the Middle West a sense of the threat of Catholicism there,
even if they seldom or never expressed the idea as firmly and emphatically as did Lyman Beecher and others. William Wisner, at
least, in 1835, dreaded the thought that "while our missionaries are
converting their thousands papal troops are coming over by hun-

---

[31] Fletcher, *Oberlin,* I, 313; Lewis Tappan, New York, Dec. 19, 1843, Feb. 1, 1844,
to Charles G. Finney, Lewis Tappan MSS.

[32] *Baptist Register,* VI (Nov. 20, 1829), 154; *Rochester Observer,* VII (April 3, 1833),
14; *New York Evangelist,* II (Sept. 10, 1831), 303; *Protestant* (New York), I (Jan. 2,
Feb. 13, 20, March 13, 1830), 1, 49, 57, 81.

dreds of thousands"; and a correspondent of Absolom Peters from Madison County proposed a huge tent and six-man team to tour the Mississippi Valley conducting protracted meetings, to seize that region from the Pope.[33] A sprinkling of correspondents and agents in western New York helped sustain the *New York Protestant Vindicator* and the *Downfall of Babylon,* as they had the *Protestant,* which these journals succeeded.

One of the favorite minor flurries of enthusiasm in the area, apparently devised by G. T. Marshall of Oswego in 1831, was the "verse a day" plan to convert France. A special paper, the *Verse Herald,* as well as the *Baptist Register,* the *Western Recorder,* and the *New York Evangelist,* all championed the scheme to send across the Atlantic eighty-six laymen, one for each Department, with Testaments for distribution, and to support their work by means of unanimous daily prayer and verse-recitation by all Christians in the United States. Thus would be made "an unsuspected though powerful assault upon the man of sin." [34]

However much anti-Catholic feeling belonged with Burned-over District ultraism, the allied nativist movement failed to become a major concern. Its periodicals circulated here in no more abundance than elsewhere, thus differing from most of the rest of the religious press. Radical enthusiasts here bestowed a good deal more attention upon Universalism than upon Catholicism as the major threat to proper religion. Nor did they, in the degree of emphasis they did grant the subject, come to equal the interest of others. The more orthodox churchmen, who spent considerable energy damning ultraists, lent as much favor or more to the antipapal cause; and persons beyond the region, in eastern centers of religious conservatism, probably enlisted even more enthusiastically in the crusade. The one group of Burned-over District zealots who gave primary attention to the question were the followers of William Miller, many of whom, like their leader, had had little interest in the multiple social reforms of the thirties. The immediately expected millennium gave the existence of Catholicism a more press-

---

[33] William Wisner, Rochester, April 7, 1835, Jonathan Pratt, Madison, Oct. 17, 1835, to Absolom Peters, A.H.M.S. MSS.

[34] Harlow, *Smith,* 59; *Western Recorder* (Utica), VIII (July 12, Nov. 22, 1831), 109, 187; *Baptist Register,* VIII (Oct. 2, 1831), 142.

ing urgency as an issue than it otherwise had. The very progress of "the Mother of Harlots" served as one of the prominent prophetic signals of the approaching judgment.[35]

Those canal-line towns which were receiving their share of immigrants reflected in proportion to their size, and in inverse proportion to their distance from the seaboard cities where the new horde centered most heavily, a more active type of nativism. Incidents in Rochester, Palmyra, and Oswego, at least, can be used to document this area's share in violence against the Irish and against the Catholic Church.[36] But few Catholic immigrants penetrated the hinterland where the potential religious excitability waxed stronger, and even in the towns, capitalists of religious conviction who would contribute to abolition, temperance, and moral reform campaigns doubtless profited from immigrant labor. William H. Seward, Thurlow Weed, and the western "conscience" wing of Whiggism generally, sustained their political strength in spite of actions sympathetic to Catholic immigrants. And as time went on, the nativist political impulse became so closely allied with conservative Whiggery in the East, and simultaneously with all the antiultra religious forces of the same section, that it could have little appeal for the reformers of the Burned-over District.[37] Hostility to Catholicism, real as it was, must thus be considered on the whole a minor, relatively inactive manifestation of religious radicalism in western New York.

Another potentially powerful impetus from ultraism bore upon education. This also was inadequately realized; and if the radicals rise in modern esteem for failing to live up to their possibilities as Catholic baiters, they fall by the same token for their relative failure to accomplish much of what their ideas portended in this more constructive line. The Presbyterians of Oneida County led in a move toward educational reform by calling a "convention of Teachers and Friends of Education" at Utica in October, 1830. At

---

[35] William Miller, *Evidence from Scripture and History of the Second Coming of Christ, About the Year 1843* (Troy, 1838), v, 141.

[36] Ray A. Billington, *The Protestant Crusade, 1800–1860, A Study of the Origins of American Nativism* (New York, 1938), 197, 215, note, 293; *Protestant*, I (Aug. 14, 1830), 261; *Rochester Advertiser and Telegraph*, March 13, 1830.

[37] Dixon R. Fox, *The Decline of Aristocracy in the Politics of New York* (New York, 1918), 374–376.

the second meeting the next year, Josiah Holbrook made a speech and received appointment as agent for the state lyceum organized during the session. Little seems to have come of efforts to study teacher qualifications and curricula of the common schools and to improve the state school law, but the lyceum movement did expand under this religious leadership. Possibly the interest of the Presbyterian revivalists in the public schools would have netted greater results had not the general public already sampled their educational benevolence in the previous decade.[38]

A greater impact on the national pattern of education came from Oneida Institute. George W. Gale began this evangelistic training school on the heels of the Oneida Revival by expanding his previous theological training of a few men who exchanged some labor on his farm for their instruction. In 1827, Oneida Presbytery came to his aid with two thousand dollars, a hundred-acre farm, and a few instructors. Twenty students the first year, and thirty the second, worked three hours and a half a day on the farm; their instructors received a half-dollar weekly with a share of any profits from the farm's produce. With an enrollment of at least seventy students by the early thirties, the school apparently provided Latin and Greek for men bound by American Education Society support but emphasized more "practical" studies based on Hebrew instead of the "heathen classics." [39] Its outright abolitionism under Beriah Green's administration made some contribution to the cause of academic freedom but led to its collapse and sale to the Free Baptists for a seminary in the early forties. From this model developed the brief campaign of the New York City Gentlemen for manual-labor schools, which Theodore Weld energized in 1832. Hence also came the basic patterns of Oberlin College, founded by upstate New Yorkers and destined to mother a multitudinous progeny of institutions in the Middle West. Gerrit Smith maintained an intermittent interest in Oneida itself and copied from it when he

---

[38] Fletcher, *Oberlin*, I, 341, 342; *New York Evangelist*, IV (May 11, 1833), 76; *Western Recorder*, VIII (Jan. 25, 1831), 13.

[39] Letter from George W. Gale, *Quarterly Register and Journal of the American Educational Society* (Andover, Mass.), II (Nov. 1829), 112; G. W. Gale, Oct. 20, 1832, C. S. Renshaw, *et al.*, July 15, 1833, S. C. Aiken, May 20, 1832, to Charles Finney, Finney MSS; *Oberlin Evangelist*, III (Dec. 8, 1841), 197; *A Sketch of the Condition and Prospects of the Oneida Institute* (Utica, 1834).

reorganized the McGraw College as an abolitionist school in 1849.[40]

But ultraists expected an early millennium and had to hasten the alleviation of evil. Formal education was a slow process compared with lecturing and publishing. Relatively few of the radical reformers persevered in a primary devotion to such institutional devices for the enlightenment of society.

A host of other social reforms experienced impulses from the energies of ultraism which overflowed its major interests. Some of these were closely allied with the larger movements but not in themselves of commanding importance. The brevity of others rendered them insignificant. A third group had prolonged histories in the nation but did not lend themselves readily to the particularly pious approach of the Yorker Yankees.

Representative of the first class was "Retrenchment," championed for several years by the *Baptist Register,* the *Rochester Observer,* and probably by the Oberlin colony in Ohio. One Finney correspondent apparently lectured widely on the subject in New York and Massachusetts, advising that parsimonious habits of dress, diet, home furnishing, and travel, adopted by all Christians in the country, could "save more than $35,000,000 annually, to devote to benevolent objects!!!" Of the second sort was the lottery reform, begun in New York about 1831 and achieved by law in about two years. A somewhat more prolonged agitation for "Boatman's Friend" organizations developed in the early thirties to parallel on the canals the earlier efforts to save ocean-going sailors.[41]

Grahamism and the associated dietary and physiological reforms approached the center of ultraist concerns less closely, but Sylvester Graham himself developed an extensive acquaintance in this area and apparently began his crusading from the same motives which recommended his program to upstate New Yorkers in the 1830's. His *Lecture on Chastity* assumed that illicit sex relations, like ex-

---

[40] *First Annual Report of the Society for Promoting Manual Labor in Literary Institutions . . . Report of Their General Agent, Theodore D. Weld* (New York, 1833), 10; Harlow, *Smith,* 61, 224–231; *Christian Contributor* (McGrawville), VI (Nov. 1, 1849), 30.

[41] *Rochester Observer,* VI (Nov. 10, 1832), 45; *Baptist Register,* XI (May 30, 1834), 57; Charles Brooks, East Bethany, Oct. 8, 1835, to Finney, Finney MSS; *New York Evangelist,* V (Jan. 4, 1834), 2; *Rochester Advertiser,* Aug., Sept., 1830, *passim.*

cess and promiscuity among married folk, were promoted by persons trying to "destroy the authority of the Bible" and to "show that marriage is not a divine institution." Of his dietary notions, he wrote Gerrit Smith in 1840 that his cause sought "in no partial manner to lop off particular branches of evil . . . but is adapted to . . . the removal as far as possible, of *every evil. . . .*" The Smiths, the Welds, the Finneys, William Goodell, and many others experimented with Graham's ideas; and some few persons, at least, sponsored the phrenology and water-cure fads of the forties and fifties, similarly seeing in them aids to physical efficiency for doing God's work on earth.[42]

The religious radicals also nodded slightly toward agitation over capital punishment and prison reform; if the "Prison Discipline Society" of the early thirties, praised by the *New York Evangelist*, probably had no broadly humanitarian program, it at least looked into prison conditions and supplied Bibles to inmates. And although concern over world peace would seem far removed from the orbit of minds which could well assume that their peaceful times would last until the early judgment day, more than a few of the religious enthusiasts played large roles in that movement. Gerrit Smith contributed to, and once became a vice president of, the Peace Society. One Oneida-Lane-Oberlin revivalist itinerant became a vigorous pacifist lecturer, and Oberlin maintained an active society, as did several counties in upstate New York. William Ladd toured the canal towns in 1840, and the Garrisonian nonresistance group apparently received some of its best support from the vicinities of Utica and Syracuse.[43] To be sure, by the time they came to support pacifism many of these Burned-over District advocates may have ceased to be ultraists. However much Christian benevolence might abhor war, strict reliance on Bible authority, customary among western New York evangelicals, yielded as much sanction

---

[42] Sylvester Graham, *A Lecture to Young Men on Chastity* (10th ed.; Boston, 1848, copyright 1837), 20; Graham to Gerrit Smith, March 4, 1840, in Harlow, *Smith*, 94; Ann C. Smith to Angelina Weld and Sarah Grimké, P.S. on Smith to Weld, July 11, 1840, Letters of Gerrit Smith to Theodore Weld, Library of Congress; Harlow, *Smith*, 46, 90, 94; Fletcher, *Oberlin*, I, 321-330.

[43] *Oberlin Evangelist*, V (May 10, 1843), 78; W. Freeman Galpin, "Reform Movements," *The Age of Reform* (Alexander C. Flick, ed., *History of the State of New York*, VI, New York, 1934), 262-264.

for Old Testament vengefulness as for New Testament nonresistance.

"I do love to meet a Yankee girl . . . especially . . . west of the Hudson. . . . She generally speaks what she thinks; nor is she fearful of thinking independently either. . . . She is less erratic in thought than the mincing prude. . . . She has none of the low tricks . . . too fashionable among many young ladies. . . ." [44] Thus spoke an editor far distant from western New York.

Not all Burned-over District folk shared this admiration for Yankee integrity in the fair sex, but ultraists for the most part seem to have sympathized. Women in western New York began with nearly equal rights in the church communion and preached in some sects from the earliest times. They fostered and abetted religious enthusiasm more largely than did men. They branched out in the ultraist period to participate strongly in temperance, abolition, and moral reform. Elizabeth Cady Stanton, Amelia Bloomer, Susan B. Anthony, Antoinette Brown Blackwell, the Grimké sisters, and others soon to lead the women's rights movement served apprenticeship in the reforms which flourished in western New York. The one-ideaism of the religious zealots, however, kept them from associating feminism with their causes as did the New Englanders, and the female vote, like so many other things the radicals wanted, could be attained only by political action, which blended poorly with religious enthusiasm. Only after the ultraist phase had passed could the women's rights enterprise take form, and that movement had very little connection with western New York's religious history. But the Seneca Falls Convention of 1848 occurred in a region which had done much to bring its purposes to the point of expression. Delayed though it was, this later crusade owed a great deal to the Burned-over District's "moral reformation."

---

[44] *Baltimore Young Men's Paper,* in *Zion's Watchman,* I (Jan. 1, 1836), 1.

Chapter 14. PERFECT SANCTIFICATION

ALL the abhorrence which now falls upon slavery, intemperance, lewdness and every other species of vice will in due time be gathered into one volume of victorious wrath against sin. . . . If you love . . . the forefront of the hottest battle of righteousness . . . set your faces toward perfect holiness." [1] This advice of John Humphrey Noyes to William Lloyd Garrison closely paralleled Charles Finney's to Theodore Weld, that he subordinate abolitionism to revivalism, and both indicate the superior logic of perfectionism over moral reform. For in exerting their zeal upon some single evil the reformers allowed their thoughts to be warped away from the comprehensive piety of their ultraist origin. Saner, more consistent minds persisted in seeking a progressively more intensive and more nearly absolute righteousness through spiritual regeneration. Perfectionism was the highroad out of ultraism. That some of the more spectacular experiments in Burned-over District history occurred along its route does not prove that its exponents were irrational fanatics but rather demonstrates their superior ability to carry originally questionable assumptions to thoroughly appropriate conclusions.

The two highest caliber mentalities to be observed in the whole story of western New York religious enthusiasms belonged to Charles Finney and John Noyes, the two leading perfectionists of the period. Possibly the ones most nearly approaching them are

---

[1] George W. Noyes, ed., *Religious Experience of John Humphrey Noyes, Founder of Oneida Community* (New York, 1923), 231.

238

discovered among the leaders of a third branch of perfectionism located in central New York. This branch had no single chieftain, unless Luther Myrick qualifies for the position, and enjoyed only a brief existence. Its history never has been (perhaps cannot be) adequately reconstructed; but it rose directly from Burned-over District ultraism and preceded and instructed the more renowned branches of the movement led by the two greater men. It will be seen that connections can be observed between the one movement in this region and the two others, one in western New England, the other at Oberlin, Ohio; but perfectionism was such an obviously logical resultant of intense revivalism that no one group can in any exclusive fashion be considered the instigator of others. All could as well have developed independently and simultaneously from common circumstances.

The liberalized Edwardean theology of New Haven and the western New York revivals allowed men to strive for their own conversion and heightened spirituality. This position differed only slightly from traditional Methodism, most significantly in the assumption, more emphatically retained from Calvinism, that conversion still, somehow, was the work of the Holy Ghost. The difference between progressive Presbyterians and the Methodists became the greater as ultraist revivalism grew within the one church and found far less favor in the other. The doctrine and practice alike of Burned-over District revivals encouraged a belief that God was *"illuminating the truth; raising ideas in the brain";* that the regenerate were guided by the Holy Spirit through the prayer of faith and must follow their impulses to the exclusion of all external authority.[2]

Conservatives who disliked Luther Myrick's tactics admitted, even when he had probably already crossed the narrow line between orthodoxy and heresy, that "his sermons were plain pungent + scriptural." They puzzled over the fact that persons then behaving infamously "10 months ago, appeared the most humble, praying, devoted + efficient Christians of any among us—the very life + soul of the Chh!" One unusually astute critic demonstrated from

---

[2] Joseph I. Foote, " 'The New Dispensation,' or Modern Antinomianism, Commonly Called Perfectionism," *Literary and Theological Review* (New York), I (Dec., 1834), 554–583, *passim.*

three sets of central New York presbytery records the practically identical meaning of orthodox doctrine gone ultraist and the dread heresy of perfectionism.[3]

Yet, however relentlessly the logic of their thoughts may tend to press people in a given direction, ideas seldom seem to react upon one another from their own unaided force alone. More often some circumstantial example inspires by contagion the transformation of already vaguely formulated assumptions into definite hypotheses or concrete action. Accordingly, although perfectionism was practically predestined to arise, the various schools in fact grew up by way of a chain of influences which connected each one to the others.

In New York City in 1828, one James Latourette left the Methodist Church and gathered about himself a following devoted to the attainment of more perfect holiness. In all probability this represented not quite the same kind of departure which soon developed upstate, but rather an attempt to realize genuine Wesleyan doctrine which seemed to be declining in the Methodist denomination. From this early group, apparently, a few disciples removed to Albany about 1830 and connected themselves with several students in Edward Kirk's itinerant training school, while a man named Abram Smith established a similar offshoot at Roundout, near Kingston, New York. Charles and Simon Lovett, John B. Foot, Chauncey Dutton, and two sisters named Annesley were prominent members of the Albany cult. The mysteriously ubiquitous Charles Weld may also have been involved and may have conveyed some suggestions to James Boyle at an early date in the thirties. Horatio Foote, too, evidently had some kind of interest in the group, possibly transmitted to Luther Myrick.

The Albany crowd were peripatetic zealots and journeyed eastward at least to Southampton, Westfield, Brimfield, Belchertown, and New Haven. To the west they penetrated central New York during 1832 and by the end of the decade were traveling as far as Ohio. Although by the latter date they had become extremists (Charles Mead, John Foot, and his sister, Ann, suffered a dose of

---

[3] Henry Snyder, Chittenango, April 1, 1833, E. H. Adams, De Ruyter, Jan. 1, 1834, to Abijah Crane, American Home Missionary Society Papers, Chicago Theological Seminary; Foote, *Literary and Theological Review*, I (Dec., 1834), 560.

tar and feathers because they slept three in a bed on their Ohio journey),[4] it is improbable that they had gone much beyond Wesleyan conceptions of holiness during the earlier tours.

Another cult sprang up in central New York about the middle of 1832. Hiram Sheldon, Jarvis Rider, Erasmus Stone, David Warren, Sophia Cook, Lucina Umphreville, and Jonathan Burt were the leaders of several local groups, spread widely over Onondaga and Madison counties. Luther Myrick's following may have coincided with or supplemented these nuclei. Charles Weld, "unobtrusively visiting" about the neighborhood in 1834, found quite a scattering of colonies and felt there had been "a·wonderful preparation for sowing the seed extensively in this region." [5]

Less evidence survives to demonstrate the existence of similar groups farther west in the state, but the New York perfectionists would scarcely have held a conference at Canaseraga in the upper Genesee Valley in 1836, if all of them had resided east of Cayuga Lake. The "sanctified ones" of Rochester, possibly led by a man named Bush, who had "set up the *spirit within* them, + put down the Scriptures," may well have been one such coterie in the west, and the Mrs. Conn of Cohocton and Wyoming County may only have been maligned by her single recorder who called her a "prophetess" and actually may rather have been another perfectionist leader.[6]

What little can be learned of the New York cults suggests that they reached their height of popularity about 1834, and that they had developed soon after this date most of the species of perfectionist behavior which both entranced and warned John Noyes and Charles Finney. But the sexual promiscuity which led to their downfall seems to have been influenced in part by the Massachusetts groups inspired by Charles Lovett.

Two vital issues rose among perfectionists, the one a question of doctrine, the other a problem of morality. The crucial point in theology was whether positive assurance of complete insulation

---

[4] George W. Noyes, ed., *John Humphrey Noyes, The Putney Community* (Oneida, 1931), 128–130.

[5] Noyes, *Religious Experience*, 187–189.

[6] Rev. James H. Hotchkin, *A History of the Purchase and Settlement of Western New York, and of . . . the Presbyterian Church in That Section* (New York, 1848), 470, 471.

from sin could be attained through regeneration. Must one strive forever toward a higher degree of saintliness without assurance that his attainments would automatically persevere? Could he never obtain any guarantee of his eventual salvation? Or would a sufficiently intense religious experience achieve for him total security against further commission of sin?

The moral issue resulted naturally from the doctrinal one. Which belief provided the better safeguard against the tendency of religious zealots to confuse heavenly and earthly love? Sexual promiscuity, however motivated, destroyed reputation and led piety far wide of its mark. John Noyes considered the doctrine of security the safer answer. He felt that the neuroticism induced by the constant struggle to achieve the unattainable, rather than the idea of security itself, caused trouble. Charles Finney took the opposite position, that a sense of inability to sin could only remove all moral restraints.

It was the experience of the New York cults, primarily, which served to instruct both men. That story suggests, contrary to the logical expectation, that Noyes may have been right and Finney wrong, at least in interpreting the developments in central New York. For this earlier school long hesitated to accept the extreme position of Noyes. In 1835 they still renounced the notion of sinlessness, which the "Yankee Saint" adopted a year earlier.[7] Their sexual experiments occurred before their belief had clearly changed and probably brought about their shift of position.

Even in 1833, they professed "to be governed in all their conduct by immediate inspiration," and denounced "the gospel . . . [and] all obligations imposed either by ecclesiastical or civil authority." They were reputed to have "openly advocate[d] a community of property" and confessed not to know "why they should love + honour + take care of *their wives more than any other woman.*" But a relentless critic, placed ideally for close observation, could not yet accuse them of promiscuity. The forty or fifty at Delphi, Onondaga County, did go into neighboring churches in groups of six or eight to interrupt worship and help in "overthrowing Babylon." Some were jailed and most suffered excommunication. The

---

[7] Noyes, *Religious Experience,* 192.

former minister at East Genoa, now a "ranting perfectionist," still attended meeting in 1835, only to harangue afterwards on the church doorstep. Such events took place quite regularly for several years in many towns within Luther Myrick's sphere of operations, mainly between Cayuga and Oneida lakes.[8]

"Spiritual Wifery" developed along with these antinomian practices, but it came rather as a by-product of the intense pursuit of greater spirituality than from belief in total sinlessness, which the New Yorkers had not yet adopted. It was in the spring of 1835 that Lucina Umphreville took up the idea "that carnal union was not to be tolerated even in marriage, while spiritual union whether in or out of marriage represented a high state of attainment." [9] Practically simultaneously, at Brimfield, Massachusetts, Maria Brown decided to demonstrate that her piety could overcome lowly desires, by proving that she could sleep chastely with her minister. John Noyes was visiting in Brimfield at the time and had warning of what was to occur. He decided in advance what the outcome would be and left in the early evening to walk home to Putney, Vermont, lest his own name become besmirched in Maria's downfall.

When news of the "Brimfield Bundling" reached central New York, the saints in this region also reacted in horror. They had denounced in convention on January first all the Noyes doctrines, on the Second Coming, security, freedom from moral law, and aversion to asceticism. A year later, the Canaseraga convention still resisted, but nevertheless publicly advocated Platonic affiliations, regardless of marital ties.[10]

During the summer of 1836, changes in both doctrine and practice came about almost simultaneously. At the Chapman homestead on the south shore of Oneida Lake, Maria Brown was visiting Mrs. Chapman and the "fascinating" Lucina Umphreville. Mr. Chapman and his neighbor, Jonathan Burt, were absent, digging on the

---

[8] E. H. Adams, De Ruyter, Jan. 1, March 20, 1834, to Abijah Crane, J. H. Rice, East Genoa, Feb. 15, 1835, and John Cross, Oneida, June 11, 1835, to Absolom Peters, and A.H.M.S. MSS, 1832–1835, *passim;* "Records of the First Congregational Church in Manlius," (MS at Onondaga County Historical Society).

[9] Noyes, *Religious Experience,* 201.

[10] *Ibid.,* 196–201; Dr. John B. Ellis, *Free Love and Its Votaries,* etc. (New York, 1870), 39.

Chenango Canal. Soon Jarvis Rider and Charles Lovett joined the party.

How it all came about, no record indicates. Possibly Maria instructed the group, suggesting how much more the willing spirit might gain from the weakness than from the strength of the flesh. Perhaps she convinced them that they, too, must be secure from sin and free to taste otherwise forbidden fruits. Or more probably, since they had to this point firmly denied security, the New Yorkers only tried to prove to Maria that they could succeed where she had failed, in the same kind of test of their highly spiritual unions. But they, too, found themselves wanting and adopted the doctrine of security for justification.

The latter interpretation seems the likely one, since both couples, Rider and Lucina, and Lovett and Mrs. Chapman, felt guilty rather than proud when Mr. Chapman came home. Chapman went after Lovett with a horsewhip but was struck blind in the act. This "act of God" probably put the stamp of authority on the doctrine of security from sin and led to its spread through the cults about central New York.[11] Soon Hiram Sheldon and Sophia Cook, Erasmus Stone and Eliza Porter, and probably other couples had cemented their formerly Platonic affiliations with the new physical sacrament. If rumor can be trusted, Martin Sweet gathered about him near Auburn a household of women, six white and one black, "deluded beings, although most of them are well educated and respectably connected," who obeyed his every whim. The negress is supposed to have been directed to run through the streets with a butcher knife, slaying whatever she met, and three of the white women were reputed to have smashed the Communion table during a neighboring service, scattering the cups and drinking the wine.[12]

John Humphrey Noyes prided himself that New Haven perfectionism was more "intellectual and civilized," but his contacts with the New Yorkers were numerous and sustained. One of his conversions occurred in a sympathetic wave of the 1830 revivals. His

---

[11] Ellis, *Free Love*, 39 ff.; Noyes, *Religious Experience*, 202.

[12] *Rochester Democrat*, paraphrased by Thomas Brothers, *The United States of North America as They Are; Not as They Are Generally Described*, etc. (London, 1840), "newsclipping" appendix, 514.

intimacy at New Haven with James Boyle, Charles Weld, Chauncey Dutton, and Simon Lovett probably had something to do with his theological development, even though he claimed with good justice that "the reaction upon myself, of my labors to convert others . . . was the immediate cause of my conviction. . . ." [13] His first *Perfectionist* magazine, inaugurated with Boyle in 1834, circulated during its two-year span among all the scattered cults in New York and probably served as their chief written communication with each other. The fact that he succeeded eventually to leadership of the Burned-over District school, bringing it into amalgamation with his own New England following, probably owes explanation mainly to Noyes's superior mental discipline and originality.

During his year at Andover Noyes had learned the Bible with amazing thoroughness, and through his studies with Nathaniel Taylor at Yale he moved with forthright independence toward the final logical conclusions of Taylor's renovations in New England theology.[14] Although he had quite a distance to travel before his beliefs became systematic and complete, he took before April, 1834, the major, bold step toward that extreme position at which the New Yorkers so long bridled. Writing to request his discharge from his missionary vow made with the "Brethren" at Andover, he explained, "I can never agree with those who suppose either in theory or *practice*—that sin is the necessary means of the greatest good— that men cannot obey the law of God—or that while they can—it is not to be expected that they will. . . . I hold in the most unqualified sense that 'he that committeth sin is of the devil.' " [15]

For three years more Noyes drifted about, both geographically and doctrinally, trying to complete his theology, argue-down opposers, and escape the irregularities which in others snared and destroyed the urge to holiness. Though he had rigorously separated himself from the sanctified bundling at Brimfield, he recognized his own affiliation "with its testimony, and its desolation came upon me like a flood." Having his own words "tried by fire," "instead of convicting me of sin, purged and healed my conscience; but it

---

13 [J. H. Noyes], *Confessions of John H. Noyes*, etc. (Oneida Reserve, 1849), 13.

14 *Ibid.*, 12, and appendix D, 79–88.

15 Noyes, New Haven, April 1, 1834, to George Champion, Brethren Papers, Andover-Newton Theological Seminary Library.

deepened my sense of responsibility, and impressed upon my spirit a sobriety and a resolution to resist corruption among professed Perfectionists. . . ." [16] During this interval he met the New York City and Albany leaders, conversed with Charles Finney, mingled with the zealous moral reformers of Gotham, and acquainted himself with Theophilus Gates of Philadelphia and William Lloyd Garrison in Boston. One by one he cast off the disturbing friendships of Dutton, Lovett, Weld, Gates, and at last Boyle, and gradually hammered out the further beliefs which helped him capture the entire eastern wing of perfectionism.[17]

His system came finally to be established, as firmly as a milking stool, on three legs. The first leg was total security from sin, defined to provide for an expectation of discipline and improvement. The second dealt with the perennial millennialism of the era in remarkably astute fashion. Upon the evidence of John 21:22, "If I will that he [John] tarry till I come, what is that to thee?" Noyes concluded that the Second Coming had taken place about 70 A.D., though in less literal manner than the orthodox of his day took for granted while expecting its future occurrence.[18] The only real Christians in the nineteenth century were those who had been rendered perfect by their descent from the saints of the year 70. All other denominations stemmed rather from the spurious postmillennial growths (presumably Catholicism) of the second and third centuries. In justifying his own duplication in the present of the first-century church, Noyes fell upon a kind of cyclical evolutionism which commenced his progressively less literal interpretation of the Bible.

This millenarian theory made good sense to a generation devoted to the theme. It could appear more reasonable than the hypotheses along the same line of William Miller, Ann Lee, the Universalists, and the orthodox Protestants. It probably constituted the most satisfactory possible explanation for perfectionism and did much to help win over the New York cults which lacked so

---

[16] Noyes, *Religious Experience*, 248.

[17] William Green, Jr., New York, Dec. 6, 1837, tò Finney, Charles Grandison Finney Papers, Oberlin College Library; *Spiritual Magazine* (Oneida), II (Jan. 10, 1850), 353 ff.

[18] *Witness* (Ithaca, Putney, Vt.), I (Aug. 20, 1837, Sept. 25, 1839), 4, 74–77.

accomplished an apologist. In addition it conformed with Noyes's third doctrine by providing a precedent in early Christianity for the communistic principle of society.

The third leg of the system had to be turned more deliberately because of personal complications. The problem beset him, as it did all his fellow seekers, of reconciling marriage with the supposed primary, supreme devotion of the sinless man to God and with the community of all saints. Noyes had been in love with Abigail Merwin, his first New Haven recruit; but Abigail deserted the group, married another man, and moved to Ithaca, New York. For a time Noyes rationalized the situation by a belief in spiritual affinities between suitable couples, regardless of earthly ties. In this way he could be connected with Abigail until the next world. But Noyes was first to last as practical-minded an individual as religious enthusiasm could produce. Heaven seemed a distant destination. Asceticism of the Shaker type, widely practiced, would only sterilize the race. On the other hand, the doctrine of spiritual affinities had proved both in Massachusetts and New York to be an unnatural test of righteousness. When it turned into actual promiscuity it could only disgust him and bring the movement into popular disrepute. Out of this dilemma Noyes emerged with his most original principle.

The reformers and the other perfectionists, he declared, "swam out a little way into the stream of spiritual experience, and finding it full of serpents and crocodiles swam back as fast as they could. I swam out and encountered these monsters, but I killed them with my bowie-knife and came out on the other side." [19] Writing to David Harrison in September, 1837, Noyes announced the master principle. The letter went on to Theophilus Gates, who published it in his journal, from whose name the "Battle-Axe Letter" gained its title:

When the will of God is done on earth as it is in heaven there will be no marriage. . . . God has placed a wall of partition between man and woman during the apostacy for good reasons; this partition will be broken down in the resurrection for equally good reasons. But woe

---

[19] Noyes, *Religious Experience,* 196.

to him who abolishes the law of the apostacy before he stands in the holiness of the resurrection! I call a certain woman my wife. She is yours, she is Christ's, and in him she is the bride of all saints.[20]

After all, he reasoned, the spiritual affinity of two was as limited as marriage itself. Furthermore, not sex but the motives which dictated its exercise determined its righteousness or sinfulness. Those few persons who had become totally sanctified would identify sex expressions and all others with their supreme religious devotion and through them would glorify God. Since all the saints were on a par together, in equal dedication to faith, communism among them in the sex relation, as in all others, was the only logical arrangement. Repeated the next year in his proposal of marriage to Harriet Holton and gradually introduced in Putney, Vermont, among a few couples in 1846, this sexual communism came to be the foundation of the entire social structure of Oneida Community.

In the spring of 1837, Noyes left his Putney home, whence he had retired under the stress of "unspiritual" wifery, and headed once more for New York City. There he fell in with Abram Smith, John Lyvere, and Jarvis Rider and set out with them for the upstate region to try to solve the difficulty of the cults in that area. Noyes and Rider after several stops arrived at Ithaca. John "had long desired to traverse the central and western parts of New York . . . the birthplace of many of the mightiest moral and political movements of the times. . . ." Abigail Merwin now lived in Ithaca, too.[21]

Nearby, at Genoa, resided a group of perfectionists able to underwrite a magazine, so once more Noyes assumed editorial leadership of the movement. The *Witness*, begun in Ithaca in August, 1837, removed with its editor to Putney, Vermont, in December of the following year, where it drew upon the inheritance of John's bride, Harriet Holton. But for the next ten years Noyes continued to grow in stature among the New Yorkers and commanded a larger following here than in his home region. Over three-fourths of the Burned-over District subscribers lived within a thirty-mile radius south of Oneida Lake.[22] When the Putney Com-

---

20 Noyes, *Putney Community*, 3.
21 *Witness*, I (Sept. 3, 1837), 3, 9.
22 Thirty-eight per cent of a list of subscribers, more than the number beyond

munity, driven from respectable Vermont, removed to the center of this very area, Noyes's organization immediately began to flourish in its proper home.

John Humphrey Noyes exhibited his genius by finding the logical absolute of ultraist assumption, and by avoiding the consequences of antinomian inspiration through the discipline of communism and the pure motives of security from sin. The second great perfectionist, Charles Finney, demonstrated his superiority by a different method. A large proportion of his amazing success derived from his uncanny ability to give the appearance of a thoroughgoing ultraist, holding extreme positions in all sincerity. Yet beneath all, probably unconsciously, he was in practice an eminently devoted listener to the counsels of that virtue so abhorred by his followers, a sense of expediency. Opportunism in his early ministry taught him the revival measures which made his fame and took him from the backwoods to the metropolis. Like Noyes he thirsted after entire holiness but dreaded the consequences made familiar in the Burned-over District. He told his wife that she might become perfect, "but that it will not answer for *him,* as it would ruin his influence." [23] He avoided the dangers of ultraist reasoning by finding the point where discretion dictated that he stop, short of the logical conclusion.

The Oberlin colony with which Finney became identified had its origins in the Burned-over District, and the Oberlinites watched with keen interest every flurry in the home territory. But the "entire sanctification" of Oberlin had even clearer connections with New York and New England perfectionism. In his Free Church pastorate in New York City, which he continued to fill during college vacations, Finney maintained contact with many of the people experimenting along the line of his thoughts. It was in that city during the winter of 1836 that Finney and President Asa Mahan prayerfully elaborated their hypothesis of holiness, and in Boston seven years later that Finney underwent his own personal reconversion to a sanctified condition.[24]

Putney in New England, were central New Yorkers. *Ibid.,* I (Sept. 25, 1839, Jan. 22, 1840), 74–77, 104.

[23] Noyes, *Confessions,* 32.

[24] Robert S. Fletcher, *A History of Oberlin College . . . Through the Civil War*

Sanctification at Oberlin did not mean that anyone could become or remain totally perfect, but merely that converts must exceed nominal Christianity by rigorous exercise of will and intelligence, to *"aim at being perfect,"* "to make the best use we can of all the light we have." It implied "entire conformity of heart and life to all the known will of God" yet supposed that "the mind may rise higher and higher, making still richer attainments in holiness at each rising grade of progress." Vision of greater heights ahead would bring "more enkindlings of desire, and more intensive struggles to advance." Man had been created able to give *perfect* obedience to God, but he could never give *whole* obedience this side of heaven, despite his *entire* dedication. Actually, Oberlin perfectionism went only a little beyond Taylor's New Haven theology in shifting emphasis away from the twin Puritan ideas of human inability and imperfect sanctification; it very nearly approximated Wesleyan Methodism freshened by a new presentation and thinly disguised in a few remnants of the old New England theology.[25]

But Oberlinism involved the most absolutely righteous social ethic which could be attained without sacrificing spirituality to more limited objectives, and the consequent radicalism made its advocates troublesome to conservative Congregationalists and Presbyterians. The Oberlin type of sanctificationists scattered through the Burned-over District constantly suffered threats or actions of excommunication and often had to face accusations which identified them too closely with the antinomian perfectionists.

The followers of the Ohio leaders in this region were probably more numerous and more influential than either of the other two groups. The *Oberlin Evangelist,* upon its foundation in 1839, en-

---

(2 vols.; Oberlin, O., 1943), I, 223; G. Frederick Wright, *Charles Grandison Finney* (Boston, 1891), 203, 207; Charles G. Finney, *Autobiography of Charles G. Finney* (New York, 1876), 347, 373.

25 Charles G. Finney, *Lectures on Revivals of Religion* (2nd ed.; New York, 1835), 389; *Lectures on Systematic Theology* (James H. Fairchild, ed., Oberlin, O., 1878, copyright 1846), 129; *Views of Sanctification* (Oberlin, O., 1840), 52; *Sermons on Gospel Themes* (Oberlin, O., 1876, delivered 1845 ff.), 413, 414; Merrill E. Gaddis, "Christian Perfectionism in America" (MS at University of Chicago, 1929), best realizes the Wesleyan influence.

joyed a great circulation in New York, maintaining agents in at least thirty villages, mostly west of the Finger Lakes. Until after 1840 the college also drew a large proportion of its clientele from the same area.[26] Mahan and Finney both preserved multitudinous friendships here with men who continued the traditions of the Rochester Revival and tended to follow the evolving beliefs of the Oberlinites. Interest in sanctification seems to have been substantial in the late thirties and to have grown greater in the early forties. Annual conventions of "non-Antinomian" perfectionists met in Rochester, Buffalo, and LeRoy in the years about the turn of the decade. George Beecher at Batavia joined the ranks, as did Seth Gates of Warsaw. The Genesee Congregational Consociation alone had twenty member churches in 1842, just before its excision from the denomination because of its Oberlinite leanings.[27]

But schism was not an outcome peculiar to quarrels over the heresy of Oberlin.

---

[26] *Catalogue of the Trustees, Officers, and Students of the Oberlin Collegiate Institute* (Oberlin, O., 1835, 1836, 1838–1840); *Oberlin Evangelist,* I (June 5, Oct. 9, Nov. 6, 1839), 104, 112, 176, 192.

[27] *Oberlin Evangelist,* III (June 23, Aug. 18, 1841), 102, 135, IV (Oct. 12, 1842), 164–167, V (March 1, 1843), 37; L. P. Judson, Buffalo, June 16, 1841, and George Avery, Rochester, Sept. 11, 1842, to Finney, Finney MSS; *Minutes of the General Association of New York* (Utica, 1842, 1843, 1844), 19, 9, 11, respectively.

Chapter 15. SCHISM

REVIVALS of religion, increasing gradually in intensity and breadth since the Great Revival of 1800, had provided the major stimulus to the growth of western New York churches. The more intense awakenings of 1826 and 1831 also provided converts to increase the membership of all denominations, but the ultraism which followed had the opposite effect. The point at which enthusiasm escaped the bounds of orthodoxy proved also to be the point at which it came to defeat its own original objective, the regeneration of increasing numbers of individuals. The mid-thirties at once brought the established churches to their crest and introduced them to the recession phase of the longer-run cycle of evangelical fervor begun in 1800 and ended during the Civil War.

The Methodist membership statistics adequately suggest the general pattern of growth of all the major evangelistic sects. Their Burned-over District conferences gained members in all except five of the twenty years before 1840, but the amount of increase varied markedly. During the twenties came three successive new peaks of growth, each larger than the last, followed at the end of the decade by a distinct relaxation of pace. But the new decade opened with the greatest gain yet, and 1831 considerably outdistanced its predecessor, while the two succeeding years exhibited diminished, but still substantial, increases, greater than any in the twenties. These four years together constituted the utmost peak in additions to membership before 1850. The middle thirties brought three years of actual decline, but a more normal rate of growth appeared in the late thirties and early forties. Another spurt developed in 1843, again followed by a couple of years of decline and a period of more steady growth in the latter part of the decade.[1]

The Presbyterian churches in the Oneida region probably reached their highest point of effective enthusiasm in 1826, with a secondary peak five years later. The most dependable source of data covers only the territory west of Oneida and Madison counties. Here the four years after 1830 netted at least eleven thousand converts, and the following five years about four thousand. The latter figure probably conceals a diminution in 1835 and 1836, for the next two years gained a reputation for revivals nearly equal to those of 1831, while the denomination nationally was smaller in 1837 than four years earlier. Presbyterian conversions during the decade seem to have approximated two-thirds the number of the Methodists, whereas during the twenties they had apparently not exceeded half of the rate of the more popular church. So much did the new measures do for the appeal of Presbyterians to the multitude.[2]

The Baptists gained more members from the revivals of the earlier thirties than did the Presbyterians, probably nearly maintaining equality with the Methodists. The period from 1827 to 1836 saw a gain in the Burned-over District of about eighteen thousand, practically the same as the Methodist increase of the same interval. The mid-thirties again showed a drop or a respite in representative associations, while the revival campaigns of Elder Knapp in the latter years of the decade brought a new increase. After leveling off in the first two years of the new decade, Baptist rolls lengthened greatly in 1843 with the Millerite flurry and declined as suddenly in the next few years.[3]

---

[1] *Minutes of the Conferences of the Methodist Episcopal Church* (New York, 1840), I, II, *passim.*

[2] Rev. James H. Hotchkin, *A History of the Purchase and Settlement of Western New York, and . . . of the Presbyterian Church in That Section* (New York, 1848), *passim;* P[hilemon] H. Fowler, *History of Presbyterianism . . . of Central New York* (Utica, 1877), 70.

[3] *Baptist Register* (Utica), V (July 25, 1828), 86; John Peck and John Lawton, *An Historical Sketch of the Baptist Missionary Convention of the State of New York,* etc. (Utica, 1837), 162–176.

Imperfect though the comparison necessarily is, it seems to indicate adequately the similar growth pattern of the major sects: a great peak following Finney's Rochester Revival, a distinct falling off in the period of increasing ultraism, a degree of recovery in the postultraist stage of the late thirties, and—in the case of Methodists and Baptists, if not of Presbyterians—a flash repetition in the years centering about 1843 of sudden increase and equally precipitous decline. This similarity also suggests that revulsion against extreme revival manners and practices, all without denominational limits, had more to do with the cycle than any peculiarities of doctrine in the different churches. The increasing immigration of European-born Catholics into the canal-line towns, and emigration of rural Yankee stock to the West, of course help to explain the broader changes of the thirties and forties. But these factors could hardly influence the shorter turns of the cycle.

In the early days when the different sects had to share meeting places all churches had been able to co-operate in promoting a season of enthusiasm, though they were apt to wrestle for the converts afterwards. Very similar behavior seems to have characterized the greater revivals of the thirties. The period of waxing zeal witnessed a primary concern for Christian piety, without too much thought for sectarian labels. But as fervor grew rampant and then declined, denominational fences underwent repair.

Charles Finney himself advised that converts "should not be taught to dwell upon sectarian distinctions, or to be sticklish about sectarian points." [4] His practice on the whole corresponded with his profession, especially in the period of the Rochester Revival, when his disregard of denominational lines seriously disturbed some of his warmest supporters. Rochester, at least, continued for several years to feature an association of ministers, who acted together for such a purpose as organizing a day of fast and prayer in time of cholera epidemic. Many of the protracted meetings of the early thirties, and even some in the later years of the decade, made a point of interdenominational support. Joint participation in many of the expanding benevolent and reform movements also alleviated prejudices and mitigated jealousies among the sects.

---

[4] Charles G. Finney, *Lectures on Revivals of Religion* (2nd ed.; New York, 1835), 369.

Co-operation naturally fell short of perfection, however, even at its maximum point, and occasional sour notes in the hymn of millennial expectancy predicted the warfare which was destined to follow. Thus a home missionary complained in 1831, at the height of a five-day meeting run by three sects, that the Baptists appointed their own meetings to garner all the converts. And the *Baptist Register,* praising the greater friendliness between churches brought about by the benevolent movements, added in the next breath that such opportunities should be utilized "for the correction of errors, and the attainment of scriptural views. . . . The liberalities of the age should not become bribes to silence." [5]

As the decade advanced, emphasis shifted more to the sectarian side. Increasingly during the years of climactic ultraism, revival notices included some hint that the church concerned was operating on its own lines, for its own exclusive benefit. Presbyterians "set forth the distinguishing doctrines of our church . . . not passing by those which are distinctly denominated Calvinistic," refused to labor among converts gone Methodist, and complained of Baptist looseness and irregularity. Baptists weakened confidence in a Presbyterian minister by spreading word that he was "not a revival minister." Again, as in the late twenties, many missionaries reported strong prejudices against the Presbyterian Church, wherever "the standard of the gospel has not long been erected . . . except by sectarians." Both Presbyterians and Baptists deplored the diminishing number of "settled" pastors and the progressively shorter terms of those who replaced them. Fickle public taste was keeping both churches in constant flux. [6]

By the middle of the decade a new order of evangelists began to appear, men who grew in favor and effectiveness in the next five years. Working always with established clergymen, they stressed orthodox doctrines and kept enthusiasm within strict limits.

---

[5] William Williams, Victory, June 5, 1831, to Miles P. Squier, American Home Missionary Society Papers, Chicago Theological Seminary; *Baptist Register,* VII (March 5, 1830), 6.

[6] B. B. Smith, Campbell's Town, March 7, 1831, James H. Hotchkin, Hector, Jan. 14, 1832, B. B. Smith, Barrington, July 2, 1833, to Miles P. Squier, and A.H.M.S. MSS, 1831–1833, *passim;* [George Peck], *The Life and Times of Rev. George Peck, D.D.,* etc. (New York, 1874), 174–178; *New York Evangelist,* IV (Nov. 30, 1833), 189; *Western Recorder* (Utica), X (Feb. 12, 1833), 27; *Baptist Register,* XV (July 27, 1838), 94.

Samuel G. Orton received most notice among Presbyterians, and an Elder Simmons, among Baptists. Jacob Knapp was a greater figure but conformed more to the earlier itinerant type. Conservatives praised these efforts, which purported to demonstrate that regeneration, after all, came from above, unsought by special means. But Charles Finney found in 1845 that revivals in the last ten years had "been gradually becoming more and more superficial." [7] Both Presbyterians and Baptists increasingly depended on established pastors of their own church in the neighborhood, rather than upon itinerants, for the conduct of protracted meetings. As early as 1833, the Presbyterian General Assembly at Philadelphia had substantially expanded its missionary work in the region instead of leaving the field mainly to the interdenominational Home Missionary Society. Two years later, Genesee Presbytery requested both the A.H.M.S. and the General Assembly mission board to support no representatives in their bounds without the endorsement of their committee on missions.[8]

Benevolent movement support began to diminish as Baptists and Episcopalians substituted denominational enterprises for cooperation with the predominant Presbyterians and Congregationalists. Indeed, the very combination upon which the great benevolent enterprises had been founded began to disintegrate. At least sixty churches in the Burned-over District, founded by New England missionaries before the Plan of Union grew prevalent in the first decade of the century, had successfully resisted amalgamation and remained in 1834 affiliated only with three or four unfederated local Congregational consociations. During that year the Genesee, Oneida, and Black River groups moved to form a state association.[9] When in the following year the Presbyterian General Assembly annulled the accommodation plan of 1808, so that no churches in the future might retain congregational features while joining a presbytery, and also declared that denominational benevolences took fiscal priority over Plan of Union activities, churches

---

[7] Charles Finney, quoted, *Oberlin Evangelist,* reprint in *Perfectionist* (Putney, Vt.), V (April 19, 1845), 12.

[8] *Rochester Observer,* VII (April 20, 1833), 16; Norris Bull, Wyoming, Sept. 9, 1835, to John Murray, A.H.M.S. MSS.

[9] *New York Evangelist,* V (June 14, 1834), 95.

once Congregational but recently Presbyterian "by accommodation" began to gravitate in the Congregational direction. A new consociation formed in the western portion of the state, and all enjoyed a steady growth. The schism of 1837 in the Presbyterian Church only accelerated the tendency. Although the Plan of Union was not officially terminated until 1852, its basic co-operative principle scarcely survived the thirties in upstate New York. After the schism of 1837, the more radical activities of Plan of Union origin came to depend for support mainly upon the newly resurrected Congregational churches of the region, while the more conservative enterprises fell almost exclusively into New School Presbyterian hands.

This strong reassertion of sectarian distinctions was in part a natural consequence of the revival cycle. It commenced at the peak of enthusiasm, whenever churches began to think of their member rolls and budgets, before ultraism became fully developed. But it was strengthened and perpetuated as ultraism progressed. For the radicalism of the reform movements and the heresy of perfectionism turned moderates into conservatives and prepared a substantial portion of each major denomination for a contest to determine which could best prove its utter orthodoxy. In addition, aside from such rivalries, ultraism eventually brought an outright decline in membership. Enthusiasm could not be perpetually sustained, and the increasingly sensational efforts to defy this religious law of gravity only generated reaction. Hastily made converts "returned to their wallowing," and churches threatened with poverty grasped the harder to fill their own pews. But both the quarrels over radicalism and heresy and the decline of fervor, much as they heightened interdenominational rivalry, did even more to generate schisms within individual sects.

Discerning critics might early have foreseen that extraordinary enthusiasm would quickly subside and leave internal conflict in its wake. Two years after the Western Revival, a correspondent reported to Charles Finney "the awful declension in Oneida Co." Local schisms had also accompanied the great evangelist's early stands in Auburn and Troy. Even while he broadened the revival impulse at Rochester, the church of his first large conquest at Rome split when its pastor could no longer hold with new measures. A church in Seneca Falls similarly divided the same year; and only two years later Third Presbyterian Church of Rochester, finding its new pastor not up to Finney's standards of piety, excluded him and a following who promptly set up for themselves. Some ministers lost churches because they were not sufficiently aggressive revivalists; others because they were too zealous. Even President Davis of Hamilton College was forced from his position on the former grounds.[10]

Such divisions were virtually inevitable, and they grew in number as ultraism advanced until they became denomination-wide clefts. Charles Finney attributed the decline of piety to ecclesiastical contests. He declared, "No doubt there is a jubilee in hell every year, about the time of the meeting of the General Assembly." [11] The decline did, in fact, gain momentum from the efforts of moderate clergymen who had merely bided their time while fervor proved too hot to handle. But fundamentally, it was predestined to occur, however much the ultraist party thought it ought not to. And when ultraists and the more stolid majority in all churches squared off against each other, everyone's fat was in the fire.

Inevitable as they were on the issue of fervency of belief alone, schisms were the more certainly guaranteed by the host of other issues raised when ultraism carried the revival impulse into fields of social reform. Teetotalism, Communion wine, secret societies, the sin of slaveholding—all these and their fellow questions helped to set at odds with each other the same radical- and conservative-minded groups in each church. Nation-wide denominations had in addition to local quarrels the difficulty of holding together their New York and New England branches and those in other parts of the broad country. Most Protestants in upstate New York disliked slavery, but not so many would excommunicate slaveholders at the expense of their church's survival as a national organization. Such

10 H. H. Kellog, Salina, March 26, 1838, to Finney, Maria Roberts, Jan. 12, and Catherine Huntington, Rome, April 4, 1831, to Mrs. Finney, E. Robinson, Sept. 24, and J. M. Goodman, Nov. 30, 1831, Seneca Falls, to Finney, Mary S. Mathews, April 24, May 16, Dec. 19, 1831, to Mrs. Finney, and S. Mathews, May 29, and O. W. Bush, June 4, 1832, Rochester, to Finney, Charles Grandison Finney Papers, Oberlin College Library; J. Brockway, *A Delineation of the Characteristic Features of a Revival of Religion in Troy*, etc. (Troy, 1827), 43 ff.

11 Finney, *Revival Lectures*, 269.

issues led radical reformers on the one hand to brand churches as harbors of sin, and the majority of each sect, on the other, to hasten toward the refuge of thoroughgoing orthodoxy.

Having first given birth to ultraism, the Presbyterian Church most promptly and emphatically set about exercises to restore its normally fashionable figure. Outside of western New York the strength of this denomination extended from its theological center at Princeton westward across Pennsylvania and southward through the Appalachian highlands to the middle and southern frontiers. Mainly Scotch-Irish in origin, and only slightly leavened by Yankee migration, this other part of the church had experienced little of the moderating interpretation of Calvinism which had characterized the entire history of New England Congregationalism. The Plan of Union of 1801 had brought an immense expansion in the reach of country from New York State into the old Northwest Territory, but it could not make the emigrant Yankees into orthodox Calvinists. Princetonian and Scotch-Irish clergymen had long had reason to believe that they had in 1801 traded in heresy for a gain in members. If solid ministers of New England origin suspected ultraism, these men viewed it with outraged alarm. From a distance, it was not apparent that only a minority of ordained pastors actually supported the radical tendencies, while the greater number clung to the middle of the road, suffering extremism in silence when it was too strong to challenge.

With this kind of national situation it was not so strange as it would seem from within the locality alone, that the major quarrel developed between the Princetonian "Old School" and men like Lyman Beecher, Albert Barnes, and the Auburn and Union seminary faculties, who themselves seemed conservative from the Burned-over District point of view. Try as they might to disclaim the radicalism within their province, these men could not allay the charge of doctrinal deviation which permitted the growth of itineracy, perfectionism, and abolition.

Through a series of heresy trials and annual battles in General Assembly the conflict raged for several years. Finally in May, 1837, when the Old School had a clear majority at the Philadelphia meeting for the first time since the battle began, four synods containing nearly half the membership of the church suffered excision. The

New School Assembly, set up after vain attempts to re-enter the old Assembly at Philadelphia, soon attracted several southwestern synods, and thus became as nearly national in breadth as was the Old School after throwing off its northernmost branch.[12]

Within western New York the schism itself had relatively little effect. The three synods of Utica, Geneva, and Genesee, excluded bodily, encompassed nearly all the churches in the region and merely became the backbone of the New School organization. Some twenty congregations split off, either entire or as seceding fragments, to join the Old School, but the conflicts so generated scarcely created a ripple among the greater controversies of the day.

The more evident quarrels accompanied the move of the New School leaders to restore their own control in the Burned-over District. Before 1837 this move was required to prove to the Old School their soundness of doctrine. Thereafter it seemed necessary to demonstrate their superior claims to national recognition and the affiliation of new western synods. As early as 1833, William Wisner, pastor successively at Ithaca and Rochester and one of the more influential and more moderate Finney supporters, spoke out against indiscriminate use of either itinerants or measures, while an A.H.M.S. pastor could make a point of boasting that his eight-day meeting "was a New England meeting as it respects order and measures." The same year Geneva Presbytery tried to force a conservative minister upon an unwilling church at Dresden. The missionary society in New York would support only the presbytery candidate, and the church applied to Finney for other aid.[13]

The full weight of A.H.M.S. funds and influence, indeed, had already shifted to the conservative side. The western New York agency in 1833 and 1834 required a new corresponding secretary: in the earlier year the New York office failed to impose a thorough-going conservative upon the locality for the position, but the next year the local agency itself requested the appointment of Sylvester Eaton, a reluctant advocate of Finney in 1831, but in general a

---

12 William W. Sweet, *The Story of Religions in America* (New York, 1930), 373–379.
13 *New York Evangelist*, IV (Nov. 2, 1833), 175; John W. Irwin, Sackets Harbor, April 15, 1833, to Absolom Peters, A.H.M.S. MSS; P. Robinson, Dresden, Jan. 31, 1833, to Finney, Finney MSS.

forthright opponent of evangelists, rather than John Frost of Whitesboro, who had "developed traits of character which would be injurious to us." A conservative forced out of his Perrinton station warned Absolom Peters against supporting the licentiate of Genesee Congregational Consociation who was to replace him. The central New York agency at Utica meanwhile declared that churches should get aid only for "such ministers as they are desirous of retaining permanently among them." Frequent changes increased expense, made the people "unstable + fastidious," and tempted ministers "to neglect the discipline of the church." By 1835, William Wisner wrote Finney that excepting five men "not a minister in this region" could be relied on "for steady persevering revival action." Throughout the decade presbytery after presbytery proscribed the various itinerant evangelists operating in the ultraist style.[14]

Revival religion and its consequent social and doctrinal radicalisms were still developing during the earlier years of this Presbyterian campaign of proscription and did not suffer extinction in the later years. But ultraists eventually had to move out of Presbyterian churches. Most of them became Congregational, either as individuals or as entire communions. Luther Myrick's Central Evangelical Association served as a similar refuge in the environs of Syracuse and Utica. Other groups remained independent, usually calling themselves Free Congregational or Bethel churches. These two types, with the Union churches eventually rising from the example of Myrick's group, numbered eighty-three in the Burned-over District by 1855. Since the Congregational Church in this state had by the late forties become almost as large as the Presbyterian, it must be concluded that the ultra-minded who departed from the New School churches made up a very respectable-sized minority. But even the Congregational Church proved uncongenial to the perfectionist-tending revivalists of western New York. The entire Genesee Consociation was read out of its church in 1844.[15]

---

[14] Medad Pomeroy and representatives of Cayuga, Bath, and Ontario presbyteries, Aurora, April 25, 1833, Henry Dwight, Geneva, [1834], Alfred White, Perrinton, Jan. 30, 1834, A. Crane, Utica, June 17, 1834, to Absolom Peters, A.H.M.S. MSS; William Wisner, Rochester, March 18, 1835, to Finney, Finney MSS; Hotchkin, *Western New York,* 172 ff.

[15] Joel T. Headley, ed., Franklin B. Hough, Superintendent, *Census of the State of*

The more loosely organized Baptist Church apparently made no effort comparable to that of the Presbyterians and Methodists to create total conformity among local congregations, so it never faced quite the same schism-breeding situation in the Burned-over District as did its rivals. Yet substantial portions of its membership eventually became abolitionists and did their full share to bring about the national schism of 1845. And within upstate New York during the thirties the same kind of divisions and controversies which wreaked havoc in sister churches had only a little less severe repercussions within this church. The *Baptist Register* at the end of 1836 found "Zion—agitated by conflicts and jealousies, and depressed by spiritual debility." [16]

Ultraism, though somewhat delayed, probably made a wider appeal in the Baptist than in the Presbyterian Church, but it ran against some resistance in many localities. Instead of producing concerted church-splitting, in this case it merely involved the mass transfer of individuals to other loyalties, at times in virtually schismatic proportions. Three separate sectarian movements of the thirties and forties gathered converts at great rates, while the orthodox churches on the whole declined. All these sectarian movements were more closely related to the Baptists than to the other major denominations, and they probably drew converts from that church in larger numbers, too.

The Freewill Baptists and the Christian Connection maintained a constant informal alliance, based upon a marked similarity of belief, membership, and attitudes. The one Arminian and the other Unitarian, they were alike liberal in doctrinal matters, and both treasured the congregational independence they derived from their predominant ancestry in New England Baptistry. Both stressed literal Bible belief and regeneration by revival techniques but cared not a fig for any other creed. Both had grown rapidly ever since their first introduction to the region. Both readily accommodated themselves to ultraist positions and practices with the one qualification, shared by the Oberlin perfectionists, that no intermediate objective should be allowed to supersede the conversion of

---

New York, for 1855 (Albany, 1857), 473 ff.; *Minutes of the General Association of New York* (Utica, 1842, 1843, 1844), 17, 9, 11, respectively.

16 *Baptist Register,* XIII (Dec. 30, 1836), 182.

sinners. The Free Baptists took over Oneida Institute in 1843 and successfully ran it as a coeducational and coracial seminary. Scattered fragments of data on individual churches indicate that their growth in the thirties paralleled, though it may not have equaled, that of their companion sect, upon which more data survive.

The *Christian Palladium,* begun in 1832 with a circulation of a thousand copies, doubled its subscriptions in the first year, the increase probably indicating equal growth of the Christian Church. By 1833 the denomination had seventy-one congregations between Onondaga County and the Genesee River, and thirty-six more farther east and west. Although some of their clergymen had stations, all itinerated either regularly or intermittently. At least six "female labourers" may be counted among the traveling evangelists. Having developed rapidly to major proportions in the climactic years of increasing ultraism and tightening orthodoxy, the church appears to have continued to profit for the duration of the decade from the disturbances of the greater denominations. Its journal attained a circulation of five thousand copies in 1839.[17]

The Millerites who gathered during the early forties came from all denominations, but in the largest numbers from the Baptist, Free Baptist and Christian churches. Like the Christians, these Adventists claimed to be nonsectarian, and noncreedal except for a literal belief in Scripture. They left their original churches only under persecution and had not thought of clerical organization even when they had "come out." But when the day passed which should have ended time, they founded a whole group of new sects instead of returning to their tormentors. For a year or two, at least, droves of persons were drawn from all the Baptist-tending sects and from Methodist groups as well, often breeding local schisms in the process.

Methodism was by profession Arminian and perfectionist, so it had little to fear from the theological innovations of ultraism. Indeed, events in the early thirties may have made it seem the logical resort for radicals. But the church had by this time become a great institution—probably the largest religious organization in the

---

[17] *Christian Palladium* (West Mendon, Union Mills), II (June, Oct., Dec., 1833), 68, 169, 197, 240, VIII (June 1, Dec. 2, 1839), 46, 234, X (Dec. 1, 1841, Jan. 1, 1842), 233, 265.

country—and had a natural interest in self-preservation which the social radicalism born in ultraism rapidly came to threaten. The episcopal organization which had so excellently managed a vast expansion could be directed even more easily than the more complicated Presbyterian mechanisms toward the suppression of dangerous tendencies. Thus the late thirties saw Methodism come about on the same conservative tack with the Presbyterians, and the episcopacy trimmed ship with an even more relentless efficiency. Abolition became the chief issue, but secret societies, teetotalism, closeness to Wesleyan concepts of holiness, and democratic procedures in church affairs all involved themselves in the quarrels which followed.

Not until 1836 did the antislavery impulse threaten the Burned-over District Methodists, but it then developed with amazing rapidity. Within eight months *Zion's Watchman* had as many active agents in the region as in all New England.[18] That same year, Orange Scott formed an antislavery society of half the clergymen in the Erie Conference. At the Oneida Conference meeting he was excluded by Bishop Hedding but gathered the attending members in a Baptist church to hear the abolition gospel. The next year he reached Jamestown, Lockport, Canandaigua, Auburn, and Cortland, forming Methodist abolition groups in each place and often generating disputes in district and conference sessions of the church.[19] George Storrs late in 1836 invaded the Utica neighborhood, moved on to Oswego as the year changed, and thence transferred to the developing antislavery stronghold about Wyoming County and the middle Genesee Valley. Genesee Conference had bred fifty abolition ministers from five a year before, now holding only forty neutrals and conservatives to oppose them. Returning to Cazenovia, Storrs organized a denominational convention dedicated to pushing abolition in all conference meetings of the church. Similar action followed in the Black River area and about Seneca Falls and Waterloo.[20]

---

[18] *Zion's Watchman* (New York), I (Aug. 3, 1836), 124.

[19] *Ibid.*, II (Aug. 26, Sept. 2, 6, 16, 30, 1837), 134–155; Lucius C. Matlack, *The History of American Slavery and Methodism, from 1780–1849*, etc. (New York, 1849), 162.

[20] *Zion's Watchman*, I (Oct. 26, 1836), 169, II (Feb. 18, March 4, 25, April 8, Aug. 12, 26, Sept. 2, 30, Oct. 14, 21, 28, 1837), 26, 27, 34, 46, 53, 134, 138, 155, 162, 167, 170.

The national General Conference of 1836 had voted nearly unanimously to stifle discussion of the issue, but Genesee Conference was forced immediately to create a committee to handle antislavery petitions. The bishop co-operated, with the understanding that no report should contradict the national position. Yet seven hundred petitions poured in demanding disciplinary rules against slavery, and Attica Quarterly Meeting directly defied the bishop with a set of totally ultraist resolves.[21]

Luther Lee, a leading lecturer in northern New York and a convincing contributor to *Zion's Watchman*, was in 1838 chosen to represent antislavery Methodists at the Canadian Conference. He suffered exclusion from the meeting, owing to the advice of conservative United States churchmen, and wrote a dramatic account of the episode in the *Watchman*. After a trial in his home conference, he was punished by appointment to Oswego, where a weak church provided inadequate support. He declined to go. Meanwhile, he twice circumvented church rules by preaching before other denominations when denied access to Methodist congregations. At the same time Troy Conference failed in an attempt to put one of its most prominent men on trial for his abolition speeches. Other men from time to time received appointments to laborious and unremunerative circuits in return for their antislavery lectures.[22] By expulsions, trials, discriminatory appointments, and ironclad control of conference meetings by the bishops, the church thus tried to restrain the urge to radicalism.

The antislavery forces gradually lost their battle for freedom of expression within the church, but they continued to expand. By 1840 the Wesleyan Antislavery Societies had coalesced in a national organization. Genesee Conference was the only one in its region to send a majority of abolitionists to that year's General Conference, but petitions signed by ten thousand laymen and five hundred preachers went to the meeting, including resolutions from both Black River and Genesee, and from five circuits within Oneida Conference. The national meetings of 1840 and 1841, however, stuck to the conservative position, so the radicals turned

21 *Ibid.*, I (May 25, June 29, Oct. 2, 1836), 81, 101, 163, II (Sept. 23, 1837), 150.
22 Matlack, *Slavery and Methodism*, 178; Charles B. Swaney, *Episcopal Methodism and Slavery*, etc. (Boston, 1926), 82–86; *Zion's Watchman*, V (Oct. 31, 1840), 173.

toward secession. Isolated communions in New England, New York, and Ohio departed between 1839 and 1842. Conventions followed at Albany, Andover, Massachusetts, and finally at Utica, in May, 1843.[23]

Here it was that the Wesleyan Methodist Church took form. Six thousand members spread across nine states pledged themselves to a broadly ultraist discipline. Teetotalism and abolition were both tests for membership. Conferences must have equal lay and clerical representation, with two delegates for every five hundred members, and instead of a bishop a president, who had no right to cast a ballot in a tie vote. A rule against secret societies went into the discipline the following year. In that one year, the Burned-over District conferences increased their numbers to a total of eight and a half thousand, while all the others in New England and the West together just exceeded six thousand. This growth of nearly 150 per cent in a year failed to continue, but in the ensuing five years the local conferences gained three times as many members as the balance of the church.[24] The movement, broad as it was, thus continued to discover its major strength in this one region.

The sudden expansion terminated abruptly because the main Methodist Church, learning a lesson from the schism, nipped it in the bud. Genesee delegates in the following General Conference pushed through a compromise but strengthened antislavery rule. The northern church was thus saved at the expense of the southern, which departed the next year.

These events checked the Wesleyan movement but failed to cure its differences with the old denomination. The Wesleyan Conference of 1844 noted that favorable action in the parent body had taken place on grounds of necessity, not righteousness—"a clear illustration of the absurdity and utter futility of *expediency,* when it is allowed to take the helm in the place of principle, and control the church on great moral questions." The Wesleyans still believed

---

[23] *Zion's Watchman,* V (Oct. 10, 1840), 162; Matlack, *Slavery and Methodism,* 200–208, 229–232, 301–305, 322–328.

[24] Matlack, *Slavery and Methodism,* 349, 363; Lucius C. Matlack, "Report of the First General Conference of the Wesleyan Connection of America," *The Debates of the General Conference of the Methodist Episcopal Church . . .* [and] *A Review of the Proceedings by Rev. Luther Lee and Rev. E. Smith* (New York, 1845), 476.

with George Storrs that "Methodist Episcopacy . . . [was] both anti-Christian and anti-scriptural." [25]

Thus ultraism in one way or another damaged every major denomination which tried to fight it. How it affected the religion of those who espoused it remains to be seen.

[25] *Ibid.*, 371; *Zion's Watchman*, V (Aug. 22, 1840), 133.

Chapter 16. THE PATTERN OF

DISPERSING ULTRAISM

RELIGIOUS ultraism reached its peak about 1836. Then it quite suddenly collapsed. For six years more, roughly coincident with the economic depression following the 1837 panic, its personnel floundered about in a period of readjustment. The time of disintegration and reorientation practically defies coherent narrative, as small groups of enthusiasts moved at different paces along variant routes away from their common position of the mid-thirties. Every crowd jostled its fellows in transit and dropped or acquired members at successive crossroads. But the causes of the collapse and the major trends of the transition phase must be investigated, both to permit an informed evaluation of ultraism and to provide an adequate understanding of developments in the following decade.

Both the nature of ultraism itself and the pressure of external circumstances helped to bring about its disintegration. Either reason alone might well seem sufficient cause to explain the result, and only the boldest determinist would hazard an attempt closely to apportion shares of responsibility between them. External forces happened in large measure to dictate the moment of the collapse and certainly bore weightily upon the changing styles of thought which accompanied the reorientation.

The period of ultraist ascendancy, indeed, had not itself occurred without the reinforcement of suitable political and economic circumstances. The revival cycle had long been inclined to an inverse conformity with the business cycle, rising with hard times and falling with good. On first sight, a peak of religious enthusiasm coinciding with the generally buoyant conditions of the early thirties would seem to be a puzzling contradiction, but closer analysis resolves the paradox.

In the first place, an extreme depression, such as came to western New York for the first time after 1837, did not serve the interests of religious fervor as well as a slighter recession. Severe panic made people focus attention upon physical survival. Although a resurgence of revivalism did come in the years following 1837, this wave had less comprehensive effects on the popular mind than the one which followed 1830. The prevalent mood of distress encouraged once-religious reform movements to take a turn toward more direct methods than those of the sin-consciousness technique.

The early thirties, despite their general prosperity, included episodic recessions and local economic maladjustments sufficient to restrain a substantial proportion of folk from any exclusive pursuit of material gain. The canal boom had subsided since 1828 about Rochester and points to the east, and the Genesee River town and vicinity, at least, felt increasingly for two years the constraints of a settling economy.[1] The constriction of credits by the Second United States Bank a little later, calculated to place upon Andrew Jackson the onus of hard times in the 1832 presidential election, while boomeranging against the bank forces in the election, brought about a degree of recession which was even more emphatically punctuated in western New York by the stilling hand of epidemic cholera.

The alien-owned land companies of the more westerly section of the Burned-over District, meanwhile, spurred on by a law of 1833 taxing the debt held by aliens on uncompleted land contracts, utilized the more prosperous years of the interval to collect substantial payments and arrearages from leaner years. In parts of the Pulteney Estate east of the Genesee and in most of the Holland Purchase west of the river, most available specie was at certain moments thus withdrawn. The highest pitch of local antirent fever to date appeared in 1834, south of the Batavia land office. With a whip hand over the company in the legislature and the prevalence of

---

[1] See earlier, pp. 72, 73.

good times, however, the lessees still felt more secure than they would in a few years.[2]

Moderate recession sufficed to generate among debtors a moderate discontent, usually falling short of direct action—a mood which could easily be diverted into otherworldliness. Among the more prosperous, it allowed the persistence of a sense that the economy and polity were fundamentally sound, to be improved by an attack on the sins of individuals more than by alterations of the social system. Yet it moderated the expectation, to which they might otherwise have entirely yielded, of prompt enrichment by concentrated money-making activities. The full swing of a speculative boom developed in western New York only from 1835 to the verge of the panic two years later, and in these years a majority of church folk had turned to conservative religious attitudes.

The most favorable kind of economic doldrums thus served to help get ultraism started. Once it gathered momentum, the coincidence of extreme prosperity, even while reducing the number of supporters, served to propel the remainder along their way. Reformer-capitalists had the more money to spend; and all the zealots could look the more eagerly toward millennial conditions within the framework of general optimism over economic affairs.

The politics of the early thirties likewise suited the mood of ultraism in subtle rather than in direct fashion. The ascendancy of Jacksonian Democracy in Washington and the Van Buren Regency at Albany might upon casual glance seem unfortunate for the religious radicals who by way of Antimasonry drifted into the opposition fold of the Whigs. Actually, the contrary was true. It was far easier to condemn all the workings and purposes of the government and to escape all responsibility for its operation, when enemies instead of friends occupied the seats of power. Again, the agnosticism of the workingmen's groups which increasingly dominated Jacksonian policies made holiness the more popular among a people bred to evangelical religion and already shunted into the opposition.

But to think of the religious radicalism and the political liberal-

---

[2] Paul D. Evans, *The Holland Land Company* (Buffalo, 1924), 364–415, *passim;* Justin Marsh, West Aurora, June 7, 1834, to Absolom Peters, American Home Missionary Society Papers, Chicago Theological Seminary.

ism of the thirties as mutually exclusive opposites is misleading. Ultraism, however much it harbored seemingly dictatorial attitudes toward other people's lives, was essentially another radical democracy, complementary to the Jacksonian brand. Revivalism was throughout the period a folk movement, contesting clerical conservatism. Complete equality, at least in theory, dwelt among the regenerate of all communions. In ideal the benevolent movements aimed to convert every last sinner and, under ultraist direction, to remove his every least sin. During the millennium and before the judgment seat, everyone, quick or dead, would realize final equality. No political party in American history has championed a doctrine so utterly leveling!

The major weakness of the religious radicals was their exaggerated concern for the individual soul. They came to believe that all evil must reside there, rather than in the environment, and they could consequently comprehend no wrong which required social amelioration. So the tremendous energy of ultraism went largely into channels where conservatives wanted it to go, safely distant from economic reforms which might raise the multitude and lower the few in this world. Their excessive individualism may have tricked these radicals into supporting the wrong party in politics, but their spirit was fundamentally one with Jacksonian Democracy, and the occasional logic of history is demonstrated by the fact that ultraism and Jacksonism rose and fell together.[3]

The optimistic mood had overextended itself in politics, economics, and religion alike when the panic of 1837 pricked the bubble. Retrenchment and confusion followed in all fields while people regained their bearings. The economy righted itself very slowly, achieving full recovery only after 1844. A revivified Jacksonian Democracy, incorporating changes appropriate to the new decade, appeared when James K. Polk entered the White House in 1845. Rather more promptly, on the whole, former ultraists discovered the new emphases which a new era required of their persistent aims and launched the isms of the forties.

[3] Ralph H. Gabriel, *The Course of American Democratic Thought: An Intellectual History Since 1815* (New York, 1940), 33–37, points up the deeper parallelism of religious and political democracy. [Calvin Colton], *A Voice from America to England,* etc. (London, 1839), vii, 107, apparently practically alone among contemporaries, sensed the situation.

The panic and the depression created the external forces which acted to disperse ultraism. Political currents became more lively as well as more confused. Banking and corporation practices, the increased public debt, lavish use of public funds in canal construction, and other issues sharpened by the business reversal became more vital questions in state politics than had existed for a decade. On the national level, 1837 accomplished what the United States Bank had failed to manage five years earlier, a wholesale reaction against the Jacksonians. The Whig-minded folk of western New York had their best opportunity to share power since the presidency of John Quincy Adams. The noisy campaign of 1840 ran up abnormal Whig pluralities for Harrison in the secure section west of the Genesee River, and carried all but six of the counties to the east within the Burned-over District, seven more than had been won against a Democrat since 1820 and nine more than Clay would capture four years later.[4] Enough votes had shifted columns to demonstrate a greatly intensified interest in the affairs of this world, and a consequently diminished concentration upon preparation for the next.

Beyond the realm of party battles, secular excitements freshly intensified by economic decline diverted attention in similar fashion. Antirent riots on the Holland Purchase reached a new crisis the year before the panic. The Holland Company, handicapped by legal restrictions on alien owners, sold most of its lands to native magnates during 1835. The new lessors proceeded rigorously with collections and evictions during 1836, generating widespread mob action which focused in Chautauqua County and in an armed raid on the Batavia land office. The fever subsided through the panic year, but the difficulty of making payments must have increased even as violence diminished.[5] Uninvestigated, but probably roughly similar, agrarian agitation appeared spasmodically through the thirties about Steuben and Wayne counties, east of the Genesee, and these areas as well as the Holland Purchase doubtless reflected some of the tenseness of the more noteworthy tenure squabbles in the Catskills and the Hudson Valley during the forties.[6]

---

[4] Charles O. Paullin, *Atlas of the Historical Geography of the United States* (John K. Wright, ed., Washington, 1932), plates 103, 104.

[5] Evans, *Holland Land Company*, 388–422.

[6] David Higgins, Kennedyville, Aug. 26, 1833, to Miles P. Squier, George King,

The Canadian Rebellion which broke out in 1837 also gained many sympathizers in upstate New York. A number of people lent active support to the rebels, in the "Caroline" episode on the Niagara River and in the comic-opera campaign of the Hunter's Lodges to capture Prescott across the St. Lawrence. Recruits to the Hunter's army came from lodges in all the major towns and many smaller ones which bordered on Canada along the Niagara, Lake Ontario, and St. Lawrence shores.[7]

No evidence has appeared to connect any individual involved in the religious movements of the thirties with these unneutral activities. The abolitionists, at least, discouraged any sympathy whatever, supposing that success of the rebellion would bring Canada into the Union and end its usefulness as a refuge for slaves.[8] And although many clergymen seem to have taken the popular side in the rent riots, evidence is lacking to establish them as leading ultraists. Probably the major support for these excitements came from an entirely different class. Yet the mere existence of such diversions evidently affected entire communities of people.

Much more solidly and directly, economic depression reacted upon religious enterprises by pinching their purses. The organized radicalisms had won the support of relatively few wealthy men and depended heavily upon the contributions of these stalwarts. The Tappan fortune practically dissolved in 1837; the Rochester capitalists lost heavily in the New York City wheat riots the same year; Gerrit Smith, the largest landlord of New York State, met severe straits in the early forties; and others with chiefly western land speculations probably suffered even more. Thereupon struggling Oberlin College almost died; the Finney family for the moment neared starvation; and Oneida Institute sold out to avoid bankruptcy.[9] Stringency of money during a considerable interval was

---

Portageville, Jan. 7, 1835 [unaddressed], and Seymour Thompson, Buffalo, Oct. 14, 1835, to Secretary Murray, A.H.M.S. MSS.

[7] Orrin E. Tiffany, "Relations of the United States to the Canadian Rebellion of 1837–1838," *Publications of the Buffalo Historical Society* (Frank H. Severance, ed., Buffalo, 1905), VIII, 65, 66.

[8] *Union Herald* (Cazenovia), Dec. 29, 1838.

[9] *Baptist Register* (Utica), XIX (April 1, 1842), 30; Ralph V. Harlow, *Gerrit Smith, Philanthropist and Reformer* (New York, 1939), 24–33; Robert S. Fletcher, *A History of Oberlin College . . . Through the Civil War* (2 vols.; Oberlin, O., 1943), I, 415–416; Henry O'Reilly, *Settlement in the West, Sketches of Rochester* (Rochester, 1838), 365.

perhaps the most decisive single factor causing the disintegration of ultraism.

Beyond the immediate scarcity of cash, few of the more consistent zealots could perceive any relationship between the state of the economy and the direction of their own thoughts. Even politics they scarcely understood except as their own designs became related to the subject. But if stronger appeals beyond the field of religion served chiefly to draw off the less loyal devotees who had lent more mass than inspiration to ultraism, the leaders themselves also underwent change, however unconsciously. Defection of their followers, diminution of their financial support, and an unobserved intrusion of the prevalent pessimism into their solidly righteous minds helped to turn their labors toward more practical channels.

Attributable in part to their experience—to the indubitable fact that their previous methods had not yet brought the millennium discernibly nearer—and in part to their gradual evolution of aim from general salvation to particular objects, this more practical trend stems also from a more modest estimate of the country's immediate potentialities after 1837.[10] The temperance forces turned from moral suasion to legal compulsion. Moral reform undertook campaigns to punish by law those who had no respect for chastity. Antislavery men gave up revivalism and its pious convictions of the sin of bondage, in favor of political moves to accomplish emancipation. Disillusion recommended less faith in the goodness and automatic accomplishments of the regenerate man and more faith in measures calculated to make men behave aright.

But ultraist points of view had become habitual with many Yorker minds, and could scarcely be obliterated by a momentary turn of events. Despite changed tactics, several characteristics of the earlier way of thought would persevere in large measure until the adults of the early thirties gradually gave way to a new generation. Most ultraists continued to be enthusiasts during and after the depression. Reform was still to be accomplished rapidly, in great strides, not painstakingly and patiently by slow, small steps. The objective continued to be an absolute, not a relative, improvement. People must still be brought to an emotionalized state of

---

[10] See Samuel Rezneck, "The Social History of an American Depression, 1837–1843," *American Historical Review*, XV (July, 1935), 662–687.

intense conviction to accomplish anything, though they might now be convinced by a variety of methods beyond the revival technique and persuaded perhaps to cast ballots rather than merely to pledge their faith.

The religious radicals also continued to be mainly one-idea men. Many of them turned about with amazing speed and frequency after 1837, but at any given moment they stuck to one cause and believed that one to be the single panacea for the ills of their age. The channels they chose to navigate, furthermore, continued more often than not to be those they had embarked upon in the early thirties. A large number, to be sure, transferred their fervor to newly current fads of European origin: mesmerism, phrenology, Swedenborgianism, or Fourierism. In the last case advocates even adopted a somewhat socialized approach to reform, substituting the small community for the individual, and experiment for preaching as a propaganda technique. But they grasped in no very realistic fashion the broader problems of an entire society and kept the movement an essentially emotional proposition, a fad, and a panacea. The other novelties took the same form. The practical turn of the reformers in the depression era carried very few of them, indeed, far enough from their earlier habits to make them effective agitators against the pervasive problems of their own society. The problems of the South, of course, were quite a different matter!

The legacy of ultraism to the forties was thus still powerful enough to balance the environmental factors making for changed expressions. This persisting legacy suggests that ultraism itself had considerable internal strength, which might have resisted even more successfully the forces of change had not inherent weaknesses co-operated in bringing about disintegration.

The ultraists had highly individualized personal inspiration and convictions which poorly matched their zeal for concerted action. As their campaigns approached extremes, their will for organization could appear to be only the desire of each person to make others conform with himself, a contention-breeding attitude which terminated effective operations. Internal strains, before the depression, had weakened the temperance movement, divided the abolition crusade into quarreling factions, put the moral reformers through painful reorganizations, raised sectarian walls, and generated conflict in every major church. "Come-outist" sects of the thirties helped to carry the revival impulse along different paths toward the enthusiasms of the forties. Another influence for change developed within ultraism was the growing, evolving antislavery impulse, much involved incidentally in the bickerings of the mid-thirties, but of great account in its own right.

Its expansion sapped the strength of other causes. Abolitionists, to be sure, usually remained the teetotalers they had been before slavery took the spotlight; in similar fashion they often retained perfunctory interest in moral reform, perfectionism, or revivals. But these became increasingly passive concerns. Slavery presented a much more convenient challenge, for it did not have to do with the transgressions of friends and neighbors. It naturally seemed also a far more enormous and dramatic evil, since the propagandists emphasized violence, miscegenation, and the pathos of the auction block. By comparison, temperance seemed nearly accomplished and revivalism only a distraction useful in the hands of conservatives to divert attention from this deepest sin.

The antislavery societies themselves experienced troubles during the late thirties, but these rose from the changing nature of the movement, not from any diminution of interest. The once-united forces split into nonresistance and political action groups, religious and nonreligious factions, one-idea and general reform camps, into stronger state organizations and two weak "national" ones, and into every conceivable combination crossing these different classi-fications. But despite such fragmentation and brief slackenings of concern owing to more spasmodic competitive excitements, the cause waxed ever stronger.

Gerrit Smith, once a zealous temperance man, scarcely longer touched that subject, or the host of others which from time to time had enlisted his attention or his benevolence. James Jackson aban-doned temperance for antislavery lecturing, until his shattered health led him to espouse hydropathy cures instead. Theodore Weld gave up temperance, manual-labor schools, and revivals to preach emancipation. Luther Myrick forsook revivalism and per-fectionism for the greater cause. James Boyle drifted into it, and out again to new ventures. A host of lesser leaders from all sects became for the time more concerned about emancipation than about the religious doctrines of their respective churches. All the schisms except the Presbyterian released people from obligations to southern confreres, so they could espouse abolition with impunity.

The growth of antislavery sentiment helped terminate ultraism merely by absorbing its personnel in the one crusade. Even more significant was the changed emphasis of that campaign. The very intensification of enthusiasm in this one religion-inspired reform led it beyond the scope of revivalism. Ultraist concentration upon freedom from sin grew to be something entirely different: the attempt of one section of the country to enforce its own moral standards upon another. Ultraist prepossession with the eradication of all evils before the millennium gave way before the more pressing urge to reconstitute this world for contemporary enjoyment.

This altered conception of reform, primarily generated by the abolitionists but reflected alike in the more practical turn of most of the other causes of the mid-thirties, drove a wedge into the ranks of the ultraists. In addition to other divisions of lesser scale, the depression period bred two broad, opposed tendencies which would run in separate parallel channels through the forties. For not all the religious-minded folk of the thirties could so easily bridge the growing gap between the reform movements and their accustomed religious beliefs. Many Oberlin perfectionists, Christians, Wesleyans, Free Baptists, regular Baptists, and Methodists, with some Presbyterians and Congregationalists, would doubtless be willing to cast a ballot for the Liberty Party or for a Conscience Whig. But they could not conscientiously follow the now non- or antireligious emphasis of the abolition leaders. Disillusioned with the movements of the thirties which led beyond their religious inspiration, they inclined to retreat into a more strict fundamentalism, where literal adherence to Scripture and exclusive concern for spiritual regeneration of individual souls forbade any great zeal for the current style of reform.[11] Still enthusiasts from long conditioning, and ever sensitive to the appeal of a new panacea,

---

[11] Finney and many followers continued to be zealous reformers while putting religion first. G. H. Barnes and D. L. Dumond, eds., *Letters of Theodore Dwight Weld, Angelina Grimké Weld, and Sarah Grimké, 1822–1844* (2 vols.; New York, 1934), I, 318 ff.

they made ready converts to the premillennial ideas of William Miller in the early forties. In this direction rode those who turned right at the great fork in the highway out of ultraism.

The left branch of the road was less well paved and ran a devious course beset with tempting side lanes, but those who took it could travel far, whereas the smooth-looking right branch ended on a precipice a few miles ahead. The less literal but more practical and experimental-minded ultraists who turned left were in the main Congregationalists of the Oberlin school or independent groups, Hicksite Quakers, a sprinkling of Baptists and Wesleyans, and a variety of Congregational or Presbyterian clergymen representing the most puissant leadership of the 1830 revivals. These groups included most of the region's antislavery leaders.

Motivated by no systematic hypothesis derived from French Revolutionary humanitarianism or in any direct fashion by any other liberalizing doctrine and untouched by the newer scientific concepts of a rarefied intellectual stratosphere, these men traveled varying distances toward liberal religion, Bible criticism, and a social gospel. Events, not ideas, pushed them along. One small step led into new circumstances which required new conclusions, and still another step. Few of them, indeed, would have chosen at the outset the positions they finally took. Here appears the grand paradox of ultraism. Its truest, most consistent, most fanatical exponents, following the logic of events and of their faith, wound up at the opposite pole of religious belief.

One movement begun in the early thirties and carried through the forties happens almost perfectly to illustrate the transition which many individuals accomplished in roughly similar fashion. Indeed, this particular evolution coincidentally provides a single thread run practically from beginning to end of Burned-over District enthusiasms, and it approximates the median course among them all.

Old Father Nash had helped Charles Finney distill the desires of backwoods folk of the pioneer era into the measures of the Western Revivals. His most direct legacy was bequeathed to Luther Myrick and the Oneida Evangelical Association. Read out of the Presbyterian Church and refused by the Congregational in the early thirties for overintense revivalism, this group commenced a perfectionist phase just before the middle of the decade. Unsectarian in its emphasis upon the abolition of all sins almost to the exclusion of creed, the group began about 1836 to focus especially upon the one sin of slavery. Although it was saturated in revivalist traditions, the organization nevertheless viewed regeneration as a state symbolized by righteous belief in current issues.

Since all the established churches temporized in order to reconcile new movements with old theologies or to maintain a national status, they appeared increasingly to be condoning sin. This association, on the contrary, was pure. What could be more appropriate than for this group to form the nucleus of the true church, free from sin: a nucleus to which right-minded congregations might adhere as they found their old denominations wallowing in evil? With such an example before them, all Christian sects would soon learn the futility of expediency, and before long all would be joined in this one Union church, where concerted action could bring the millennium to pass forthwith.[12]

Where the idea of the Union church originated it is difficult to discover. Ezra Stiles Ely's proposals of the late twenties for a Christian Political Party should perhaps be considered an antecedent. The *New York Evangelist* in 1836 noted experiments in this direction by a group in Connecticut. A letter on the subject reached Gerrit Smith in December, 1835, but he apparently failed to become associated with the local enterprise in that direction for three more years. Whether Luther Myrick came to this logical conclusion of his earlier positions independently or gathered inspiration from abroad cannot be determined, but he apparently began to be active very early, if not at the start of the movement.[13] His reorganized Central Evangelical Association, with fifteen ministers, eight licentiates, and seven churches, resolved in July, 1835, that "*union of feeling and sentiment* . . . can never be obtained till . . . [churches] abandon their exclusive creeds, and incorporate

---

[12] J. W. Adams to J. Bushnell, July, 1837, in *Union Herald*, April 20, 1838; *New York Evangelist*, VI (Dec. 5, 1835), 277.

[13] *New York Evangelist*, VII (Feb. 13, March 26, 1836), 27, 50; *Baptist Register*, 1835, *passim*; Arnold Buffum, Philadelphia, Dec. 7, 1835, to Smith, Gerrit Smith Papers, Syracuse University Library, cited in Harlow, *Smith*, 197 ff.; Smith's name first appears in this connection in *Union Herald*, June 22, 1838; *Baptist Register*, XVI (June 14, 1839), 69.

nothing in their articles that will shut off their fellowship with any true child of God." [14] In May, 1836, he established the *Union Herald* at Cazenovia, devoted to church union, abolition, and perfectionism.

The members of the association became agents for the *Herald* and agitators both for abolition and for sinless, nonsectarian community churches. Antislavery leaders of various denominational origins joined this congenial company as it gathered headway during the late thirties. James C. Jackson, Silas Hawley, Gerrit Smith, William Goodell, Beriah Green, George Storrs, and John Keep, and when the movement spread into Massachusetts, Joshua Himes, John Collins, and George Ripley, became affiliated. A convention at Syracuse in August, 1838, gathered sixty apostles from central New York "for the purpose of . . . adopting the most feasible methods, to annihilate the existing denominational distinctions. . . ." Other meetings followed at Cazenovia and Rochester, the latter indicating a considerable extension into the western reaches of the state. During 1839 at least three congregations in the region inaugurated unionism, and Gerrit Smith planned another at Peterboro. Other assemblies convened within four years at Penn Yan, Apulia, Auburn, Syracuse, and Groton, Massachusetts. By 1843, Alder Creek, Preble, Penn Yan, Albany, Sherburne, Oswego, Peterboro, and Canastota had Union churches, while most of the once religion-inspired antislavery leaders in the region had joined the movement. [15]

Early in 1843, William Goodell moved from Utica and his editorship of the *Friend of Man* to the country village of Honeoye, situated in the hill country south of Rochester. Here he built a Union congregation and began publishing the *Christian Investigator*, a journal which soon had 1,300 paid subscribers, mainly west of Oneida County. Goodell's slogan, "Pro-slavery, or Apparently Neutral Churches, are Anti-Christian," covered an ample program. He proposed separate *"Antislavery action"* in home and foreign missions, seamen's relief, and all associated endeavors, in order to

---

[14] *New York Evangelist*, VI (Oct. 3, 1835), 248.

[15] *Union Herald*, Aug. 24, 1838, and 1836–1842, *passim* (file incomplete); *Christian Investigator* (Honeoye, 1843–1848).

punish the old line benevolent societies for "pro-slavery" positions. His church, composed of former Methodist Protestants and Congregationalized Presbyterians, called itself "the church of God at Honeoye" and made the actual living of Christian morals the exclusive test of membership, interpreted by clauses on the millennium, teetotalism, and abolition.[16]

Myrick, Goodell, and their followers considered themselves statesmen in church polity rather than saviors of individual souls. They angled for entire congregations, and, prospectively, for denominations. Their difference from earlier sects which also claimed a nondenominational bearing was fully appreciated at least by the Christians, whose *Palladium* observed, "A union of the sects is one thing, and a union of the saints another, and a very different thing. If the sects are ever united it will be by *human* policy; and their union will prove their destruction. . . ."[17] More explicitly, to make abolition the test of godliness was to destroy evangelical religion.

Before long, the unionists were turning upon the orthodox sects the same criticisms which Protestants had long used against Catholicism: their origins and policies were unscriptural; their revivalism, failing to stress specific sins, "lays as broad a foundation for superstition . . . as that of the second and third centuries which ripened into Romanism." Because clerical influence seemed most conservative, unionists believed, "There can be no Spiritual Christian Union under a system where ministers claim the exclusive right of religious teaching. . . ."[18] In their own churches the Union congregation elected the preacher, dispensing with ordination. It was only consistent to permit lay management of marriage and the other sacraments.

When Liberty Party campaigning invaded the Sabbath, and other churches refused their pulpits, Gerrit Smith preached the political gospel on the village green, and the *Oberlin Evangelist* applauded him for it. He incidentally began at this point rationalizations which finally led him to seventh-day notions. George

---

[16] *Christian Investigator*, I (Feb., May, Sept., Nov., 1843), 1, 32, 63, 78.
[17] *Christian Palladium* (Union Mills), VIII (July 1, 1839), 73.
[18] *Christian Investigator*, I (Oct., 1843), 65–70; *Union Herald*, Aug. 24, 1838.

Bush of New York City, successively a Presbyterian, abolitionist, unionist, Swedenborgian, and spiritualist, described exactly how the unionists reacted in a letter to Smith in 1845:

You have been led, as I have, to unexpected results. In attacking one weak spot of the current system, you found that there were a good many others in the near neighborhood, till at last it became difficult to tell what was not rotten.[19]

Other antislavery leaders and reformers of other types underwent a similar transformation during the forties. John Humphrey Noyes, who himself intensified the revival impulse into perfectionism, and perfectionism into a nonliteralist, practical-minded communism quite opposed in spirit to the religion he started from, could see the trend in others better than in himself. He traced the reformer's usurpation of the Bible, from the Communion wine, through abolition and nonresistance, to women's rights, where "the Misses Grimké . . . declared independence of the authority of Paul." The reformers became infidels because they were too impatient "to wait on the slow movements, by which God and the Bible are working out redemption for man." Instead they "learned at last to trample on the Bible boldly, whenever they conceive that it crosses the path of their favorite enterprises for human improvement." [20] He also realized that the mingling of Quakers, Unitarians, Universalists, and transcendentalists with the once-orthodox reformers had a bearing on their change. Burned-over District zealots had on the whole little affection for, or patience with, William Lloyd Garrison and his followers, but even in fighting his principles of reform they were put in a way to think along new lines.

Few contemporaries observed that this kind of change was a broad, general tendency or understood how it happened. The membership of the two diverging strands of ultraism spent more of their time cursing than explaining each other. But one Presbyterian, observing the numbers of abolitionists who wandered from the fold, admitted that "there was no doubting the realness and eminence of their piety, while their integrity was a marvel and a

---

[19] *Oberlin Evangelist* (Oberlin, O.), V (Nov. 22, 1843), 190; George Bush, New York, Aug. 6, 1845, to Smith, Gerrit Smith MSS.

[20] John H. Noyes, *The Berean: A Manual for . . . Those Who Seek the Faith of the Primitive Church* (Putney, Vt., 1847), 16, 19.

charm." Antoinette Brown Blackwell, one of the first four college graduates of her sex and probably the first ordained woman minister in the country, had preached to a Wesleyan Methodist Church in Wayne County, but soon became Unitarian. She wrote to Gerrit Smith in the early fifties, "What will you say Mr. Smith at my getting more and more unorthodox? Will you be sorry about the part you took at the ordination?" About the same time, Elizabeth Cady Stanton decided that since the *New York Observer* had dubbed her an infidel she ought to "look up [her] associates," Tom Paine and Fanny Wright! James Birney's last letter to Smith in 1857 stated that he had long since "lost all confidence in mere beliefs as necessary to happiness hereafter." [21]

Theodore Weld had written Birney in 1842, "That a vast amount of what passes for truth in the religious world, is not taught in the Bible and is utterly contradicted by reason seems clear to me." In 1843, when Lewis Tappan learned something of Weld's heretical trend of thought and that he believed some of the antinomian perfectionists to be pious, while his wife, Angelina Grimké, was flirting with Millerism, he asked Charles Finney to "write a faithful letter to brother Weld." But a few months later, after further conversations with Theodore, Tappan himself could ask, "Why has Christianity made so little progress . . . provided it has been understood and obeyed? . . . Shall we abandon the churches . . . or mix with other professors + do them all the good we can." [22]

The forces making for increasingly liberal religious beliefs in the Burned-over District were perhaps even broader. Every extreme revivalist must have seemed to damn a goodly portion of apparently righteous folk. Each succeeding ultraism assumed sanctity for the few and eternal fire for the many. All the schisms pro-

---

[21] P[hilemon] H. Fowler, *Historical Sketch of Presbyterianism* . . . *of Central New York* (Utica, 1877), 160; Antoinette L. Brown, Hopedale, Mass., Jan. 18 [?], to Smith, Gerrit Smith MSS; E. C. Stanton to Elizabeth S. Miller, Sept. 20, 1855, in Theodore Stanton and Harriet S. Blatch, eds., *Elizabeth Cady Stanton as Revealed in Her Letters, Diary and Reminiscences* (2 vols.; New York, 1922), II, 61; Birney to Smith, Oct. 29, 1857, Dwight L. Dumond, ed., *Letters of James Gillespie Birney, 1831–1857* (2 vols.; New York, 1938), II, 1175.

[22] Weld to Birney, May 23, 1842, in Dumond, *Birney Letters*, II, 693; Tappan, New York, Dec. 24, 1843, to Charles Finney, and to Theodore Weld, March 8, 1844, Lewis Tappan Papers, Library of Congress.

duced ungentle name-calling. In the wake of each excitement came some proportion of disillusion and despair. One panacea after another proved too feeble to save the world immediately. The sloughing-off process by which common men and women departed from revival religion must have been more significant at the time than any surviving evidence can indicate.

But the idealistic strain and habit of strong conviction were deeply ingrained by tradition and experience. Successive disappointments only led to an increasing willingness to try some other method to save the world. The isms of the forties developed along two lines, one fundamentalist and the other modernist, both grounded in the history of the preceding decade and both dedicated anew to the redemption of American society.

BOOK VI

Aftermath: 1840-1850

I have felt great sympathy with all true hearted Second Advent believ-
ers in their great disappointment at the non appearance of their
Lord + Master . . . [but] it was not necessary that Christ should be
visible *to our fleshly eyes, in order that he should reign in the world.*
. . . Who cannot see + feel that we have entered upon a new era. *. . .*
Truth . . . is finding its way into the most secret recesses of Church +
State + is most surely working the overthrow of both. . . . Now I can
see why the judgment is antecedent to the coming of the son of Man,
for it is clear that Truth must sit in judgment upon all human organiza-
tions . . . before he can triumph over all error. . . . Your bodies +
mine will probably go down to the grave, before God's everlasting king-
dom shall fill the earth. The epoch at which we live is the epoch of
Judgment—a time not *of triumph, but of deep trial, conflict + travail*
of spirit.—ANGELINA GRIMKÉ WELD, JAN., 1845, MS LIBRARY OF CONGRESS

Chapter 17. THE END OF THE WORLD

CHRISTIAN enthusiasts through the ages had anticipated an early millennium: a thousand years of heaven on earth which were to precede Christ's Second Coming, the day of judgment, and the end of this world. Occasional variant interpretations had reversed the sequence, putting the Advent before the millennium. When William Miller's ideas became popular both the Shakers and John Humphrey Noyes had adopted such premillennial doctrines. But no recent belief had specified so dramatic an event as did the Millerites: the literal appearance of Christ, the ascent of the saints into heaven, and the descent of the wicked into hell. Nor had any sizable group of folk adopted such ideas so wholeheartedly since the early days of the Roman Empire. Probably well over fifty thousand people in the United States became convinced that time would run out in 1844, while a million or more of their fellows were skeptically expectant.[1]

This most sensational movement in Burned-over District history happened not to originate in the region and was at no time a peculiarly localized phenomenon. It began and expanded during the thirties in northeastern New York, Vermont, and western Massachusetts. Only when it reached Boston in 1839, did it receive general publicity, and it achieved epidemic proportions in New England before it did elsewhere. Several indeed of its few historians

---

[1] Clara E. Sears, *Days of Delusion, A Strange Bit of History* (Boston, 1924), 244; Francis D. Nichol, *The Midnight Cry* (Washington, 1944), 204.

have been content to treat it as an almost exclusively Yankee affair. But before the end of 1844 it had spread over the entire Northeast, supporting journals in New York, Philadelphia, Cincinnati, Cleveland, Rochester, and Montreal. Once in Washington, D.C., three thousand people gathered on the mere false rumor of Father Miller's presence in town, and traveling preachers took the message also into Michigan, Illinois, and Wisconsin.[2]

It is impossible to estimate the number of Adventists in western New York, let alone to compare this one area with others. But the excitement probably gathered its main support where the way was paved for it; and it is possible, despite the earlier start in the parent section, that this area may nearly have equaled New England. These two regions together undoubtedly exceeded all others, for all the antecedent movements had flourished primarily in the Burned-over District and secondarily in rural New England. So also had the Christians, Freewill Baptists, Wesleyan Methodists, and regular Baptists. Those earlier developments bred the mentality to which Adventism appealed and these sects for the most part contained it.

It is equally likely, though beyond complete demonstration, that the Millerites hailed chiefly from rural areas, as did their predecessors, despite the appearance of urban strength lent by the mobs who attended city meetings and the journals printed in the various metropolitan centers. Whatever its relative strength may have been in this one region, however, Adventism became an integral portion of Burned-over District history, thoroughly interrelated with the other rural manifestations of religious enthusiasm.

William Miller in many respects typified the Yankee Yorkers of his generation. Four years after his birth in 1782, his family left Pittsfield, Massachusetts, to settle in Hampton, just over the Vermont line in Washington County, New York. His parents, neither impoverished nor ignorant, afforded for him a common-school education, which he improved by wide reading in the libraries of several neighboring gentlemen. He became a Royal Arch Mason

---

[2] Albert C. Johnson, *Advent Christian History* (Boston, 1918), 108 ff.; Theodore Weld, Washington, Jan. 22, 1843, to Angelina G. Weld, in G. H. Barnes and D. L. Dumond, eds., *Letters of Theodore Dwight Weld, Angelina Grimké Weld, and Sarah Grimké, 1822–1844* (2 vols.; New York, 1934), II, 965, 966.

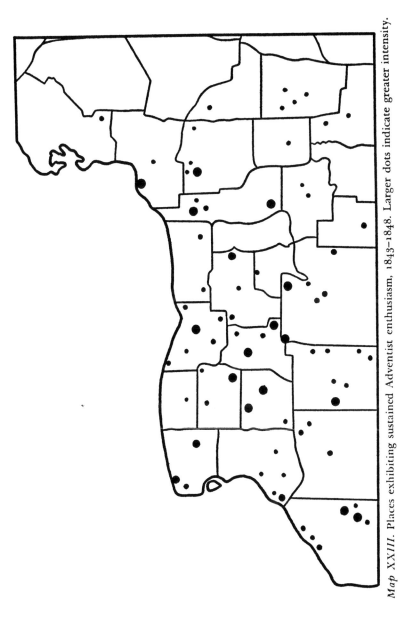

Map XXIII. Places exhibiting sustained Adventist enthusiasm, 1843–1848. Larger dots indicate greater intensity.

and a good Democrat and advanced from constable and justice to sheriff of Poultney, Vermont. Having been commissioned a militia lieutenant in 1810, he naturally went to war two years later, participating in the battles about Lake Champlain. Upon his return from the army, he paid off his mother's mortgage at Low Hampton, bought a two-hundred-acre farm nearby, and built a substantial two-story house. By the mid-twenties he had attained a position in the community which entitled him to sit at table with LaFayette when the hero reached the neighborhood on his semi-centennial tour.[3]

Though he came of a line of Baptist preachers, Miller as a youth professed deism; but an army fever epidemic and the deaths about him in battle turned his thoughts to immortality, while the miraculous victory of Plattsburg he felt compelled to consider divinely ordained. During a local revival in 1816 he joined the Low Hampton Baptist Church and soon became its leading member. His early skepticism had probably been rather a fashionable, youthful adventure than a firm-rooted conviction. Yet it sufficed to give him the zeal of a new convert upon his return to his fathers' faith.

Feeling a necessity to justify his new belief by logical analysis, he set out to demonstrate to his own satisfaction that the entire Bible was pure revelation. The test would be its absolute consistency, showing one authorship through a multitude of scribes. So he proceeded to an exhaustive study of Scripture, guided by nothing but a concordance and the fervent desire to prove his preconceived conclusion by resolving all apparent contradictions. He labored constantly for fourteen years.

Fully literate but scarcely learned, he exercised a naturally fertile imagination within the scope of prevailing religious notions. He became preoccupied with the millenarian prophecies in part because his contemporaries thought largely in those terms; in part also, no doubt, because prophecy was the most convenient theme about which the whole Bible might conceivably be reconciled. He found, as he anticipated, that "God in his wisdom has so interwoven the several prophecies, that . . . they tell us the same

---

[3] Sylvester Bliss, *Memoirs of William Miller*, etc. (Boston, 1853), 1–84, is the chief original source of all biographical information.

things. . . . There never was a book written that has a better connection and harmony than the Bible. . . ."[4]

His accumulating data pointed inescapably to a pre- instead of a postmillennial Advent. Aside from this change of emphasis, shared by several contemporaries, Miller achieved no startling novelty. His doctrine in every other respect virtually epitomized orthodoxy. His chronology merely elaborated and refined the kind of calculations his contemporaries had long been making but became more dramatic because it was more exact, and because the predicted event was more startling. On two points only was he dogmatically insistent: that Christ would come, and that He would come about 1843. Though he himself preached a physical appearance, others might anticipate a spiritual one only. Miller never argued "the physical destruction of the globe," but others might devise their own interpretations of such incidental points. No details about the exact nature of the Advent greatly concerned the leader or most of the followers until it became necessary to explain the disappointment.[5]

Nor did Miller of his own volition from first to last specify a date for the event. For years he said "about 1843," and only in that January did he hazard the statement that this year (from March 21, 1843, to March 21, 1844, owing to calendar changes) must see the end of time. He frankly admitted his error when the latter date passed, and only under pressure from others and very late in the season did he sanction "the tenth of the seventh month," calculated by the Jewish calendar to be October 22, 1844.[6]

William Miller was temperamentally conservative: an ingenious logician with a resourceful mind; not an inspired prophet but a solid, sober, sincere student, driven only by the irresistible conclusions of patient research; and withal, an utterly literal-minded soul. In the early years of his campaign he exhibited a humility equaled in Burned-over District annals only by Daniel Nash. When an intimate friend reported the doctrinal vagaries of a neighbor,

4 William Miller, *Evidence from Scripture and History of the Second Coming of Christ About the Year 1843: Exhibited in a Course of Lectures* (Troy, 1838), iv.

5 William Miller to George Bush (n.d.), Miller, Low Hampton, April 28, 1841, to Gilbert R. Gladdings, William Miller Papers, Aurora College Library.

6 Bliss, *Miller*, 172; Nichol, *Midnight Cry*, 158, 171, 206–213.

Miller replied: "If as good a man as you say father West is, can twist the scriptures to accomodate his views . . . why may not old br Miller do the same and neither of them know it?" But like Father Nash, Father Miller developed from genuine humility a sense of mission which could eventually overbalance his natural character and make him contentious and uncharitable. He could account for his influence only "by supposing that God is supporting the *old mans* work, wicked imperfect and ignorant as he is." "I know my own weakness, + I do know that I have neither power of body or mind, to do what the Lord is doing by me as an instrument." [7]

By 1831 Miller felt absolutely confident of his grasp on final truth. He began issuing local warnings about the Advent. Baptist, Methodist, and Congregational ministers in northern New York and western Vermont invited him to lecture, for his message greatly assisted their protracted meetings. Two years later, when he received his license to preach as a Baptist clergyman, his views had already been systematically presented in the *Vermont Telegraph,* while at least eight pastors had adopted the doctrine. In 1835 he secured a testimonial endorsed by forty ordained Baptist ministers, scattered from the Adirondacks to the Connecticut Valley and from Canada to western Massachusetts. His lectures were published in book form in Troy in 1838 and began to circulate far beyond the circle in which the author moved. By 1839 Miller had probably delivered eight hundred sermons in a constantly enlarging radius. Though he had reached Rome, New York, the previous year, most of his correspondence still continued to originate in Vermont, New Hampshire, and western Massachusetts.[8]

The Advent movement became a general, organized enterprise instead of a casual, local one, just at the turn of the new decade. In November, 1839, Joshua Himes discovered Miller at a Christian convention held at Exeter, New Hampshire. The next month Father Miller invaded Boston. Himes, the minister of Chardon Street Chapel, and previously an evangelist, temperance, and abolition crusader, unionist and Garrisonian, had made his con-

---

[7] William Miller, Low Hampton, July 21, July 27, 1838, to Truman Hendryx, and Montpelier, Nov. 17, 1838, to William S. Miller, Miller MSS.

[8] Testimonial, March 19, 1835, and *passim,* Miller MSS.

gregation the virtual center in New England of every variety of enthusiastic reform. Whether he was immediately convinced of the new doctrine is debatable; but he promptly realized its potency as a revival measure and espoused it so wholeheartedly that conviction must soon have come if it was at first lacking. Himes became the manager and publicity agent of the enterprise, founding journals, arranging camp meetings, and finally devising the extensive tours of a group of evangelists, with the biggest tent the country had even seen.[9]

Other powerful men enlisted practically at once. Charles Fitch, a Congregational minister and Oberlin perfectionist who had held important pastorates in southern New England, including Marlborough Street Chapel in Boston, and had recently moved to Newark, New Jersey, wrote Miller in 1838 to clear up his doubts on two points. In 1840 he was forced to resign his charge and commenced itinerating as an Adventist. He immediately attempted to win over the Oberlinites by a personal visit and a series of debates in the *Oberlin Evangelist*. A number of students soon left that college to preach the message in their western New York home areas. Josiah Litch, a prominent New England Methodist, joined up in 1838 and provided one of the most active pens of the movement. His pamphlets gained notice, and his articles, columns, in *Zion's Watchman* during 1839. Later he edited the *Signs of the Times* in Boston, perhaps the most influential Adventist magazine. Miller, Himes, Fitch, and Litch were the "Big Four." They succeeded in sweeping New England by 1843 and simultaneously inaugurated projects to reach farther afield.[10]

Only during 1843 did the leaders direct attention to western New York and make Rochester the center of Burned-over District Adventism; but Millerite notions had by that time been noised about for several years and had grown popular enough to provide adequate preparation for a concerted campaign.

Father Miller had a few personal connections in the region. A

---

[9] Bliss, *Miller*, 139; Sears, *Days of Delusion*, 60–62.

[10] *Midnight Cry* (New York), IV (June 1, 1843), 81, V (Dec. 1, 1843), 167, VI (Oct. 31, 1844), 142; *Oberlin Evangelist* (Oberlin, O.), II–IV (1840–1842), *passim*; *Zion's Watchman* (New York), V (Feb. 9, 1840), 33; Everett Dick, *Founders of the Message* (Washington, 1938), 33.

nephew near Oswego interested his minister in the *Lectures on the Second Coming,* and the two men circulated copies in their own vicinity and northward into Jefferson County. A clerical colleague named Truman Hendryx corresponded with Miller through the thirties from pastorates in Cayuga County and Bradford, Pennsylvania. When Hendryx was considering a location in Wayne County, Miller wrote a complete description of the locality from personal knowledge of the area. These letters do not certainly prove that Hendryx was an Adventist, but he did attempt to arrange for Miller's appearance at Hamilton, where he would have met the most influential New York Baptists. The *Baptist Register* took notice of Miller from the beginning of 1837 and championed full discussion of his doctrine, without endorsing the specific time, for "It cannot be unwise . . . to keep before our minds the reality of the event . . . to prepare for it as though it were to transpire the present year." That other papers in the region also listened is clear. A Broome County correspondent asked Miller in 1839 to verify or renounce his newspaper's announcement that Miller had acknowledged a hundred-year error in reckoning.[11]

Doubtless emigrant Vermonters also carried the belief with them. One who reached Attica in 1839 circulated Miller's book and built a zealous knot of adherents who besought the author to come and preach to them. An apparently similar situation had brought the old man to Rome the year before. Some circulation of the volume was reported from Madison County in 1838. One clergyman at least must have read Miller's first articles in the *Vermont Telegraph,* for he began preaching The Coming in Chautauqua County in 1833. Others in his neighborhood bought the *Lectures* upon publication and wrote Miller for further guidance from time to time.[12] The new cause had thus struck a few roots

11 Truman Hendryx, Chestertown, March 8, 1834, Locke, Feb. 11, 1835, Justus Taylor, South Rutland, March 6, 1839, William Storrs, Harpursville, Sept. 2, 1839, James Chalmers and Silas Guilford, Fair Haven, Oct. 20, 1840, Jan. 6, 1841, to Miller, Miller MSS; *Baptist Register* (Utica), XIV (Feb. 17, 1837), 2, XV (July 13, 1838), 86, XVI (Oct. 4, 1839), 134.

12 Clark Flint, Attica, July 19, Aug. 11, 1840, March 27, 1841, Ambrose Nash, Attica, April 4, 19, 1841, Emerson Andrews, Rome, March 20, 1838, Justus Taylor, Hamilton, July 20, 1837 [1838], L. M. Richmond, Lebanon, April 25, 1842, A. B. White, Ellington, Nov. 20, 1839, Isaac Fuller, Harmony, Jan. 31, 1840, to Miller, and Miller to Hendryx, Feb. 8, 1833, Miller MSS.

into the Burned-over District even before its organization began to function in New England.

From 1840 to 1843, while the leaders concentrated on the area farther east, sentiment developed rather rapidly in central and western New York, without the benefit of organizational forcing. By casual contagion from the Champlain and Hudson valleys, where Miller had long been making tours, interest expanded westward and continued to enlarge the concentric rings of his influence.

The *Palladium,* state magazine of the Christian denomination, though its heaviest circulation was in the Finger Lakes region, had in 1834 been moved to Union Mills in the lower Mohawk Valley. There Joseph Marsh, a self-educated itinerant preacher with over fourteen years' experience in western New York, assumed its editorship in 1839. Almost immediately he interested himself in the premillennial doctrines already popular in his new location, and through his editorship he gradually swung large portions of his denomination into the Millerite movement, just as did Joshua Himes in New England. Only in July, 1843, was he relieved of his editorial post for overemphasizing Adventism. A large number of his articles on the subject came from L. D. Fleming, also one of the most successful Christian-itinerants in western New York during the early thirties. Fleming had taken a large church in Portland, Maine, in 1839 and was one of the earlier converts in eastern New England. He resumed his itinerancy in this region after 1842 and seems to have been one of the more powerful preachers and pamphleteers in the crusade.[13]

Probably no other journal with circulation focused in the Burned-over District espoused the cause as did the *Palladium,* but *Zion's Watchman* and the *Union Herald* both lent substantial space to discussions of the theme. The *Baptist Register,* while temperately refuting Miller's chronology, constantly urged study of his ideas and once even gave the full front page to a Millerite chart. To those who advised disciplinary action against the premillen-

---

13 *Christian Palladium* (Union Mills), IX, X, XI (1841, 1842), *passim; Gospel Luminary* (West Bloomfield), II (Jan., 1826), 25; Joseph Marsh, Union Mills, Oct. 17, 1841, March 11, April 1, 1842, and L. D. Fleming, Portland, Me., Dec. 5, 1839, Dec. 9, 1840, March 16, 1841, Newark, N.J., Jan. 19, Sept. 26, 1842, Boston, Oct. 10, 1842, to Miller, Miller MSS.

nialists in the sect, the *Register* recommended the patient test of time. Its invariably sensible editorial staff estimated in June, 1842, that three hundred Baptist clergymen were preaching the Advent, while more were leaning that way daily. Well may they have dreaded to force a schism out of which the orthodox could conceivably emerge in the minority! [14]

But the propaganda of the journals, pro and con, would have netted few converts had the labors of itinerant preachers not enlivened discussion. Christian, Baptist, and Methodist parsons lived among poor folk; and the early forties were depression years, which sent multitudes of Americans westward. Not all the migrants hopped at once from seaboard to frontier: as many, or probably more, merely moved a state or even a few counties farther west in pursuit of a new start. A considerable number of Adventist clergymen, Christians predominating, left the reservoir of emigration in western New England and eastern New York during these years. Since they expected time to continue little longer, they could have been motivated only by the desire to gain the souls of their emigrating parishioners.

Fourteen can be counted who became itinerant lecturers in the Burned-over District. The work of these less famed men found reinforcement in the occasional tours of more renowned figures. George Storrs, late a zealous Wesleyan abolitionist, conducted tent meetings in Albany and Utica in the fall of 1842, and Miller himself swung through the Mohawk Valley once each winter for three successive years, finally reaching Utica in December, 1842. The poor man was giving his utmost. He estimated in 1841 that he had delivered 627 hour-and-a-half lectures and made 5000 converts in a single year.[15]

With the assurance early in 1843 that time had begun its final year, the movement everywhere redoubled its energies. From Feburary 28 until April 1 the most brilliant comet of the nineteenth century lowered nightly on the horizon. This symbol recalled other astronomic disturbances—a display of shooting stars

---

[14] *Baptist Register*, XIX (June 17, Sept. 9, Oct. 28, 1842), 73, 122, 149.

[15] *Christian Palladium*, XI, XII (1842–1844); *Midnight Cry*, IV, V (1843–1844); Miller MSS; William Miller [signature deleted], Low Hampton, May 19, 1841, to Truman Hendryx, Miller MSS.

in 1833 and an unusual aurora borealis in 1837—and led the visionary to discover multitudinous "signs of the times" about them as the last year advanced. The number of anxious watchers undoubtedly leaped upwards under such stimuli. But the ablest apologist of Adventism seems to be correct in his assertion that Millerite journals paid less attention to these omens than did the secular press of the day. To sincere believers, "whether He sends this [comet] as the messenger of His fury, is immaterial," for they knew that in any case "He will be revealed in flaming fire, taking vengeance on them that know not God." Their faith rested "on the word of God, and such things are not needed to confirm it. . . ." [16] No other enthusiasts of the half century, in fact, stuck so closely and exclusively to the Bible as did the Millerites.

After the beginning of 1843, the flood of Adventist itinerants in the Burned-over District compensated for any earlier inferiority to New England. At least twenty-five spent here the major part of the fifteen months before the supposed final limit of time. They criss-crossed the entire area on single tours and in teams, meeting at their route junctions for larger sessions. Some came upon Himes's orders, mainly from New England. Several returned to their home areas from Oberlin College. Others gave up local charges to spread the message more effectively. Many more than these retained their pastorates but gravitated about their own station almost as constantly as the full-time travelers.[17]

Little opposition seems to have disturbed this rapid spread of the premillennial doctrine. Place after place, begging Father Miller to come himself or send a substitute, emphasized the unanimous desire of pastors and flocks of all sects to hear him.[18] The Advent movement's most distinctive feature was in fact its extreme closeness to orthodoxy. Any church might profit from hearing the message, whether or not it chose to follow the letter of the doctrine. For all expected some grand event soon, either the Advent or the

---

[16] *Signs of the Times* (Boston), March 29, 1843, 28; *Midnight Cry*, April 13, 1843, 9; both in Nichol, *Midnight Cry*, 135, note, 136, 137.

[17] Whitney R. Cross, "The Burned-over District, 1825–1850." (MS at Harvard University, 1944), 349–358.

[18] Silas Guilford, Fair Haven, Jan. 2, Clark Flint, Attica, April 9, I. C. Brownson, Jan. 11, and S. W. Paine, April 15, Warsaw, A. Chapin, Jamestown, Jan. 12, James Huntington, Rome, Jan. 15, 1843, to Miller, Miller MSS.

millennium, and all should prepare. Every Protestant sect in the region, excepting possibly the Episcopal and the Presbyterian, achieved a new height of revival fervor and conversions in 1843.

Not until 1844 would harmony cease and schism grow. For this very reason the number of actual Adventists cannot even be adequately guessed. Many of those who gathered to hear the Millerites came "from curiosity" and continued attendance to "hear the *truth*" from orthodox clergymen.[19] Others merely enjoyed the show, especially when the itinerant was feminine. The young blades at Preston Corners speculated over Sister Rice, whether she "was an *angel*" or "if she once was an angel she had fallen from her first estate," and "Saml Noyes + Holmes flipped a cent to see which should go home with her the last *night*." [20]

On June 23, 1843, Joshua Himes, the great tent, and a group of lecturers descended upon Rochester. L. D. Fleming, who knew the region well, may have been responsible for the wise decision to launch the larger-scale operations at this point. Advertisement of the meeting proceeded for a month in advance; crowds drifted into town from the countryside and even sailed in from Canada. The tent, designed to accommodate three thousand people, was erected near the center of town. Himes, Fitch, Fleming, and Thomas F. Barry provided the heavy oratorical artillery, supported by small-fire troops gathering from the area with a constantly changing membership. Barry, a Christian preacher from Portsmouth, New Hampshire, had been Miller's chief lieutenant in Maine since 1839. From this time on, Rochester became his headquarters, and he was said personally to have converted a thousand in the Genesee city.

Fleming began editing the new journal which Himes established, until Joseph Marsh came from the *Christian Palladium* to relieve him. The *Voice of Truth and Glad Tidings of the Kingdom at Hand* promptly became the co-ordinating instrument for the Advent workers and believers in all western New York. Two years later, after all the specified terminal dates had expired, a Univer-

---

19 Hiram Weed, Sharon, April 15, 1843, to George P. Kaercher, George Jacob Kaercher Papers, Cornell Collection of Regional History.

20 George A. Throop, Preston Corners, April 23, 1843, to Dan Throop, George A. Throop Papers, Cornell Collection of Regional History.

salist magazine noted that the *Voice of Truth* remained "one of the most profitable papers in the state," with receipts doubling expenses.[21]

The tent meetings continued two weeks, drawing daily assemblies reported to run from five hundred to several thousand, while prayer meetings and Bible classes took place concurrently in Talman Hall. One day a wind squall broke fifteen guy chains and several inch-thick ropes of the tent, during meeting. Luckily, the tent toppled to windward and raised on the leeward side, so the audience passed out unharmed. The city at large raised a hundred dollars to repair the traveling tabernacle, while Himes lectured to newly roused thousands in the municipal market. The apparently miraculous lack of injury in the accident made it seem that the Millerites enjoyed a charm, and the contributions of substantial citizens to the repair fund added reputation in the locality. But Rochester, unlike most cities, had given a fair hearing throughout, restraining rioting opponents.[22]

The tent and some of its crew moved on to Buffalo and into Ohio. Less had been expected of Buffalo because of the "mixed character" of its society, but even there the stand provoked great interest and the authorities afforded protection from annoyances. By November, however, it had become clear that the cause languished in the Lake Erie port while it still developed at the Ontario port of Rochester. Barry filled Talman Hall to its capacity of two thousand every Sunday of the summer, and Fleming stayed to help well into July.[23]

Both men urged Father Miller to come to Rochester. Fleming wrote, "You could go to no place where a little of your labors would do more good at present than here." Barry reported that *"thousands"* gathered to witness baptisms in the Genesee every Sabbath. Elon C. Galusha, son of one of the greatest Baptist preachers in the country, added a postscript to Barry's letter. "Father . . . preaches all but the time. Should you come this way it may be the means

21 *Western Luminary* (Rochester), IV (July 26, 1845), 240.

22 *Voice of Truth and Glad Tidings of the Kingdom at Hand* (Rochester), XI (July 29, 1846), 36; *Midnight Cry*, IV (June 8, 29, July 13, 1843), 88, 129, 160.

23 *Midnight Cry*, IV (Aug. 17, 1843), 201, V (Sept. 28, Nov. 30, 1843), 46, 135.

of calling into the field an able Laborer tho it be at the 11th hour."[24]

In November Miller arrived. For a week he spoke twice daily to overflowing audiences. A worker passing through mentioned the contrast with Syracuse whence he came; even New York City, with fifteen times the population, had no more believers than Rochester. Farm and village folk from the hinterland swelled the urban crowds. One convert later recalled how widely the doctrine spread at this time in his home community, Victor, estimating at five hundred the faithful in the vicinity of that village of two hundred folk.[25]

Miller's actual appearance in the western part of the state redoubled the demands made upon him. Buffalo, Syracuse, Batavia, Auburn, Utica, Lockport, Ithaca, Niagara Falls, and a host of smaller places begged him to come, each claiming special reason to be regarded as particularly vital spots for his attention. He did go to Lockport, upon Elon Galusha's invitation, and stayed ten days. Then he devoted eight days to Buffalo, six to Lewiston, and a week to Penfield, just northeast of Rochester. Apparently the solidity of sentiment in the entertaining congregation was a strong criterion for selecting his stands. The Penfield Baptist Church had three hundred members, almost unanimously premillennialist. The weary old man may well have preferred at this late date to comfort and bless the saints rather than fight for new converts. Back in Rochester again, he gave five more lectures as the calendar turned to 1844. He had promised to stop briefly at Auburn and Syracuse on the return trip but may have changed his plans.[26]

One of the significant results of Miller's visit was the conversion of Elon Galusha. The son of a governor of Vermont, he held master's degrees from two universities, had championed the estab-

---

[24] L. D. Fleming, Rochester, July 13, 1843; Thomas F. Barry, E. C. Galusha, Oct. 16, 1843, to Miller, Miller MSS.

[25] *Midnight Cry*, Nov. 23, 1843 [n.p.], V (Nov. 30, 1843, March 28, June 27, 1844), 135, 295, 400; J. N. Loughborough, *The Great Second Advent Movement*, etc. (Washington, 1905), 139.

[26] H. B. Skinner, Buffalo, Sept. 25, Elon Galusha, *et al.*, Lockport, Oct. 2, David Bernard, Penfield, Nov. 21, William Collins, *et al.*, Lewiston, Nov. 21, Hugh Hancock, Syracuse, Nov. 24, David Bernard, Nov. 27, C. B. Hotchkiss, Auburn, Nov. 27, John Mitchell, Clyde, Dec. 4, David Bernard, Dec. 15, T. F. Barry, Rochester, Dec. 25, 1843, to Miller, and *passim*, Miller MSS, 1843.

lishment of Hamilton Seminary, and was a trustee of the Columbian College at Washington. He had ministered to influential congregations successively at Whitesboro, Utica, Rochester, Perry, and Lockport and as a missionary had established the Baptist Church in Buffalo. For nineteen years he presided over the state missionary convention, the skeletal organization of his denomination in New York. He began the discussion of abolition among Baptists, had been president of the American Baptist Antislavery Society since its origin, and had represented his church at the world antislavery convention in London in 1840. Upon his death in 1856 the Perry church declared that Baptists owed "to him more than to anyone else" their institutions of learning and benevolent societies. He was a giant among the Baptists, and one of the most influential individuals ever to join the Adventist movement. Not long after Miller's visit, Galusha was forced by the action of other ministers, contrary to the will of the majority of his church, to resign his Lockport pastorate. Thenceforward he too joined the Advent itinerants and regularly drew thousands to hear him.[27]

The last three months of remaining time (the first three of 1844) saw the movement swell in many neighborhoods. If the Genesee country prospered most, the groups about Oswego, Ithaca, and Warsaw grew nearly as fast, and several other vicinities lagged only slightly behind the leaders. Collections for the Baptist Missionary Convention dwindled in the western part of the state, since it was idle "to talk about the spread of the gospel . . . just as the Saviour is to . . . wind up the affairs of this world!" The Harmony Baptist Association in Cattaraugus and Chautauqua counties supposed it would next gather together "with the great association of the redeemed in the new earth. . . ."[28]

Yet these months failed to produce any fanatical excitement. Meetings became larger and converts more numerous: Elon Galusha was reported to have brought eight hundred souls to regeneration at one session in Rochester in early March. But none

---

[27] Mary B. Putnam, *The Baptists and Slavery, 1840–1845* (Ann Arbor, Mich., 1913), 21; *Baptist Register*, III (July 7, 1826), 75, XIX (Nov. 11, 1842), 158; Charles W. Brooks, *A Century of Missions in the Empire State*, etc. (Philadelphia, 1909), 135–139; "History of the First Baptist Church at Perry," *Minutes of the Genesee Baptist Association for 1861* (Buffalo, 1861), 15.

[28] *Baptist Register*, XXI (March 22, 1844), 27; *Midnight Cry*, V (Sept. 21, 1843), 37.

seems to have quit earning daily bread, prepared ascension robes, or gathered on hills or in cemeteries the better to swing aloft with the heavenly chariot. Nor does any evidence suggest any loosening of morality during these last days. After all, no hour had been set; even in specifying the year following March 21, 1843, Miller had not absolutely denied the possibility that the "vision" might "tarry" a few days.

In a number of vicinities these three months even witnessed declining fervor: laborers about Utica and Syracuse became discouraged, Auburn had more adherents in the jail than at large, the Watertown and Batavia groups were slipping away, and in Buffalo and Clyde many brethren had departed for the navigation season on the canal.[29] Indeed, ever since Miller's visit the preceding fall, the conditions under which the Advent could best be preached had been changing throughout the Burned-over District.

Previously, everyone wished to hear the message, whether or not they chose to believe it. But Miller reported from Rochester that "the clergy in the city begin to arouse themselves, not for the salvation of souls, but to save their walls of partition between the sects and the churches. . . . The cry now is *'disorganizers,' 'Schismatics,' 'Unitarians,'* and *'covenant breakers.'* "[30] The *Baptist Register,* though it reported Utica Adventist meetings in early 1844, had six months earlier ceased printing notices of the revivals induced by Millerite preachers about the state. Influential orthodox Baptists had forced Galusha to resign all his denominational positions as well as his Lockport church. Marsh had long since been driven from the *Christian Palladium.* The movement had in the last year gained such proportions that orthodoxy could no longer afford to sponsor it merely to gain from its heavy evangelistic artillery.

The Adventists responded like other, earlier ultraists. They had the light and were superior to sectarians. Opposition could only emanate from deliberate sinfulness. "The Whore of Babylon" must have meant the Protestant as well as the Catholic Church! Elon Galusha, when later invited to return to his Lockport church, stated the position admirably:

---

[29] *Midnight Cry,* V (Feb. 8, May 16, 1844), 232, 352; *Voice of Truth,* II (May 25, June 1, 8, 1844), 46, 68, 72.

[30] Miller letter, in *Midnight Cry,* Nov. 23, 1843.

We could not live under a ministry which should not, prominently, set forth these truths—much less under one opposed to them. Besides . . . we could not . . . walk with a church which in any way . . . countenances slavery . . . [or] tolerates . . . Freemasons . . . [or] any species of gambling . . . [or] raises monies for religious purposes, by pampering the vanity and voluptuousness of community, by *fairs, pleasure parties* or other similar means. . . .[31]

In January, 1844, the leading men gathered in New York City to form a state Second Advent Association. Though explicit statements guarded against a sectarian appearance, this was inevitably a step toward a new church organization. By April the *Voice of Truth* was calling outright, "Come out of her, my people!"[32]

Thus the very months which witnessed the peak of Adventist growth set the bounds which would limit it. Wherever the impact of the doctrine had been strong enough during 1843 to swing over large segments of the regular churches, the cause was safe from the full consequences of the denominational reaction, for the size of the Adventist group gave it strength to survive, making local churches think twice about excommunications. Conversely, where insignificant minorities had been influenced during the earlier period of harmony, the old sects were able effectively to eliminate or at least to quarantine the fever. The spring of 1844, then, was a period of selection and consolidation, predestining the campaign to reach a point of diminishing return. Most of the main-line canal towns, except Rochester, and many of the other larger communities of western New York experienced a marked decline in enthusiasm. But in the Genesee city and valley, in Lockport and Oswego, and in wide stretches of the hill country lying on either side of the upper Genesee River, the movement continued to gain momentum for a time.

How much the falling-off which did occur owed to the stubborn continuation of time after March, 1844, cannot be determined. Millerite sources indicate little disappointment; but the almost cheerful apologia generally adopted—"if the vision tarry . . . we had better be found watching till then, then [*sic*] to relieve our-

---

[31] *A Correspondence between the Baptist Church and the Advent Brethren of Lockport, and Elders Webster and Galusha,* etc. (Lockport, 1845), 13 and *passim.*
[32] *Midnight Cry,* V (Jan. 11, 1844), 196; *Voice of Truth,* I (April 27, 1844), 46, 47.

selves from . . . a momentary expectation of the great event . . ."
—undoubtedly concealed a considerably dampened ardor, at least
in some quarters. Only in September did Miller and Himes reluctantly endorse the new calculations pointing to October 22.[33] It
seems quite probable, however, that disillusion did less to limit
the extent of the excitement than did sectarian opposition. For
the summer following the disappointment witnessed in selected
localities the greatest outburst of fervor yet aroused, leading toward
the final climax of October 22, 1844.

At least thirty roving preachers labored all that summer and
fall. Every few weeks five or ten of them converged at an appointed
site for a camp meeting. Father Miller and the great tent crossed
the state in July, stopping at Cooperstown, Rochester, and Buffalo.
Other sessions met at Manlius, Oswego, Volney, Port Byron, Seneca
Falls, Canandaigua, Urbana, Fairport, Scottsville, Adams Basin,
LeRoy, Porter, Lodi, and Gerry. The name of a village served for
identification, but the actual site of the meeting lay usually in open
country several miles from town. Farm families journeyed in for
Sunday when they could not spend the week. Even with a generous
allowance for exaggeration, week-end attendance must usually
have run in the neighborhood of a thousand. Including several
other similar sessions designated as conferences, over twenty-five
camp meetings gathered west of the Catskills after May of 1844. If
the estimate of one Adventist historian correctly records the total
in the country that year, the Burned-over District must have
sponsored close to half of all such assemblies.[34]

The largest and longest of the camps, near Scottsville on the
bank of the Genesee, ran for several weeks in July and August.
Nine tents held the permanent staff, with families and followers.
Miller was there part of the time, and Himes and eight other
clergymen, apparently quite constantly. Four women took part in
the exhorting, and other preachers attended irregularly. The
women conducted a jewelry collection to underwrite extra publications. Weekday sessions were small because of the wheat harvest,

---

[33] *Voice of Truth,* II (May 11, 1844), 53, III (Sept. 25, 1844), 140; *Midnight Cry,* III
(Oct. 10, 1844), 152.
[34] Dick, *Founders,* 80.

but the crowds reached from four to five thousand on Sundays.[35]

Devoted and excited bands of zealots in all the camp areas absorbed the last frantic appeals of the Indian summer season. In more remote, isolated spots, others read them in the *Midnight Cry* and the *Voice of Truth*. Joseph Marsh went nearly sleepless in October, converting his weekly into a semiweekly, printing a hundred thousand extra copies in three weeks. Unsolicited contributions covered all the extra expense.[36]

The behavior of these poor souls who based every hope on this world's ending on October 22 has been a fascinating and controverted subject. How should people who expected to behold their Lord in the flesh and to witness the holocaust of the wicked world as they rose into heaven conduct themselves during their last days and hours on earth? The legend which grows out of the careless folk taste for fun, color, and drama descends to us brimful of zestful humor at the expense of the Millerites. The extraordinary situation encouraged observers alien to the movement to let their imaginations run riot: conceiving what kinds of things they might choose to do with their last hours, they passed on these conceptions as good stories, which in time collected an aura of hoary respectability and served for the truth.

Thievery, murder, lasciviousness, and insanity; the preparation of ascension robes in such numbers as to boom the textile markets; gatherings in cemeteries (where the saints of the past must be gathered up), and on hill tops and hay stacks (to make the ascent easier); the abandonment of business, distribution of money, and reckless scattering of possessions—these indictments against the Adventists, grown in folklore, have commonly been written into history without close examination.

So far as immorality is concerned, a little reflection has more validity than any amount of prejudiced contemporary evidence. The whole movement developed from an utterly literal but absolutely logical study of Scripture. However simple their reasoning, Millerites were consistent thinkers above all else. How could sincere watchers for the coming of "the Bridegroom" possibly

---

[35] *Midnight Cry*, VI (Aug. 1, 8, 1844), 21, 22, 30.
[36] *Voice of Truth*, III (Oct. 2, 9, 10, 12, 17, 1844), 144–166.

bring themselves to sin on the very eve of the judgment? Every article of their faith led them in the opposite direction. No more moral and righteous people would seem ever to have inhabited this earth.

The latest student of the movement, furthermore, has successfully demonstrated by laborious research in the records of New England insane asylums that no greater proportion of Millerites than of other people became mental cases in the period.[37] No hint exists in reliable sources relating to western New York that such a charge was even seriously made in this region. Nor does any scrap of genuine evidence substantiate the myth of the ascension robes.[38] Tradition has it that the Rochester saints covered Cobb's Hill, just at the edge of town, on the last day;[39] but no notice for such a gathering was served in the *Voice of Truth*. Even if the location was utilized, it could scarcely be considered strange, when many years since have witnessed Easter morning services on the same spot.

No absolute proof exists on any of these points. They simply present the fundamental problem of historical analysis: which sources may one trust? Many serious charges may be made against the religious enthusiasts of the Burned-over District, but they were never guilty of conscious misrepresentation. Where there is reason to condemn them, the case can almost invariably be put together from their own writings. One seems to get closer to sensible explanations by reading the words of the zealots themselves, than by relying upon opponents. The Millerites admitted, directly or indirectly, sufficient errant behavior before and after October 22. That which they did not admit, probably never happened. This probability is increased by the fact that the *Baptist Register,* an opposition organ whose attitude was generally intelligent on this as on other questions, in a careful description of the Millerites on the last day said nothing of any species of fanaticism.[40]

What the saints did do during these last hours was to gather almost continuously in their accustomed places of meeting and pray

---

[37] Nichol, *Midnight Cry,* 337–348.

[38] My own research substantiates Nichol's conclusions, *Midnight Cry,* 370 ff.

[39] Carl Carmer, *Listen for a Lonesome Drum, A York State Chronicle* (New York, 1936), 136.

[40] *Baptist Register,* XXI (Nov. 1, 1844), 154.

for themselves and for their unregenerate contemporaries. Naturally they had little thought of future needs on earth. Indeed, had they been parsimonious with their goods they would have seemed weak in the faith. Many, perhaps most, at the very end "abandoned their worldly occupations." [41] But their time and property were not recklessly squandered. Rather, both alike poured abundantly into the selfless enterprise of proclaiming the message to still-unawakened thousands.

As early as July, Joseph Marsh had advised his readers to "dispose of *all* you have which you do not actually need for the present wants of yourself and family, and for the prosecution of your lawful business . . . to aid in sending out the truth to the perishing. . . ." On October 10 he quoted with approval the sign of a Philadelphia tailor: "This Shop is closed in honor of the King of Kings, who will appear about the 23rd of October. Get ready, friends, to crown him Lord of all." A week later he reported the constant meetings in Rochester, the "deep searching, sanctifying influence of the truth. . . . Never . . . seen the like before. . . . The Lord is evidently doing up his last work. . . . A few days more and our faith will be lost in vision." Both Miller and George Storrs, and doubtless the other leaders, too, had given the same advice as did Marsh; and the saints in New York City, Toronto, and Onondaga County, at least, like those in Rochester, acted upon it literally "through God's abundant grace to forsake *all* and venture *all*." [42] This was the extent of Millerite fanaticism before and during the day of reckoning.

When October 22 passed into history, the believers found themselves in dire straits. Joseph Marsh was too ill to write and resumed publication only on November 7. Another editor in the region who had published briefly at Oswego and Lewiston had bought his press on credit and devoted all current income to extra copies. Now he had to sell out to meet his debts. The *Midnight Cry* resumed publication on October 31, carrying advice for all to return

[41] *Voice of Truth*, III (Oct. 10, 1844), 152.

[42] *Voice of Truth*, II (July 27, 1844), 99, III (Oct. 10, 17, 1844), 152, 161; Orlando Squires, Amboy, Nov. 4, 1844, J. O. Orr, Toronto, Canada, Oct. 31, 1844, John G. McMurray, New York, Dec. 25, 1844, to Miller, Miller MSS; *Midnight Cry*, VI (Oct. 31, 1844), 142.

to work and provide for their families while time lingered on. Joshua Himes announced plans for relief committees. "We must not permit them [the poverty-stricken] to be dependent upon the world, or that portion of the professed church, who scoff at our hope. . . ."[43]

Had others behaved as well as the saints, the ordeal would have been less heroic. At Ithaca, Dansville, Scottsville, and Rochester, mobs stormed the Adventist meeting places, wrecking or burning as they could. In Loraine thirty black-faced ruffians, egged on by the Methodist minister, attacked the congregation with clubs and knives. Tar and feathers abounded in Toronto, Canada.[44] One itinerant wrote Miller from LeRoy, "The cup of iniquity was not full. I was back in the country . . . no mobs, but O what week was that in all our large villiages [sic] + cities . . . did our boasted land of liberty ever know so much religious persecution in so short time. . . . We must have something to make the world hate us, if this be it Amen. The Lord's will be done." Pulpit, press, dignitaries, and rowdies alike gave currency to "falsehoods, and . . . all manner of evil about us . . . we have become a proverb and byword in the land. . . ."[45]

But poverty and persecution could be borne with relative ease. Martyrdom had often been glorified in the Christian past. Shock, grief, and perplexity were the greater troubles. Could any group in history have prepared for themselves a more vicious trap? a more sudden, more abysmal disenchantment? Not merely did the single doctrine of the present Advent come into question, but faith in the whole Bible, the literal reading of which had created their distinctive belief. If they admitted error, they must also place themselves "in the dark concerning a large portion of the Scriptures."[46] Faced with an intellectual alternative utterly impossible for minds of their character and training, the more sincere Millerites could only hold to the substance of their faith. There could

---

[43] *Midnight Cry*, VI (Oct. 31, Dec. 19, 1844), 142, 196–197.

[44] *Voice of Truth*, IV (Nov. 7, 1844), 167, V (March 5, 1845), 27, 28; J. O. Orr, Toronto, Canada, Oct. 31, 1844, to Miller, Miller MSS.

[45] James D. Johnson, LeRoy, Dec. 9, 1844, to Miller, Miller MSS; *Voice of Truth*, IV (Nov. 7, 1844), 167.

[46] N. Hervey, Salem, Mass., Nov. 28, 1844, to Miller, Miller MSS.

be no major error, only some slighter misinterpretation attributable to still-fallible human judgment. The emotional experience
of martyrdom reinforced the same conclusion. Rendered the more
peculiar by failure of their expectations, they could only consider
themselves even more than formerly, the Lord's chosen people.

Probably most of their parent churches tried to recover them,
although some congregations did immediately exclude or attempt
to punish all participants in the movement and William Miller
himself was excommunicated from the Low Hampton Baptist
Church. But the *Baptist Register* struck the attitude which seems
to have been more prevalent: a firm but tactful invitation to "receive the welcome embrace of your brethren," upon admitting
error. But such kindness from a "sin-tolerating and polluted
church" [47] must have seemed to the saints to be persecution redoubled; and refusal of honestly extended offers of friendship must,
on the other side, have rendered the orthodox even more hostile.

For those who had been thoroughly convinced, return to orthodoxy offered no solution. Of course, the great excitement had gathered all kinds of adherents, among whom those with deep and
abiding conviction were perhaps the minority. The majority of
the watchers of October 22—the lukewarm, the partially interested, and the guilt-conscious ones who had feared the judgment
day for excellent reasons—these slipped out of the Adventist ranks,
either to slink back into the old churches or to abandon evangelical religion. The falling-off after the great disappointment, though
not always directly attested by the Millerites, was indirectly pointed
out in many ways. It must have been substantial.

But those "who had oil in their vessels" were certainly a respectable number in western New York, and they remained steadfast. Their problem, once they recovered from the first thought-
sterilizing dejection, was to discover an adequate explanation for
the failure of October 22. Where did the error in reckoning occur?
Unfortunately for a movement which had been in origin strongly
nonsectarian, no one explanation could satisfy even a clear majority
of the faithful; and from the variety of hypotheses adopted came
more feeble, fragmentary sects than had grown out of any other

---

[47] Bliss, *Miller*, 288; *Baptist Register*, XXI (Nov. 8, 1844), 158; *Voice of Truth*, VI
(April 23, 1845), 26, 27.

cause in Burned-over District history. Unfortunately, too, for a record thus far clear of extraordinary fanaticism, some of the theories led directly to the most spectacular irregularities of the period.

George Storrs had brought about a degree of schism among New England Adventists between March and October, 1844, with a peculiar set of doctrines involving both mesmerism and "the annihilation of the wicked." Apparently he considered eternal torment in hell to be an un-Godlike sentence for the unregenerate and thought rather that they would experience painless extinction at the Advent. Departed souls of ages past had been suspended in trance until the judgment day. Whether he himself, or only his misunderstanding followers, developed these ideas farther is not clear, but some Massachusetts believers held that "Christ is not intercession for the impenitent. Hell is not yet made. God's people cannot sin." Storrs's New England following apparently held together after October 22 sufficiently to carry the annihilation of the wicked into the beliefs of the Advent Christian Church. But Storrs himself announced in February, 1845, that the whole movement had been propagated by mesmeric trances. The bulk of Millerite preachers, who had suspected him earlier, were of course embittered by this accusation of themselves, and it is unlikely that any considerable number of people escaped the great dilemma along this route.[48]

Several groups in New England, Pennsylvania, and Ohio, and a substantial sprinkling of western New Yorkers, after a period of floundering joined the Shakers. One of the leading itinerants in the Utica neighborhood took this course and led a group with him, including the nephew of William Miller who had first circulated the Advent message in the area. Shakerism had constantly been a final resort for the most pious victims of every religious excitement since the Great Revival of 1800, and it prospered up to the middle of the century, for the most part on the strength of such additions.[49]

---

[48] Nichol, *Midnight Cry*, 192, 283, 455; Abel Wood, Westminster, Mass., June 11, 1844, William Miller to I. E. Jones, April 14, 1844, Miller MSS; Storrs's letter in *The Morning Watch*, quoted in Sears, *Days of Delusion*, 242, 243.

[49] Anna White and Leila S. Taylor, *Shakerism: Its Meaning and Message*, etc. (Columbus, O., 1904), 170, 171; George W. Peavey, Watervliet, Oct. 25, 1848, to Miller, Miller MSS; I am indebted to Mr. and Mrs. Edward Andrews, lifetime students of Shakerism, for confirmation on this point.

The accretion from Millerism was probably the largest since the early days, as well as the last of major importance.

But such answers involved too great a change in fundamental beliefs to serve for the bulk of the faithful. Substantial numbers, probably the great majority, followed one of two general hypotheses. Which main branch drew the larger support and consequently deserves to be considered the more direct lineal descendant of the original Millerites, it seems impossible to determine.

The saner, more conservative crowd, led by most of the greater original preachers of the movement, merely assumed that an error had occurred in calculating the last day. Miller, Himes, Litch, Sylvester Bliss, Elon Galusha, L. D. Fleming, and others met in April, 1845, at Albany to form an Adventist organization. They created a committee to examine candidates for the ministry, asked congregations to set up as churches, accountable to God alone, and resolved to proceed with lectures and Sabbath schools, but to abandon camp meetings.

This General Conference of the Second Advent Believers of America served to hold in a loose affiliation for at least two decades most of this branch of the movement. Internal friction prevailed during its history, finally leading in the 1860's to the formation of three sects: the Advent Christian Association, the Life and Advents Union, and the Church of God. The trouble from the start was the multiple disagreement on chronology. Certain of the leaders apparently commenced immediately to abandon the notion of a particular time, preferring to be constantly ready for an event of unknown date.[50]

William Miller's own attitude on the question is uncertain. Probably after October 22 he lost the position of eminence which had previously made his word the ultimate sanction for believers, so the tendency of the Albany group cannot be taken certainly to reflect his personal desires. He had little to do with most western New Yorkers, apparently because they insisted more zealously than the leaders of the Albany Conference upon setting new days every few months. On the other hand, he could write to Himes in

---

[50] *Voice of Truth*, VI (April 9, May 21, 1845), 13, 57–62, X (June 17, 1846), 89–94; Bliss, *Miller*, 301 ff.; William W. Sweet, *The Story of Religions in America* (New York, 1930), 407.

November, 1845, that "anything which will prove Christ near, and the nearer the better" would satisfy him. In 1848, lingering near the death which came only after two more tortured years, he still considered "the present state of the world a hundred fold more evidence than forty three" and wished he were still young enough to "shake the world tremendously." [51]

Joseph Marsh and the bulk of western New Yorkers who stuck with this side of the dividing movement agreed that the time must have been wrong but heartily resisted the General Conference for several years. Not only did they prefer a particular time, however many times it must be altered, to an indefinite postponement, but they also felt that this degree of organization denied the faith by making provision for the future. Adventism would thus become a sect, soon inevitably to harbor all the evils known in the old ones: creedal tests, clerical supervision, and expediency. This group for a time held separate conferences, continued to organize camp meetings despite the Albany pronouncement to the contrary, and tried over and over again for a number of years to whip up once more the great stir of 1844, upon fixed dates.[52] But enthusiasm could not be forever prolonged, and this band or number of bands probably in time followed Galusha's lead instead of Marsh's and joined the General Conference. They may have continued some sense of closer kinship among themselves and perhaps largely constituted the Church of God, when it later emerged. The Advent Christian Association, in contrast, was mainly of New England origin; although a Worcester group interested in a date in 1851 joined the sect, it apparently inherited the remaining conservatives of 1845, who had abandoned the setting of a definite time, and borrowed from them the commanding article of its creed.[53]

But none of the groups which approached affiliation with the General Conference became fanatics as did their other fellows of 1844. Indeed, the whole process of organization had been motivated mainly by fear of what the "spiritualizers" would do to the move-

---

[51] William Miller, Low Hampton, Nov. 15, 1845, to Himes, Robbins Miller to Himes, July 23, 1848, Miller MSS.

[52] *Voice of Truth*, IV (Nov. 7, 1844), 165, V (Feb. 12, March 5, 12, 1845), 10, 21–28, 32–35, VI (May 21, June 4, 1845), 57–62, 73–79, IX (Jan. 7, 1846), 9–16.

[53] Nichol, *Midnight Cry*, 454–456.

ment, if left to command it unopposed. An error in time, whatever its exact amount was considered to be, gave no justification for different conduct from that which preceded the tenth of the seventh month. But the second branch took the dangerous position that the Lord had come on October 22, only not in the expected fashion. Most of the bands which thought in this fashion wound up eventually in the Seventh-Day Adventist Church, if they survived at all the irregularities of conduct to which their doctrines led them.

William Miller himself had written in 1836, "I did not think the door would be closed until about A.D. 1839—but what does this general apathy mean. After the door is shut—he that is filthy will remain so. There will be no use . . . to warn people of their danger." [54] If he forgot this prospect in the excitement of forty-three and forty-four, others apparently did not. The extremist line of reasoning was such an automatic response in such widely separated quarters just after October 22 that it must have been present in many minds in the interval. Too soon to have spread by contagion from a single or a few sources, expressions of the idea rose in Portland, Maine, Boston and Springfield, Massachusetts, New York City, and Utica, Rochester, and Chautauqua County, upstate.[55]

Joseph Marsh's lead article on October 2, 1844, had mentioned that soon "the door of salvation will be forever closed." His first editorial after the disappointment admitted that "we have been mistaken in the *nature* of the event . . . but we cannot yet admit that our great High Priest did not *on that very day,* accomplish all that the type would justify us to expect." [56] Indeed, it was a natural conclusion. "When the day passed + our eager eyes saw not the Lord, strong in our confidence we felt the Lord had robed us in wedding garments, + *some event* had transpired equal . . . to that which our faith had anticipated." In this view, the Adventists had "stumbled over the body of Christ, looking for a litteral

---

[54] William Miller, Low Hampton, Dec. 23, 1836, to Truman Hendryx, Miller MSS.

[55] Clarkson Goud, Topsham, Me., Jan. 14, Alexander Edmunds, Portland, Me., April 5, C. S. Clemons, Boston, Feb. 17, J. H. Shipman, West Springfield, Mass., Feb. 28, H. E. Jones, Brooklyn, July 1, C. Swarthout, Utica, Nov. 21, 1845 (and in *Voice of Truth*, Dec. 18, 1844), S. Fenton, Collins, Dec. 10, 1844, to Miller, Miller MSS.

[56] *Voice of Truth*, III (Oct. 2, 1844), 145, IV (Nov. 7, 1844), 165.

[*sic*] coming, which we never shall see. . . ." [57] He had come only in the spirit, but He had come. The door was shut.

Some added that He came in this fashion purposely to try the saints, "fanning out the chaff from the wheat." Most who believed in the spiritual Coming and the end of hope for the wicked had the complementary idea that the saints were already selected and certain of salvation. Not a few went even farther: God's chosen people had entered the millennium which followed judgment day and instead of inhabiting heaven, as they had anticipated, had been allowed to enjoy heavenly privileges on earth. The many varieties of doctrine associated with these notions of the shut door, the spiritual Coming, and the present millennium led many of the most zealously sincere Millerites into remarkable extravagances, which contrasted markedly with their generally circumspect behavior up to the tenth of the seventh month.

The number who followed these theories cannot be ascertained, but it was certainly substantial, and may even for a time have been the majority of the faithful. In western New York alone, at least eight prominent lecturers drew their personal followings in this direction, and sizable bands developed certainly in Oswego, Utica, Syracuse, Seneca Falls, Rochester, Springwater, and Collins. The assurance from the other side, that the brethren here were mainly faithful to Miller, protested a little too much; and the repeated warnings against fanaticism and incidental comments indicating its presence reinforce the impression that such sentiments were far more popular than the more respectable and verbal branch of the movement cared to admit.[58]

What happened to these folk can be about as well imagined as described. One formerly renowned preacher fell into conduct "not becoming a civil man." Another was taken into custody with stolen goods and proved to have kept "a very bad house." About Collins, the spiritualizers "in addition to kissing and embracing . . . practice promiscuous lodging. . . . We have heard them say they are immortal, cannot die, and have got to raise up spiritual chil-

---

[57] C. S. Clemons, Boston, Feb. 17, C. Swarthout, Utica, Nov. 21, 1845, to Miller, Miller MSS.

[58] *Voice of Truth,* V (March 19, 1845), 37–40, VI (May 14, 21, June 11, 1845), 52, 63, 64, 81–85, and *passim.*

dren. . . ." At Rochester an entire conference engaged in foot washing and indiscriminate kissing, but "The *fruits* of the meeting," Marsh was happy to report, "have not been as deleterious" as usual in such gatherings. Miller's nephew wrote him how the saints about Oswego "split up into all kinds of Isms from Millerism to Spiritualism, Peavyism shut door feet washing Holy Salutation Praying for the Destruction of Sinners and many other sentiments —hardly any two Believe alike. . . ." [59]

At Springwater came the crowning episode in this region. Twenty or more people gathered in "the House of Judgment." When Marsh and Elder Hill visited the place, one of the members was testing his hostess's consecration to God by making "licentious advances." And in the Miller manuscripts there survives an amazing document, dated "Springwater Valley May 11th . . . at the house of Jugement [*sic*] by the command of the Lord who sits here upon his throne for thee William Miller." It describes

the work of God . . . now being wrought . . . in this household where Gods Car is moving forward with its wheels of burning fire in our midst utterly consuming every vestige of our old nature. . . . Many times every day for months past have we had communications from God by those whom he takes away in the visions of the Spirit among us as Paul was sometimes several at one time. . . . Yours from the fathers flaming bar sealed with the spirit and stamped with the impress and truth of God Almighty by the authority of him with whom thou hast to do by the household of faith.[60]

William Miller believed that "wicked and designing men" caused such abominations; but Joseph Marsh, who had himself just recovered his senses in time to switch to the safer side before he could be contaminated, saw the case more clearly:

Our brethren who have taken the lead in producing these evils, were once devoted, humble, and godly disciples of Christ, faithfully engaged in proclaiming his coming. . . . They were *honest* christians. . . . They followed their honest convictions . . . and the *natural*, the *un-*

---

[59] *Voice of Truth*, VIII (Nov. 19, 1845), 528, IX (Dec. 31, 1845), 2, XIII (Dec. 2, 30, 1846), 5–7, XIV (April 7, 1847), 15; S. Guilford, Fair Haven, Feb. 23, 1846, to Miller, Miller MSS.

[60] *Voice of Truth*, VII (Sept. 10, 1845), 449, X (May 6, 1846), 45, XIII (March 17, 1847), 93; Springwater Valley, Livingston Co., N.Y., May 11 [?], to Miller [unsigned], Miller MSS.

avoidable, honest result has produced the train of evils which exist among us.

They had merely failed to understand the Bible aright.[61]

Many of the spiritualizers apparently exhausted their religious intensity in their various aberrations, but a scattering of groups survived through the late forties to be gathered into the Seventh-Day Adventist Church. Among the spiritualizers who had revelations or inspirations were O. R. L. Crozier, who edited *Day Dawn* at Canandaigua for a time after 1845, and Hiram Edson of Port Byron. These two formulated a variant of the shut-door theory which made of the tenth of the seventh month an intermediate judgment, symbolizing Christ's elevation to a more significant position in heaven. In Maine, meanwhile, Ellen G. Harmon had been enjoying visions and had gathered a following which fraternized considerably with Seventh-Day Baptists. Contact was somehow established between the Maine and the New York groups and Ellen Harmon, now Mrs. White, ratified the Crozier interpretation by a revelation. The failure of the physical appearance in October, 1844, had to do with the abandonment by believers of the proper Sabbath, and observance of the seventh day would help yet to bring Him in the flesh.

The Whites and several lieutenants, probably upon Hiram Edson's invitation, moved to Oswego in 1848 and issued *Present Truth* (later the *Advent Review and Sabbath Herald*) irregularly for several years from their temporary locations in Oswego, Auburn, Saratoga Springs, and Rochester. Edson, S. W. Rhodes, John Loughborough of Victor, and several other local stalwarts, toured the countryside through the early fifties, harvesting for this sect most of the remaining sheaves from the bumper crop of "spiritual" interpretations which had grown after October 22, 1844. A persuasive instrument in the process was the continued shut-door doctrine, which made it impossible for any to come to salvation who had not believed before the intermediate judgment. The faithful would thus be a small band, distinguished by exclusively held rights to enter heaven upon the full Advent. Only after several years did the Seventh-Day Church make the necessary compromise

[61] *Voice of Truth*, IX (March 4, 1846), 76.

with expediency and devise a theory under which new generations of unregenerate souls might be allowed the privilege of conversion and entrance into the true church.[62]

The Seventh-Day Church probably centered quite heavily in western New York during the fifties, gathering strength through emigration from New England; but emigration continued westward, and after the Civil War its membership had probably become very largely middle western. Similarly, the Church of God soon became localized in the Pacific Northwest.

David M. Ludlum, historian of the enthusiastic movements in Vermont, aptly describes the Millerite flurry as "the summation of all the reforms of the age." [63] An immediate judgment day was the shortest possible cut to millennial perfection, the boldest panacea of the era. Such a simple solution to all earthly problems could have appeared only among a people bred to a buoyant optimism. But that is not the whole story. The movement developed in a specific atmosphere of deep pessimism. While it aimed at the final accomplishment of all reform in a single stroke, it was actually the compensatory dream of persons who had abandoned lesser reforms in despair. An escape mechanism, it negated the more broadly popular idea of positive action to solve contemporary difficulties. Basically founded upon similar premises and objectives, it yet ran counter to the other campaigns of its era.

The excitement attained general vogue during a severe economic depression. The "perilous times" described by II Timothy 3:1–7 were indications of the end, and Father Miller in 1838 believed that this prophecy had been fulfilled. "Are not our rich men perfectly infatuated with stocks of all kinds? and monopoly is the order of the day. To grind down the poor and heap treasure together for the last days." [64] The journals circulating in upstate New York regularly printed reports of poverty, distress, and disaster among calculations of the time and essays on the omens of the Advent.

---

[62] Nichol, *Midnight Cry*, 457–465; Dick, *Founders*, 251–259; Elmer T. Clark, *The Small Sects in America* (Nashville, Tenn., 1937), 50 ff.; Otis Nichols, Dorchester, Mass., April 21, 1846, to Miller, Miller MSS.

[63] David M. Ludlum, *Social Ferment in Vermont, 1791–1850* (New York, 1939), 251.

[64] Miller, *Lectures on the Second Coming*, 269, 270.

Since this premillennial doctrine demanded of believers an utter literal-mindedness, which was apparently coupled as a rule with inadequate education and slight prosperity, the Millerites represented a class particularly sensitive to depression. With a few prominent exceptions, the movement was in western New York probably a more purely rural interest than most of the other enthusiasms of the period, while the poorer areas of the countryside also supported it most wholeheartedly. One convert, a Steuben County postmaster, described conditions which must have contributed to the popularity of the cause:

Nearly one-half of our population want bread. What grain there is . . . can't be had without money, and that is not to be had. Five days ago, about 150 men went under arms to a distiller of whiskey, ten miles from where I live . . . and demanded his grain and pork. Finally, he gave up about 3000 bushels, and 50 barrels of pork, and the poor settlers divided it among themselves and gave their due bills. Such things will be in the latter days.[65]

The Millerites themselves, while recognizing external conditions as a signal of their great expectation, seldom indicated, if indeed they realized, the effect of depression upon their willingness to believe. Miller used the tokens of the approaching judgment related to "profane history," only "to convince the men of the world," not at all to support his doctrine.[66] The dramatic idea drew men's minds inward, not outward. Its attraction lay in its striking contrast with drab reality. While it seems certain that economic ills contributed heavily to the growth of the movement, the prophecies placed no marked emphasis on such matters. Astronomical peculiarities received passing notice and politics an occasional nod, but the burden of proof that the time of fulfillment was at hand rested upon the events of religious history. Here, too, Adventism was the product of a pessimistic mood.

William Miller was in the beginning a "High Calvinist" Baptist, entirely unsympathetic toward the enthusiastic crusades of the twenties and thirties. He thought "these fireskulled, vissionary [sic], fanatical, treasonable, suicidal, demoralizing, hot headed set of *abolitionists*, are worse if possible than Anti-Masonry—and if

---

[65] *Midnight Cry*, IV (April 27, 1843), 32.
[66] William Miller, Low Hampton, Nov. 28, 1834, to Truman Hendryx, Miller MSS.

they go on in this way they will set our world on fire, before the time." He disliked the "Birchard stile" evangelism. "Negro's, drunkards and brothels, together with Magazines, Newspapers and tracts" were distracting the ministry. If they had "their Bibles + *concordance,* with a common English education . . . they would feed more sheep . . . tell more truth and learn more their dependence on God." [67]

Yet he recognized the work of the thirties as a significant portent, possibly subduing his prejudices in the interests of popularity. His first two headings in the list of signs pointed to the evangelistic progress of recent decades: "This gospel of the kingdom shall be preached in all the world as a witness and then shall the end come"; "The Pouring out of the Holy Spirit and last reign of grace." A third, "Even to the time of the end . . . knowledge shall be increased," was fulfilled by "the fifty different moral societies." [68]

But these signs had been first described in 1832 and put in final form six years later. As the movement progressed, less emphasis fell on these promising omens and more on sourer notes, closer to Miller's own personal beliefs. The breaking and scattering of churches; reluctance to imbibe sound doctrine; the spread of seducing beliefs like Shakerism, Catholicism and free thought; false prophets and teachers; and the "scattering of holy people"— such occurrences received increasing attention. Miller's lieutenants and followers, many of whom in this region at least had been zealous reformers in the thirties, came to the Advent position later than did Miller himself. Few of them, indeed, indulged in expressions about favorable signs. Rather, they found the world beyond rescue, legislatures corrupt, and infidelity, idolatry, Romanism, sectarianism, seduction, fraud, murder, and duels all waxing stronger. One of the chief reasons for a sudden terminus was the feeling "that every associated body . . . when once occupied . . . has never been regenerated; but has fallen into pollution." Church and state alike had filled "the cup of iniquity" and were "now fitted for destruction." [69]

---

[67] William Miller, Low Hampton, Feb. 25, March 22, 1834, Feb. 11, 1835, Oct. 26, 1837, July 27, 1838, to Truman Hendryx, Miller MSS.

[68] Miller, *Lectures on the Second Coming,* 267-269.

[69] Miller, *Lectures on the Second Coming,* 267-271; *Midnight Cry,* IV (June 15,

This kind of pessimism rose from the failure of ultraism to re-deem civilization. Far worse, the campaigns against sin had now progressed beyond their religious inspiration and had become cor-rosives, eating up genuine piety. The Protestant denominations had been proving their kinship with the "Mother of Harlots" by their dead formalism and hopeless addiction to expediency instead of truth. Above all, the alarming growth of Catholicism was "un-dermining and sapping the foundation of every religious sect . . . [and] of every civil government. . . ." [70]

But economic depression and disillusionment with reform do not alone suffice to explain the amazingly rapid growth of the premil-lennial excitement. More important yet was the fact that the Mil-lerites profited from two generations of rising enthusiasm. Their doctrine, some of whose consequences achieved distinction even among Burned-over District heresies and eccentricities, was nearest to strict orthodoxy of all the creations of the period. On every sub-ject but the millennium the Adventists found the same Bible meanings others found and held to them more rigidly than did most. Their peculiarity lay not in radical change from traditional notions but in intensified adherence to them. The only difference between pre- and postmillennialists was a slight degree of literal-mindedness applied to the prophecies of the Second Coming.

The Millerites cannot be dismissed as ignorant farmers, liber-tarian frontiersmen, impoverished victims of economic change, or hypnotized followers of a maniac, thrown into prominence merely by freak coincidences, when the whole of American Protestantism came so very close to the same beliefs. Their doctrine was the logical absolute of fundamentalist orthodoxy, as perfectionism was the extreme of revivalism. A Universalist editor concluded in 1845, much as must be concluded a century later, "The follies of 1843 . . . will continue to be so long as professing Christians retain in their faith all the elements of this fatal delusion. . . . The *gulli-bility* of the people remains, though the predictions and computa-tions of Miller have all failed." [71]

July 27, 1843), 110, 182, VI (Aug. 22, 1844), 52; *Christian Palladium,* VIII (Aug. 1, 1839), 104, 105.
[70] Miller, *Lectures on the Second Coming,* 141.
[71] *Western Luminary,* IV (May 17, 1845), 158.

All Protestants expected some grand event about 1843, and no critic from the orthodox side took any serious issue on basic principle with Miller's calculations. The *Oberlin Evangelist* considered this an age of expectation, in which a universal interest in the prophecies had been stimulated by moral and social reforms. Its only question was a shade of doubt about rendering days into years in the Biblical oracles of Daniel and John. The editors proclaimed that "Bros. Miller and Fitch may be wrong, but they are not knaves, or dunces." George Bush, soon to become a Swedenborgian, had a different objection. "Whoever attacks Mr. Miller on his point of *time,* attacks him on his strongest point. . . . He is mistaken in the event to occur." John Humphrey Noyes held that the Adventists "hear the same voice we have heard, that God is coming into the world and the day of judgment is at hand; but to them the voice is not clear enough to save them from the delusions of their own imagination." Angelina Grimké Weld believed that a preliminary era of judgment had been inaugurated in 1844, to pave the way gradually for the millennium.[72]

But men cannot remain long poised on the logical absolute of any doctrine. Like climbers advancing on a mountain ridge, they either attain a new reach of broader ground, retreat, or fall into the abyss below. Fragmentary Adventist churches survived the debacle and achieved some degree of stability by skillful retreats from the apex of their positions. But the majority of those who had sought the very narrow path of perfect logic fell off the precipice. For them, this was the end of enthusiastic religion. The road out of ultraism to the right thus terminated abruptly; but the one to the left continued some distance farther.

---

[72] *Oberlin Evangelist,* III (Feb. 17, May 26, 1841), 28, 85, V (Jan. 18, 1843), 15; Loughborough, *Second Advent,* 111; Nichol, *Midnight Cry,* 447; *Spiritual Magazine* (Putney, Vt.), I (Nov. 15, 1846), 137.

Chapter 18. UTOPIA NOW

THE two bands of enthusiasts emerging from ultraism in the late thirties both continued during the early forties their quest for the regeneration of American society. The greater depths of economic depression at the beginning of the new decade made both alike concentrate their energies anew and hasten their steps. As their pace increased, however, their ways diverged ever farther. The group traveling to the right sought an escapist's short cut to the millennium, looking to supernatural forces for miraculous change. The crowd going left, having departed from the literal rendition of their religious tradition, could make a somewhat more realistic approach to the problems of this world. In their view, too, the millennium would come immediately, but it would be a Utopia built by mortal hand and brain, of earthly materials, established in the midst of contemporary society.

Moreover, when once the former ultraists journeying on the leftward branch progressed beyond the confines of orthodoxy, they found a goodly company of strangers going their way. In their new assault on the evils of the world they were joined by others who had never been religious enthusiasts. For revival religion, even at its height, had never obtained complete sway in western New York. Freethinkers had for a few years even supported a periodical in the enthusiastic city of Rochester! [1] Masonry had discovered many

---

[1] *Liberal Advocate* (Rochester), 1832–1833.

champions who became distrustful of all movements toward churchly influence in politics or personal mores. Most persistently aggressive of the enemies of revivalism and all its works had been the flourishing Universalist Church.

Students of American culture and church historians alike have quite neglected the Universalists, and the oversight seems to be a serious one. They greatly exceeded the Unitarians in their area of effective influence and may have been more numerous as well. Their impact upon reform movements and upon the growth of modern religious attitudes might prove to be greater than that of either the Unitarians or the freethinkers. And their less sophisticated, more homely warfare upon the forces fettering the American mind might be demonstrated to have equaled the influence of the transcendentalist philosophers. In the Burned-over District, at least, they played a highly significant role, and no hint appears to suggest that they behaved abnormally in this one region.

The Universalists, like the orthodox Yorkers, were good Yankees. They had the tender conscience, the intense concern for the community, the preoccupation with a perfected society, long grown in the Puritan tradition. But their generously conceived heaven had room for sinner as well as saint. Christ had died to atone for the original sin of all men. Regeneration, then, could be no Heavenly miracle, sorting the saved from the damned, but rather betokened a growth in morality which could as well be gradual as instantaneous. Such a theology might easily accord with the opinion, as orthodox doctrine did not, that evil was the consequence more of social maladjustment than of individual sin.

Zealous reformers these liberals were, but in a sharply different style from the ultraists. Much as they hated Negro bondage, they considered abolitionists to be fanatics and believed that slavery must be handled by practical remedies looking to the benefit of southern whites as well as blacks. No more temperate group inhabited western New York, but none fought more bitterly the organized temperance societies with their petty tyrannies. Often in this region aligned with both Masons and Democrats, Universalists attacked debtor prisons, blue laws, the inequities suffered by workingmen, capital punishment, and extortion by land speculators, while they fumed over revivals, anti-Catholicism, and dictatorial benevolent societies of all types.[2]

Orestes Brownson, for one, journeyed while in this area from the bosom of Universalism into a temporary alliance with the "infidel" Workingmen of New York City, where he espoused programs of economic and political change designed to bring about fundamental alterations in American society as a whole.[3] His reaction was not strange, but only rather more extreme than that of his fellows. Many of his upstate companions followed Robert Owen's ventures with keen interest, and some nearly established a community similar to New Harmony in all but religious orientation, at Williamsville, near Buffalo, in 1827. The largest periodical of the sect in the region carried an editorial in 1837 entitled "Science and Christianity," which could almost as well have been written a hundred years later.[4]

The Universalists acquired recruits in increasing numbers through the thirties, as people became satiated with protracted meetings and revivals. More important, they provided a leadership in reform for others beyond their church membership: disillusioned revivalists and enthusiastic reformers who had outgrown their original religious inspiration. Universalists usually led in taking up the new intellectual currents introduced from Europe and in adapting them to the needs of liberal reform. They acquired in turn from their new allies attitudes originally grown in ultraism: a goodly dose of one-ideaism to make them risk all on one panacea at a time, and a strong tendency, novel with these liberals, to seek the ideal, absolute form of their single obsession rather than to follow the rule of expediency in all things. Perhaps the broader tendencies of the age operated in the same direction.

With the encouragement of Universalists and other liberals, a series of new ideas spread about during the late thirties and early

---

[2] [George Rogers], *Memoranda of the Experience, Labors, and Travels of a Universalist Preacher*, etc. (n.p., 1846), 353 ff.; *Gospel Advocate* (Buffalo), V (Feb. 24, 1827), 62; *Evangelical Magazine and Gospel Advocate* (Utica), II (Feb. 5, 1831), 42, III (May 12, Aug. 11, 1832), 147, 254, V (Oct. 11, 1834), 326.

[3] Arthur M. Schlesinger, Jr., *Orestes A. Brownson, A Pilgrim's Progress* (Boston, 1939), 13–27.

[4] *Gospel Advocate*, V (June 23, 1827), 198, VI (March 1, 1828), 73; *Evangelical Magazine*, VIII (Aug. 18, 1837), 262.

forties. Phrenology, mesmerism, land reform, Fourierist communism, and Swedenborgianism all helped to direct Burned-over District enthusiasm into new channels. None of these had any peculiar development in this single region, though all prevailed more in the Northeast than elsewhere in the country. But all worked themselves into the point of view of the liberal type of thinkers in this area and persisted for several years.

At least one phrenologist was lecturing in western New York in 1836, and LaRoy Sunderland of *Zion's Watchman* probably became a "phrenopathist" and then a mesmerist before his partner, George Storrs, became a Millerite. Interest in this fad seems first to have reached epidemic proportions, however, with the tour of the Scotch lecturer, George Combe, begun in 1837. Following the canal line, he attracted large audiences at least in Syracuse and Buffalo and even found a few societies organized to sponsor him. Clerical opposition he found so strong as to discourage the naturally eager sympathy of physicians and other liberal thinkers.[5] But the Universalist press gave him prompt and hearty support, as did the Noyes perfectionists and many former ultraists. The *Baptist Register* admitted debates on the subject, but with a pronounced editorial frown. Orson Fowler, founder of the Fowler and Wells publishing house, destined to become a mainstay of this movement and others of related nature, grew up in western New York and began his career as a phrenological lecturer in the region early in the history of the cause.

Phrenology paraded as a science based on natural law. No doubt many of its popularizers were ill-equipped to deal even with pseudo science; but however much imagination flourished in the propagator or credulity in his audience, the belief definitely discouraged supernatural interpretations of human conduct. As one man reported to George Combe, sinners had according to this system to be deemed "unfortunate rather than criminal: as 'moral patients' . . . rather than fit subjects for punitive justice."[6] Possibly this fad of pseudoscientific nature did as much as geology or biology to undermine revealed religion.

---

[5] George Combe, *Notes on the United States of America during a Phrenological Visit in 1838–1839–1840* (2 vols.; Philadelphia, 1841), I, 148, 170, II, 70–84.
[6] *Ibid.*, I, 131.

Soon after the first phrenologists entered western New York, mesmerism began to rouse a similar curiosity among the same groups of people. To some folk mesmeric trances appeared to be a species of magic or trickery; to others reared in superstition they seemed the work of departed spirits. Others thought that the phenomena of the trance revealed hidden powers in stronger minds which could prevail over weaker ones. The more intellectually sophisticated considered mesmerism to be a new revelation, "opening a passage from the highest point of physical science, into spiritual philosophy"; a "connecting link between the sciences which treat of those subtler powers of nature . . . and the science of life, animal and eternal." Like phrenology, it seemed "a foundation on which a form of society might be built which would result in the regeneration of the whole human family." [7]

Both of these pseudo sciences reinforced Universalist religious doctrines and suggested that natural laws rather than whimsical miracles embodied God's purposes for humanity. They also stimulated speculations about the constitution of the human mind and its correspondence with the similarly constituted universe. Persons thinking along these lines quite as a matter of course extended their search to discover the laws of social organization which related to the nature of the individual and the universe. The severe depression of the early forties served to focus attention upon economic subjects, particularly land reform and communism. For the liberal reformers these two causes temporarily provided a sociology to match the supposed sciences of phrenology and mesmerism.

George and Frederick Evans had come to western New York from England in 1820, bent on developing their interests in free thought, land reform, and communism. They joined in the Workingmen's and antimonopoly movements of the early thirties and studied the communism of Robert Owen and the Shakers. George edited a journal at Ithaca for a time before he joined the New York City radicals and founded the *Workingman's Advocate* in the metropolis. By the forties he was the leading land reformer in the

---

[7] Mary B. A. King, *Looking Backward* (New York, 1870), 170; John H. Noyes, *The Berean: A Manual for the Help of Those Who Seek the Faith of the Primitive Church* (Putney, Vt., 1847), 65; H. J. Seymour, Westmoreland, in *Spiritual Magazine* (Putney, Vt.), II (Aug. 15, 1847), 109.

country. Frederick joined the Shakers and rose to leadership of that church in the same decade.[8] Possibly these two brothers had roused some early upstate support for their ideas; the agrarian agitations of the mid-thirties in the Hudson Valley would seem to indicate a persevering concern with problems of land ownership.

Yet neither the "agrarian" socialist land reform notions of the New York City labor radicals in the thirties, nor George Evans's "national" reform of the forties which anticipated the homestead system, seem to have appealed widely in upstate New York. The one was perhaps too drastic a plan for farmer landowners, and the other may have seemed geographically remote to a long-settled people. Or possibly the historians of land policy have paid insufficient attention to the ideological aspects of their subject to realize the possible connection in people's minds between rent wars and homesteading theories.[9] Perhaps a genuine interest in the subject did exist here, which has merely not been discovered.

Such a hypothesis would explain Gerrit Smith's otherwise paradoxical advocacy of land reform. He not only donated a large number of virtually worthless plots on the fringes of the Adirondacks to help support free Negroes but also during his term in Congress sponsored bills for the free distribution of western land. Of course Smith may have been a rare exception, not the mouthpiece of a general concern. He may have been prodded into his attitude by Beriah Green, who wrote him about banking monopolies in 1840, or by his conservative uncle, Daniel Cady, who taunted him for his deep concern for poor blackfolk while, as the greatest landholder in the state of New York, he contributed to the poverty of white folk.[10]

Probably land reform of other sorts appealed less than might have been the case in this region, in part because communal ownership proved to be a much more entertaining subject for

[8] Marguerite F. Melcher, *The Shaker Adventure* (Princeton, 1941), 157, 178, 179, 275–278; Arthur M. Schlesinger, Jr., *The Age of Jackson* (Boston, 1945), 182, and *passim*.

[9] Paul D. Evans, *The Holland Land Company* (Buffalo, 1924), and David M. Ellis, *Landlords and Farmers in the Hudson-Mohawk Region* (Ithaca, 1946), fail to approach this angle of the subject.

[10] Ralph V. Harlow, *Gerrit Smith, Philanthropist and Reformer* (New York, 1939), 31–32, 242–257.

speculation. Ordinary folk knew enough of the technicalities of land ownership, in an area whose apportionment of real estate had been substantially accomplished, to prevent the growth of unrealistic dreams along that line. A scheme to avoid the pitfalls of private ownership was far more appealing. The pitfalls of communal arrangements being unknown to most men, their imagination could soar unrestrained as they contemplated the Fourierist plans.

Though pleasantly mysterious, however, communism was not inordinately strange to the Burned-over District. Most people by the early forties must have had some slight cognizance of Jemima Wilkinson's New Jerusalem and of the several Shaker colonies in the state. Liberals, at least, had interested themselves in New Harmony and in Fanny Wright's project at Nashoba. A number in the region maintained contact with the developing ideas of John Humphrey Noyes, and many no doubt had some knowledge of the Mormon United Order.

Liberals in the region thus had ample preparation when in the depth of the depression the theories of Fourier began to receive extensive publicity. Albert Brisbane, a product of the locality, gave the movement its initial impetus in the *New York Tribune* and also lectured at Utica, Syracuse, Seneca Falls, and Rochester. Dr. Alexander Theller, a filibuster in the 1837 Canadian Rebellion, Edwin Stillman, a former Noyes perfectionist, and one Theron C. Leland spread the doctrine from Rochester, while a lawyer named Alonzo Watson roused interest about Watertown. A convention at Rochester in August, 1843, gathered together several hundred delegates and launched the active organization of phalanxes in the area.[11]

The agitation quickly reached the proportions and acquired many of the characteristics of a religious revival. By April, 1844, nine units were contemplated within fifty miles of Batavia, and Leland estimated that twenty thousand persons west of Rochester

---

[11] Arthur E. Bestor, Jr., "American Phalanxes: A Study of Fourierist Socialism in the United States (with Special Reference to the Movement in Western New York)" (2 vols.; MS at Yale University, 1938), 25, 26, 30, 38, 46, 64, 68, 69, 85, and *passim*. This is a thorough and dependable study to which I am indebted more heavily than specific citations can suggest. George W. Noyes, ed., *John Humphrey Noyes, The Putney Community* (Oneida, 1931), 160; John H. Noyes, *History of American Socialisms* (Philadelphia, 1870), 268–272.

awaited opportunity to enter communities. Farther east the enthusiasm was probably little less intense. The Watertown area started a phalanx in the spring, and others in central New York made plans which failed to reach maturity.[12]

Several members of the Throop family, spread over Madison and Cortland counties, led one such venture. Their comments indicate the kind of people the movement attracted and the style of their thoughts. The family were abolitionists, Washingtonian temperance advocates, lawyers and teachers by profession, students of phrenology, physiology, and anatomy, opponents of "sectarian" religion, and devout, though liberal, Episcopalians. DeWitt Throop, of Sherburne, entitled one two-hour lecture, "The destiny of Man + the means God has provided for raising man to his proper station." His brother, George, of Preston Corners, grew "stronger and stronger in the belief that if it is not the true system which God designed for the human species . . . it is a great improvement on the present Isolated system." George delighted to see "such a man as G. Smith throw off the shakles [sic] + Expose . . . the hypocrisy of the churches. . . . I hate *Bigotry*. . . . I want a faith the bow of whose promise embraces the children of every clime, country + tongue upon one Broad + general Basis of Philanthropy." Brother William, of East Hamilton, presided over the founding of a Hamilton Fourier Association in December, 1843. He reported a month later the abolition, Washingtonian, and Fourier meetings he attended, "all in one sense aiming at the same great center." "First make all *sober* then equal + the Philosophy of Fourier carried out will do the rest." A disagreement over the appraisal of the proposed site of the community set the Hamilton scheme at rest, but George took comfort that "in the hearts they have acknowledged the doctrine to be true. . . . It is the grand and Angelic theme comeing [sic] down to suffering humanity. . . ."[13]

No community achieved actual establishment on the Fourierist plan in this central New York area, but that the doctrine appealed

12 Noyes, *Socialisms*, 268; see map XXIV.

13 D. D. W. C. Throop, Sherburne, Aug. 7, 1843, to George, George A. Throop, Preston, Oct. 4, 1843, to DeWitt, William H. Throop, East Hamilton, Jan. 7, 1844, George, March 17, 1844, to DeWitt, George A. Throop Papers, Cornell Collection of Regional History.

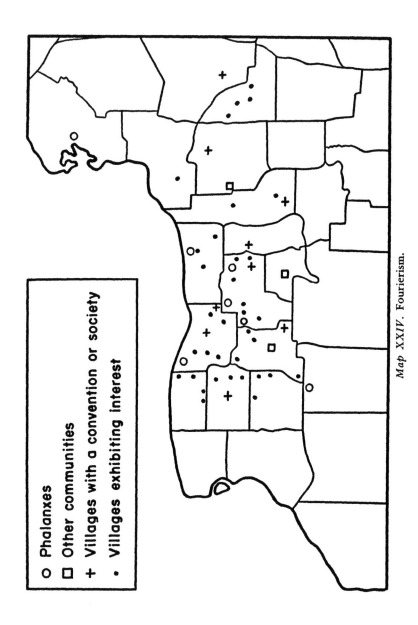

Map XXIV. Fourierism.

widely is witnessed by reports in 1847. Farther west and north, phalanxes had by this time risen and fallen, leaving a lingering disillusionment; but Cayuga, Onondaga, Oneida, Cortland, and Madison counties appeared to two New England itinerants to be a superb field for cultivation. The farmers of the vicinity listened eagerly, and antirenters and "national" reformers thereabouts would make powerful allies. Here was "more wealth, refinement, freedom of thought, general intelligence . . . than among either our village or farming population in New England." Utica and Kings Ferry, on Cayuga Lake, had active associations, trembling on the verge of community-founding.[14]

But it was the earlier flush of enthusiasm about Rochester that yielded five of the six Fourierist colonies in upstate New York. All commenced in the spring of 1844, as did the sixth, near Watertown. The five lay in a wide circle about the city on the Genesee: Clarkson, a few miles west on the Lake Ontario shore; Mixville, about fifty miles up the river valley; Bloomfield, twenty miles to the southeast; Ontario, between Canandaigua and Manchester; and Sodus, on the lake shore, thirty miles east.

These western New York phalanxes, like the rest of the forty-odd of their type in the United States, had brief careers, wherein an early excess of fervor led to extreme disillusionment. By 1847 Rochester was the least receptive spot in the state for lecturers on association, and most of the area to the west was little less hostile. During their short history, however, the communities founded here demonstrated a certain similarity to the region's religious ventures, beyond their waxing and waning emotions. The American Industrial Union, a confederation of the six colonies in New York State, was the only effective co-ordinating organization to appear among all the communist projects of the period.[15] The Yankee Yorkers, fundamentalist or liberal, habitually formulated their plans in large, orderly designs, with mechanisms meant to function for all of society whenever it might be converted to the panacea of the moment.

---

[14] *Harbinger* (New York and Boston), V (July 24, Sept. 18, Oct. 9, 16, 1847), 98, 235–240, 304.

[15] *Harbinger*, V (Oct. 23, 1847), 317; Bestor, "Phalanxes," 81; Noyes, *Socialisms*, 272–275.

All sorts and conditions of people seem to have joined the communal experiments. One of the chief reasons for the broader appeal of Fourierism, compared with Owenite communism in the twenties, was the lack in the later variety of any pronounced religious skepticism. Liberals in religion and urban residents no doubt led the movement. Universalists and Quakers probably participated more fully than the members of any other church, and capital to inaugurate the colonies probably came largely from an urban middle class. But a majority of the residents seems to have been farmers and laborers, and no class lines are featured in the literature of the movement. Many of the members had served apprenticeship in the religion-dominated reform movements of temperance, abolition, or perfectionism. Probably more of them entered the venture out of need than out of principle. Indeed, though the plans of the Burned-over District phalansteries were hastily drawn and certainly in some cases economically unsound, the more serious difficulty seems to have been the incompatibility of liberal and orthodox groups within the communities. At least, a schism in the Sodus colony over the question of Sabbath observance preceded and brought on its most pronounced economic difficulties.[16]

A seventh and independent colony in the region, located near Skaneateles, lasted three years and apparently had a degree of economic success. John A. Collins, formerly a Massachusetts Antislavery Society agent, was its prime mover. The experiment was nearer to the Owenite than the Fourierist type, with a prejudice against religion which the *Harbinger* considered its most serious error. With total community of goods, a "no-government, or nonresistance principle," and "the largest liberty . . . [and] the broadest principle of democratic equality," the venture nevertheless failed, because, according to its founder, its principles were "false in theory and pernicious in their practical tendencies. They might . . . do very well if men were angels, and angels Gods; but human nature is too low, too selfish and too ignorant for relations so exalted."[17]

---

16 Bestor, "Phalanxes," 4–14, 49–53, 99, 109–111, 218–221; *Harbinger,* I (Sept. 27, 1845), 247, 254, II (Jan. 31, 1846), 126; *Western Luminary* (Rochester), IV (Nov. 29, 1845), 379.

17 *Harbinger,* I (Sept. 27, 1845), 253; *Friends Weekly Intelligencer* (Philadelphia),

Yet another community distinct from the phalanxes was planted near Buffalo in 1842 by the Amana Inspirationists from Germany. This one, like several other religious communisms of foreign sectarians, had a lengthy and successful history, though it removed to Iowa in 1854. But its foreign origin and separate development remove it from direct relationship with causes native to Burned-over District society.

Most famous of all early American socialisms was John Humphrey Noyes's Oneida Community. This, too, was primarily a religious enterprise, not to be confused with the Fourierist projects. Noyes acknowledged his indebtedness both to the Shakers and the Fourierists, but these examples only supplemented his original concept of primitive Christian communism. Oneida was remarkable both for the scale and perseverance of its economic success, and for its unique combination of religious, economic, and social beliefs. It deserves more extensive study than it has yet received, and far more than the proportions of this investigation allow. But its history must at least be sketched and its leading principles summarized in order to clarify its position among the other religious movements of the region. Indeed, it is veritably the keystone in the arch of Burned-over District history, demonstrating the connection between the enthusiasms of the right and those of the left.

Noyes's colony gathered at Putney, Vermont, in the early forties. A nucleus of his own family and several neighbors was swelled by persons like George and Mary Cragin who fled the licentiousness of the New York perfectionists. The group's religious services began in 1840, and three years later a financial partnership commenced among four couples. The estates of John's father and his wife's grandfather, rather large for the times, fortunately made available in the same years nearly thirty thousand dollars and several properties. Other associates added smaller amounts to form a joint-stock company, superseding the partnership, in March, 1845. On November 6, 1846, the band adopted a set of principles for social union, declaring a total communism under God, through the lieutenancy of John Noyes. The Cragins and Noyes's at the same time joined in one family and three other couples composed

III (Aug. 29, 1846), 172; Communitist (Skaneateles Community, Mottville), I, no. 25 (May 21, 1845).

a second home. These two households amalgamated the following spring.[18]

But staid Vermont could not tolerate complex marriage. Two sympathizers apparently turned renegade and advertised the communal proceedings in the village. In October, 1847, Noyes suffered arrest on charges of *"adultery* and *fornication."* A month later he forfeited his bond and departed from his home state, leaving thirty-one adults and fourteen children to straggle after him into central New York. Meanwhile, the New York perfectionists, who for a decade had been looking increasingly to Noyes's leadership, had begun to prepare a refuge at Oneida.[19]

Both Noyes himself and George Cragin as his representative had made periodic tours in the more westerly region for several years, working to unify the various cults with similar notions. After several preliminary consultations, conventions met at Lairdsville, Oneida County, and Genoa, Cayuga County, in September, 1847. At the first meeting, Noyes laid bare the full extent of practice in marital communism at Putney and received a pledge of support from thirty-six New York State delegates. At the second, a committee was selected to plan a community here on the Putney model.

Jonathan Burt of Chittenango had recently undertaken purchase of a forty-acre timber lot and mill site in the newly opened Oneida Indian Reservation. Five families who had come together near Hamilton joined Burt, just as Noyes was fleeing Vermont. Another group had formed at Oneida Depot and now purchased adjacent land. Small colonies from Lairdsville and Syracuse followed suit. Thus about as many Yorkers as Vermonters participated in founding the new community. The first issue of the *Spiritual Magazine* at the new location recorded sixty-five members. By January 1, 1849, the number had risen to eighty-seven, and in another year it had doubled this figure.[20]

With a decade of thought and planning, several years of experi-

---

[18] Noyes, *Putney Community*, 46–74, 201, 205, 206; Pierrepont Noyes, *My Father's House, An Oneida Boyhood* (New York, 1937), 5.

[19] Noyes, *Putney Community*, 282, 283, 302, 393; Rev. Hubbard Eastman, *Noyesism Unveiled: A History of the Sect Self-Styled Perfectionists, etc.* (Brattleboro, Vt., 1849), 36.

[20] *Spiritual Magazine*, II (Aug. 5, 1848), 200; *First Annual Report of the Oneida Association, etc.* (Oneida Reserve, 1849), 1; *Second Report* (1850), 1.

ence, and relatively abundant resources, Oneida Community was launched with steam already at full pressure and paddle wheels turning full speed ahead. The canny Yankee acumen of its founder augured well for its material prosperity, and good fortune conspired to bring as an early convert Sewall Newhouse, the inventor of the era's best small animal trap.

Perhaps because he had never concerned himself primarily with ideal economic conceptions, Noyes did not aim to accomplish any particular degree of self-sufficiency in the colony and never suffered from the agrarian emphasis of many Utopian socialists. Trap manufacturing brought prosperity and silver plate production continued it to modern times. No other American communism enjoyed such an economic success. Shakerism was self-destructive and had passed its peak. The Mormons had yet to reach theirs, but at no time did they make their United Order into a full communism. All the Owenite, Fourierist, and spiritualist colonies experienced sudden and early collapse. Several religious communities of European origin did succeed and persist on a small scale, by practically isolating themselves from American society, but none approached in prosperity or in significance the adventure of the perfectionists in central New York.

But economic matters were incidental to the original colony. Noyes stated the philosophy of the community in this fashion:

> Our warfare is an assertion of human rights; first the right of man to be governed by God and to live in the social state of heaven; second the right of woman to dispose of her sexual nature by attraction instead of by law and routine and to bear children only when she chooses; third, the right of all to diminish the labors and increase the advantages of life by association.[21]

The primary aim, then, was religious. Unlike Owen and Fourier, Noyes believed with the evangelists that personal sanctification must precede social regeneration. Or at least, as he came to modify his original position, the two must go on together.

The Oneida members thought of themselves as saints, purified by repeated, intense religious experiences and disciplined by a prolonged search for true righteousness. They were a Bible congrega-

---

[21] J. H. Noyes, Jan. 21, 1848, in Noyes, *Putney Community*, 368.

tion, the only genuine descendants of the original primitive Christian church. Secure as they were in sinlessness, moreover, they had progressed beyond any need for literal adherence to Scripture. The letter of the Bible was a mere preliminary instruction for the unsaved and striving multitudes. Their standard of perfection, by contrast, was a progressive, not a fixed measure. They sought absolute fellowship between men and total love of God, but what kind of behavior met these tests in ideal fashion might change on an ascending scale as they grew in capacity and judgment. Sinless perfection did not mean the end of spiritual growth.

Had such flexible standards of ideal conduct remained open to the vagaries of individual interpretation, Oneida's history would indeed have been as brief as that of the secular communities, and of the other perfectionists beyond the Noyes group. But the colony emphasized its organization; and organization meant the unquestioned acceptance by all associates of John Noyes's discipleship to God.[22] The enterprise was, at least in theory, a thoroughly dictatorial theocracy. Yet it utilized democratic procedures, and no trustworthy source indicates any tyrannical action by the leader. Noyes must have been tactful and persuasive as well as firm and righteous. The extraordinary success of the community is almost exclusively attributable to the singularly large mold of its founder's character. He must surely be ranked as one of the geniuses of his generation.

Even saints secure from sin were not proof against the minor frictions which in other communities developed into great controversies. But Noyes solved this problem satisfactorily. A system of "mutual criticism" kept irritations at a minimum and renewed dedication to higher spirituality. Like the other distinctive practices of Oneida, this ritual began at Putney on a small scale, after lengthy preparation. The germ of the idea had come from Noyes's membership in the Brethren Society of Andover Seminary.

Love for the truth and for one another had been nurtured and strengthened till it could bear any strain. We could receive criticism kindly and give it without fear of offending. . . . We had studied the Bible system-

---

22 J. H. Noyes, Nov. 11, 1847, to Mary J. [Noyes] Mead, Noyes, *Putney Community,* 298.

atically for ten years, and were trying to express our conclusions in appropriate external forms.

Like the Catholic confessional, mutual criticism apparently utilized as a religious ordinance an inborn need for release from the conscience, placing upon a perpetual basis the satisfied feeling of redemption which orthodox Protestantism had to realize irregularly in periodic revivals. One member, who in the process "felt as though he were being dissected with a knife . . . ," testified, "These things are all true, but they are gone, they are washed away." [23]

The perfectionist religion of Oneida, though it developed directly from the ultraism of the thirties, did not continue the emphasis upon reform movements which others derived from the same impulse. The conclusions of Noyes on this subject, as on many others, developed in the direction of antirevivalistic attitudes. He felt that temperance reformers were trying to enforce a non-Biblical morality. The abstinence pledge, furthermore, was an artificial device calculated to eliminate evil without piety, when the real sin was not alcohol but rather "a disease of the drunkard's heart." Temperance could be a problem in political economy, but not legitimately a religious question. The signing of the pledge, moreover, confirmed "the self-complacency that is natural to men who have reformed themselves." All the reformers refused "to recognize the principle that every valuable form of outward amelioration holds a secondary and dependent relation to Spiritual Life." [24]

In many ways, Oneida Community developed a balanced philosophy which co-ordinated the best elements from the diverse theories of social regeneration of liberals and ultraists. Viewing these opposite approaches, Noyes concluded:

A millennium arranged in accordance only with either of the two . . . would be decidedly *simplistic* (to borrow a word from our friends of the Harbinger.) The great ideas of both must be *combined* in the right proportions, and in one living organization, before the Kingdom of Heaven can come.[25]

---

[23] From *Mutual Criticism* (1849, 1876), in Noyes, *Putney Community*, 100, 101.
[24] *Spiritual Magazine*, I (April 15, 1846), 19, II (May 15, June 1, 1847), 9, 24–26.
[25] *Ibid.*, I (Jan. 15, 1847), 161–162.

Persons perpetually sanctified, near to the heavenly state of being, could scarcely be expected to share the physical and mental ills common to sinful humanity. By implication, perfectionism demanded a belief in faith healing, and Noyes was not the man to stop short of a logical absolute. Thus Putney and Oneida folk provided a precedent for Christian Science.

As early as 1838, the *Witness* carried an article on victory over death. Elaborate testimony was gathered at Putney to demonstrate that Noyes and Mary Cragin saved one Harriet Hall, pronounced incurable by doctors, to live thirty years longer at Oneida. An attempt to heal the tuberculosis of a young woman, however, was a total failure, only to be explained by her own and her neighbors' lack of faith. Repercussions of this episode contributed to the hostility which produced the hegira from Vermont. In New York, George W. Robinson testified to the cessation of his own multitudinous infirmities upon his conversion in 1845, and Horace Burt, Jonathan's brother, removed from an asylum at Worcester, Massachusetts, had his evil spirit conquered and tamed by Noyes in 1849.[26]

Most interesting and distinctive of the Oneida practices, however, was the sexual communism, instituted originally on religious grounds and perpetuated by social justifications. Like many of the other sexual experiments of the period, complex marriage started because intensely spiritual people discovered an incompatability between absolute good will among all regenerate beings and the exclusive attachments of a man and woman physically and legally bound together.

Noyes recognized the danger of perverted solutions of this problem. He held himself aloof from the early perfectionist experiments in spiritual wifery and constantly warned of the consequent evils. He held the strayed sheep in abhorrence but apparently was ready to pardon upon evidence that one had been an innocent accomplice or had undergone a change of principle. George and Mary Cragin had had extensive experience in religious adultery but became pillars of the community. The Belchertown, Massachusetts, cult

---

[26] E. Douglas Branch, *The Sentimental Years, 1836–1860* (New York, 1934), 353; Noyes, *Putney Community*, 63, 240–273; *Perfectionist* (Putney, Vt.), V (March 22, 1845), 4; *Spiritual Magazine*, II (Oct. 15, 1849), 280–282.

was by 1843 held in high repute by Noyes. A substantial number of once-errant central New Yorkers eventually became members of Oneida Community.

The difference between complex marriage at Oneida and the looseness Noyes disapproved may seem insignificant to the casual modern observer, but it was great in the eyes of the community. Complex marriage was "organized" instead of fortuitous: in other words, it came under Noyes's direct supervision. More important, it was inspired by "true spirituality." "Whoever meddles with the affairs of the inner sanctuary . . . [otherwise motivated] will plunge himself into consuming fire." [27]

Total sanctification should precede freedom of association. This, at least, was the original belief. When no significant tokens appeared of the final physical resurrection among the saints which Noyes expected, he

perceived for the first time that there was interaction between life and environment; that increased life tended to improve environment, and improved environment to increase life. He therefore announced his belief that Complex Marriage was one of the means by which the resurrection power would be let into the world.

He always maintained that "the Putney Community instead of causing the flood [of spiritual wifery] built the ark, and that it set about the work not a moment too soon." [28]

Noyes was an omnivorous student and inclined to experiment. Robert Dale Owen's *Moral Physiology* began his interest in birth control. This concern became an obsession when his wife lost four out of five babies through premature births in the first six years of their marriage. Lengthy thought and experiment recommended the practice of male continence as the basis of a unique practice of selective breeding, carried on at Oneida for at least twenty years.

So long as the amative and propagative functions are confounded sexual communion carries with it physical consequences that take it out of the category of purely social acts. . . . But let the act of fellowship stand by itself and sexual communion differs only by its superior intensity and beauty from other acts of love. The self-control, retention of life and ascent out of sensuality that must result from making free-

[27] From *Bible Communism*, in Noyes, *Putney Community*, 122.
[28] Noyes, *Putney Community*, 194–195.

dom of love a bounty on the chastening of physical indulgence will elevate the race to new vigor and nobility.

Male continence . . . opens the way for scientific propagation. We are not opposed to procreation. . . . But we are in favor of intelligent, well-ordered procreation. The time will come when scientific combination will be freely and successfully applied to human generation.[29]

The time Noyes spoke of may never come, but it is difficult to escape a degree of sympathy with his purposes. No one with an appreciation of the last century's advance in genetics and the merest concern over the present difficulties of an apparently perverse human race can consistently call the sexual experiments of the Oneida Community less than noble in aim. In this respect as in others, the Oneida beliefs demonstrate the way in which essentially rational attitudes could develop out of a background of revival religion. The tendency is only more sharply defined here than in the companion movements stemming from ultraism.

John Humphrey Noyes and his fellows concerned themselves only with their own perfection, not with making over the world about them. But this attitude did not betoken total indifference to the salvation of society in general. Like the Fourierists and the transcendentalists, they believed that the good example of the absolute ideal, however small its embodiment, would be the most persuasive propaganda. Once men knew the nature of righteousness, they could not but follow automatically. Noyes never doubted that the community was constantly "growing in confidence, and love, and assurance that God will give us the kingdom."

What if there is not another bright spot in the wide world, and what if this is a very small one? Turn your eye toward it when you are tired of looking into chaos, and you will catch a glimpse of a better world.[30]

---

[29] *Witness* (Ithaca, Putney, Vt.), I (Sept. 23, 1837), 22; Noyes, *Putney Community*, 114.

[30] J. H. Noyes to G. W. Robinson, in Noyes, *Putney Community*, 193.

Chapter 19. WORLD WITHOUT END

THE Fourierist collapse and the Millerite disenchantment left western New Yorkers momentarily without a generally accepted recipe for the immediate redemption of American society. Only the Oneida perfectionists preparing a haven for John Humphrey Noyes held among their small number a theory not yet deflated by the test of experience. But the same years which brought the earlier panaceas to nought witnessed the growth of fresh ideas, which after a brief interval would fuse into a new hypothesis for the attainment of millennial happiness and inaugurate yet another religious excitement. The Swedenborgian faith composed a new synthesis, utilizing both the heritage of ultraism and the newer notions of mesmerism, Fourierism, and phrenology. Swedenborgianism in turn yielded place to spiritualism.

Emanuel Swedenborg had not been unknown in the United States before the 1840's. The half-legendary Johnny Appleseed is supposed to have been a Swedenborgian missionary. At least one upstate New Yorker had been interested in the great mystic before the turn of the century. But through a series of apparent coincidences, his ideas now became an enthusiasm "as palpable and portentous as that of Millerism or the old revivals." [1] Fourierism had apparently been tinged with this religion during its transporta-

---

[1] George Peck, *Early Methodism within the Bounds of the Old Genesee Conference*, etc. (New York, 1860), 126 (James Parker); John H. Noyes, *History of American Socialisms* (Philadelphia, 1870), 539.

tion and transformation into an American system, and a new English edition of Swedenborg's works in 1845 probably made them fairly widely available to Americans for the first time. But the growth of interest in mesmerism during the preceding decade probably did most to create the Swedenborgian vogue.

Mesmerism led to Swedenborgianism, and Swedenborgianism to spiritualism, not because of the degree of intrinsic relationship between the three propositions but because of the assumptions according to which American adherents understood them. The religious liberals of the forties had grown beyond dependence on the letter of Scripture. After their fashion, they had espoused science as the grand highway to knowledge and happiness. But they lived in an era of romantic idealism. Before they ever heard of Mesmer or Swedenborg, they expected new scientific discoveries to confirm the broad patterns of revelation as they understood them: to give mankind ever-more-revealing glimpses of the pre-ordained divine plan for humanity and the universe. They expected that all such new knowledge would demonstrate the superiority of ideal over physical or material force, and that it would prove the relationship of man's soul to the infinite spiritual power.

So it was that the leftward-tending former ultraists, the Universalists, and many of the Quakers, studied lowly animal magnetism and made it point to higher things. Mesmerist phenomena were explainable only by "some grand and fundamental law of our being that has hitherto escaped detection." Clairvoyance was a new science, "the true philosophy" of the age, wherein "the *spiritual*" was the "region of *causes*," and "the worlds of matter and of mind" were joined. The trance was "so near an approximation to the state of spirits divested of the body" that it illustrated the basic laws of the spirit world. It seemed, indeed, as if mesmerism had "been developed in this age with the *express design* of confirming the message of Swedenborg. . . ."

But the proof of the new religion's truth and the breadth of its appeal depended ultimately upon its attestation by "the voice of Reason and the voice of Revelation." [2] And in remarkable fashion,

---

[2] George Bush, *Mesmer and Swedenborg; or The Relation of the Developments of Mesmerism to the Doctrines and Disclosures of Swedenborg* (New York, 1847), vi, 13, 17, 160; *Spiritual Telegraph* (New York), June 5, 1852.

Swedenborgianism, as Americans construed it, satisfied a considerable variety of different senses of what was reasonable and divinely ordained. John Noyes ably explained its popularity:

Swedenborgianism went deeper into the hearts of the people than the Socialism that introduced it, because it was a *religion.* The Bible and revivals had made men hungry for something more than social reconstruction. Swedenborg's offer of a new heaven as well as a new earth, met the demand magnificently. . . . The scientific were charmed, because he was primarily a man of science, and seemed to reduce the universe to scientific order. The mystics were charmed because he led them boldly into all the mysteries of intuition and invisible worlds. The Unitarians liked him, because, while he declared Christ to be Jehovah himself, he displaced the orthodox ideas of Sonship and tripersonality. . . . Even the infidels liked him, because he discarded about half the Bible. . . . His vast imaginations and magnificent promises chimed in exactly with the spirit of the accompanying Socialisms.[8]

Swedenborgianism was thus a belief which made a great, if rather vague, synthesis of all the more liberal religious doctrines and many of the scientific and sociological ideas of its day. Yet it retained the indispensable element of revealed religion, an utter faith in the close relationship of the natural and the supernatural. This philosophy, whose sire was American Universalism, and dame, European mysticism, was a true cousin of transcendentalism, bred from the brother Unitarianism and the sister European idealism. The fame of the New England cousin has pre-empted attention so exclusively as to leave the provincial cousin in total obscurity. But Swedenborgianism had no peculiar relationship to the Burned-over District and cannot in this study receive the independent investigation it deserves. It served here merely as a catalytic agent, operating briefly to carry old elements into a new compound.

A group of men about New York City, some of whom had long been moving in sympathetic vibration with upstate religious currents, provided Swedenborgianism with its American formulation; George Bush, professor of "occult therapy" at New York University, and once Presbyterian, reformer, and church unionist, was probably the major leader. Associated with him were James Boyle,

---

[8] *Oneida Circular,* in Noyes, *Socialisms,* 538–539.

now preaching in a Methodist Protestant church, studying medicine, and lecturing on phrenology; Theophilus Gates, the Philadelphia "Battle-Axe"; LaRoy Sunderland, coeditor of *Zion's Watchman;* Theodore Weld and perhaps his brother Charles; and Andrew Jackson Davis, a yokel from Poughkepsie trained in the exercise of the clairvoyant trance by several Universalists. Davis met Swedenborg's ghost during a trance and with Bush's aid had in considerable measure plagiarized Swedenborg's writings in his trance-dictated *Great Harmonia,* which became a kind of testament for the movement. John Noyes testified that Brook Farm transcendental-Fourierists were also involved in the process.[4]

The ideas of this circle spread promptly among leading Universalist clergymen. John Murray Spear, Adin Ballou, Charles Partridge, Thomas L. Harris, William Fishbaugh, S. B. Brittan, and others served as editors and itinerants to circulate the new theology upstate and elsewhere after 1845. Andrew Jackson Davis himself traveled widely at least from New England to Ohio and became quite intimately acquainted with western New York. The Oberlin perfectionists exhibited at least a passing interest, and though John Noyes studied it in a skeptical mood, other New York perfectionists probably greeted it less critically.[5] Allegiance to the Swedenborgian notions did not apparently demand any severance of old religious associations, so no schism occurred at the time among Universalists and Quakers in western New York to serve as a quantitative measurement of the movement's popularity. But it seems safe to assume, on the evidence of preceding and succeeding developments, that a great many in these liberal churches and also many former ultraists had become essentially Swedenborgian by 1848.

American Swedenborgianism provided a leadership, a theology, and a set of social concepts which required only a mechanism for

---

[4] Noyes, *Socialisms,* 537–550; Harris E. Starr, "George Bush," Allen Johnson and Dumas Malone, eds., *Dictionary of American Biography* (21 vols.; New York, 1929–1936), III, 347; John B. Ellis, *Free Love and Its Votaries; or American Socialism Unmasked,* etc. (New York, 1870), 406–409; George W. Noyes, ed., *John Humphrey Noyes, The Putney Community* (Oneida, 1931), 171.

[5] Andrew J. Davis, *The Magic Staff: An Autobiography of Andrew Jackson Davis* (New York, 1857), 279, 300, 338, 355 ff., 414, 470, 477, 512; *Perfectionist* (Putney, Vt.), V (May 3, 1845, Jan. 3, 1846), 15, 84.

communication with the dead to become spiritualism. Before the appearance of the Fox sisters, it was a liberal, intellectual, somewhat rationalistic movement. Transformed into spiritualism by the discovery of devices of communication, it remained substantially unchanged in nature in the eyes of the persons who followed the slight alteration. The presumably substantial numbers of Swedenborgian-minded liberals in western New York were responsible for taking up the episodic experience of the Fox sisters and creating from it a new religious enthusiasm.

But contact with departed spirits had a far wider appeal and attracted persons of all types and persuasions. The formerly revival-minded folk in the Burned-over District, persons indoctrinated in enthusiastic religion of the more fundamentalist type, but disillusioned by the failures of ultraism and premillenarian prophecy, were probably more numerous than the liberals. Only the existence of this larger potential following could have made western New York any more sensitive to the appeal of spiritualism than other portions of the Northeast proved to be.

In December, 1847, a respectable Methodist farmer named John D. Fox moved with his family to a small frame house at Hydesville, near Newark, New York. According to gossip, he had in times past been known to imbibe too freely, while his wife was renowned as one steeped in superstition. One son was a blacksmith in Newark, and a mature daughter, Mrs. Leah Fish, taught music in neighboring Rochester. Margaretta, aged fifteen, and Katie, twelve, lived at home. The local lore attributed a ghost to the house before the time of the Fox habitation, but this was probably an afterthought of the neighbors. Folk legend has little memory for chronology.

A succession of weird rappings in the night disturbed the family's slumbers during March, 1848. After a month of such difficulties, the girls discovered that the spirit would answer questions and that it was infallibly omniscient. With the neighbors gathered to witness the scene, the spirit finally related his history, by simple negatives and affirmations to the painstaking questions put by Katie and Margaretta. The body of a peddler, murdered by a former occupant of the house, had been interred in the cellar and his essence left to guard the premises. Excavation the following summer revealed certain remains to substantiate the tale, but no one outside the family saw this evidence. A committee of investigators in Buffalo later found that the girls produced the knocks with their toe joints, but this knowledge had no effect on the already well-developed popular faith.[6]

The entire episode would doubtless have remained a local, transient superstition, had not Mrs. Fish immediately introduced Katie and Margaretta into Rochester and Auburn society. At Rochester, Isaac Post, a Quaker reformer, discovered systematic responses to letters of the alphabet; and Charles Hammond, a Universalist preacher, became the first writing medium. Soon the spirits demanded public seances, which accordingly began during November, 1848. At Auburn, E. W. Capron became the first public lecturer on spiritualism.[7]

The Fox girls were fraudulent, but innocent: the victims of an invention begun as a childish prank and perpetuated when adults took it seriously. Their elder sister, Leah Fish, probably saw prospects for a livelihood in the rappings and may fairly be considered a deliberate impostor. Post, Hammond, Capron, and most of their associates in both Auburn and Rochester were sincere religious zealots, satisfied that they had discovered a new faith which combined the popular appeal of direct supernatural revelations with a rational concept of this world and the hereafter.

At first the spirits spoke only through people acquainted with Margaretta and Katie Fox, but soon others discovered powers as mediums. The more dignified merely wrote under external direction, but as the sensational news spread over the country, rappings, table moving, speaking in tongues, and the involuntary operation of musical instruments became almost commonplace experiences. Crowds visited Auburn, Newark, and Rochester. Horace Greeley came and lent columns of the *New York Tribune* for publicity. During 1849 and 1850 the Fox sisters themselves traveled about the Northeast. The Swedenborgian-Universalist ministers swung

---

[6] Frank Podmore, *Modern Spiritualism: A History and a Criticism* (2 vols.; London, 1902), I, 179–183; [D. M. Dewey], *History of the Strange Sounds or Rappings Heard in Rochester and Western New York, and Usually Called the Mysterious Noises!* etc. (Rochester, 1850), 14–20, 52, 58.

[7] [Dewey], *Rappings*, 19, 23; E. W. Capron, *Modern Spiritualism: Its Facts and Fanaticisms*, etc. (Boston, 1855), 63, 88, 95, 99; Uriah Clark, *Plain Guide to Spiritualism, A Handbook for Skeptics, Inquirers*, etc. (Boston, 1863), 27, 28.

over practically to a man and became editors and speakers for the new cause.

By 1851 seven papers devoted themselves to this subject; six years later sixty-seven had sprung forth. A prominent judge, a governor, and many other leaders of society joined the movement. Camp meetings and conventions assembled in Ohio, New York, and New England. At the height of the flurry, about 1855, there may have been between one and two million persons adhering in some degree to the movement, though not all, presumably, were totally convinced. At least three state legislatures considered or took measures during the decade to protect the gullible from unscrupulous mediums.[8]

Spiritualism had throughout its existence a dual attraction. Its Swedenborgian adherents were men of relatively wide education, experienced in the progressive reforms of the day and broadened beyond the narrow limits of orthodox, evangelistic religion. To such persons, this seemed a rational, nonsectarian faith, seeking "to preserve the good and true, and build up a heavenly order on earth modled [sic] after the angel spheres." It recognized the Bible, "without accepting plenary inspiration or infallibility," and maintained the essentials of Christianity, "without believing the orthodox trinity or vicarious atonement." It involved no councils, tracts, priesthoods, or theological schools, while allowing complete freedom of individual conviction. It encompassed all measures dedicated to human improvement on this earth and provided as well a warmly satisfying and eminently democratic view of immortality. It answered the prayers of the whole generation of evangelists by inaugurating the millennium on earth.[9]

Men of this mind apparently had little to do with sensational seances but received revelations from the spirits in heaven of men great on earth, by allowing their writing hands to be guided supernaturally. Thus, Isaac Post presented sermons by Elias Hicks, Emanuel Swedenborg, George Fox, George Washington, Thomas

[8] Podmore, *Spiritualism*, I, 183, 214–250; Capron, *Modern Spiritualism*, 204–207; [Dewey], *Rappings*, 34; George Lawton, *The Drama of Life after Death, A Study of the Spiritualist Religion* (New York, 1932), 292–293.

[9] U. Clark, ed., *The Spiritual Register for 1859*, etc. (Auburn, 1859), 17; Clark, *Plain Guide*, 76, 202–203, 281.

Jefferson, and Benjamin Franklin. These discourses, after attesting the genuineness of spirit messages, commented upon the earthly mistakes of each man and adapted the advice to a current morality, such as the semiconsciousness of a good Quaker might dictate. A large part of the movement's literature devoted itself to highly sophisticated discussions of man's nature and the problems of society. Representative articles in the *Shekinah*, for instance, were entitled, "Science of History," "Elements of Spiritual Science," "Education for the People," "The Death Penalty," and "Instinct of Progress." [10]

This religion of spiritualism, dominant at first and strong until the late fifties, may be compared in appeal with the Christian Science of a later date. Some of its adherents very probably lived to become followers of Mary Baker Eddy. Few, in any case, remained active spiritualists very long. For many, if not most, of the more sophisticated minds connected with it, this was probably a further step on the path to religious modernism of some variety. Its scientific manner, social awareness, Biblical and historical criticism, and eager attention to current speculations must have tended to obliterate any remnants of literal-mindedness and orthodoxy still imbedded in the mentalities of its converts.

By far the greater number of spiritualists found a very different appeal in the notion of direct influence from the departed. Except for the Second Coming, contact with spirits was a more sensational idea than any before experienced in a generation of upheavals. Many common folk, led from one enthusiasm to another, had become hardened against ordinary religious inspiration, and driven far from their moorings in orthodoxy.

Yet they yearned for a greater marvel which would satisfy their preternatural desires and succeed where other panaceas had failed. Reared as they had been in superstition and little educated toward its removal, they gloried in this greater mystery which exceeded in appeal the tricks of the magician at the county fair. They were "merely 'sign seekers'; distinguished chiefly for their love of monstrosities . . . [who] watch[ed] and listen[ed] for sights and

---

[10] [Isaac Post], *Voices from the Spirit World, Being Communications from Many Spirits, by the Hand of Isaac Post, Medium* (Rochester, 1852); *Shekinah* (New York), I, 419–420 (1853); the titles could be matched in *Spiritual Telegraph*, 1853–1855.

sounds of ultramundane origin." At the same time, they enjoyed contemplation of a universal, friendly life after death, wherein persons still maintained intimate interest in the doings of this earth. Probably too, they could secure through one medium or another Heavenly sanction for the realization of almost any suppressed desire.[11]

The temptations of mediumship led many to experiment with their own resources, and as the number increased the quality of the supernatural messages and visitations deteriorated. Gradually the degenerating popular wing of spiritualism spread an evil reputation over the whole. Scattered groups and colonies of believers have survived even to the present in the more remote rural areas of western New York. Since 1860, however, the number has been small, and their history has been one of ignorant credulity, irresponsible occultism, and complete isolation from current vogues of thought.[12]

The Burned-over District contained its full share of both types of spiritualists, a total larger apparently than any other region in the United States. A count of mediums in 1859 revealed 71 in New York, to Massachusetts' 55 and Ohio's 27. Lecturers were more numerous but distributed in the same proportions, geographically. The same survey estimated affiliations with spiritualism, nationally, at nearly a million and a half. New York, with 350,000, had more than twice as many adherents as any other state. The distribution within the upstate area of the lecturers and mediums noted in the survey suggests, as does the whole preceding history of religious fervor in the region, that spiritualism was much stronger here as a popular than as an intellectual movement, and that it was more rural than urban.[13] Like its predecessors, the enthusiasm persisted rather in mature, stabilized neighborhoods than in the isolated areas of more recent settlement.

The dual nature of the spiritualist religion probably becomes more apparent in retrospect than it was at the time. During the heyday of the epidemic the two groups presumably intermingled

---

[11] "The Shekinah," editorial, *Shekinah,* I (1853), 86; Clark, *Plain Guide,* 47; Lawton, *Life after Death,* 170.

[12] Lawton, *Life after Death,* 144, 181, and *passim.*

[13] Clark, *Spiritual Register,* 23–27. See map XXV.

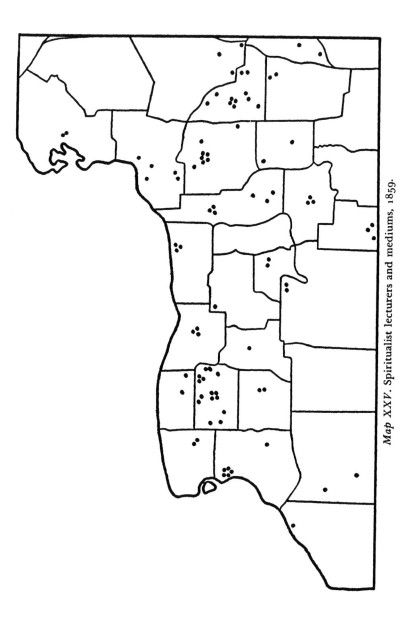

Map XXV. Spiritualist lecturers and mediums, 1859.

and exchanged influences. From the mixture grew a number of transient phenomena which must be noted in a history of religious aberrations.

Extreme fervor, whatever its exact nature, had periodically run over into experiments in sex relations. This had happened with revivalism, perfectionism, and Adventism, and now took place again. Certain of the early perfectionists became converted to the new doctrine and some transfers direct from Adventism probably occurred as well. Evidence therefore supports the contention of spiritualists that free love was "a philosophy originating in religious fanaticism before modern spiritualism was known." Apologists for the movement also made much of the fact that French socialism introduced some unorthodox sex practices.[14]

While both of these theories are presumably sound as partial explanations, American spiritualism seems to have encouraged more widespread participation in such experiments than had any previous movement. For this quantity of eroticism, at least, the nature of the belief bears a degree of responsibility. The intellectuals of the new faith were noted advocates of sex equality and, probably more than other women's rights champions, frankly recognized aspects of equality beyond property or political safeguards. In addition, both mediums and clients were quite possibly even more overwhelmingly feminine than the intensely enthusiastic groups of earlier decades. The larger amount of irregularity may merely reflect the predominance of feminine reactions to emotional tension. Even more distinctly than had perfectionism, furthermore, this belief encouraged the idea of a mystical kind of spiritual affinity, different from and more pure than sexual or legal relationships. The number of irresponsible people who became mediums may have fostered the use of occult resources for a sanctimonious justification of earthly desires, under the guise of the doctrine of spiritual affinities.

While indications are that sex irregularity occurred in scattered portions of western New York, the more famed experiments were combined with socialism and spiritualism in several community enterprises farther afield. Berlin Heights, Ohio, was probably the

---

[14] *Oneida Circular*, Nov. 16, 1851, quoted, Noyes, *Socialisms*, 568–569; Capron, *Modern Spiritualism*, 380; Clark, *Plain Guide*, 137.

most renowned free-love colony. The venture of the Nicholses and Stephen Pearl Andrews at Modern Times, Long Island, had also for a time a somewhat similar reputation. But at least one project tinged with some degree of eroticism originated in the Burned-over District.

During 1849 an "Apostolic Circle" gathered in Auburn, under the leadership of James Scott, a Seventh-Day Baptist minister from Brooklyn, Thomas L. Harris, an English-born Universalist-Swedenborgian minister, and a Mrs. Benedict, a local medium. Some of the members had been Adventists; others, perfectionists. In October, 1851, about a hundred of these folk settled in the Mountain Cove Community at Fayette, Virginia. The colony disbanded during the following year, but Harris led a fragment to Amenia, in Dutchess County, New York. In 1865 he and his followers moved to Harmonial City in the Kiantone Valley, near the Lake Erie shore in Chautauqua County. But by this time Harris had developed new beliefs, and this Brocton community cannot be called a spiritualist undertaking.

After the Civil War, Lily Dale, a thoroughly spiritualist but not an erotic community, sprang up on Chautauqua Lake. This and a couple of other once-communist centers of spiritualist inspiration survive as camp grounds, where faithful adherents still gather every summer.[15]

Spiritualism, the last great excitement in the region, like Antimasonry, the first, was thus an enthusiasm incorporating several points of view, manifested in a variety of fashions. Contact with departed spirits was a mere device, convenient for many purposes. The uses to which the mechanism was put depended upon the persons involved. And the diverse mentalities of those persons had been alike developed amidst the lengthy history of religious emotionalism in the Burned-over District.

---

[15] Lawton, *Life after Death*, 371 ff.; Capron, *Modern Spiritualism*, 111–129; William S. Bailey, "The Harris Community: Brotherhood of the New Life," *New York History*, XVI (July, 1935), 278–285.

Chapter 20. THE PASSING ERA

MOVEMENTS rising from attitudes deeply ingrained in a multitude of minds could not cease, any more than they could begin, abruptly. The evolving religious emotionalism of western New York carried some people along with it but left at each stage an inheritance of individuals, or even their descendants, whose ability to adjust to further novelty stopped at that given point. In spite of the pressure of events, many persons lived out at least the latter half of their span bitterly resisting change. Consequently, only the hand of death, gradually claiming increasing numbers of the generations which had matured between 1800 and 1850, could finally terminate the phenomena of the half-century.

Spiritualism enjoyed a great vogue for more than a decade. Even earlier enthusiasms continued in evidence for some time. Perfectionism, embodied in the Oneida form, lasted in its purity for a quarter-century. As in the case of spiritualism, changed remnants of the original system remain today. The Adventist sects failed after 1850 to achieve great prominence but survived in miniature. The Wesleyans persisted as a perfectionist branch of the Methodist Church. Abolition, temperance, and the lesser crusades of pious origin grew and prospered under altered methods, long gathering support from persons indoctrinated with the ideas of the thirties. Mormonism developed in its western locale to become the most successful religion of American origin.

A few new occurrences of the old sort took place after 1850, but the declining number of people still devoted to earlier attitudes made them feeble resurgences of the former fervency. Masonry had recovered from the ill effects of the Morgan episode and was now only one of several flourishing fraternal orders. During the last few years before the Civil War, the evangelistic brotherhood staged a second, weak antimasonic crusade.[1] Revivalism had steadily declined since the impasse of 1844, but during the depression of 1857 a nation-wide awakening transpired for the last time. This had no particular affinity for the Burned-over District, however, and was quite different in nature from its predecessors.[2] One more local schism disturbed the Methodist Church. A group of clergy and laymen in the Genesee Conference apparently suffered disfavor and inconvenience under the episcopacy, because of their unfashionably strict adherence to the original discipline and their uncompromising insistence upon now-outdated conceptions of holiness. They were, in fact, survivors of 1830, untouched by intervening events. They seceded and formed the Free Methodist Church in 1860.[3]

With the exception of these small movements and in spite of the perpetuation here of sectarianisms originated during the three decades past, the mid-point of the century marks the end of important religious upheaval in the Burned-over District. The only groups which continued to embody on a noticeable scale the ideas originated in the past thirty years of enthusiasm had moved, or were moving, westward.

Agrarian culture survived the Civil War in the West more strongly than in upstate New York. The parallel between Yankee-settled areas of the Middle and Far West in the third quarter of the century and the Burned-over District in the second is an imperfect one, but more nearly true than a comparison drawn within this one region alone. New religious phenomena, somewhat similar

---

[1] C[harles] G. Finney, *The Character, Claims and Practical Workings of Freemasonry* (Chicago, 1887, copyrights 1869, 1879), testifies in its three editions to surviving antimasonic feeling.

[2] Merrill E. Gaddis, "Christian Perfectionism in America," (MS at University of Chicago, 1929), 380; Samuel W. Dike, "A Study of New England Revivals," *American Journal of Sociology*, XV (Nov., 1909), 364.

[3] Gaddis, "Perfectionism," 428; B. T. Roberts, *Why Another Sect?* etc. (Rochester, 1879), 19-23, 44, and *passim*.

to those experienced here before 1850, later developed under conditions at least slightly reminiscent of western New York in the period of its spiritual experiments. But the main currents of thought in this region had now flowed beyond that part of the stream wherein religious emotionalism readily flourished.

Events on the national scene, particularly the Mexican War and the gold rush, tended here, as elsewhere, to intensify awareness of political and economic issues, turning concentrated attention away from religious questions. The long depression after 1837 gave way to renewed prosperity during the late forties and early fifties. Railroads finally won ascendancy over canal transportation, while the agricultural and processing businesses in upstate New York began to decline, at least relatively, before western competition. Manufactures began to specialize geographically, and markets correspondingly widened. The canal-line cities had been growing constantly, gradually shifting the earlier ratio of urban and rural population. Increasing numbers of Europeans, seldom sympathetic with the isms of the period now passing, entered the region and started to spread beyond the major cities.

After a decade of rapid development, industrial revolution boomed with the stimulus of the Civil War. The idealism which the antislavery crusade had gradually absorbed found its exclusive aim apparently accomplished. Victory hardened concepts of morality into moribund forms, preventing the wholesale transfer of energies to new campaigns. War, reconstruction, urbanism, and industrialism took a heavy toll of the settled scheme of social ethics grown in the more quiescent agricultural economy of western New York. Spiritual and crusading zeal flagged during an interval of readjustment to a new society.[4]

It is not difficult satisfactorily to explain the decline of fervor on such external grounds. A changing civilization quite naturally altered religious attitudes, along with others. But internal factors had operated to create the enthusiasm in the first quarter of the century, and a retrospective view of the second quarter suggests that internal causes bore also upon its decline.

Apparently, religious extravagances and sensationalism made

---

4 David M. Ludlum, *Social Ferment in Vermont, 1791–1850* (New York, 1939), draws a set of conclusions with which these agree essentially.

enemies as well as friends and finally bred sore disillusionment among advocates. Furthermore, the extreme emotionalism of the climax period happened to develop along lines whose continuations ran counter to the direction of the original impulse. The pious reformer soon came into conflict with the zealous evangelist and turned against him his own artillery. The reformer left the old faith and eventually lost his driving motivation. The stalwart evangelist retreated into a more rigorous fundamentalism, which went equally wide of the original mark.

Enthusiastic religion in western New York was thus heavily responsible for its own demise. Its venturesome proponents were radicals who dared to form their plan for living upon the logic of their convictions and face all consequences heroically. Unfortunately, their unparalleled vitality and courage aided mankind to make slight, if any, progress along the wearisome road toward Utopia. For the assumption that sin must be attacked primarily in the individual, rather than in society, misled these zealots into a futile expenditure of their energies. The wastage, in channels leading only to self-destruction, of a potent motivation which if applied to the political, economic, and social problems of the era might have accomplished great things, is probably the chief debit in the account of religious enthusiasm.

Again, ultraism must answer for a marked decline in neighborly charity and humankindness, apparent wherever it flourished. Moreover, it flouted as often as it sustained the ideas of personal liberty cherished in a democracy. And the greatest trial of democratic government in the United States traces in a considerable measure to this source.

Nevertheless, the American tradition has been greatly enriched by the legacies of this kind of radicalism. The Mormon Church, several Adventist denominations, two species of Methodism, and a sprinkling of spiritualist groups survived the period. The thirteenth and eighteenth amendments of our Constitution, though currently of no great significance, were at least once important, each in its time. Both developed from movements inspired in the same fashion. Oneida Community was one of the most daring social experiments in our national history. Courageous nonconformity, whatever its purposes, ought of itself to constitute a precious heritage to the twentieth century. Finally, religious enthusiasm, even as it destroyed itself, built a path—perhaps followed by as many persons as traveled any other route—toward the more modern conceptions of liberal religion which the zealots had originally so consistently abhorred.

Possibly at least the greater of these achievements may compensate for the destruction wrought when fires of passion raged in the Burned-over District.

Appendix. NOTES ON MAPS

ALL of the maps reproduced here, with the exception of III and IV, have been plotted on a mimeograph outline of suitable size to show clearly the portion of New York State being studied. The two exceptions have been designed within the same external lines, but have no internal political boundaries. The original of the mimeographed outline is the flyleaf map in New York Mercantile Union, *Business Directory* (New York, 1850). The original has rail, road, and canal lines and certain geographical features omitted in tracing. Omission of the Finger Lakes creates a slight distortion of county lines in the central part of the map. The county boundaries are those of 1850, substantially unchanged today except for the creation of Schuyler County from parts of Steuben, Chemung, Tompkins, Seneca, and Yates. During much of the period under review, Wyoming was still within Genesee County and Chemung within Tioga. Other changes of boundary in the interval were slight.

Maps I and II are based upon a comparative analysis of population in 1820 and 1835. Thomas F. Gordon, *Gazetteer of the State of New York*, etc. (Philadelphia, 1836), *passim*, contains county-by-county tables which give township population in both years, as well as area in acres. When towns had been divided in the interval, calculations were made for the earlier date and for growth by combining in one unit the two or several towns involved. This process cannot, of course, be exactly accurate but was deemed to provide generally reliable data.

Map III was prepared by ruling off in squares the entire area to be considered and dividing the total value of manufactures by the total number of squares, to secure a common unit of area and value. The arrangement of city and county lines was made to conform as closely as possible with geographic location. Figures on manufactures are compiled from the *Census of the State of New York, for 1835*, etc. (Albany, 1836), *passim*. The census is not paged but has a leaf number for each county, with the counties in alphabetical order. Dollar value is recorded for each township by industries, with county totals for each column. Twenty types of manufacture are recorded, so the totals are reliable as a general index of industrial activity even though the survey is presumably not all-inclusive.

Map IV represents a rough estimate of the proportions of farm market areas served by the various canal cities. Differentiation in productivity of land has been accounted for approximately by adopting three sizes of area units. The counties of Niagara, Orleans, Monroe, Wayne, and Genesee and the northern part of the tier of counties adjacent to the south have been divided into small squares. The area south of the northern line of Steuben County, extended east and west across the state, has been divided into squares equaling two of the first units, assuming half as many fully productive acres as in the counties first named. The land between these two sections and that east of Wayne County has been assigned a value of one and one-half. The total units so secured have been divided into the average total tolls for the four years 1837, 1840, 1845, and 1850, omitting extra-state goods paying toll at Buffalo and Oswego. The zones have been proportioned to the resulting figures for Lockport, Rochester, Syracuse, Rome, and Utica and the remaining toll value has been assigned to the central area which no city dominated. Geographical arrangement roughly conforms with the probable actual market, considering branch canals, river valleys, railroads, and topography. Toll figures are from the *Report of the Auditor of the Canal Department of the Tolls, Trade and Tonnage of the New York Canals* (Albany, 1854), 122–125.

Data for map V were compiled from the *Census of the State of New York, for 1845* (Albany, 1846), *passim*. The eastern portion of the map has little significance, as 1845 is too late to measure the nativity of early settlers there. For most of the region south of Lake Ontario, however, these figures should provide a reasonably good index for the origins of the population. Map VI represents a summary of economic conditions and has no specific sources.

Rolla M. Tryon, *Household Manufactures in the United States, 1640–1860, A Study in Industrial History* (Chicago, 1917), 304, 305, provides figures upon which maps VII and VIII are based. Data for maps IX and XI, and X and XII, respectively, are contained in the

"Annual Report of the Superintendent of Common Schools," [A. C. Flagg], *Legislative Documents of the Senate and Assembly of the State of New York*, 53d session, I, no. 31 (Jan., 1830), 43–45; and the "Annual Report of the Superintendent of Common Schools," [J. C. Spencer], *Documents of the Assembly of the State of New York*, 64th session, IV, no. 100 (1841), 46–47. The figures from which map XIII is compiled are given for each county, arranged alphabetically, in separate columns for private schools, academies, and colleges, in the *Census of New York State, 1845, passim.* The calculations for map XIV used figures in J. D. B. DeBow, Sup't., *The Seventh Census of the United States: 1850*, etc. (Washington, 1853), lxiii and 126.

The *Seventh Census* tabulates illiteracy figures separately for the native- and the foreign-born, for the first time. Map XV, compiled from figures on pages xli and 118, is therefore the clearest indication of native-born illiteracy, even though it comes at the end of the period. Map XVI attempts to approximate similar information for 1840. Illiteracy figures from the *Compendium of the Enumeration of the Inhabitants and Statistics of the United States . . . from the Returns of the Sixth Census*, etc. (Washington, 1841), 1–65 *passim*, 83–123, 136, 185, and 343, have been rendered in percentages to form the main legend of the map. Superimposed upon this picture of total illiteracy is a set of lines which show areas where low literacy figures are explained by large percentages of foreign-born. The latter data are also from the *Sixth Census*, 83–123.

Maps XVII and XVIII are derived from county election returns recorded in Edwin Williams, *The New York Annual Register* (New York, 1830), 73–76. For map XIX, Andrew Jenson, *Latter-Day Saint Biographical Encyclopedia*, etc. (2 vols.; Salt Lake City, 1901), vol. I, *passim*, gives a number of sketches of early Mormon members from New York. Data in a clipping collection belonging to Donald Perry, *Enterprise Press*, Shortsville, N.Y., helped to identify a few adherents. David Whitmer, *An Address to All Believers in Christ*, etc. (Richmond, Mo., 1887), *passim*, gives further information, particularly on the first church groups formed. Over ninety letters were written to Finney during his six months' sojourn at Rochester in the winter of 1830–1831. The places within this region which solicited his aid or interest have been noted on map XX, from the Charles G. Finney Papers at the Oberlin College Library, *passim*.

O. L. Holley, *The New York State Register for 1843* (Albany, 1843), 69–102, gives town and county figures on Stewart's run for the governorship on the Liberty ticket in 1842. The county totals have been used in the shadowing, and the township figures were scanned for unusually high proportions of Stewart polls among the total cast, to form map XXI. The sources for map XXII are varied. Wesleyan Methodist churches are listed in Joel T. Headley, ed., Franklin B. Hough, Supt., *Census of the State of New York, for 1855* (Albany, 1857), 462–463. The location of Christian Union churches and centers of interest in union has been ascertained through an accumulation of articles, notices, and letters in *Union Herald* (Cazenovia, N.Y.), vols. II–IV, no. 30 (May 16, 1837–Nov. 26, 1840), and vol: VI (May, 1841–April, 1842); and in the *Christian Investigator* (Whitesboro, Honeoye, N.Y.), vols. I–VI (1843–1848), *passim*. Congregational churches recently changed from Presbyterian are located from a tabulation made of individual congregational histories given for every Presbyterian church west of Madison County by the Rev. James H. Hotchkin, *A History of the Purchase and Settlement of Western New York, and of the Rise, Progress, and Present State of the Presbyterian Church in That Section* (New York, 1848), *passim*. Methodist abolition sentiment, aside from that expressed in the formation of Wesleyan congregations, has been judged from correspondence addressed to the editor of *Zion's Watchman* (New York), vols. I–II (1836–1837), and vols. V–VI (1840–1841), *passim*.

Information on Adventism must be gleaned from a few periodicals. From the *Christian Palladium* (Union Mills, N.Y.), vols. VIII–XII (1839–1843), *passim;* the *Midnight Cry* (New York), vols. I–VII (1842–1844), *passim;* and the *Voice of Truth, and Glad Tidings of the Kingdom at Hand* (later *Advent Harbinger* and yet later the *Advent Harbinger and Bible Advocate;* Rochester, N.Y.), vols. I–XVIII (April, 1844–June, 1849), *passim,* an assortment of over 400 notices, letters, and reports has been gathered, each of which indicates Millerite strength or weakness in a given place, in definite fashion. Fourierist locations noted on map XXIV are taken directly from Arthur E. Bestor, Jr., "American Phalanxes, A Study of Fourierist Socialism in the United States (with Special Reference to the Movement in Western New York)" (2 vols.; MS at Yale University, 1938), vol. I, 17, 24. Map XXV is made possible by a list of mediums and lecturers with addresses, published in U[riah] Clark, ed., *The Spiritualist Register for 1859: Facts, Philosophy, Statistics of Spiritualism* (Auburn, N.Y., 1859 [?]), 23, 24, 27.

INDEX

[An author index (including titles of anonymous works, manuscript collections, and serials) has been incorporated in this general index, to provide convenient reference to footnotes, in lieu of a formal bibliography. Since most references to notes are bibliographical only, the letter "n," following the page number, ordinarily differentiates the bibliographical from the text references. The first and complete citation of each source in each chapter has been indexed. Abbreviated titles follow the author's name only when two or more items are involved. Newspapers are listed under place of origin. Journal titles in the index indicate use as a primary source, since articles in scholarly journals may be traced adequately from author entries.]

Abolition, *see* Antislavery movement
Academic freedom at Oneida Institute, 234
Accommodation plan: of Plan of Union, 19; as a pressure toward Presbyterian organization, 49; annulled, 256. *See also* Plan of Union
Adams, John Q., President, 116, 272
Adams, John Q., of Auburn Theological Seminary, 102n
Adams (Jefferson Co.), 151, 188; sectarian rivalry in, 45
Adams Basin (Monroe Co.), Millerites at, 304
Address of General Union for Promotion of a Christian Sabbath, 134n
Advent, *see* Premillennialism
Advent Christian Association formed, 311-312
Advent Christian Church, 310

Adventism, *see* Premillennialism
Adventist churches, 353, 356
Adventist General Conference, Burned-over District resistance against, 312
Advent Review and Sabbath Herald, 316
Agrarianism, 327; and Antimasonry, 117
Agriculture: social maturity of, in economy of western New York, 56; in Utica area, 63; journalism of, 104
Aiken, Rev. S. C., and C. G. Finney, 164
Albany, 39, 75, 104; growth of, 56; perfectionists at, 192, 195, 240-241; Edward Kirk at, 195; Millerites at, 296; *Cultivator,* 104
Albany Regency, 116, 270
Albion, *Orleans Advocate,* 54, 120n; *Orleans Telegraph,* 117n
Allegany County, Mormons in, 148
Allegheny Valley, soils of, 70
Allen, Ethan, 8

Amana Inspirationists, 333
Amenia (Dutchess Co.), community at, 352
American Antislavery Society founded, 219. *See also* Antislavery movement
American Baptist Antislavery Society, 301
American Baptist Home Missionary Society, 24; *Annual Report of*, 24n
American Bible Society, 25; Charles Weld as agent of, 196; *Annual Report of*, 25n
American Citizen, 107, 221
American Education Society, 26, 128, 234
American Female Moral Reform Society, 230. *See also* Moral reform movement
American Home Missionary, 105
American Home Missionary Society, 22ff., 24, 26, 47, 50, 128-129; federation process of, 22; strength in western New York, 23; and sectarian rivalry, 47; in Monroe County, 48; revival system of, 49; denominational apportionment of aid, 49-50; ministers of, in public schools, 92; and Antimasonry, 121, 123, 124; and Presbyterian Board of Missions, 135; and Free Church movement, 166; and temperance, 213-214; conservatism of, 260-261; New York State papers of, MS, 35n, 49, 92n, 121n, 127n, 141n, 153n, 176n, 190n, 214n, 240n, 255n, 270n; *Annual Report of*, 22, 22n
American Industrial Union, Fourierist, 331
American Protestant Society, 195
American Protestant Vindicator, 108n
American Revolution, New England religion during, 7
American Society for Promoting Observance of the Seventh Commandment, 229. *See also* Moral reform movement
American Temperance Union, 215. *See also* Temperance movement
American Tract Society, 25; *Annual Report of*, 25n
Amherst College, 98
Anarchy, ultraist view of, 207
Andover Theological Seminary, 45, 158, 245; Society of Inquiry, papers of, MS, 129n, 153n. *See also* Brethren Society
Andrews, Edward, 310n
Andrews, Stephen Pearl, 352
Angelica Presbytery: license of Augustus Littlejohn, 193; Records of, MS, 194n
Annesly sisters, 240
Anthony, Susan B., 237

Anti-Catholicism, 84, 231-233; distinguished from political nativism, 232; in Millerite movement, 320. *See also* Nativism
Antimasonic Inquirer, 73
Antimasonic movement, 3, 16, 35, 71, 74, 75, 135, 144, 352; environment and, 76; described, 114-120; agrarian nature of, 117; and temperance, 117; and religion, 117, 121, 124, 125, 136, 137; class distinctions in, 122; and benevolent movements, 123; layman revolt in, 123; and millennialism, 123; and Rochester Revival, 154; William Miller on, 318; the second, 354. *See also* Antimasonic Party
Antimasonic Party, 79, 116, 270; history of, 116; program of, 116
Antirent feeling, 71, 269, 272, 331
Antirent war, in Hudson Valley, 272, 327
Antislavery movement: abolitionist phase of, 16, 35; in religious press, 105; Luther Myrick in, 193; Charles Stuart and, 195; origin of immediatism, 220; New York societies in, 221; in western New England, 223; and millennialism, 224; environment and, 226; Oneida Institute and, 234; McGraw College and, 235; Canadian Rebellion of 1837, 237; women in, 237; threat to Methodist Church, 264-265; and Union Church movement, 279; William Miller on, 318-319; persistence of, 353
    other references: 103; environment of, 76; and perfectionism, 193; ultraist attitudes in, 205; abolition crusade and, 217; British, in West Indies, 218; influence on ultraism, 224-225, 276-277; changes in 1840's, 225-226, 274, 276-277; strength in Burned-over District, 226; and nativism, 233; benevolent societies for, 280-281; ended, 355
Anxious bench, the, 181ff.
"Apostolic Circle," formed at Auburn, 352
Appleseed, Johnny, 341
Apprenticeship, as education, 98
Apulia (Onondaga Co.), 196
Arcade (Wyoming Co.), temperance in, 130
Arminianism: in Methodist Church, 15; trend toward, in New England theology, 27; and Antimasonry, 121
Ascension robes, 302, 305-306
Attica (Wyoming Co.), 71, 124; Millerites in, 294

Auburn, 107; New England settlement in, 6; C. G. Finney at, 154, 163; Burchard revival in, 188; perfectionists at, 244; schism in, 257; abolitionists at, 264; Millerites at, 302; spiritualists at, 346, 352
Auburn prison, 136
Auburn Railroad, 67
Auburn Theological Seminary, 101-102, 128, 129, 156, 158, 259; and moral reform, 230
Avon (Livingston Co.), 42-43

Bacon, Ezekiel, 205n
Bailey, William S., 352n
Bainbridge (Chenango Co.), 142
Baldwin, Johnson, 129
Ballou, Adin, 344
Baltimore (Md.), Jacob Knapp in, 196
Baptist Church: and camp meetings, 8; education of ministers, 8, 26, 101-102; growth of, 9, 13, 23-24, 253; missions of, 18ff., 23ff.; state missionary convention of, 24; and Antimasonry, 118ff.; and benevolent movements, 135-136; and temperance, 214, 216; and abolition, 221-224; and moral reform, 230; schism of 1845, 262ff.; and Millerites, 288, 296, 301-302
Baptist Education Society, of New York, Annual Report of, 26n
Baptist General Tract Society, 25
Baptist Register, 24n, 47n, 107n, 120, 120n, 127n, 132, 148n, 169n, 177n, 197n, 198n, 216n, 253n, 273n, 294n; characterized, 105-106; and Mormons, 148; on Rochester Revival, 169; on millennialism, 201; and moral reform, 230; anti-Catholicism in, 231; verse a day plan in, 232; and abolition, 223-224; and retrenchment, 235; quoted on sectarianism, 255; and Millerites, 294-296, 302, 306, 309; and phrenology, 325
Barnes, Albert, 259
Barnes, Gilbert H., *Antislavery Impulse,* 158n, 177n, 218n; and D. L. Dumond, *Weld-Grimké Letters,* 80n, 167n, 187n, 204n, 218n, 277n, 288n
Barrett, Lyman, 129
Barry, Thomas F.: at Rochester, 298-299
Batavia, 70-71; Masonry in, 114; antirent controversy in, 269; Millerites at, 302; Fourierism about, 328; *Advocate,* 114
Bates, Ernest S., 89n
Bath (Steuben Co.), 76

"Battle-Axe Letter," quoted, 247-248
Beecher, Charles, 28n, 151n, 218n
Beecher, George, 251
Beecher, Lyman, 27, 159, 231, 259; and temperance, 130; on Rochester Revival, 156; at New Lebanon Conference, 163; accord with C. G. Finney, 164; and women's equality in church, 177
Belchertown (Mass.), perfectionists at, 240, 338
Belden, A. Russell, 37n
Bellamy, Joseph, 27
Beman, Nathaniel, 231; at New Lebanon Conference, 163; quoted on revival measures, 183
Benedict, David, 102n
Benedict, Mrs., 352
Benevolent movements, 24-28; journalism of, 26, 105; and theology, 28-29; and layman revolt, 136; and religious enthusiasm, 136-137; and humanitarianism, 165; and C. G. Finney, 165; and millennialism, 200; interdenominational support of, 254; William Miller on, 318. *See also* Benevolent societies *and individual movements*
Benevolent societies, 40, 47, 165; female, 38; Presbyterian domination in, 47; May anniversaries of, 133; antislavery, 280-281. *See also* Benevolent movements *and individual societies*
Bergen (Genesee Co.), Burchard revival in, 188
Berkshire and Columbia Missionary Society, 21
Berlin Heights community, 351
Bernard, Elder David, 123n
Bestor, Arthur E., Jr., 328n, 361
Bethel churches, origin of, 261
Bible circulation, 126-127
Bible societies, support of, 127
Billington, Ray A., 84n, 233n
Binghamton, 62, 75; Burchard revival in, 188
Birney, James, unorthodox beliefs of, 283
Bissell, Josiah, Jr., 75, 134, 154, 212; characterized, 133
Black River Canal, 63
Black River Congregational Association, 191-192
Black River Valley: Universalist Church in, 18; isolation of, 62-63; Daniel Nash in, 160; Methodist abolition in, 264
Blackwell, Antoinette Brown, 237; unorthodox beliefs of, 283

Bliss, Sylvester, 290n, 311
Bloomer, Amelia, 237
Bloomfield (Ontario Co.), Fourierist phalanx at, 331
Boatman's Friend Societies, 235
Book of Mormon, 81, 144, 145
Boonville (Oneida Co.), Western Revival in, 153
Boston (Erie Co.), Patching heresy in, 39
Boston (Mass.), 51; slight migration from, 6; Mormons in, 148; C. G. Finney visits, 164; Kirk revivals in, 195; Jacob Knapp in, 196; William Miller at, 292
Bourne, George, 218, 231
Boyle, James, 240, 245, 246, 276, 343; career of, 189-191; and Charles Weld, 196
Boyle, Laura Putnam, 189
Bradley, Joshua, 12n
Branch, E. Douglas, 88n, 338n
Brethren Society: of Andover Seminary, 336; J. H. Noyes and, 245; papers of, MS, 245n
Brief Account of Divisions in the Presbyterian Church in Troy, 163n
Brigham, Clarence S., 103n
Brimfield (Mass.), perfectionists at, 240
Brimfield bundling, the, 243
Brisbane, Albert, 328
Brittan, S. B., 344
Brockway, J., 163n, 174n, 258n
Brocton community, 352
Brodie, Fawn M., 139n
Brook Farm, 344
Brooks, Charles W., 26n, 301n
Brothers, Thomas, 244n
Brown, Amos, 124
Brown, Maria, 243, 244; and the Brimfield bundling, 243
Brownson, Orestes, 106, 189; quoted, 134, 137; beliefs of, 324
Buffalo, 71, 75, 154; sectarian rivalry in, 45; economic development of, 56, 59, 63, 74; Burchard revival in, 188; perfectionist convention at, 251; Millerites at, 299, 300, 302, 304; Owenite community plans in, 324; phrenology at, 325; Amana colony near, 333
Burchard, Jedediah, 152, 160, 178, 187, 192; and business operations during revivals, 180; rates for services, 187; career of, 188-189; antagonism of C. G. Finney toward, 188-189
Burchard, William, 51
Burned-over District, use of term, 3, 152

Burnt District, *see* Burned-over District
Burt, Horace, 338
Burt, Jonathan, 241, 243, 334
Bush, George, 342n, 343; and James Boyle, 190; quoted on Union Church, 282; on Millerites, 321
Bush, perfectionist, 241
Butler, Frances, *see* Kemble, Frances

Cady, Daniel, 327
Calvin, John, 45
Calvinism, 15; and Antimasonry, 121; modified, 159; and religious optimism, 199
Campbell, Alexander, 145n, 148; quoted, 145-146
Campbellites, *see* Disciples of Christ
Camp meetings: denominational attitudes on, 8; Millerite, 304-305
Canadian Rebellion of 1837, 273
Canal, *see* Erie Canal, Chenango Canal, etc.
Canandaigua, 70, 76, 139; Morgan trial in, 114; as leading village, 139-140; Methodist abolition at, 264; Millerite camp meeting at, 304
Canaseraga (Allegany Co.), perfectionist convention at, 241, 243
Candler, Isaac, 8on
Cape Vincent (Jefferson Co.), 188
Capital punishment, ultraism and, 236
Capron, E. W., 346, 346n
Carlton, Frank T., 92n
Carmer, Carl, 3n, 34n, 306n
Caroline episode, 273
Catholic Church, 17, 232, 319; antipathy to, 43, 231-233; foreign-born membership of, 83; in urban and rural areas, 233. *See also* Anti-Catholicism *and* Nativism
Cattaraugus County: Mormons in, 148; Millerites in, 301
Cayuga County: Luther Myrick in, 192; Fourierism in, 331
Cazenovia (Madison Co.), 107; sectarian rivalry in, 45; Luther Myrick at, 191; Methodist abolition at, 264; Union Church meeting at, 280; *Abolitionist*, 107
Census: of New York, of 1835, 87n, 359; of 1845, 18n, 360; of 1855, 63n, 261n, 262n, 361
of United States, of 1840, 360; of 1850, 103n, 360; of 1860, 149n; of 1860, MS, 150n

Central Evangelical Association, 187, 261; and Union Church movement, 279. *See also* Oneida Evangelical Association

Central Sunday School Union, 129

Centreville (Allegany Co.), 49

Champlain (Clinton Co.), Horatio Foote at, 194

Chapman, Mr., 243, 244

Chapman, Mrs., 243, 244

Chardon Street Chapel, Boston, William Miller at, 292

Chautauqua County, economic development of, 74; antirent riots in, 272; Millerites in, 294, 301; spiritualists in, 352

Chemung Canal, 70

Chenango Canal, 62, 63

Chenango County, population of, 62

Chenango Valley, 62

Cholera epidemic: and temperance, 214; and recession of 1832, 269

Christian Church (Christian Connection), 38; development of, 15-17, 262-263; journalism of, 106; and Antimasonry, 121; and benevolent movements, 135-136; and Millerites, 288

Christian Contributor, 106, 235n

Christian Examiner, 164n

Christian Investigator, 107, 218n, 280n, 361; established, 280

Christian Palladium, 263n, 281n, 295n, 361; characterized, 106; circulation of, 263; quoted on Union Church, 281; and Millerites, 295

"Christian Party in Politics," 132-135, 207-279. *See also* Sabbatarianism

Christian Science: perfectionist precedent for, 338; and spiritualism, comparable, 348

Church membership: growth of, 9; and Antimasonic movement, 124; cycles of gain in, 252-254. *See also individual denominations*

Church of God (Adventist), formed, 311-312

Cincinnati (Ohio), Theodore Weld at, 219

Cities: and Erie Canal, 56-57; growth of, 355

Civil War, 217, 354; and industrial revolution, 355

Clark, Elmer T., 317n

Clark, Uriah: *Plain Guide to Spiritualism*, 346n; *Spiritual Register*, 347n, 361

Clarkson (Monroe Co.), 124; Fourierist phalanx at, 331

Class distinctions: in Antimasonry, 122; in benevolent movements, 136

Clay, Henry, 272

Cleaveland, Dorothy K., 63n

Cleveland, Stafford C., 33n

Clinton, DeWitt, 3, 153

Clyde (Wayne Co.), Millerites in, 302

Cohocton (Steuben Co.), 160; James Boyle at, 191

Colgate University, *see* Hamilton Seminary

College attendance, 98, 101

Collins, John A., 107, 280; quoted, 332

Collins (Erie Co.), Millerites in, 314-315

Collyer, Robert H., 229n

Colton, Calvin: *Revivals of Religion*, 79n; *Thoughts on the Religious State of the Country*, 41n, 186n; *Voice from America*, 15n, 271n

Columbian College, 301

Combe, George, 82n, 325, 325n

Communion: closed, and Antimasonry, 122; wine controversy, 105, 216, 258

Communism, 326; and Shakerism, 32; and Jemima Wilkinson's colony, 33, 35-36; Owenite, 143; knowledge of, in Burned-over District, 328

Communitist, 107, 333n

Community of the Publick Universal Friend, *see* Communism *and* Wilkinson, Jemima

Conable, Rev. F. W., 15n, 48n, 121n

Congregational Church: in western New England, 7; in Great Awakening, 7; and camp meetings, 8; ministerial education in, 8; social dominance of, 9; missions system, 18ff., 21; intolerance in, 46; and Plan of Union, 50n; early bias against Masonry, 122; abolition in, 221-222; and moral reform, 230; schism over perfectionism, 251; state association formed, 256; and Plan of Union activities, 257; as resort of Presbyterian ultraists, 261; *General Association of New York, Minutes of*, 251n, 262n

Conn, Mrs., 191, 241

Connecticut, post-1815 revivals in, 11-12

Connecticut Baptist Missionary Society, 24

Connecticut Congregational Association, 18; *Address to New Settlements*, 14n

Connecticut Missionary Society, 19ff.; revenues of, 20; *Reports of*, 20n

Connecticut Valley, slight migration from, 6

"Conscience" Whigs, *see* Whig Party
Constitution of United States, amendments of, 356
Convention of Teachers and Friends of Education, 233
Conversion: as test of church membership, 41; ultraist doctrine of, 198-199
Cook, Sophia, 241, 244
Cooperstown, Millerites at, 304
Correspondence of Baptist Church and Advent Brethren of Lockport, 303n
Cortland, Methodist abolition at, 264
Cortland County: church growth in, 13; Luther Myrick in, 192; Fourierism in, 329, 331
Cortland Presbytery, and temperance, 130
Cowdery, Oliver, 39
Cragin, George, 231, 333, 334, 338
Cragin, Mary, 204, 231, 333, 338
Cross, Whitney R.: "Burned-over District," MS, 297n; "Mormonism," 143n; "Rochester," MS, 59n, 89n, 116n
Crozier, O. R. L., 316
Cultural agencies, as education, 98
Cumorah hill, 144

Dansville, Millerite persecution at, 308
Dartmouth College, 98
Davis, Andrew Jackson, 344, 344n; and James Boyle, 190; itinerary of, 344
Davis, President, removal from Hamilton College, 258
Day Dawn, 316
Deism, 18; in New England, 7; of William Miller, 290
Delphi (Onondaga Co.), perfectionists at, 242-243
Demaree, Albert L., 104n
Democracy: Jacksonian, 79, 116, 117, 168, 270; workingmen in, 270, 324, 326; Jeffersonian, 79; and religion, new measures and, 173; and radicalism, 199; ultraism and, 207; millennialism and, in ultraism, 207; and abolition, 222; of ultraism and Jacksonism, paralleled, 270-271
Democratic Party, 79; and Masonry, 121; "Barnburners" in, 226
Democratic Republican Party, 79
Denominational affiliation: in Antimasonry, 222; in dispersing ultraism, 277-278
Denominationalism, 40ff., 135, 254-255; and decline of benevolent movements, 256ff. *See also* Sectarian conflict

Denominational schism, in religious press, 105. *See also* Schisms *and individual denominations*
Depressions, *see* Economic depression
Dewey, D. M., 346n
Dewey, Orville, 176n, 199n
Dick, Everett, 293n
Dike, Samuel W., 354n
Dill, Rev. James H., 21n
Disciples of Christ (Campbellite Church), 15; and benevolent movements, 135
Dixon, William Hepworth: *New America,* 82n; *Spiritual Wives,* 89n
Doolittle, Mary Antoinette, 32n
Dow, Lorenzo, 10, 10n
Dow, Peggy, 10
Downfall of Babylon, support in Burned-over District, 232
Dresden (Yates Co.), 33
Dumond, Dwight L., 222n, 283n
Duncan, John M., 80n
Dunkirk (Chautauqua Co.), 74
Dutton, Chauncey, 240, 245, 246
Dwight, Timothy, 27, 80n

East Genoa (Cayuga Co.), perfectionists at, 243
Eastman, C. G., 189n
Eastman, Rev. Hubbard, 334n
Eaton, Sylvester, 175n, 260
Economic depression: and revivals, 12; and isms, 273; and Millerite movement, 317-318. *See also* Panic of 1837
Economics, innocence of ultraists in, 274
Eddy, Mary Baker, 348
Edson, Hiram, 316
Education: denominational differences in, ministerial, 8; elementary, 89ff., 92-93; of religious enthusiasts, 93; private school, 93, 96; of Mormons, 143; ultraist influence in, 233-235; and millennialism, 235
Edwardean theology, 7, 27, 239
Edwards, Jonathan, 7, 27, 160, 164, 180
Edwards, Jonathan, II, at New Lebanon Conference, 163
Election of 1840, 272
Ellicottville (Chautauqua Co.), intolerance in, 44
Ellis, David M., 327n
Ellis, Dr. John B., 243n, 344n
Elmira, 75
Elsbree, Oliver W., 27n
Ely, Ezra Stiles, 134, 135, 135n, 279
Emancipator, 221

Emigration, *see* Migration

Enthusiasts, characteristics of, 202

Entrepreneurs: and benevolent movements, 136; and anti-Catholicism, 233

Episcopal Church, 9; in Finger Lakes country, 67; and benevolent movements, 135

Equality, in democracy and millenarian anarchy, 207

Erie Canal: 3, 12, 55, 62, 65, 70, 74, 78, 79, 113, 139; projected, 5; impact of, 56ff.; and cities, 56-57; and regional development, 59; tolls, 59, 63; and rural life, 84; and Antimasonry, 116; and Sabbatarianism, 132; celebration of, 132, 153; and Rochester Revival, 154-155; towns, and anti-Catholicism, 233; decline of boom from, 269, 355; *Report of Auditor of*, 56n, 359

Erie County: revivals of 1819, 11; church growth in, 13; journalism, 64-65; economic development, 74

Erie Railroad, and southern tier prosperity, 69-70

European-Americans, *see* Migration

Evangelical Magazine, 106, 106n, 148n, 324n

Evangelical Recorder, 11n, 26n

Evangelists, *see* Itinerants

Evans, Frederick S., 32; career of, 326-327

Evans, George H., career of, 326-327

Evans, John H., 141n

Evans, Paul D., 71n, 79n, 270n, 327n

Excommunications, in early churches, 37

Fairport (Monroe Co.), Millerites at, 304

Faith healing, J. H. Noyes and, 338

Fanaticism, of Millerites, 314ff.

Fayette (Seneca Co.), 146

Federalist Party, 79; and Antimasonry, 116

Female moral reform, *see* Moral reform movement

Female seminaries, 89

Financial scandal, of Jacob Knapp, 197

Finger Lakes: canalization of outlets, 66; as early freight routes, 66

Finger Lakes country: soils of, 5; settlement in, 5; revivals of 1819 in, 11; the Friends in, 17; Universalist Church in, 18; population of, 66; prosperity of, 66; economic development of, 66-70; perfectionist cults in, 191

Finney, Charles Grandison: mention of, 3, 4, 10, 11, 13, 27, 51, 75, 114, 120, 122, 133, 153, 162, 173, 175, 176, 178, 185, 188, 189, 191, 196, 204, 212, 231, 238, 241, 242, 246, 251, 257, 261, 273, 278, 283

beliefs and attitudes: theology, 158ff.; revival experience and theology, 160; urban theory of evangelism, 166; progressive ideas, 168; and women's equality in church, 177; and "prayer of faith," 179; views of conversion, 199; quoted on ministerial education, 202; quoted on sin, 205-206; advice on abolition, 225; adopts Grahamism, 236; perfectionist reasoning, 249; quoted on sectarian controversy, 254; quoted on superficial revivals, 256; quoted on Presbyterian General Assembly, 258

personal and biographical references: and Oberlin College, 101; description of, 151; conversion, 151-152; ministerial training, 152, 158-159; travels after Western Revival, 154; in Rochester Revival, 155, 168-169; travels after Rochester Revival, 156; career and influence, 156-158; ordination, 159; at New Lebanon Conference, 164; conferences in New York City, 164; evolving style, 164ff.; relation to environment, 169

personal and other influences: and Daniel Nash, 161-162; and "Holy Band," 162; accord with L. Beecher, 164; and Nathaniel Taylor, 165; and benevolent movements, 165; and Free Church movement, 166-167; and Jedediah Burchard, 188-189; and James Boyle, 190; and Luther Myrick, 193; and Horatio Foote, 194-195; associates in Western Revival, 195-196; and Charles Weld, 196; conversion of Theodore Weld and Charles Stuart, 218; and Theodore Weld, 219

revival usages of: oratorical gifts, 152; preaching techniques, 175-176; and business during revival, 180; and anxious bench, 181; rates for services, 187

writings of: papers, MS, 75n, 107n, 133n, 151n, 174n, 186n, 198n, 219n, 246n, 258n, 360; *Autobiography*, 3n, 51n, 151n, 173n, 181, 186n, 218n, 250n; "Can Two Walk Together," 160n, 174n; *Free Masonry*, 120n, 354n; *Sermons on Gospel Themes*, 199n, 250n; *Lectures to Professing Christians*, 202n; "Sinners Bound," 160n; *Revival Lec-*

Finney, Charles Grandison (*cont.*) *tures*, 160n, 174n, 199n, 212n, 213n, 250n, 254n, *Systematic Theology*, 203n, 250n; *Views of Sanctification*, 250n
Finney revivals, *see* Western Revival and Rochester Revival
Fish, Mrs. Leah, 345ff.
Fishbaugh, William, 344
Fisher, Vardis, 142n
Fitch, Charles, 293; at Rochester, 298
Fleming, L. D., 80, 295, 311; at Rochester, 298
Fletcher, Robert S., 89n, 156n, 207n, 218n, 249n, 273n
Foot, Ann, 240
Foot, John B., 240
Foote, Horatio, career of, 194-195, 240
Foote, Joseph, 239n
Fort Niagara, William Morgan at, 114-115
Fourier, Charles, 335
Fourierism: 275, 325, 333, 340, 341; development of, 328-332; religious attitudes in, 332; and Swedenborgianism, 341-342
Fowler, Orson, 325
Fowler, P. H., 10n, 189n, 253n, 283n
Fox, Dixon Ryan: *Decline of Aristocracy*, 79n, 115n, 233n; "New York a Democracy," 79n; *Yankees and Yorkers*, 6n, 81n
Fox, George, 347
Fox, John D., 345
Fox, Katie, 345ff.
Fox, Margaretta, 345ff.
France, plan for conversion to Protestantism of, 232. *See also* Verse a day plan
Franklin, Benjamin, 348
Free Churches, 166; James Boyle at New Haven, 190; Herman Norton and, 195
Free Congregational churches, origin of, 261
Freedom of speech, and abolition, 222
Freemasonry, 79, 322; officeholding and, 115; social privilege in, 117. *See also* Antimasonry
Free Methodist Church, 354
Free thought, 319, 322; in foreign-born groups, 83
Freewill Baptist Church: and camp meetings, 8; revivals in 1819, 11; growth of, 13, 15, 16, 262-263; woman preaching in, 38; and Antimasonry, 121; and benevolent movements, 135-136; and Communion wine, 216; and abolition, 221-222; and Oneida Institute, 234; and

Millerites, 288; *Minutes of General Conference of*, 16n, 216n
French, J. H., 62n
French Revolution, and decline of clerical influence, 132
Freudians, pseudo-, 88
Friend of Man, 107, 223n
Friends, the, 33; migration from New England, 17; in religious experiments, 17; settlement in Boston, Erie Co., 39; and benevolent movements, 135; influence on religious reformers, 282; and Fourierism, 332; and Swedenborgianism, 344
Friends Weekly Intelligencer, 332n
Frost, John, 261; at New Lebanon Conference, 163
Fundamentalist trend, out of ultraism, 277-278

Gabriel, Ralph H., 271n
Gaddis, Merrill E., 250n, 354n
Gale, George W., 151n, 152, 153, 155, 158, 162, 163, 164, 167, 168, 174n, 178, 188, 189n, 219, 231; at New Lebanon Conference, 163; and manual labor schools, 234
Galpin, Horace, 45
Galpin, W. Freeman, 236n
Galusha, Elon, 223, 224, 311, 312; career of, 300-301; at Rochester, 301
Galusha, Elon C., 299
Garrison, William Lloyd, 217, 218, 238, 246; and James Boyle, 190; hastens abolition, 220; and early New England abolition, 223; nonresistance movement of, 236; influence on religious reformers, 282
Gates, Seth, 251
Gates, Theophilus, 190, 246, 247, 344
General Conference of Second Advent Believers, formed, 311
General Union for Promoting Observance of the Christian Sabbath, 134. *See also* Sabbatarianism
Genesee Baptist Association, Minutes of, 125n, 221n, 301n
Genesee Conference, Methodist Church: and abolition, 265; revolt in, 354. *See also* Antislavery movement *and* Methodist Church
Genesee Congregational Consociation: and moral reform, 230, 251; exscinded, 261
Genesee country, 35; settlement in, 5-6;

Great Revival in, 10; revivals of 1819 in, 11; the Friends in, 17; Universalist Church in, 18; Wilkinson followers in, 34; early emotionalism in, 51; use of term, 66; Millerites in, 301, 303

Genesee County, 11

Genesee Farmer, 73, 104

Genesee fever, 5

Genesee Presbytery, denominationalism in, 256

Genesee River, Erie Canal crossing of, 59

Genesee Sunday School Union, 129

Genesee Synod: and moral reform, 230; and schism of 1837, 260. *See also* Presbyterian Church *and* Schisms

Genesee Valley, 66-67; soils of, 5; Shakers in, 33; soils of upper, 70; and Rochester, 70; prosperity of, 70; Mormons in, 148; Methodist abolition in, 264

Genesee Valley Canal, 72

Geneva, 76

Geneva Presbytery, conservatism of, 260

Geneva Synod, and schism of 1837, 260. *See also* Presbyterian Church *and* Schisms

Geneva tract agent, 127

Genoa (Cayuga Co.), perfectionists at, 248, 334

Gerry (Chautauqua Co.), Millerites at, 304

Ghent, Peace of, 5

Gillet, Moses, 164, 178; and New Lebanon Conference, 163

Gold hunting, by Joseph Smith, 142

Gold rush, 355

Goodell, William, 107, 217, 218, 280, 281; adopts Grahamism, 236; unionist program of, 280-281

Gordon, T. F., 56n, 358

Gospel Advocate, 45n, 106, 121n, 127n, 153n, 177n, 200n, 324n; quoted on temperance, 131

Gospel Luminary, 16n, 38n, 128n, 177n, 295n; characterized, 106

Graham, Sylvester, 235, 236

Granger, Francis, 116

Great Awakening, the, 7, 10, 33, 163, 185; separatists of, 15

Great Harmonia, Andrew Jackson Davis', 344

Great Revival, the, 9, 10, 13, 20, 23, 28, 30, 38, 163, 166, 185; in Burned-over District, 10-11; about Palmyra, 140

Greeley, Horace, 116; and spiritualism, 346

Green, Beriah, 280, 327; conversion to immediatism, 220; at Oneida Institute, 234

Green, Mrs. William, 231

Grimké, Angelina, *see* Weld, Angelina Grimké

Grimké, Sarah, 237

Groveland (Livingston Co.), Shaker Community at, 33

Guilford (Vt.), 38

Haight (Allegany Co.), 193

Half-way Covenant, 7

Hall, Basil, 8on

Hall, Harriet, 338

Hamilton, Milton W., 103n

Hamilton (Madison Co.), Jacob Knapp's relations in, 197

Hamilton Baptist Missionary Society, 24

Hamilton College, 102, 218, 258

Hamilton Fourier Association, 329

Hamilton Seminary, 102, 106, 196, 301; and moral reform, 230; and abolition, 233

Hammond, Charles, 346

Hampshire Missionary Society, 21; *Annual Report of*, 21n

Harbinger, 331n; on Skaneateles Community, 332

Harlow, Ralph V., 8on, 129n, 192n, 199n, 213n, 273n, 327n

Harmon, Ellen, *see* White, Ellen Harmon

Harmonial City Community, 352

Harris, Thomas L., 344, 352

Harrison, David, 247

Harrison, William Henry, 272

Harvard University, 101

Hawley, Silas, 280

Hebrew language, in Oneida Institute curriculum, 234

Hedding, Bishop, 264

Hendryx, Truman, 294

Herald of Salvation, 44n, 153n

Heresy, influence of protracted meetings on, 184

Hicks, Elias, 347

Hicksite controversy, 17

Hill, Elder, 315

Himes, Joshua, 148, 280, 295, 297, 299, 304, 307, 311, 312; at Utica, 234; career of, 292-293; and William Miller, 292; at Rochester, 298

Holland Land Company, 5, 72, 272; land donation to churches by, 49

Holland Purchase, 37, 269

*Holland Purchase Baptist Association,
Minutes of,* 221n
Holley, Myron, 121
Holley, O. L., 63n, 360
"Holy bands," 162, 176; use of "prayer
of faith," 179; and pastoral visiting, 180
Home manufactures, decline of, 84
Homer (Cortland Co.): New England set-
tlement in, 6; Burchard revival in, 188
Hooker, Edward, papers of, MS, 182n,
189n
Hopkins, Samuel, 27
Hotchkin, Rev. James H., 10n, 13, 20n,
37n, 141n, 187n, 241n, 253n, 361
House of judgment, at Springwater (Liv-
ingston Co.), 315
Howard (Steuben Co.), 129
Howitt, Emanuel, 81n
Hubbard, Silas, 49
Hudson, David, 34n
Hudson and Erie Boat Line, 132
Humphrey, President, at New Lebanon
Conference, 163
Hunter's lodges, campaign of, 273
Hutchinson, Anne, 38
Hydesville (Wayne Co.), spiritualism be-
gun at, 345

Illinois, migration to, 141
Illustrations of Masonry, by William
Morgan, 114
Immigration, *see* Migration
Imperfect sanctification, doctrine of:
preserved in ultraism, 204; and per-
fectionism, 241-242. *See also* New Eng-
land theology *and* New Haven theology
Individualism, excess of, in ultraism, 206,
271, 356
Industrial revolution, and Civil War, 355
Infected district, 3, 120
Inquiry meetings, 181ff.
Institute of Practical Education, 155
Interdenominational relations, *see* De-
nominationalism *and* Sectarian rivalry
Intolerance, in ultraism, 205-206
Irvine, E. E., 62n
Isms, 14, 71; about Utica and Rochester,
65; environment and, 66, 76, 82-84, 98;
in Susquehanna watershed, 70; journal-
ism and, 103; decline of, 284, 355-356
Israel, lost ten tribes of, 81
Ithaca: New England settlement in, 6;
sectarian rivalry in, 45; Burchard re-
vival in, 188; Abigail Merwin in, 247;

J. H. Noyes in, 248; Millerites at, 301,
308
Ithaca and Owego Railroad, 70
Itinerants: Universalist, 18; support of
Congregational, 20; Connecticut, 20-21;
New England Baptist, 24; and journalism, 109; as mission method, 135; Mormon, 148-150; training schools for, 155-
156; of Western Revival, 162; and settled clergy, 175, 183; praying techniques, 175-176; pastoral visiting of,
180; use of anxious bench, 182; methods
of starting revivals, 182; and protracted
meetings, 183; characterization of, 185-
188; significance of, 197; theological
training of, 202; and temperance, 213;
and abolition, 219; of late 1830's, 255-
256; proscription of, 261; Millerite, 296,
297, 304. *See also* "Seventy, the"

Jackson, Andrew, 113, 116
Jackson, James C., 276, 280
Jacksonian Democracy, *see* Democracy,
Jacksonian
Jamestown, Methodist abolition at, 264
Jamesville (Onondaga Co.), Luther My-
rick at, 191
Jefferson, Thomas, 132, 347-348
Jefferson County: Vermonters in, 6;
growth of, 63; C. G. Finney in, 152;
Kirk revivals in, 195; Millerites in, 294
Jenson, Andrew, 360
Jerusalem (Yates Co.), 33
Johnson, Albert C., 288n
Johnson, Col. Richard M., and Sabbath
mail controversy, 134
Journalism: Antimasonic, at Rochester,
73; New York State, 102-103; of benev-
olent societies, 105
Judgment day, *see* Millennialism *and*
Premillennialism

Kaercher, George Jacob, papers of, MS,
298n
Keep, John, 280
Keller, Charles R., 7n, 20n, 38n
Kemble, Frances A., 87n
Kentucky: Baptists in, 24; Great Revival
in, 7, 9
Kidd, Captain, 80
Kimball, Heber, 143
King, Mary B. A., 133n, 154n, 326n
Kirk, Edward, 195; and Albany perfec-
tionists, 195, 240; itinerant training
school of, 195

Kirtland (Ohio), 144; Mormon Church at, 149
Knapp, Elder Jacob, 192, 253, 256; and Augustus Littlejohn, 193; career of, 196-197; ideas of, 197; and abolition, 224; letter to William Colgate, MS, 197n; *Autobiography*, 197n; *Evangelical Harp*, 197n
Kneeland, Abner, 106
Krout, John A.: "Early Temperance Movement," 8on, 130n, 214n; *Prohibition*, 82n, 130n, 212n

Ladd, William, 236
Lairdsville (Oneida Co.), perfectionist convention at, 334
Lancaster (Pa.), C. G. Finney at, 154
Land companies, payments to, 269
Land reform, 325-327
Land values, in Genesee country, 141
Lane rebels: Theodore Weld and, 219; Gerrit Smith and Charles Stuart on, 220
Lane Theological Seminary, 219, 222
Lansing, Dirck, 155, 167, 229; at New Lebanon Conference, 163
La Rochefoucauld-Liancourt, Duke de, 34n
Latourette, James, 240
Latter-Day Saints, *see* Mormon Church
Lawton, George, 347n
Layman: the revolt of the, 45; in Antimasonry, 123; in benevolent movements, 136; in Western Revival, 154
Leavitt, Joshua, 231
Lecture on Chastity, by Sylvester Graham, 235
Lectures on the Second Coming, by William Miller, 294. *See also* Miller, William
Lee, Luther, 42, 45, 50, 223; punishment for abolitionism, 265; *Autobiography*, 42, 43n
Lee, Mother Ann, 31, 33, 246. *See also* Shakerism
Leland, Theron C., 328
LeRoy: perfectionist convention at, 251; Millerites at, 304
Letters of Rev. Dr. Beecher and Rev. Mr. Nettleton, 163n, 205n
Lewis, John L., diaries, MS, 204n
Lewis County, growth of, 63
Lewiston (Niagara Co.): William Morgan at, 114; William Miller at, 300
Leyden (Mass.), 38

Liberal Advocate, 322n
Liberator, 217
Liberty Party, 226, 277, 281
Library facilities, 93, 97
Life and Advents Union, formed, 311
Lily Dale Community, 352
Litch, Josiah, 293, 311
Literacy, 93-100; of Smith family, 142. *See also* Education
Literary and Theological Review, 229n
Literacy, 93-100; of Smith family, 142.
Little Falls, C. G. Finney at, 154
Littlejohn, Augustus, 187, 192; career of, 193-194
Lockport, 75; development of, 71-72; Methodist abolition at, 264; William Miller at, 300; Millerites at, 303, 304; Millerite persecution at, 308
Lottery reform, 235
Loughborough, J. N., 300n, 316
Lovett, Charles, 240-241, 244
Lovett, Simon, 240, 245-246
Low Hampton (Washington Co.), Mormons in, 148. *See also* Miller, William
Ludlum, David M., 7n, 39n, 121n, 223n, 317n, 355n; on Millerites, 317
Lundy, Benjamin, 217
Lyceum movement, 234
Lyons (Wayne Co.), 39; as canal port, 65
Lyvere, John, 248

McCall, Ansel J., papers of, MS, 37n
McCall, Benajah, 36
McCarthy, Charles, 115n
McDowall, John R., 226, 229, 230
McDowall's Journal, 107, 229, 229n
MacGill, C. E., 56n
McGraw College, 235
McKelvey, Blake, 67n, 127n, 149n, 154n
Mack family, 139
MacLear, Martha, 89n
Madison Baptist Association, Minutes of, 214n
Madison County, 126; Baptist missionaries in, 24; sectarian rivalry in, 45; economic development of, 59-62; Luther Myrick in, 192; perfectionists in, 241; Millerites in, 294; Fourierism in, 329, 331
Mahan, Asa, 161, 161n, 249, 251
Male continence, at Oneida Community, 338
Malin, Margaret, 36
Malin, Rachel, 34-36
Malone circuit, Methodist Church, 43

Manchester (Ontario Co.), 139, 146; development of, 140-142; migration from, 141

Manlius (Onondaga Co.), 67; New England settlement in, 6; Luther Myrick at, 191; Millerites at, 304; "Records of First Congregational Church," MS, 243n

Manual-labor schools, 234ff.; Theodore Weld, agent for, 219

Manufactures and manufacturing, at Utica, 64; at Rochester, 72-73; and religious history, 84; changing nature of, 355

Marion (Wayne Co.), James Boyle at, 190

Marks, David, 35

Marks, Marilla, 13n, 16n

Marsh, Joseph, 106, 295, 302, 305, 307, 312, 313-314, 315-316

Marshall, G. T., and verse a day plan, 232

Martineau, Harriet, 8on, 206, 206n

Masonry, see Freemasonry and Antimasonry

Massachusetts: post-1815 revivals in, 12; literacy in, 93

Massachusetts Baptist Missionary Society, 24

Massachusetts Missionary Society, 21

Matlack, Lucius C.: American Slavery and Methodism, 223n, 264n; Antislavery Struggle, 223n; Report, First General Conference, Wesleyan Connection, 266n

Matthias, the prophet, 39

May, Samuel W., and Augustus Littlejohn, 193

Mayhew, Henry, 142n

Mead, Charles, 240

Mead, Sidney E., 28n, 151n

Melcher, Marquerite F., 32n, 327n

Merwin, Abigail, 247, 248

Mesmerism, 275, 325; various appeals of, 326; and Swedenborgianism, 342

Methodist Church: descriptive references: ministerial education, 8; emotionalism in, 8, 9, 15, 16, 263-264, 265ff.; growth of, 10, 12-13, 14, 252-253; journalism of, 26; doctrines of, 27, 239-240; preachers of, 37, 38

and reform movements: Antimasonry, 121; Sunday-school unions, 129; benevolent movements, 136; temperance, 214; abolition, 222-223, 264-265 and schisms and secessions, 38, 354,
356; Wesleyan, 265-266; sectional, 266 Minutes of General Conference of, 11n, 46n, 253n

Mexican War, 355

Michigan, migration to, 141

Middlebury College, 98, 101

Middletown (Vt.), 38

Midnight Cry, 293n, 361; resumes publication, 307

Migration: non-Yankee, 4-5; European, 83, 84, 254; Pennsylvania, 67; westward from New York, 71, 83, 141, 254; Adventists in, 317; enthusiasts in, 354 Yankee, 4-6, 71; later, 83; of particular sects, 15, 16, 17, 18, 23; influence of, 11, 54

Military Tract, settlement in, 5

Millard, David, 51

Millennialism, 79, 200-201; as optimism, 79; and revivals, 79, 168-169, 183-184; and Antimasonry, 123; in Mormonism, 146; of Jacob Knapp, 196; and ultraism, 200, 202; and temperance, 211-212; and abolition, 217, 224; and anti-Catholicism, 231-233; and education, 235; of J. H. Noyes, 246; history of, 287; universality of, 320-321. See also Premillennialism, Miller, William, and Millerites

Miller, Rev. James A., 16on, 193n

Miller, Samuel, papers of, MS, 50n, 164n, 216n

Miller, William, 80, 180, 187, 193, 246, 278, 295, 304, 307, 311; and Antimasonry, 123; and Mormons, 148; anti-Catholicism of, 232-233; personal reference, 288-292; doctrinal orthodoxy of, 291; spread of ideas of, 292; publication of lectures of, 292; and Burned-over District, 293-294, 296, 299-300, 304; conversions by, 296; protest against intolerance by, 302; excommunicated, 309; on continuing time, 311-312; and shut-door doctrine, 312; deplores fanaticism, 315; social attitudes of, 317-319; papers of, MS, 80n, 123n, 149n, 291n; Lectures on Second Coming, 233n, 291n. See also Premillennialism and Millerites

Millerites, 16, 108, 201, 253, 341; environment and, 76, 263, 288; journalism, 106; anti-Catholicism, 232-233; Angelina Weld and, 283; beliefs and attitudes of, 287, 296-297, 317ff., 320; number and geographical distribution of, 287, 288,

292ff., 303; westward migration of, 296; response to persecution, 302-303; disillusionment and consequences, 303-304, 308-310; camp meetings, 304-306; fanaticisms, charged and actual, 306, 307, 310-314; and Shakers, 310-311; and ultraism, 321; and spiritualism, 351; and "Apostolic Circle," 352. *See also* Miller, William, *and* Premillennialism

Mills, Samuel, 49

Ministers, influence of, 101

Mitchell, William, 183n

Mixville, Fourierist phalanx at, 331

Modernist tendency in ultraism, 278

Modern Times Community, Long Island, 352

Mohawk River, canalization, 59

Mohawk Valley, 59; migration route, 5; A.H.M.S. aid in, 49; C. G. Finney in, 153; Millerites in, 296

Monarchy, ultraist view of, 207

Monroe Baptist Association, Minutes of, 224n

Monroe County: early revivals in, 11; misrepresented religious destitution, 48; journalism in, 64-65; manufactures, 72-73; Bible campaign, 127; Sunday-school union, 128

Montezuma swamp, canal ports, 65

Moral law, and democracy, 207

Moral reform movement: female, 226-231; in Burned-over District, 230; and perfectionism, 230-231; women in, 237; legal compulsion in, 274

Morgan, William, 114, 115, 122. *See also* Antimasonry

Morgan episode, 354; appeals of, 115. *See also* Antimasonry

Mormon Church, 16, 114, 138, 353, 356; geographical and environmental analysis of, 76, 138ff., 149ff.; and spiritual wifery, 84; westward movement and appeal in West, 138, 146-150; doctrines and attitudes, 144-146; missions and converts, 148-150; at Kirtland, Ohio, 149; persecution of, 150; United Order of, 335

Moscow (Livingston Co.), 49, 124

Mountain Cove Community (Fayette, Va.), 352

Murray, Orson, 223

Mutual criticism, at Oneida Community, 336-337

Myrick, Luther, 107, 187, 240-241, 243, 261, 276, 278, 281; career of, 191-193;

and Augustus Littlejohn, 193; and Horatio Foote, 195; and perfectionism, 239; and Union Church movement, 279

Naples (Ontario Co.) Presbyterian Church: and temperance, 214; "Record Book," MS, 121n, 214n

Narrative of the Revival of Religion, 153n, 176n, 204n

Nash, Daniel, 152, 153, 162, 164, 175, 187, 189, 278, 291; characterized, 160-161; praying technique of, 161, 179; and C. G. Finney, 161-162; and prophecy, 179-180; and James Boyle, 190-191; and Luther Myrick, 192; death of, 192; and Horatio Foote, 194

Nash, Daniel, Jr., 187, 192

National reform, 327, 331. *See also* Land reform

Nativism, 83, 231-233; and abolition, 83; journalism of, 108; and Whig Party, 233. *See also* Anti-Catholicism

Nativity: of Mormons by states, 149-150; New England, and emotional religion, 67

Nettleton, Asahel: and New Lebanon Conference, 163-164; and women's equality in church, 177

Newark (N.J.), James Boyle in, 190

New England: Great Awakening in, 10; Methodism in, 14; sectarians of, 15-16; Congregational missionary societies, 21; Shaker communities in, 31; precedent for Antimasonry, 122; temperance societies, 130; Sabbatarianism, 132; abolition origins in, 220-222; Millerite beginnings in, 287; origin of Advent Christian Association, 312. *See also* Migration, *individual denominations and movements, and states of New England*

New Englanders: and New York public schools, 93; at New Lebanon Conference, 163

New England theology, 27-28. *See also* Edwardean theology, New Haven theology, *and* Calvinism (modified)

New Genesee Farmer, 104

New Hampshire, migration from, 6

New Hampshire Missionary Society, 21

New Harmony Community, 324

New Haven (Conn.), perfectionists at, 240

New Haven Theological Seminary, 27, 245

New Haven theology, 239, 250; and

New Haven theology (*cont.*)
Finney doctrines, 159-160. *See also* New England theology, Taylor, Nathaniel, *and* Noyes, John Humphrey
Newhouse, Sewall, 335
New Jersey: post-1815 revivalism in, 12; literacy in, 98
New Jerusalem (Yates Co.), and Joseph Smith, 143. *See also* Jerusalem
New Lebanon (Columbia Co.), 31-32; Shakers at, 30; conference at, 163-164, 173, 177
New Lights, 7. *See also* Great Awakening
New measures, 160, 173; origin of, 161; and benevolent movement, 165-166; evolution of, 165-167; and Rochester Revival, 168-169; prayer in, 178-179; and protracted meetings, 183; and itinerants, 185; and ultraism, 198. *See also* Finney, Charles Grandison, *and* Nash, Daniel
New School, Presbyterian Church, *see* Presbyterian Church, New School
Newspapers, number, circulation, and content, 65, 102-103
New York City, 39; C. G. Finney at, 154, 164, 167; Millerites in, 300
New York Evangelist, 107, 107n, 155n, 192n, 200n, 213n, 221, 255n, 279n; C. G. Finney and, 156; Daniel Nash and, 160; on Rochester Revival, 169; on temperance, 212-213; and Communion wine, 216; anti-Catholicism in, 231; and verse a day plan, 232; and prison reform, 236; on Union Church movement, 279
New York Female Benevolent Society, 229
New York Magdalen Society, 229
New York Mercantile Union, 358
New York Observer, 13n, 17n, 46n, 105, 283
New York Protestant Vindicator, 232
New York State: literacy in, 98; journalism, 102-103; natives in Utah Territory in 1860, 149-150
New York State Baptist Missionary Convention, 24
New York State Temperance Society, 214
New York Tribune, and spiritualism, 346
New York University, 343
New York wheat riots of 1837, 273
Niagara County, misrepresented destitution of religious services in, 48
Nichol, Francis D., 287n
Nichols, Thomas L., 352

Nominating conventions, Antimasonic, 115-116
Northampton (Mass.) Community, James Boyle at, 190
Norton, Herman, 133, 187, 195
Norwich (Chenango Co.), denominational co-operation at, 42; *Peoples Advocate*, 42n
Nott, President Eliphalet, 80
Noyes, George W., *Religious Experience of John Humphrey Noyes*, 190-191n, 238n; *John Humphrey Noyes, Putney Community*, 241n, 328n, 344n
Noyes, Harriet Holton, 248
Noyes, John Humphrey, 108, 186, 192, 204, 231, 238, 241, 242, 341, 344; journals of, 107; and Mormons, 148; and James Boyle, 190-191; and Charles Weld, 196; on the millennium, 200-201; doctrines of, rejected in New York, 243; and the Brimfield bundling, 243, 245-246; and New York perfectionists, 244ff., 248-249; doctrines of, 245-249; on infidelity in reformers, 282; on Millerites, 321; on phrenology, 325; and Oneida Community, 333-340; on Oneida beliefs, 335; estimate of, 336; on temperance, 337; on complex marriage, 338; on male continence, 339-340; theory of reform of, 340; on Swedenborgianism, 343, 344; *American Socialisms*, 191n, 328n, 341n; *Confessions*, 201n, 245n; *The Berean*, 282n, 326n. *See also* Noyes, George W. (writings compiled by), *Witness, Perfectionist, Spiritual Magazine, Oneida Community, and Perfectionism*
Noyes, Pierrepont, 334n

Oberlin (Ohio), 156; perfectionism of, 231, 239, 249, 250; and moral reform, 231; and retrenchment, 235; and Swedenborgianism, 344
Oberlin College, 101, 224, 297; New Yorkers at, 101; Oneida Institute influence upon, 234; and peace movement, 236; *Catalogue*, 101n, 251n. *See also* Finney, C. G.
Oberlin Evangelist, 108, 199n, 230n, 251n, 282n, 293n; editor in seduction case, 231; circulation in Burned-over District, 250-251; applauds Gerrit Smith, 281; and Millerites, 293, 321
Ogdensburg Presbytery, and temperance, 130

Ohio: Baptist missionaries in, 24; literacy in, 98; antislavery society and James Boyle, 190
Ohio Valley, Shaker communities in, 31
Olds, Gamaliel, and Richard S. Corning, 179n, 189n
Oliphant, J. Orin, 27n
Olive Branch, 128n
Oneida (Congregational) Association, Report of, 334n
Oneida Community, 191, 193, 341, 356; doctrinal origins of, 245-248; beliefs and practices at, 333-340; duration of pure form of, 353
Oneida County: Connecticut settlement in, 6; Great Revival in, 10; church growth in, 13; Baptist missionaries in, 24; economic development, 59, 62, 64; journalism in, 64-65; Luther Myrick in, 192; Augustus Littlejohn in, 193; Fourierism in, 331. *See also* Utica *and* Rome
Oneida County Presbyterians, education convention, 233
Oneida County revival, *see* Western Revival
Oneida Evangelical Association, 187, 193, 278. *See also* Central Evangelical Association
Oneida Indian Reservation, 334
Oneida Institute, 129, 168, 224, 263, 273; Theodore Weld at, 219; Beriah Green as President of, 220; influence in education, 234-235; *Sketch of Condition and Prospects,* 234n. *See also* Gale, George W.
Oneida Lake, perfectionists near, 248
Oneida Presbytery: and Western Revival, 162-163; and Jedediah Burchard, 189; and Luther Myrick, 191; and Charles Weld, 196; and Oneida Institute, 234
Oneida Revival, *see* Western Revival
One-ideaism: and temperance movement, 216; and women's rights, 237; among Universalists, 324. *See also* Ultraism
Onondaga County: Luther Myrick in, 192; perfectionists in, 241; Fourierism in, 334
Ontario County, revivals of 1819 in, 11
Ontario Fourierist Phalanx, 331
Ontario Presbytery, and temperance, 130
Opinion, excessive regard to, in ultraism, 206
Optimism, and credulity, 82; in ultraism, 199-200

O'Reilly, Henry, 273n
Original sin, and human perfectibility, in ultraism, 200
Orleans (Jefferson Co.), Daniel Nash in, 160
Orleans County, temperance in, 131
Orton, Samuel G., 256
Oswego, 75, 201; economic development of, 63, 65, 69; anti-Catholicism in, 233; Methodist abolition at, 264; Millerites in, 294, 301, 303, 304, 314-315; Seventh-Day Adventists at, 316
Oswego County, 66
Oswego River, canalization, 59
Otsego County, Great Revival in, 10
Otsego Presbytery, and temperance, 130
Otto, Jacob, 49
Owen, Robert, 324, 326, 335
Owen, Robert Dale, *Moral Physiology,* 338
Owenism, and Shakerism, 32
Owenite community, planned at Williamsville (Erie Co.), 324

Paine, Thomas, 283
Palmyra (Wayne Co.), 39, 70, 132, 139; economic development of, 65, 140-142; James Boyle at, 190; anti-Catholicism at, 233; *Herald,* 132n, 140n; *Western Farmer,* 132n, 140n; *Wayne Sentinel,* 140n
Panic of 1837, 55, 215, 268, 271. *See also* Economic depressions
Parker, James, 35
Parker, Joel, 167; and C. G. Finney, 166; *Lectures on Universalism,* 44n; *Signs of the Times,* 120n
Parker, Robert A., 88n
Partridge, Charles, 344
Pastoral visiting, as a new measure, 180
Patch, Sam, 154
Patching, Talcott, 39
Paullin, Charles O., 272n
Paul Pry, 127n
Peace movement, ultraists and, 237
Peck, George: *Early Methodism,* 8n, 15n, 34n, 341n; *Life of,* 42n, 175n, 255n
Peck, John, and John Lawton, 253n
Penfield (Monroe Co.), William Miller at, 300
Penn, William, 81
Pennsylvania: post-1815 revivals in, 12; Baptist missionaries in, 24; literacy in, 98
Penn Yan, Wilkinson followers in, 34

Perfectionism, 353; and Shakerism, 32; environment and, 76; and spiritual wifery, 84; Luther Myrick's, 192-193; and abolition, 193; Horatio Foote and, 195; and Charles Weld, 196; and moral reform, 238; relationship between branches of, 239-240; vital issues of, 241-242; and Union Church movement, 279; New York, and J. H. Noyes, 334; meaning in Oneida Community, 335-336; and spiritualism, 351; and "Apostolic Circle," 352

Perfectionist, 149n, 245, 256n, 338n, 344n; James Boyle and, 190

Perkins, Ephraim, 174n

Perry, Donald, 360

Perry (Wyoming Co.), temperance in, 130

Peterboro (Madison Co.), 192; abolition convention at, 221

Peters, Absolom, 135, 220, 232, 261

Phelps, William, 143

Philadelphia (Pa.), C. G. Finney at, 154; Beecher and Finney agree at, 164

Phrenology, 236, 275, 325; scientific pretenses of, 325; development of interest in, 325

Pilgrims, sect in Vermont, 39

Pioneer Line stage coaches, 133, 134

Plan of Union, 9, 18-19, 23, 24, 27, 40, 46, 49, 259; churches under, 26ff., 168; disintegration of, 256-257. *See also* Accommodation plan, Presbyterian Church, American Home Missionary Society, *and benevolent movements*

Podmore, Frank, 346n

Politics, challenges to temperance, 216; and ultraism, 270; issues in, of late 1830's, 272

Polk, James K., 271

Pompey (Onondaga Co.), 67

Population, growth of, 56, 59, 60-63

Port Byron (Wayne Co.), Millerites at, 304

Porter, Eliza, 244

Porter (Chautauqua Co.), 304

Post, Isaac, 346, 347, 348n

Poultney (Vt.), William Miller in, 290

Pratt, Orson, 143

Prattsburg (Steuben Co.), New England settlement in, 6; temperance in, 130

Premillennialism, 193, 201, 278; and Shakerism, 32; before Millerites, 287; appeal of, 297-298; and spiritualism, 345. *See also* Millennialism, Miller, William, *and* Millerites

Presbyterian Church, 114; ministerial education in, 8, 101-102; prestige of, 9, 46-47; growth of, 9, 41, 46-47, 253; and revivals, 13, 155, 183, 239; General Assembly of, 19, 21, 135, 256; *Report of Board of Missions of General Assembly*, 20n; schism of 1837 in, 27, 257, 259-260; New School, 27-28, 257, 259-261, 260; domination of benevolent societies, 47, 135; pastoral visiting in schools, 92; journals, 106-107; and Antimasonry, 121, 123; and tract campaign, 126-127; and Sunday-school union, 128-129; and temperance, 131, 216; and abolition, 222; and moral reform, 230; and anti-Catholicism, 231; Oneida Education Convention of, 233; ultraist schismatics from, 261ff.

Present Truth, 316

Priest, Josiah, 8on

Priestcraft Exposed, 48n, 130n

Prince, Walter F., 144; "Psychological Tests," 144n, 145n; "A Footnote," 145n

Princeton College, 98, 102

Princeton Theological Seminary, 101, 158; and Asahel Nettleton, 164

Prison Discipline Society, 236

Prison reform, ultraists and, 236

Prohibition, *see* Temperance

"Promiscuous assemblies," 177

Propaganda, Antimasonic, 120; temperance, 214

Protestant, 108n, 231, 231n, 232

Protestant Crusade, the, *see* Nativism *and* Anti-Catholicism

Protracted meetings, 183ff.; and itinerants, 185; interdenominational support of, 254

Pulteney Estate, 34, 269

Punchard, George, 10n

Puritans, 7; doctrinal survival in ultraism, 204

Putnam, Mary B., 224n, 301n

Putney (Vt.), Noyes's community at, 333-334

Quakers, *see* Friends, the

Quarterly Register, 17n, 101n, 105, 128n, 234n

Radicalism in religion: denominational alignment of, 135-136; basic assumptions of, 199; ultraism as, 201. *See also* Itinerants *and* Ultraism

Railroads, and canal competition, 63; development of, 355
Reading (Pa.), C. G. Finney at, 154
Reconstruction, 156
Reed, William, 42n
Reform: literature in farm journals, 104; ultraist methods of, 199-200; and piety in conflict, 356. *See also* Benevolent movements *and particular reforms*
Religious education, in public schools, 92
Religious journalism, 48, 105ff., 108-109, 221
Religious liberalism, a product of ultraism, 357
Religious warfare, *see* Sectarian conflict *and* Denominational schism
Reminiscences of Rev. Charles G. Finney, 155n, 174n
Republican Party, 116
Retrenchment, 235
Revival cycles, 12, 30, 173, 268-270
Revivalism, 12, 354; doctrine of salvation in, 27-28; environment and, 76, 154-155; and Antimasonry, 124-125; and benevolent movements, 136-317; and humanitarianism, 168ff., and millennialism, 200; and democracy in ultraism, 207; and church membership, 252
Rezneck, Samuel, 274n
Rhode Island: migration from, 6; post-1815 revivals in, 11
Rhodes, S. W., 316
Rice, Sister, 298
Rider, Jarvis, 241, 244, 248
Rigdon, Sidney, 143-144
Rights of Man, 221
Ripley, George, 280
Roberts, B. T., 354n
Robinson, George W., 338
Robinson, William A., 22n
Rochester, 71, 75, 84, 156, 167; New England settlement in, 6; branch of Baptist tract society, 25; economic development, 56, 63, 65, 67, 70-73; isms about, 65; cultural agencies, 73; politics in, 116; Sunday schools in, 128; Sabbatarianism at, 132; Burchard revival at, 188; Jacob Knapp at, 196; abolition at, 222; anti-Catholicism in, 233; perfectionism at, 241, 251; ministerial association, 254; schism in, 258; decline of canal boom at, 269; Union Church movement in, 280; center of Adventism, 293, 298-299; Millerites in, 299, 300, 303, 304, 308, 314-315; freethinkers in,

322; Fourierism in, 328-329, 331; spiritualism in, 346; *Daily Advertiser*, 33n, 141n, 212n; *Gem*, 104n; *Telegraph*, 190n
Rochester Observer, 44n, 107, 127n, 136, 155n, 214n, 256n; on Rochester Revival, 169; on Sabbath observance, 132-133; and abolition, 217, 220; anti-Catholicism of, 231; and retrenchment, 235
Rochester Revival, 75, 114, 154-156, 211, 254; and Antimasonry, 154; and Sabbatarianism, 154; and temperance, 154, 168-169; and canal commerce, 154-155; influence of, 156; character and significance, 168-169; millennialism in, 168-169; and protracted meetings, 183; and church membership, 254
Rogers, George, 44n, 182n, 324n
Rome, 75, 153; economic development of, 59, 62, 63, 64; Burchard revival in, 188; schism in, 257
Roundout (Ulster Co.), perfectionists at, 240 ·
Russell, Elbert, 17n
Rutgers College, 98

Sabbatarianism, 126, 132-134, 154; Sabbath tract sales criticized, 127; mail controversy, 134ff.; Fourierism and, 332
Sackets Harbor (Jefferson Co.), 188
St. John, Robert P., 34n
St. Lawrence County, Vermonters in, 6
St. Lawrence University, 18
Salina (Onondaga Co.), 67
Sanctification, doctrine of, 159-160, 250
Schisms: ultraism and, 257-258; and antislavery movement, 277. *See also* Presbyterian Church *and* Methodist Church
Schlesinger, Arthur M., Jr. *Age of Jackson*, 135n, 327n; *Orestes Brownson*, 189n, 324n
School enrollment, 89ff. *See also* Education *and* Literacy
Schroeder, Theodore: "Matthias the Prophet," 39n; "Erotogenetic Interpretation of Religion, " 89n
Schulz, Christian, 80n
Scott, James, 352
Scott, Orange, 223, 264
Scottsville (Monroe Co.), Millerites at, 304-305, 308
Sears, Clara E., 287n
Second Advent Association, 303

Second Awakening, 7. *See also* Great Revival

Second Coming, *see* Millennialism *and* Premillennialism

Secret societies, early agitation against, 122. *See also* Antimasonry

Sectarian conflict, 40, 43, 44-46, 114. *See also* Denominational relations

Seductions: case of Augustus Littlejohn, 194; case of Horatio Foote, 195; case in Oberlin, 231

Seeley, Miss, 201

Seldes, Gilbert, 89n

Seneca County, Yankee nativity in, 67

Seneca Falls: Woman's Rights Convention of 1848, 237; schism in, 258; abolition in, 264; Millerites in, 304, 314; Fourierism at, 328

Seneca Lake, Jemima Wilkinson's colony on, 33

Seneca River, canalization of, 59

Separatists: in western New England, 7; of Great Awakening, 15

Seventh-Day Adventist Church: origins of early members, 313; origins of, 316-317

Seventh-Day Baptist Church, 316

"Seventy, the," abolitionist itinerants, 219-220, 223

Seward, William H., 82n, 116, 233

Sex communism: Noyes doctrine of, 247-248; at Oneida Community, 338-339

Sexes, ratio in population, 87

Sex experiments: in perfectionism, 241, 242, 244; and spiritualism, 351ff.

Shakerism, 31ff., 319, 326-327, 333, 335; communities, 30; doctrines, 31-32; growth of, 31-32, 310-311; model for eccentricities, 32; products marketed, 33; relation to other Burned-over District movements, 36; and Joseph Smith, 143

Shaw, William, 51

Shekinah, 348, 348n

Sheldon, Hiram, 241, 244

Shut-door doctrine: of Millerites, 313; and Seventh-Day Adventist Church, 316

Signs of the Times, 293

Simmons, Elder, 256

Skaneateles, 67; Community, 332-333

Smith, Abram, 248

Smith, Gerrit, 76, 80, 202, 217, 236, 276, 280, 281, 283; in Western Sunday School Union, 129; and Luther Myrick,

192; on Communion wine, 216; and abolition, 220, 221; land donations of, 226; and Oneida Institute, 234; and peace movement, 236; losses in depression, 273; and Union Church movement, 279; and land reform, 327; papers of, MS, 129n, 192n, 206n, 213n, 279n; letters of, MS (in Library of Congress), 236n

Smith, Hyrum, 142

Smith, Joseph, 39, 81, 114, 138, 142, 143, 146; personal reference, 142-145. *See also* Mormon Church

Smith, Joseph, family, 138, 139, 141, 143

Smith, Joseph, Sr., 142

Smith, Lucy, 142

Smith, Nathaniel, 187, 195

Smith, Peter S., 192

Snow, Lorenzo, 143

Society for Promoting Manual Labor Schools, Report of, 235n. *See also* Weld, Theodore

Sodus Bay: Shaker community, 30; Sodus Canal project, 33; Fourierist phalanx, 331

Southampton (Mass.), perfectionists at, 240

Southern tier: settlement in, 4; economy of, 63, 69-70; isms in, 70

Spaulding, Solomon, 81, 144

Spear, John Murray, 344

Spiritual Clarion, 107

Spiritualism, 16, 356; and Shakerism, 32; environment and, 76; and spiritual wifery, 84, 351ff.; and Swedenborgianism, 344-345; appeal of, 345, 347; origin of, 345-347; extent of, 347, 349; sensationalism in, 348-349; decline of, 349; duration of, 353

Spiritual Magazine, 108n, 201n, 246n, 321n, 326n, 334

Spiritual Telegraph, 342n

Spiritual wifery, 84, 339; in perfectionism, 243ff.; in spiritualism, 351

Sprague, William B., *Annals of American Pulpit*, 102n; *Religious Ultraism*, 205n

Springwater (Livingston Co.), Millerites in, 314-315

Stacy, Nathaniel, 35n, 8on

Stanton, Elizabeth Cady, 237; unorthodox beliefs of, 283

Stanton, Henry B., 155n, 219

Stanton, Theodore, and H. S. Blatch, 283n

Starr, Harris E., 344n

Stauffer, Vernon, 7n, 122n

Stearns, Bertha-Monica, 104n
Stearns, John G., 123n
Steuben County, antirent feeling in, 272
Stewart, Alvan, 221
Stewart, I. D., 11n, 16n, 38n
Stillman, Edwin, 328
Stillwell, Lewis D., 6n
Stone, Erasmus, 241, 244
Storrs, George, 223, 264, 280, 307, 325; quoted on Methodist Church, 266; as Millerite, 296, 310
Strang, James J., 143
Streeter, Russell, 175n, 189n
Stuart, Charles, 176, 217; and C. G. Finney, 195-196; as religious activist, 218; abolition lecturer, 220; on abolitionism, 221
Stuart, James, 43n
Sunday mails, campaign against, see Sabbatarianism
Sunday-school movement, 126, 128ff.
Sunderland, LaRoy, 223, 325, 344
Superintendent of Common Schools, Report of, 92n, 360
Susquehanna River, migration route, 4, 66
Susquehanna Valley: revivals of 1819 in, 11; soils of, 69; and isms, 70
Swaney, Charles B., 223n, 256n
Swedenborg, Emanuel, 35, 341, 342, 347
Swedenborgianism, 275, 325, 341-347; James Boyle and, 190
Sweet, Martin, 244
Sweet, William W., 260n, 311n
Syracuse, 64, 75; economic development of, 56, 63, 65, 67, 69; Jacob Knapp in, 196; Garrisonian nonresistance in, 236; Union Church meeting at, 280; Millerites in, 300, 302, 314; phrenology in, 325; Fourierism in, 328

Tappan, Arthur, 107, 165, 166, 213, 218, 219, 220
Tappan, Lewis, 107, 165, 166, 190, 216, 218, 219, 220, 283; papers of, MS, 108n, 166n, 225n, 283n
Taylor, Nathaniel, 27, 159, 245, 250; theology of, 164; and Tappan brothers, 165. *See also* New Haven theology
Teetotalism, *see* Temperance movement
Temperance movement, 16, 103, 126, 130ff., 136, 211-217; environment and, 76; and European immigrants, 83; and Antimasonry, 117; the pledge of, 130, 212ff., 215; denominational and doctrinal support of, 130, 215; teetotalism in, 131, 215, 258; and Rochester Revival, 154, 168-169; and ultraism, 211; Theodore Weld and, 219; women in, 237; legal compulsion in, 274; J. H. Noyes on, 337; persistence of, 353
Tent, the Millerite, 293, 298-299, 304
Theller, Alexander, 328
Throop, DeWitt, 329
Throop, George, 329; papers of, MS, 298n, 329n
Throop, William, 329
Tiffany, Orrin E., 273n
Tonawanda Railroad, 71
Toronto (Ont.), Millerites at, 308
Total abstinence, *see* Temperance movement
Tracts, in public schools, 126-127
Tract society of New York, 126
Transcendentalism, 340; and Swedenborgianism, 343
Troy, 39, 75, 156; C. G. Finney at, 154, 163; schism in, 257
Tryon, Rolla M., 359
Turner, Frederick J., 5n, 82n, 117n

Ultraism: general references, 187, 191, 197, 198ff., 268, 322
  qualities of: meaning, 173; paradoxes in, 201-202; thought processes in, 203; political and social angles of, 206-208; causes of decline, 268ff.; environment and, 270; equalitarianism of, 271; persevering traits of, 274-275; and religious liberalism, 283
  and reform movements: temperance, 211, 212-214; abolition, 217, 220, 224-226; moral reform, 226-227; education, 233-235; Grahamism, 235-236; peace, 236-237; women's rights, 237; perfectionism, 238-239
  and churches: membership, 252ff.; rivalry among, 255; schisms, 257ff.; Methodist, 264; Wesleyan Methodist, 266
  and succeeding movements, 274-277; mesmerism, 342; spiritualism, 345
Umphreville, Lucina, 241, 243, 244
Union Church movement, 192, 261, 279-281. *See also* Myrick, Luther
Union College, 102
Union Herald, 107, 191n, 221, 273n, 361; established, 280; and Millerites, 295
Union Theological Seminary, 254

Unitarian Church, 7, 18; intolerance toward, 43-44; and benevolent movements, 135; influence on religious reformers, 282

United States Bank, and 1832 recession, 269

Universal Friend, the Publick, *see* Wilkinson, Jemima

Universalist Church, 232; growth of, 17, 18, 44-45, 324; journalism of, 18, 106; and ultraism, 18, 282, 323; intolerance toward, 43-44; and Antimasonry, 121; doctrines and attitudes of, 323-324; and phrenology, 325-326; and mesmerism, 326, 342; and Fourierism, 332; and Swedenborgianism, 344

Urban: support of anti-Catholicism, 231; theory of evangelism of C. G. Finney, 166

Urbanism, analysis of types of, 75-76

Utah Territory Census, 1860, MS, 148, 150n

Utica, 84, 167; early revivals in, 11; Baptist tract society at, 25; intolerance in, 44; economic development of, 56, 59, 62-65, 73, 75; isms about, 65; Sunday-school union, 129; Sabbatarianism in, 132; Female Missionary Society, 152; Western Revival in, 153; religious expenditures at, 153; abolition in, 220, 222, 264; abolition convention of 1835, 221; synod of, and moral reform, 230; education convention at, 233; nonresistance movement in, 236; synod of, and schism of 1837, 260; agency of A.H.M.S., 261; Wesleyan Methodist Church formed at, 266; Millerites at, 296, 302, 314; Fourierism at, 328

Van Buren, Martin, 116

Van Deusen, Glyndon, 115n

Vermont: youth of migrants from, 6; migration into, 7; post-1815 revivals in, 12; University of, 98; economy in 1816, 138-139; migration from, 139

Verona (Oneida Co.): Western Revival in, 153; Daniel Nash and Luther Myrick in, 192

Verse a day plan, 232

Verse Herald, 232

Victor (Ontario Co.), Millerites at, 300

Virginia, Baptists in, 24

Voice of the Shepherd, 107

Voice of Truth, 107, 108, 108n, 298, 299n, 305, 361

Volney (Oswego Co.), Millerites at, 304

War of 1812, 11, 113, 130; William Miller in, 290

Warren, David, 241

Warren (Warren Co.), Luther Myrick at, 191

Warsaw (Wyoming Co.): temperance in, 130; abolition at, 224; Millerites at, 301

Washington, George, 347

Washington (D.C.), Jacob Knapp in, 196

Washington·County, William Miller in, 288

Washingtonian temperance movement, 216. *See also* Temperance movement

Water-cure fad, 236

Waterloo (Seneca Co.), abolition at, 264

Watertown: Millerites in, 302; Fourierism at, 328-329, 331

Watertown Presbytery, and temperance, 130

Watkins Glen (Schuyler Co.), James Boyle at, 190

Watson, Alonzo, 328

Wayne County: prosperity of, 66; antirent feeling in, 272

Weed, Thurlow, 80, 80n, 116, 120, 133, 233

Weeks, William R.: *Letter on Protracted Meetings*, 153n; *Pastoral Letter*, 153n; *Pilgrim's Progress in Nineteenth Century*, 165n, 181n, 189n

Weld, Angelina Grimké, 80, 237; unorthodox beliefs of, 283; on Millerites, 321; letter of, MS, 286

Weld, Charles, 240, 241, 245, 246, 344; career of, 196

Weld, Theodore, 80, 165, 167, 168, 176, 187, 204, 222, 231, 238, 276, 344; and woman's equality in church, 177; and James Boyle, 190; and Charles Weld, 196; as religious "activist," 218; and origin of immediate emancipation, 218ff.; personal loyalties of, 219; and abolition, 220, 222, 225; and moral reform, 229; and manual-labor schools, 234; unorthodox beliefs of, 283; papers of, MS, 176n, 196n, 218n. *See also* Barnes, G. H., *and* D. L. Dumond

Wells, Ashbell, 129

Wesleyan Methodist Church, 265-266, 288, 353

Westchester and Morris County Associated Presbyteries, 21
West Dresden (Yates Co.), temperance feeling in, 131
Western (Oneida Co.), 13, 153; in Great Revival, 10. *See also* Western Revival
Western credulity, 80
Western Education Society, 26
Western folkways, 79-80
Western Luminary, 299n, 332n
Western New England, religious enthusiasm in, 7
Western New York Baptist Missionary Magazine, 11n, 24n, 102n
Western Recorder, 25n, 48, 107n, 127n, 132, 134, 156n, 178n, 199n, 232n, 255n; characterized, 106-107; Daniel Nash and, 160; anti-Catholicism in, 231; and verse a day plan, 232
Western Reserve (Ohio), abolition in, 220
Western Revival, 13, 23, 50, 114, 153, 160, 162, 166, 173, 178, 187, 191, 195, 218, 234, 257, 278; circumstances of, 153-154; sensationalism of, 162-163
Western Sunday School Union, 129
Westfield (Mass.), perfectionists at, 240
West Otto (Cattaraugus Co.), Mormons in, 148
Whig Party, 79, 116, 270; "conscience" group, 226, 233, 277; and nativism, 233
White, Anna, and L. S. Taylor, 32n, 310n
White, Ellen Harmon, 316
Whitesboro (Oneida Co.), 155, 156; C. G. Finney at, 154
Whitmer, David, 360
Wilkinson, Jemima, 33ff., 144; property management of, 35-36; relation to Burned-over District movements, 36; papers of, MS, 33n
Williams, Edwin, 360
Williams, John, papers of, MS, 41n
Williams College, 98
Williamson, Charles, 34
Williamson (Wayne Co.), 39

Wilmington (Del.), C. G. Finney at, 154
Winchell, 39
Wisner, William, 260, 261; on anti-Catholicism, 231-232
Witness, 204n, 246n, 340n; established, 248; on faith healing, 338
Women: as preachers, 37-38, 177, 263, 304; church membership of, 38, 177; status of, 84-89; ratio to men, 87; and sex attitudes, 87-88; in revivals, 177, 178; and preachers, 186-187; in temperance, 215, 237; and moral reform, 229, 237; in abolition, 237. *See also* Women's rights movement
Women's rights movement, 237; spiritualism and, 351
Woods, Leonard, 203n, 216n
Woodstock (Vt.), 39
Woody, Thomas, 89n
Workingman's Advocate, 326
Workingmen's Party, *see* Democracy, Jacksonian
Wright, Benjamin, 151
Wright, Elizur, Jr., 120, 120n, 220; papers of, MS, 220n
Wright, Frances, 283
Wright, G. Frederick, 151n, 250n
Wyoming County: New England settlement in, 6; Mrs. Conn in, 191; abolition in, 264

Yale College, 98. *See also* New Haven Theological Seminary
Yankee credulity, 181-182
Yates, J. V. N., 126, 134
Young, Brigham, 143
Youngs, Benjamin S., 32n

Zion's Watchman, 107, 108, 108n, 148-149n, 214n, 221, 264n, 265, 293n, 361; and Mormons, 148; established, 223; circulation in Burned-over District, 264; and Millerites, 293, 295

Printed in the United States
59730LVS00003B/1-75